CW00566336
1675

First published in 1988.

All photographs and drawings in this book not otherwise credited are from the National Railway Museum.

British Library Cataloguing in Publication Data

Jenkinson, David
British railway carriages of the twentieth century
Vol. 1: The end of an era, 1901-22
1. Railroads—Great Britain—Passenger-cars—History
I. Title
625.2'3 TF455

ISBN 0-85059-912-1

Patrick Stephens Limited is part of the Thorsons Publishing Group, Wellingborough, Northamptonshire, NN8 2RQ, England

Printed in Great Britain by The Bath Press, Bath, Avon
Typeset by MJL Limited, Hitchin, Hertfordshire

10 9 8 7 6 5 4 3 2 1

By the same author

Rails in the Fells: a railway case study
An Illustrated History of LNWR Coaches
The Power of the Duchesses
The Power of the Royal Scots
Profile of the Duchesses
Modelling Historic Railways
Eric Treacy's LMS

With F.J. Bellwood
Gresley and Stanier

With N.H. Campling
Historic Carriage Drawings in 4mm scale

With R.J. Essery
Locomotive Liveries of the LMS
The LMS Coach
An Illustrated History of LMS Coaches
An Illustrated History of LMS Locomotives (4 volumes)
Midland Carriages: an Illustrated Review
An Illustrated Review of Midland Locomotives (2 volumes)

With Gwen Townend
Palaces on Wheels (Royal Saloons at the NRM)

With R.J. Essery and V.R. Anderson
Portrait of the LMS

Title spread *Wolverton (LNWR) at its apogee, c 1904. Five twelve-wheel clerestory diners, three semi-Royals and two more than adequate brake composites lined up for inspection — or maybe a special working — show Edwardian elegance at its best.*

Front endpaper *Departed glories of a lost era: a typical London and North Western American Boat Train at Liverpool (Riverside) station early in the 1900s, with hardly a speck of dust in sight and staff lined up in almost military precision.*

Rear endpaper *Taken at Fort William, c 1920, this quintessentially Scottish view shows a totally North British Railway array of solidly constructed 'no-nonsense' carriages and the equally purposeful 4-4-0 engines which pulled them.*

Contents

Author's introduction

It is said that Brahms, in explanation of the fact that he waited until he was in his 40s before tackling his first symphony, remarked that it was because he was conscious of the spirit of Beethoven looming over his shoulder. Now, apart from a great love of his music, just about the only thing I have in common with Brahms is a beard; but I know how he felt. Let me explain.

Anyone attempting to write a general account of British railway carriages cannot help but feel the presence of that superb artist/author, the late Cuthbert Hamilton Ellis, who was the first to try and till the soil of carriage history to any depth — and, in my view, his is still the finest model for the rest of us to follow. His definitive work on the nineteenth century came out as early as 1949 and even the revised version, taking the story forward to 1914, appeared as long ago as 1965. They are, however, still the standard works and nothing quite like them has appeared since, perhaps surprisingly. It was therefore with a sense of considerable pride, mixed with some anxiety and overtones of inadequacy, that I received the publisher's invitation to write this present work bringing the story to the present day, especially when I was given some 300,000 words, well over 1,000 illustrations and three volumes to play with! It seemed at first to be an awful lot of space to fill, yet I soon had to come to terms with what to leave *out*, so it seemed prudent to launch the work with a few words of general explanation as to emphasis.

I have said elsewhere* that, in my view, the railway carriage is above all something in which people *travel*. It is also, of course, a piece of applied technology and I am well aware that some carriages carry no people at all, being filled with luggage, parcels, mail or what have you; but when the 'bottom line' is drawn, the railway carriage is a fundamental socio-economic artefact in a way which the locomotive can never be and the freight vehicle only rarely. Of all the pieces of plant and machinery which go to make up the complexities of the total railway, the carriage is always that part of the system which is most familiar to most people. In this context, I must of course exclude the rather specialized case of the dedicated railway enthusiast who will regularly know a great deal more about many aspects of the railway than will the typical traveller. Obviously, I hope that these *aficionados* will also find my comments to be of interest.

There will, therefore, be no great fleet lists in these pages and there will certainly be no attempt to mention every single carriage ever built; there is, in fact, a considerable literature addressed to this sort of thing already — see the Bibliography. There will, however, be much reference to people, whether it be their travelling needs, changing social attitudes, criticisms and so forth or, in the more practical sense, the skills, quality and craftsmanship of the many, largely anonymous folk who built (and still do for that matter) some of the vehicles which will be featured. There will also be a fair bit of technology, for it would be absurd to write of vehicles without explaining something of the 'how and why it works' aspects. At the same time, however, I have tried my best not to assume too much pre-knowledge on the part of readers. In consequence, I have in this first volume tried to explain the essential background technology of the twentieth-century railway carriage in terms which do not demand a degree in engineering or a post-graduate qualification in applied physics. If by so doing I cause those of my readers who do have more detailed knowledge of the subject to feel somewhat cheated, then I am sorry to upset them; but I do not apologize for the basic approach I have chosen.

Essentially, I have attempted to provide an overview, concentrating on trends, developments and general principles which seem to be valid, rather than addressing all the minutiae. Above all I have tried to inject a degree of historical perspective into the story, which is why I have set the scene for the whole series by devoting its first chapter to 'The Victorian Inheritance', as I have elected to call it. It is rare that history obliges us by sorting itself out in terms of precise and tidy dates on the calendar. The railway carriage is no exception and the twentieth-century story would be utterly incomprehensible without first reviewing, even briefly, those years of Queen Victoria's reign when the carriage 'grew up'. Much that was Victorian lasted well into the twentieth century, so it would be quite wrong to exclude from the survey the essential overture to all that which followed. Unlike much in our modern world, railway technology has rarely been of the 'throw away after five years of use' kind!

Before concluding these preliminaries, I must place on record my especial gratitude to Dr Neil Cossons, Director of the Science Museum, and Dr John Coiley, Keeper of the National Railway Museum, for giving me, as a public servant, both their permission and encouragement to undertake this task, albeit as a private venture. This has been especially valuable in the realm of permission to use

**An Illustrated History of LNWR Coaches,* OPC, 1978.

much illustrative material from the archives, for without the availability of the vast picture collections of the NRM these books would be immeasurably disadvantaged. It may therefore safely be assumed that unless credited to other sources, all pictures in this book have been taken from the NRM collections. Irritatingly, however, some of the pictures whose historic interest demands inclusion have not quite captured the whole of the carriage, but readers may rest assured that the odd instances of cropped buffer heads and the like are neither the fault of the museum nor the publisher.

My immediate museum colleagues have also given me much support in this context and although this is no more than they already give to others, it is still much appreciated. Philip Atkins and John Edgington have been particularly helpful with the picture research, the NRM studio photographers have printed many newly-found views, and particular thanks must go to my dear friend and colleague Gwen Townend, not only for acting as my 'guinea pig' non-specialist reader but also for typing the bulk of a long and complicated manuscript in her own time — largely because she is one of the few people who can actually read my appalling handwriting! Finally, very warm thanks go to my good friends Bob Essery and Barry Lane for vetting every word of the manuscript.

Notwithstanding all caveats, this is still very much my own personal compilation. Happily, I have had absolutely no pressure brought upon me by the publisher to 'make it like . . .' and I have done *all* my own research. Thus, any mistakes are mine and where choices of emphasis were necessary, these too are subjectively based.

David Jenkinson,
Knaresborough, North Yorkshire

'. . . *the railway carriage is above all something in which people* travel.' *And if you were a reasonably well-heeled family in 1911, even the rather unfashionable Lancashire and Yorkshire Railway could offer this stylish Family Saloon for your delectation. It was wholly typical of the best achievements of British carriage builders during the first quarter of the twentieth century.*

THIRD
THIRD
M&GNJR
THIRD
8
THIRD
THIRD

FIRST
FIRST

THIRD
THIRD
N. E. R. 1453
THIRD
THIRD

1. The Victorian inheritance

Unlike many manifestations of human ingenuity, the railway carriage has a fairly precise beginning. While the railway idea, as such, may be lost in the mists of antiquity — it certainly goes back some 4-500 years — the history books tell us that the first *people* officially to travel on a railway train did so in South Wales between Swansea and Mumbles in 1807, drawn by a horse. Prior to that time, railways were purely for things and the human species came a very poor second place in the reckoning.

The development of the 'steam railway' proper, in effect from the opening of the Liverpool and Manchester Railway in 1830, was very much a Victorian phenomenon, and it is a matter of fact that the enthusiastic demand for railway transport by people came as something of a surprise to certain parts of contemporary society. That it still does so in some establishment circles is, perhaps, outside this immediate discussion! Be that as it may, however, the railway carriage 'came of age' during the Victorian expansion of the mechanized railway and it is impossible to comprehend its twentieth century development without devoting some small space to 'setting the background'.

The railway carriage drew its main inspiration from the early nineteenth-century road coach — indeed, the words 'coach' and 'carriage' have their origins in the road transport business. The two words are more or less interchangeable and both will be used, somewhat indiscriminately, in this compilation. Indeed, much of the vocabulary, specific to the subject, derives from other sources, so it will not do any harm to start with a few more definitions of terms which will appear quite regularly in these pages. Take, for instance, windows, which were always called 'lights' because they let in the light. There were 'fixed lights' (ie non-openable), usually surrounded by some sort of frame; there were 'drop lights' (windows which opened by being lowered, ie 'dropped', in their surrounds); and there were 'quarter lights', usually set on either side of a door and so called because, initially, they were shaped like a quarter circle, harking back to stagecoach days again. There were also 'top lights', 'deck lights' and several others — more of which in their proper time.

Top left *Archetypal Victorian four-wheeler from the Midland & Great Northern Joint Railway — third class No 3. The five-compartment third class was probably the most common single type at this time, whether on four or six wheels. Note the retention of oil lamps.*

Middle left *'Chariot ended' six-wheel first class No 15, with two lavatories and featuring half-compartments ('coupés') at the vehicle end, was an unusual but nevertheless typical nineteenth-century Highland Railway coach.*

Left *This North Eastern Railway six-wheel third class No 1453 with two central lavatories was a quite 'up-market' third class type in late Victorian times. Its body styling is wholly characteristic of traditional British practice — see Chapter 7.*

This terminology withstood the transfer to the railway environment, even after carriage shapes had changed quite markedly. So too did other words and phrases which were often either anatomically or architecturally derived. Thus the 'waist' of a carriage was its middle portion just below the window; while 'eaves', 'cornice', 'gutter', 'floor', 'ceiling', 'dado' and even 'clerestory' had obvious roots in buildings and retained their basic connotations virtually unaltered.

The carriage itself started its purely railway form as a somewhat basic box, in effect three stagecoach bodies joined together and mounted on one set of four wheels. Each section was called a compartment and the whole unit was essentially a pure conveyance with not much thought for added amenity; thus it remained, in essence, for some forty years or so. But there were boxes and boxes, some distinctly better than others — and this was almost entirely as a result of the differential price structure in terms of paying for one's journey. The various distinctions were designated by the word 'class' which has developed unfortunate sociological connotations in recent decades, yet whose origins are no more than the root of the perfectly logical 'classification'.

The railways 'classified' their passengers according to how much the customers were prepared to pay, and in this they did no more than follow accepted road custom. Thus, first class developed from the old 'inside' seats of the stage coach. There could be no rooftop 'outside' seats on a steam-drawn train — the speed was too great and the danger of hitting fixed structures too high — so a cheaper option was offered in the form of a covered compartment of a considerably more spartan nature. Typically it would have wooden seats, few, if any, windows (save for those in the door) and probably little or nothing in the way of artificial light. Since more people could be packed in, the status and price somewhat equated with the old rooftop conveyance of the stagecoach. It was known as second class.

The cheapest form of conveyance was a third class carriage. This was the absolute provisioning — an open-topped box on wheels, frequently devoid of seats and possibly with a few holes in the floor to let out the rain-water. It was frightful but, amazingly to modern-day travellers, it was popular. But then, the alternative form of conveyance in pre-railway days for the least wealthy, other than walking, was to ride on the slow moving (maybe 1-2 mph average) 'commercial' horse-drawn merchandise wagons which plodded their way along our roads. The increased speed of the railway and its eventual cheapness compared with road would obviously commend itself even in those spartan circumstances, however basic the accommodation offered. In due course, Gladstone's famous 1844 Act compelled the often reluctant railways to roof over even the third class carriages, but it was well into the last quarter of the nineteenth century before these miserable vehicles improved much further on a nationwide basis.

If there was a significant date above others, it was probably the year 1875 when the Midland Railway decided to abolish second class by upgrading its third class carriages to 'better than second class' standards but without increase in charge. Simultaneously — or near enough as to make no practical difference — it admitted third class passengers to *all* its trains and this again was something almost revolutionary. Hitherto, third class passengers were more often than not accepted only grudgingly by the railways. Obliged as they were by Gladstone's 1844 Act to provide at least *one* third class service per day at one old penny (0.4p) per mile, stopping at all stations — the famous 'Parliamentary' trains — many railways fulfilled their obligation but literally, interpreting the word 'day' as embracing 24 hours, thus allowing them to run the 'Parliamentary' at the most inopportune times — often in the middle of the night. Not without reason did the immortal W.S. Gilbert write those words into the Mikado's 'punishment and crime' song: '. . . we only suffer to ride on the buffer of a Parliamentary train'! They were pretty awful.

It was against this sort of background that the Midland delivered its *coup de théâtre*. When the Midland, having abolished second class, additionally reduced first class fares to second class levels without loss of carriage quality, the shock waves reverberated round the railway world. Of course, the effect on other systems was not immediate. Some improvements would have happened anyway and it is always dangerous for a historian to try and date with precision the point at which quantum changes occur; but if one wants to assign a 'conception' date for the first essentially twentieth-century *attitude* to rail passenger travel, then the activities of the English Midland Railway during the late 1870s seem to mark as good a single point in time as any.

In effect, the MR introduced a two-class only approach — the basic twentieth-century subdivision — with a built-in assumption that the lower of these two classes still merited essentially comfortable accommodation. However, the high quality of the 'soft third class' of the British railways — most of them eventually copied the Midland — was still a source of wonderment in many overseas countries well into the present century. That it took until as late as 1956 for the last vestiges of three-class accommodation to vanish in Britain (mostly retained on a few boat trains) is part of the main story to be considered later. But for older readers who remember it and have perhaps wondered at this curiosity, it does explain why during much of the first half of the present century, most British trains were, somewhat puzzingly, labelled 1st and 3rd Class only.

So much, for the moment, for the social aspect of the railway carriage; in this survey, classes of accommodation will be quoted as they were known at the time the vehicle was built. 'Third' class did not become 'second' in Britain until well into the period covered by the third volume, so references to 'second' class in this first part do, indeed, relate to a threefold subdivision.

Just as it took nearly half a century for the railways to develop a fairly civilized attitude to people, so too did it take longer than is generally realized for the vehicle itself to improve. The basic four-wheeler had a long and not entirely praiseworthy run in the nineteenth century, and many were built in the early part of the twentieth too, but eventually the demand for greater speed and safety gradually caused changes to occur. The combination of factors was a little subtle, involving both social and technological aspects, but the end product was to set the pattern for twentieth-century development just as in the socio-economic field thus far discussed.

The railway carriage is, fundamentally, a very stable vehicle and can be made very large and very heavy, subject mainly to the maximum dimensions imposed by fixed structures (bridges, tunnels, etc) and the maximum weight per axle permitted by the railway itself. The extent to which the carriage could be 'expanded' was probably not fully appreciated in early steam days, and in any case the early locomotives were often too feeble to pull much above a string of typical four-wheelers; but the potential for development was there.

The first increase in size was generally to a six-wheel type, often with enhanced width and height as well. This would clearly allow more 'people per carriage', but it is doubtful if the actual cost or weight per seat was less than with the four-wheeler. In fact, the contrary was probably the case. However, the six-wheeler was more comfortable at the higher speeds which competition (and the passenger) was forcing; its greater weight gave it greater safety in the case of accidents and there was, in general, rather

Top *Great Northern Railway No 2653, built in the late 1890s, was one of the several approaches to the use of eight wheels which did not involve the use of bogies. Only the first class had access to the lavatories. Some of these carriages lasted until the 1930s.*

Above *London & North Western Railway 42-foot eight-wheeler No 469 was one of many hundreds which employed Francis Webb's patent 'radial' axle at both ends of the vehicle as an alternative to pivoting bogies — see Figure 2a, page 16. It has lavatories and luggage space as well as three classes of accommodation.*

more space below the floor to fit the various ancillary equipment which was increasingly being provided, particularly in the realm of braking.

It is not too widely known that the legalized automatic braking of all passenger trains was quite a late arrival on the scene. Not until well after the Newark Brake Trials of 1875 did the railways seriously address themselves to the problem. It took some time to get things organized, nationally, after this date and even then there was not total agreement about the best system (see Chapter 2); but as far as the carriage was concerned, it meant that extra equipment had to be carried, increasing the weight.

The demands for increased amenities (see below), the growing need in absolute terms for more passenger capacity and the desire for still greater speeds together combined to force the carriage above the six-wheel configuration during later Victorian days. The Americans had had an answer since the 1830s, but Britain was slow to take it up. Essentially it involved mounting a much longer carriage on two separate sets of wheels (known as 'bogies' in Britain but, confusingly, 'trucks' in America), one at each end and free to pivot relative to the carriage body itself. Once again, applied technology provided part of the reasoning. The typically British six-wheeler, like its four-wheeled counterpart, had a virtually rigid wheelbase (see Chapter 2). This meant that there were restrictions regarding the radius of curvature it could traverse. The precise mathematics need not concern us for the moment but suffice to say that in the context of British civil engineering it posed no serious problems. British lines were well engineered (some would even say 'over engineered'), had gentle curvature and were generally easily graded.

In America, by contrast, as part of the 'opening up' process of that vast continent, the early railways tended to be pushed through as expeditiously as possible and this included a 'low cost' element. More pronounced curvature and more severe gradients were accepted (to save money) and this had important consequences in both locomotive and carriage devevelopments in North America, one early end product of which was the carriage bogie. This device was introduced in order to permit larger vehicles to traverse more severe curves than they could do were the wheelbase rigid. Each pivoting bogie acted as an independent four-wheel 'carriage' so, self evidently, the bogie coach could get round a sharper corner than a rigid six-wheeler.

William Stroudley's London Brighton & South Coast Railway first class carriage No 77 built in 1889. The bogies were quite primitive (note the spoked wheels), but for their time the vehicles were very spacious, each compartment being almost eight feet square.

This was not such an acute problem on the well engineered lines in Britain, the six-wheeler was a cheaper option than the bogie carriage and the British railways muddled along quite happily as before. Thus, it was not until 1874 that the first bogie carriages appeared in Britain and, yet again, it was the English Midland Railway which introduced them into this country. That the bogies were also of patently American inspiration was no coincidence either, and bogie vehicles eventually became the norm in the twentieth century.

What took some time for the British railways to appreciate — and in this respect it is worth recalling that even the enterprising Midland built mostly six-wheelers down to 1900 — was that the bogie carriage had other advantages besides that of getting round curves more easily. For one thing, its 'ride' quality (ie freedom from unwanted jerks and jolts) was better, since it could be made larger and heavier; also, because of the vast area of empty 'sub-floor' space between the bogies, it could also have attached to it, a fair quantity of ancillary equipment. This latter advantage was to become dominant, which conveniently links to the third principal twentieth-century feature established in late Victorian days — improved passenger amenity.

The human species is a curious animal. Give it something better and it immediately bends its mind to thinking of yet further improvements, and railway carriages are no exception to the general rule. Thus, no sooner had the railways demonstrated that a better standard of seat comfort was possible than the passengers began to ask or even demand that other things, too, be considered. These grouped themselves into three principal categories, all connected with fundamental bodily functions — some almost unmentionable in polite Victorian circles — but none the less vital!

There was the lavatory for starters. The ever expanding railway network, together with the consequential longer transit times between more distant centres, meant that calls of nature could not be ignored. The train (unlike its stagecoach predecessor) was not able to call at any convenient roadside hostelry, so travellers had to rely on the often inadequate provisioning at station stops and risk the train leaving too soon! This was not really very dignified, so some of the more enterprising railways in the long-distance business started to incorporate lavatories on their trains.

In 1873, the North British Railway (NBR), closely followed by the London and North Western Railway (LNWR) in the same year, introduced sleeping cars to cater for a second vital bodily function and in 1879 the Great Northern Railway (GNR) put into service the first British dining car service between London and Leeds, which took care of the third basic bodily need. Hamilton Ellis has dealt with much of this in his own books so there is no need to concern ourselves further here, but sufficient has probably been said by now to appreciate that much which we now take for granted in the late-twentieth-century travelling environment was established by the privately-owned railways of later Victorian Britain from the 1870s onwards. Of course, it was stimulated by competition for patronage between the various private systems and often had to await the ability of the mechanical engineers to provide more swift-moving and powerful locomotives to haul the extra weight, but very little that we now regard as 'normal' in terms of twentieth-century rail travel had not been foreseen by our Victorian predecessors.

Naturally, although the fundamental ideas were first sown in the 1870s, it took some time for them to be universally adopted. Take inter-vehicle connections, for example. Clearly, if all passengers were to be able to gain access to a lavatory or partake of the facilities of the dining car, some means of getting from one carriage to another was essential. This meant a 'gangway' between the ends of adjacent vehicles and some form of passageway (or 'corridor') along the length of the vehicle itself to gain access to the gangway. Interestingly, the first recorded British example of this facility was on the pair of Royal Saloons provided for Queen Victoria in 1869 by the LNWR. It is said that she would not use it, save when the train was stationary!

We shall have cause to re-consider Royal travel later, more than once, but it is interesting to note that when the LNWR pioneered inter-vehicle connections in 1869, it transpired, and not for the last time, that where the Monarch led, the subjects followed. Thus, by the end of the nineteenth century it was becoming the norm that on long distance trains it should be possible to move along the length of any one vehicle without hindrance and, preferably, be able to move *between* vehicles, by means of a gangway, to gain access to other facilities.

It took time, and full 'corridor' trains were not really introduced to any real extent until the 1890s — and then not for all services. Indeed, the pioneering Midland did not venture its first corridor train until 1898 and in this rather significant respect it was behind some of its larger, longer distance rivals, notably the Great Western Railway (GWR) and the LNWR.

Now, although so far mention has not been made of other late Victorian improvements such as better lighting and heating — these will be considered in later chapters because they continued to form the basis of the first twentieth-century developments — what should now seem abundantly clear is that the railway carriage 'came of age' during late Victorian times and, in its bogie form, became the basis of most of the important twentieth-century innovations. The bogie carriage allowed for the insertion, between the bogies and below the floor, of most of the extra equipment needed for the 'servicing' of the more elaborate vehicles, such as gas cylinders (for cooking and lighting), batteries (for storage of electricity) and brake apparatus. By the end of the last century, most of the bigger railways had 'adopted' the bogie carriage, or were in the process of so doing, simply because it made sense so to do. The four-wheel and six-wheel vehicles were not dead, but they were surely dying. That they took so long about it may be attributed perhaps more to the innate conservatism of the British than to any particular merits the carriages may have possessed. They were still, of course, cheaper to build, but that was not everything when the new century dawned.

Thus, on the first day of the twentieth century the 'nature of the beast' was probably apparent to all who took interest in these things and, by way of preliminaries, there only remains one final area to consider before launching into our main subject area. I refer to the 'train' itself.

The 'train' is a fundamental word in the study of railways. That a vast number of people use it when they really mean 'locomotive' or 'carriage' is beside the point — the 'train' is the end product when it comes to carrying the people about in rail-borne vehicles. In railway terms, the word means an assembly of vehicles, connected together and doing,

American influence on British practice during the nineteenth-century was particularly represented by the importation of typically American-styled carriages. Pullman was the best known practitioner (see Chapter 12), but this view shows South Eastern Railway first class 'Car No 35', built by the rival American Gilbert Car Company for the SER boat trains in 1892. The livery and decoration, also typically American, were applied in the USA before shipment and were described at the time as being dark lake, almost chocolate, with sage green bogies. The cars were later acquired by Pullman.

Classic late Victorian practice with profound twentieth-century influence — East Coast Joint Stock third class No 13, with side corridor and lavatories, built in 1898 and shown here as LNER No 41810. Its 'twin', ECJS No 12, is preserved at the National Railway Museum, York.

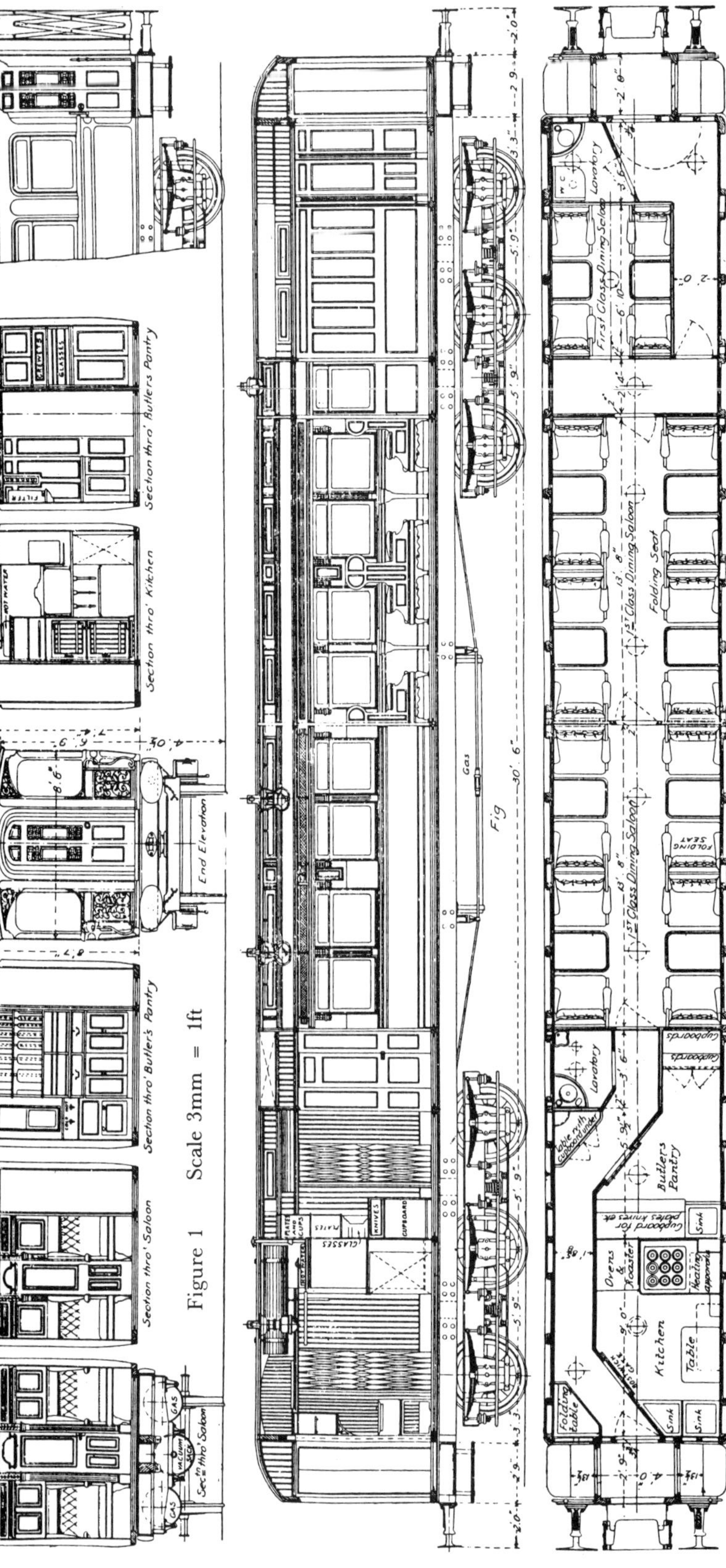

Figure 1 Fin de siècle — *the late Victorian twelve-wheeler in the form of the classic Wolverton (LNWR) 65 ft 6 in long dining and sleeping carriages, introduced in the mid-1890s. This drawing shows details and layout of the first type built, the first class dining cars of 1895. A slightly later example is shown in the picture on page 108.*

Above right *Victorian inheritance I — the long-lived characteristics of many typically humble Victorian-styled carriages are exemplified by this view of no fewer than a dozen of them at Kittybrewster as late as the mid-1920s on the former Great North of Scotland Railway, then part of the LNER. Some of the carriages still carry GNSR livery.*

Right *Victorian inheritance II — the Great Western Railway found considerable use for its turn-of-the-century clerestory coaches for many decades after they had seen the first flush of their youth. Here, at Southcote Junction, Reading, is a typical cross-country working to Newbury in 1931. Note the much shorter windows of the centre vehicle, of older vintage than the two end examples.*

collectively, a useful job of work. In the beginning of passenger railways it merely reflected, in passenger terms, a number of vehicles (of whatever class) whose sole object was to convey people from 'A' to 'B'. In the fundamental sense it still does, but by later Victorian times, three quite distinctively different categories had begun to emerge in Britain and are relevant to the twentieth-century story.

Firstly, the long-distance train is totally different from its short-distance 'home to work' counterpart. This was not at first apparent (surprisingly), but by the start of the present century the railways appreciated the fundamental difference which existed between a vehicle in which one was anticipating to spend several hours (or even the bulk of one day) and that with which one's acquaintanceship was but transitory, for maybe an hour or even less. In between the two was a sort of intermediate third category — not quite long-distance and not quite transitory, but nevertheless distinguishable. These three broad categories are fundamental to the understanding of British railway carriage design, for they resulted in the provision of distinctly different vehicle types.

Put at its simplest, the long-distance train is 'strong' in amenity and the short-distance train is 'high' in seating capacity, with the intermediate train lying somewhere between the two. In British terms, the ultra-long-period operations (several days and nights) of the Americas, Australia or Asia were not relevant, but the railways were more than aware of the differing needs of potential patrons at an early stage; their response varied accordingly.

All these various differentiations had been identified — and the solutions to some extent arrived at — by the start of the twentieth century, so the 1900s started, in effect, with the various problems identified. The carriage had 'grown up' and the new century dawned with all to play for. It will be the object of the remainder of this survey to review the extent to which it was successful.

Machine Shop.

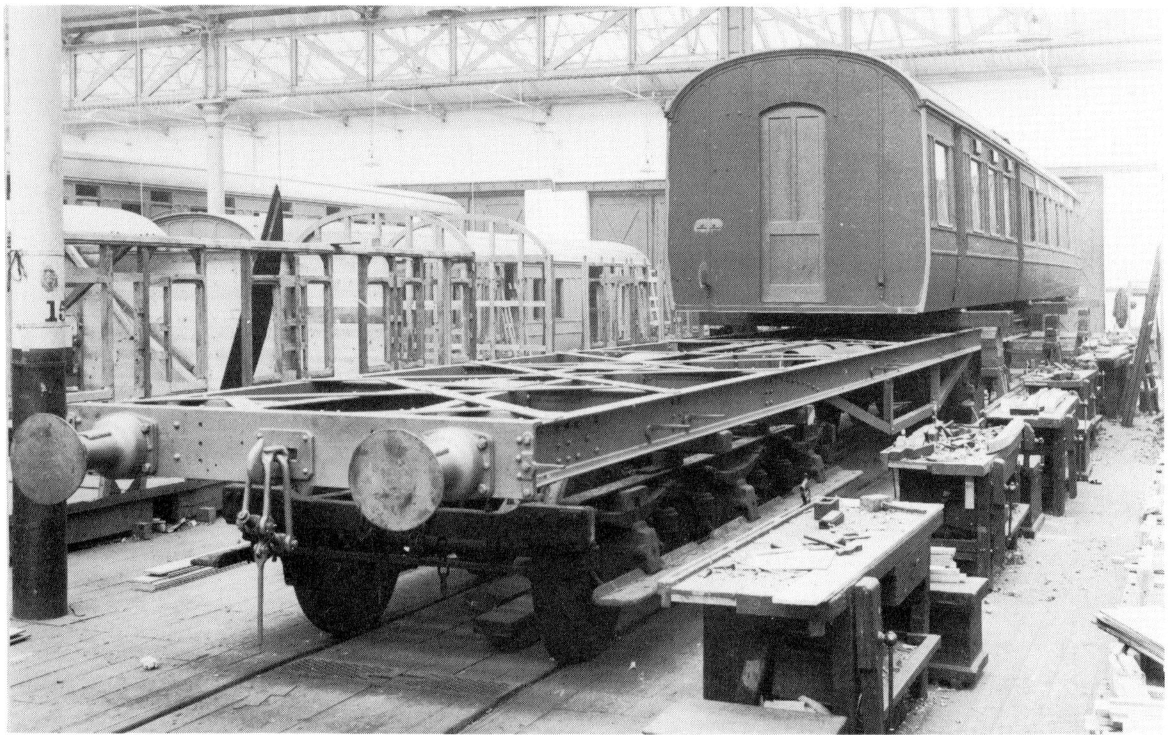

THIRD CLASS
DINING SALOON
FIRST CLASS

2. The carriage as a vehicle

The traditional British railway carriage consisted of two basic components, the chassis and the body. It was normal to build the two components separately and then, at some quite late stage in the process, offer up the body for fixing to the chassis, at which point the final stages of adding interior fitments, ancillary components, etc could begin, finishing with the all-essential painting and decoration. This approach, while not uniquely British, was in marked contrast to the form of construction generally adopted in America, where a form of 'integral' construction was adopted from an early stage. Although used widely in North America and possessing several advantages, this form of construction only achieved significance in Britain during the period covered by the first volume of this survey in the shape of Pullman Cars (Chapter 12), and is therefore left out of consideration until that part of the book.

Bearing in mind the dangers of such a generalization, the railway carriage tended to be either British (perhaps, more accurately, European) or American in terms of its basic structural form for something like the first half of the twentieth century and, certainly as far as British practice is concerned, the separate body/chassis form was all but universal until the 1960s. Although a great number of detailed variations did exist, not to mention an ever-increasing move towards extensive pre-fabrication of components and semi-mass production of whole vehicles in the case of the larger companies, the fundamental structure of the vehicle itself remained little changed. It happily withstood the changeover from 'all-wood' bodies through 'part-wood/part-metal' to 'all-metal' without significant alteration to the basic principles. Consequently, given a fundamental understanding of how the early twentieth-century coach was put together, it is readily possible to appreciate the subsequent evolutionary stages. These latter were really quite slow and the late Victorian/early Edwardian carriage builders would have had little real difficulty in comprehending the vehicles of the mid-1950s. They might have been surprised at their greater size, the considerable changes in their interior decor and the move towards considerably simpler colour schemes, but that would be about all.

It has been seen in outline how the twentieth-century railway carriage was born during the last decade of the previous century in terms of concept and utilization. It is now necessary to turn to a consideration of how it actually worked. As in the case of concept, so too in the case of constructional methods, the ideas stemmed from late Victorian times. This detailed account, therefore, must also commence with a look at the turn of the century situation in terms of carriage building. For ease of comprehension, the various principal elements are separated into chapter and sub-headings; the various specific words and terms will be introduced as they become relevant and since the railway carriage is, in all its manifestations, always a vehicle, it seems logical to look first at its fundamental component, the vehicle chassis.

The underframe

The largest single part of the vehicle chassis is known as the underframe. It is the essential foundation of the whole vehicle, regardless of the precise body type, and to it are fixed, in one form or other, all the other components (wheels, axles, brakes, etc) which go to make up the whole. Frequently, the word underframe is used to denote the whole assembly, but in this book the word 'chassis' will be used to differentiate the whole from its constituent parts.

The underframe itself is basically a rectangular structure, the size of which reflects the length and width of the body which will, in due course, be fixed to it. Most railways arrived at various standardized sizes to suit several different body configurations, but few if any of the individual companies settled down to one basic underframe for all requirements. Neither did the different railways agree between themselves as to the optimum length which should be used for a particular carriage type. There was thus considerable variation in length and width at all times, even though all of them had to fulfil the same basic purpose.

The underframe had to have, above all, great

Above left *Six-wheel underframes, both all-steel (left) and composite wood and steel (right), under construction at the York works of the former North Eastern Railway.*

Middle left *The classic British form of carriage construction — body unit mounted on a separate chassis. The example illustrated is a twelve-wheel M & GSW first class dining carriage at Derby works in 1920, and the underframe itself is of the angle-trussed kind — see page 18. To the left can be seen the framing of a typical compartment coach* (BR LMR).

Left *A somewhat dramatic solution to the underframe of heavy twelve-wheelers was adopted at York by the NER, and was likened by many to the girder construction of the various Tyne bridges! The style is well shown on NER first and third class dining car No 3753. Note the almost complete filling of the space between the bogies with ancillary apparatus. This type of underframe may still be examined in the preserved East Coast Royal Saloons at the NRM — see Chapter 13.*

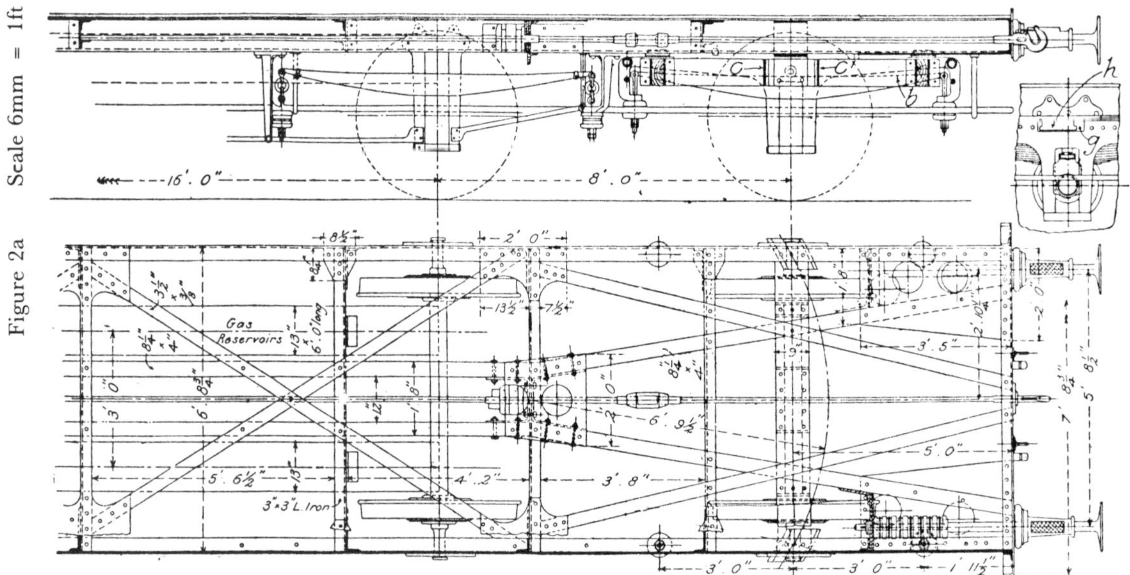

Figure 2a *Probably the most sophisticated of the non-bogie eight-wheel carriage underframes was Webb's LNWR radial pattern. Although by then obsolete, it was still quite widespread on the parent system at the start of the twentieth century.*

strength. To achieve this it was built in the form of a horizontal girder with very strong outer side-members (known as 'solebars') and equally strong outer end cross-members ('headstocks'). There would, typically, be additional longitudinal and cross-members, often associated with diagonal 'braces' to give extra strength in the more vulnerable areas where greater stress might be expected to occur. The essential requirement was to produce a framework which remained rigid and free from distortion. In this latter context, the most likely eventualities to be guarded against were too much drooping at the ends and rising in the middle (known as 'hogging' or 'hog-backed'), the opposite effect (known as 'sagging or 'sway-backed'), or a tendency to get out of square horizontally as a result of the forces exerted by the buffing and drawgear (see page 25). In point of fact, it was common for underframes to be constructed with a deliberate amount of 'hogging' which would be forced horizontal by the weight of the bodywork on top; otherwise 'sagging' would result!

In terms of material, underframes progressed from all-timber, via a combination of timber and iron (later steel) to all-steel. All three approaches could be seen at the start of the century but the all-steel underframe fairly rapidly assumed dominance. The all-wood underframe can be regarded as basically obsolete in carriage terms by the twentieth century, but many carriages which spent most of their lives operating between 1900 and the mid-1930s (often later) did make use of a composite form. In most cases these would employ oak, reinforced with iron or steel plates and brackets.

The precise nature of a particular underframe was governed by two principal considerations, namely the nature of the buffing and drawgear (see below) and the length, wheelbase and number of wheels to be employed. In this latter context, there was a fundamental distinction between a four-wheel or six-wheel chassis and one which was to be carried on a pair of bogies.

The four-wheel and six-wheel arrangements carried the wheels and their supporting equipment mounted directly on the underframe. This type of arrangement had been virtually, but not quite, superseded by the present century for most of the better passenger-*carrying* vehicles, but remained in use for some lesser services and for passenger-*type* vehicles (luggage vans, etc) well into the modern age. The presence of either the centre set of wheels (six-wheelers) or the relatively short length of the vehicle (four-wheelers) meant that there was less intrinsic risk of sagging at the centre.

The bogie underframe, however, was different. The underframe was supported at each end on the bogies and, in the case of longer carriages, there was a considerable unsupported length between the bogies which would have a natural tendency to sag. To prevent this, the underframe was strengthened along the solebars (and sometimes also along the centre longitudinals) by an ancillary framework, usually

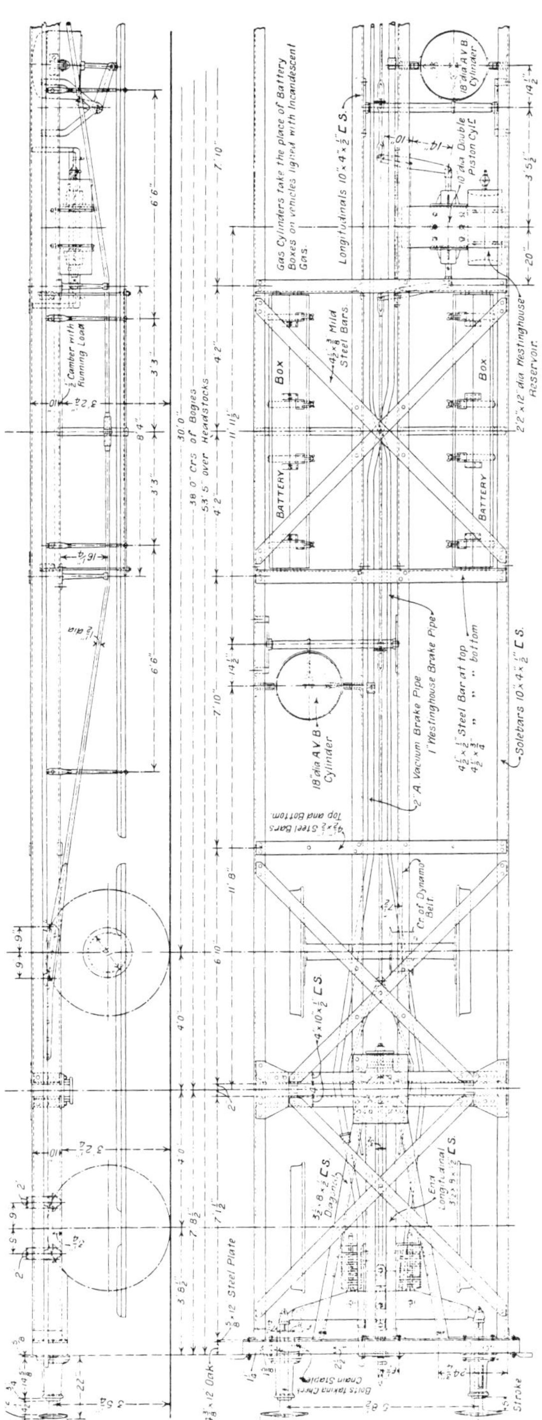

Figure 2b Scale 4.5mm = 1ft

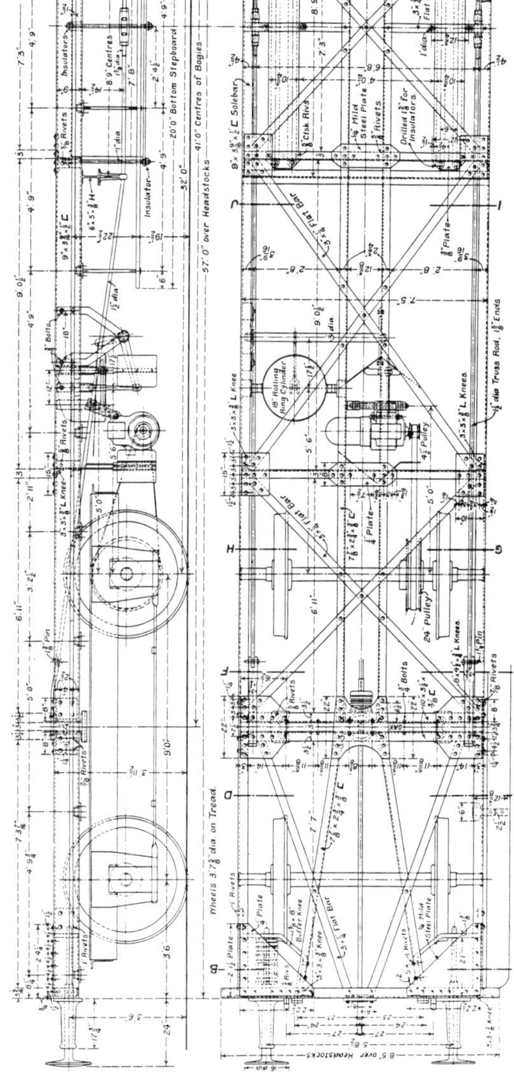

Figure 2b *These two part elevations and plans show characteristic 'round bar and queen-post' bogie underframes of the Midland (54-footers,* circa *1910) and the LNWR (57-footers,* circa *1913) respectively. Their considerable similarities are far more important than the superficial differences.*

known as 'trussing'. This consisted of vertical members (usually referred to as 'queen-posts') and horizontal or slightly diagonal members known as 'truss-rods'. The appended diagrams and pictures show some typical arrangements.

The tendency for the underframe to drop in the centre puts the queen-posts into compression and the truss-rods into tension and, provided the stresses and dimensions are calculated properly, this combination of forces maintained the top of the underframe in a flat horizontal configuration. In Britain, this was normally achieved by one of two basic methods. The older solution — and entirely typical of the start of the century — was to make the queen-posts quite substantial (sometimes even decorative) and to make the truss-rods of round bar section, typically 1-1½ inches in diameter. Somewhere along its length, the truss-rod would be 'broken' and a 'turnbuckle' inserted. This and the end of the truss rod itself were threaded in the manner of a conventional nut and bolt so that when the turnbuckle was rotated it either increased or decreased the tension in the truss rods, the latter being fixed at their outer ends (ie those nearest to the bogies) to the underframe itself. Thus the integrity of shape of the underframe could be maintained.

This method (generally known as a 'roundbar and queen-post' or 'turnbuckle' underframe) was augmented and finally superseded by the second common method — the so-called 'angle-trussed, all-steel' underframe. In this arrangement, the stresses were met in more or less the same way but without the need for adjustment by turnbuckle. This was achieved by making the whole of the trussing out of angled steel sections, usually 'L'-shaped and permanently bolted together in such a way as to ensure almost total rigidity of the whole assembly with almost no distortion — other than any which had been 'planned in' — taking place when the bodywork was put on top. This form of construction appeared quite early in the century — well before the railway grouping — and had become the British norm by the Second World War.

By this time, experiments in integral construction had begun to appear and welding was replacing the bolted-together form of fixing in some cases. These developments will be mentioned in their due historical sequence.

Springing and suspension

The carriage wheel was fixed to the underframe in one of two ways. It was either attached direct (in the case of four-wheelers and six-wheelers) or fixed to the bogie frame which in turn was separately attached to the underframe. Either way, the first and most critical factor was to fix the wheel in a firm housing which would nevertheless allow it to accept some form of springing to cushion the shocks. Known as primary suspension, this was the only form of wheel suspension which could be contrived on a non-bogie vehicle.

The method adopted could trace its beginning to the very origins of the steam railway and, in the use of leaf springs, to the preceding road-coach era. As a principle it more than stood the test of time, increased weights and stresses being regularly matched by improved materials and methods of manufacture. Basically, two wheels were mounted on an axle which was allowed to project well beyond the outer faces of the wheel itself. These outer extensions (known as 'journals') were machined to the appropriate diameter and were carried inside an axlebox — a closed container in which were the axle bearings. Within the axlebox, the journals were kept cool in rotation against their bearings by means of lubricating oil. In earlier days, lubrication had been achieved by 'packing' or 'stuffing' the axlebox with semi-solidified grease, relying on frictional heat to melt the grease and afford lubrication. This method was still quite widespread at the turn of the century on freight vehicles, but the oil axlebox was much better and almost universally employed for passenger stock during the period of this survey. It was essential for really high-speed operation.

The axlebox itself was carried in a rigid metal frame — or axleguard — fixed to the underframe (or to the bogie side), within which it was free to slide up and down between parallel vertical 'guides'. Shocks were usually taken up by means of a leaf spring fixed to the top of the axlebox and anchored to the underframe or bogie frame at the outer ends by means of movable links or 'scroll irons'. It will be appreciated that as a spring flexes its length varies slightly, so the outer ends must be given some freedom of movement. The term 'spring hanger' is often used as an alternative to scroll iron.

The axlebox itself should be not only free to move up and down in the axleguard but also have some lateral movement — quite commonly the groove in the axlebox is about 1 inch wide while the guide itself would be some ¾ inch thick. On six-wheelers, the centre axle had to be given rather more lateral movement, or side play, typically ⅝-¾ inch either side of the centre line in order to assist in traversing curves; as a result of this, the centre scroll irons were often of different design to allow for this extra lateral movement which, of course, also applied to the ends of the springs themselves.

With a bogie vehicle, each bogie acted as an independent four-wheel truck and in most British examples the primary suspension was exactly as described above using leaf springs. However, many bogies in North America used a form of compensating beam between the two axleguards on the same side of the frame as a substitute for two independent leaf springs — see Figure 6. Each end of this compensating (or equalizing) beam was anchored to one axlebox. Therefore, when, for example, the left-hand axlebox rose in its guide, the right-hand box would fall and the vertical shocks were most commonly damped by coil springs between the equalizing beam and the fixed frame. This type of bogie was used in Britain, but to nothing like the extent of the leaf spring version. It was particularly popular with the Pullman Company (Chapter 12) and, indeed, was the first type of bogie used by the Midland Railway in 1874. All references in this book to 'American' pattern bogies should be taken to infer this form of springing.

Regardless of its primary suspension, the bogie itself was a sort of miniature underframe and was built along much the same principles, although some

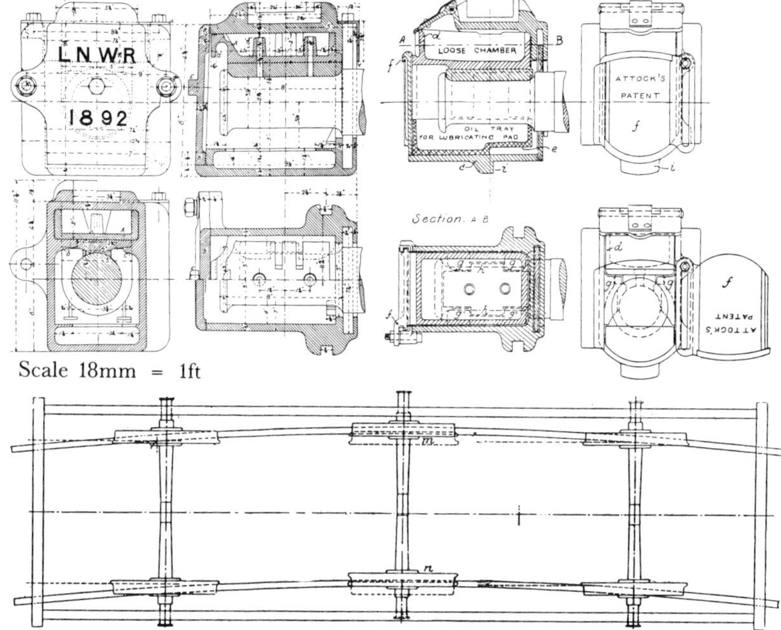

Figure 3 *Oil axleboxes were developed late in Victorian times and in widespread use at the start of the present century. The examples shown are the LNWR standard and the Attock (Lancashire and Yorkshire Railway) types; other railways mostly used similar forms.*

Figure 4 *Exaggerated diagram showing the behaviour of a typical six-wheel chassis on a curve. This drawing shows, at 'm' and 'n', the lateral displacement of the centre axle.*

Right *Detail view showing the leaf springs, spring hangers, axlebox and axleguard of a typical NER six-wheel carriage.*

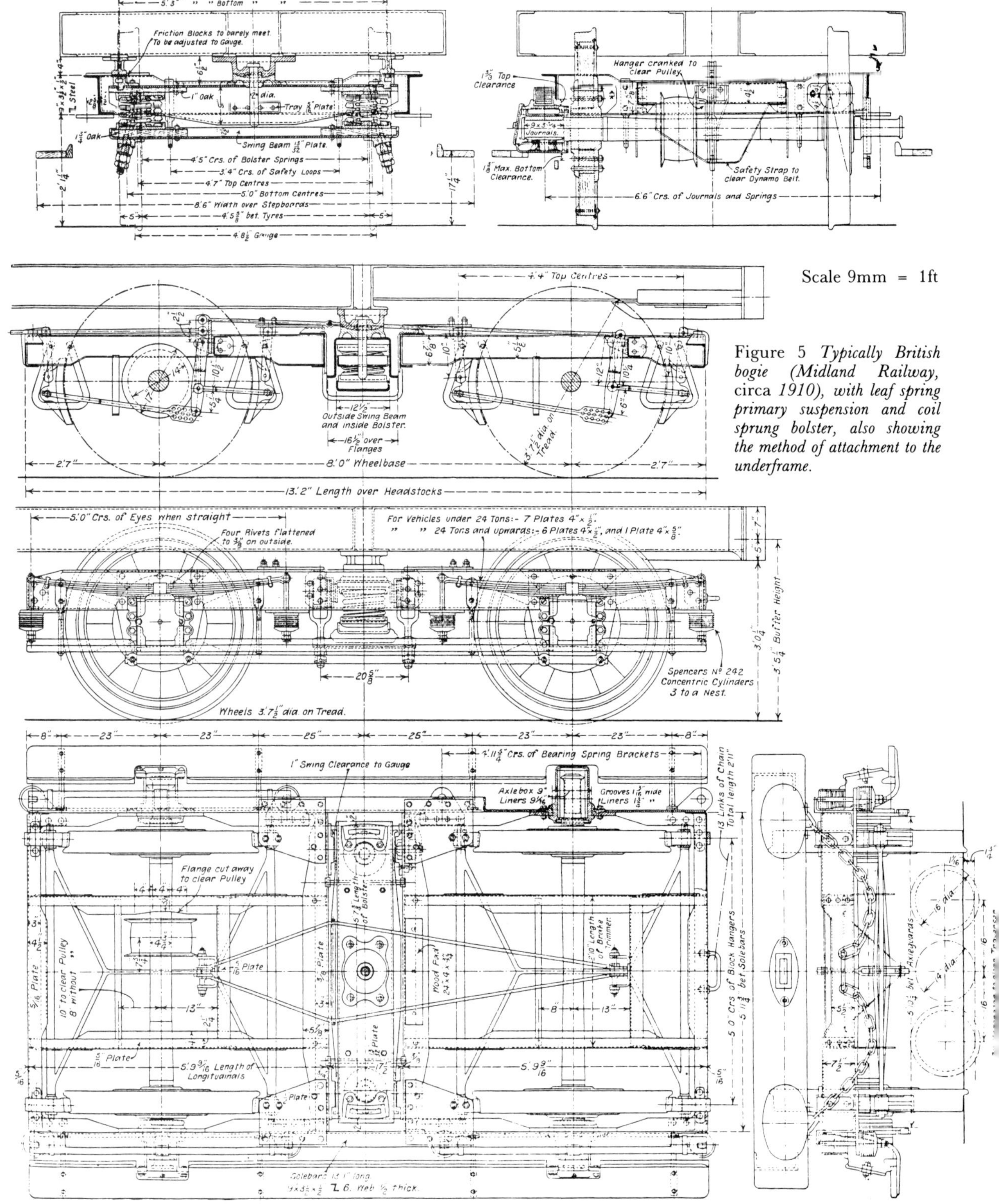

Scale 9mm = 1ft

Figure 5 *Typically British bogie (Midland Railway, circa 1910), with leaf spring primary suspension and coil sprung bolster, also showing the method of attachment to the underframe.*

bogies — again often the American type — were built with a mainframe cast in a single piece. It was, however, in its mode of attachment to the main underframe that the bogie displayed its advantages, in suspension terms, over a rigid wheelbase vehicle.

The essential component was known as a 'bolster'. This was a form of metal swinging plank set between and parallel to the two axles. It 'hung' from the bogie mainframe, usually on four rods (two at each end) known as 'swing links'. The centre of the top of the bolster carried the pivoting mechanism, the other part of which was fixed to the main underframe. Thus the weight of the carriage was carried through the pivot to the bolster and, via the swing links, to the bogie frame itself. In effect, the carriage, although appearing to bear down on top of the bogie, actually hung from it.

The swing links themselves were set in a trapezoidal shape which assisted the carriage on corners, when there is a natural tendency for the body and underframe to move to the outside of the curve by centrifugal force. This movement caused the outer swing links to adopt a more vertical position and the inner ones a slightly more inclined orientation. As a result, the bolster itself (to which was fixed the carriage body and underframe) tilted slightly inwards and the whole carriage 'leaned' into the curve — precisely what the passenger wanted for greater comfort and somewhat analogous to the leaning action of a cyclist or the banking of an aeroplane when cornering.

Although free to move within the bogie frame, the bolster itself was not permitted unlimited freedom. There were usually restraining blocks fitted to the carriage at each side to limit the maximum amount of 'tilt' — mainly to prevent the carriage underframe coming into contact with the wheel rim — and the bolster itself carried its own independent springing at each of the outer ends of the swing plank. This 'secondary' suspension, as it is known, was either in the form of transverse double leaf elliptical or powerful coil springs. Thus on a bogie carriage there were, interposed between the passenger and the wheel, at least three devices all of which helped to smooth the ride — the primary suspension, the tilting action of the bolster and the secondary suspension.

Thus, the bogie carriage was intrinsically more comfortable, particularly on curves, than a four or six-wheeler, quite apart from its other advantages. It also meant that curves could be taken more quickly without causing passenger discomfort. It can be demonstrated that the discomfort threshold is reached far sooner than the safety equivalent as far as vehicle speed is concerned so the bogie coach really did allow much higher speeds to be achieved. In practice, of course, the natural tendency of the bogie carriage to adopt a leaning position on curves was often supplemented by raising the outer rail of the track itself — superelevating as it is known.

LNWR carriage bogies undergoing overhaul at Wolverton Works during early LMS days, August 1930. Little had changed for thirty or more years — neither would it do so for a similar or longer period. The nature of the swing bolster plank itself is very apparent from the example in the foreground.

Finally, although written in the past tense, it should perhaps be made clear that the substance of the above paragraphs still applies to the bulk of bogie vehicles on the modern railway — refined, of course, by many later improvements.

Before leaving the bogie itself, a few words about the effect of axle loading will not come amiss. The main purpose of adding wheels to a carriage was to ensure that no one axle bearing was subject to overload as weight increased. A typical turn-of-the-century British figure for coaching stock in this respect was about 6 tons per axle or a little more. This gave, typically, 12, 18 and 24 tons as fairly characteristic weights for carriages of four, six or eight wheels respectively. The railways, however, were having to build coaches heavier than 24 tons, so the next logical step was to introduce *six*-wheel bogies, capable of carrying up to 36-40 ton carriages. As the twentieth century progressed, permitted axle loadings gradually increased until some 10 or more

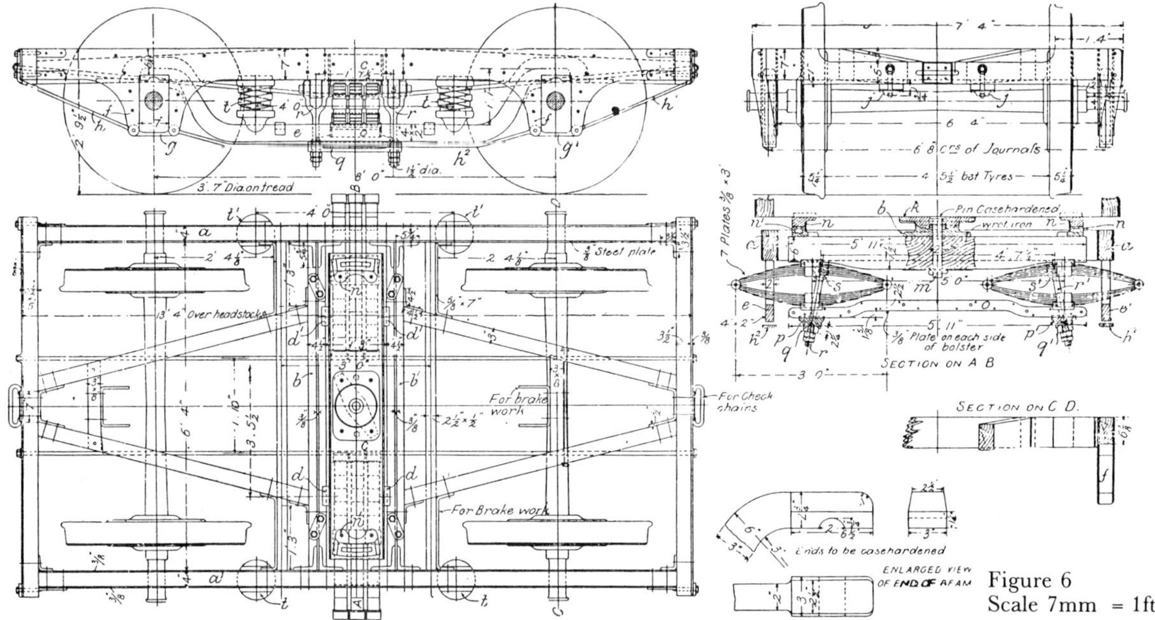

Figure 6 *'American' pattern bogie with compensating beam primary suspension and transverse leaf bolster springing. The cross-section at AB shows the characteristic trapezoidal nature of the swing links on the bogie bolster, regardless of the form of primary suspension adopted.*

Figure 7 *These two diagrams show typical British six-wheel bogie designs. They represent (above) the Caledonian 'Grampian' stock of 1905 and (below) the final LNWR design of 1907, used for almost twenty years and even being fitted to some early LMS standard stock.*

tons per axle could be accepted. Thus, by the late 1930s it was possible to put 40-ton coaches on eight wheels — a weight which would have been pushing at the limits for a *twelve*-wheeler at the start of the century. Not surprisingly, the late twentieth century figure is higher still.

The six-wheel bogie itself was much the same as the four-wheel version and came in conventional or 'American' pattern as far as primary suspension was concerned. In the case of the American type, each side of the bogie carried two equalizing beams (one between each adjacent pair of wheels), both of which were anchored to the centre axlebox but free to move semi-independently. The bolster of a six-wheel bogie followed similar principles as for a four-wheeler but generally took an 'H' shape in plan — two transverse planks between and parallel to the axles joined by a central longitudinal member which carried the bogie pivot. This would have eight rather than four swing links and two sets of bolster springs on each side.

Carriage wheels and axles

These, the most fundamental components of the carriage chassis, are of far more than passing interest. They bear the brunt of the 'wear and tear' and, since even at 60 mph a typical 3 ft 6 in wheel makes 480 revolutions per minute, it is subjected to considerable stress. It must therefore be both strong and well balanced, not to say adequately supported by its bearings and springs.

Today, carriage wheels are made from cast steel discs on to which are 'shrunk' the separate steel 'tyres' which carry the wheel tread and flange, and this has been true for much of the present century. However, the era dawned with a very different sort of wheel in general use for carriages, the so-called 'Mansell' wheel, named after its inventor and characterized by its wooden centre section (see Figure 8).

Visitors to the National Railway Museum at York find it a constant source of surprise that quite heavy carriages were mounted on what they describe as 'wooden wheels' and there seems to be some lack of understanding of the considerable advantages possessed by the Mansell wheel. Although steel wheels were introduced very soon, the Mansell wheel was still being fitted to some new carriages until at least the late 1930s and remained in service for many years beyond that. Indeed, at least two of the NRM's Mansell-wheeled carriages withstood the full rigours

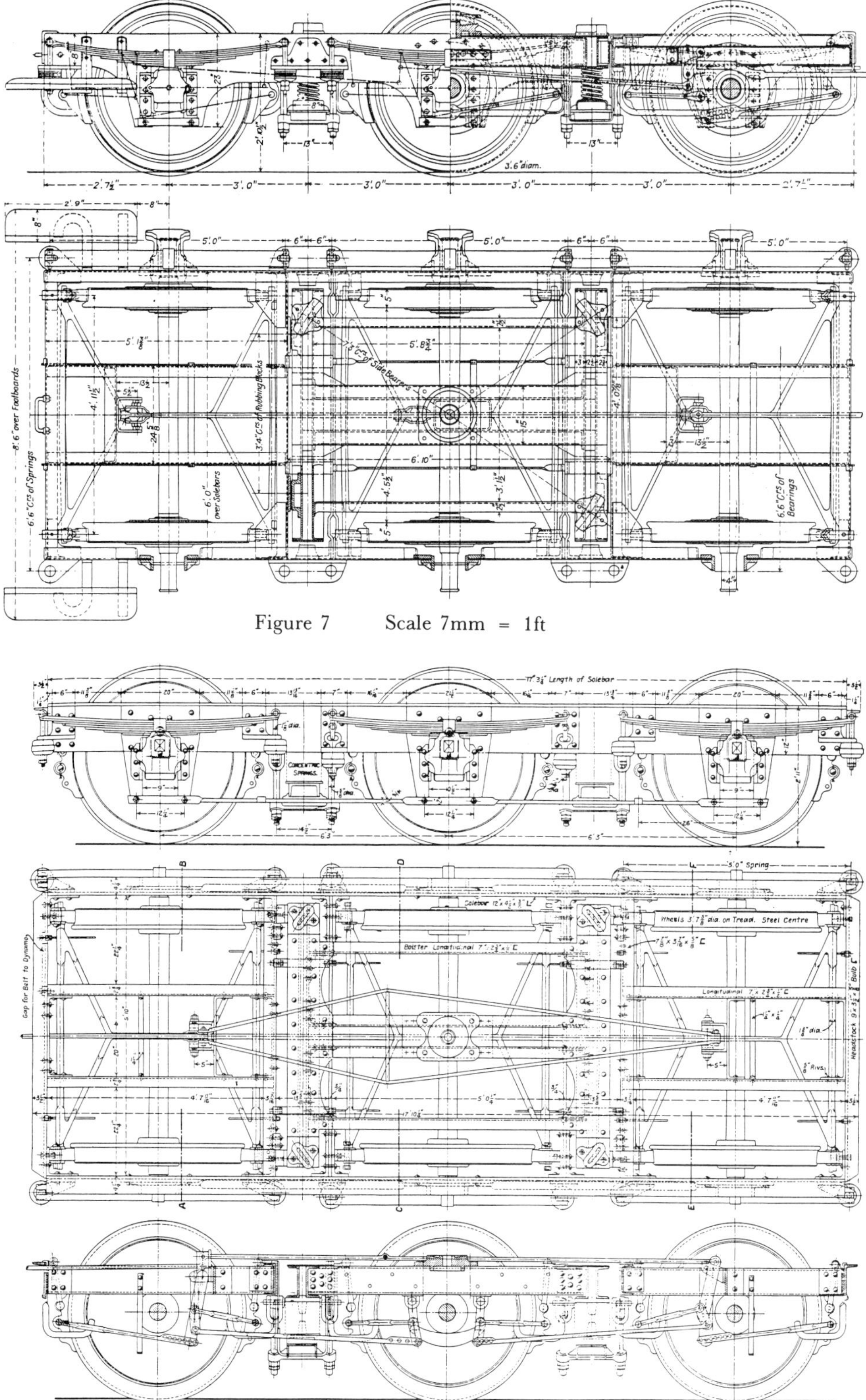

Figure 7 Scale 7mm = 1ft

Fitting carriage wheels to axleboxes at Wolverton, circa *1930; once again a practice hardly changed for nigh on a century, save for the method of wheel construction.*

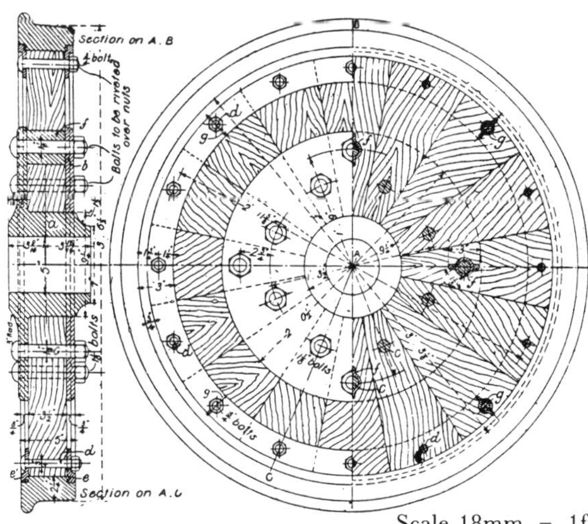

Scale 18mm = 1ft

Figure 8 *Typical Mansell wheel construction as adopted by the Great Eastern Railway.*

of the current BR examination and were cleared for 70 mph running as recently as 1979.

The Mansell wheel was not solid wood. It consisted of a forged iron centre boss round which was fitted the wooden disc proper which itself was made from many separate timber segments (normally 16) which in turn were surrounded by retaining iron rings at the outer circumference. These rings also held the outer circumferential *steel* tyre. Individual railways adopted their own slight detailed design variations, but did not part from the general principle.

Turning now to the advantages of this somewhat complex wheel form, they were considerable when viewed against contemporary criteria:

1 The tyre fastening was very safe even if the tyre should break into a number of separate pieces — a real enough if not very common risk — because each separated piece would remain attached to the wheel unless the retaining ring also broke. This was a very unlikely eventuality.
2 The whole circumference of the tyre was supported by the wooden disc. This somewhat 'insulated' the tyre and caused less noise transmission to the carriage interior and less of the characteristic 'ringing' sound.
3 The tyres could be allowed to wear down in thickness to a considerable extent without danger.
4 The wheels were relatively easy to make and needed little skilled labour.
5 The slight elasticity of the wooden centre, compared with a rigid steel disc, probably made the wheels somewhat less vulnerable to the stresses and shocks caused by passing over the very numerous rail joints (characteristic of the early part of the century) at the higher speeds then becoming common.

In due course, the obvious advantages (to modern-day eyes) of the one-piece cast steel disc wheel gradually became paramount in new vehicle construction, but this had to await the ability to make the right sort of steel; and it is not too fanciful to state that without the Mansell wheel, the early twentieth-century railways would have found it much harder to meet the ever growing public demand for more amenities (ie heavier coaches) and higher speeds (ie more stress on the moving parts).

Regardless of wheel type, the twentieth-century carriage always employed steel axles and even at the turn of the century a desired tensile strength of some 40 tons per square inch was required for any one axle. At this time, several interesting tests were demanded of the steel, including the ability to be bent double when cold without fracturing and an ability to withstand, also without fracturing, a ton weight dropped on it from a height of 20 ft, five times in succession, the axle being turned between each blow and supported only on two bearings some 3 ft 6 in apart.

It was thus an extremely rare thing for axle failure to occur, and such was the quality of workmanship that axles bearing a date stamp as early as 1908 have fully withstood the full rigours of present-day BR scientific ultrasonic stress testing when such institutions as the National Railway Museum have sought to operate vintage vehicles on the main lines.

Buffing and drawgear

The buffing and drawgear represent, after the wheels themselves, the most important part of the carriage chassis.

The traditional British coach carried buffers mounted on the headstock, one at each at the four corners of the underframe. Their purpose was multifold. Firstly they existed to absorb the momentum of moving vehicles by forming an elastic medium between carriages and wagons as they came into contact. For this reason they needed to be strongly sprung, and thus acted as a form of shock-absorber.

A second function was to stabilize the coach in motion in several important ways. The conventional British form of coupling carriages together was by means of an adjustable screw coupling (see below) and this was tightened up so as just to bring the buffer heads of adjacent vehicles into contact, or even slight compression. The friction generated by this contact, albeit usually made less by 'greasing' the buffer heads, tended to keep carriages steady when running at speed, particularly on curves and when negotiating pointwork and junctions. Additionally, the compression between the buffer heads also damped down most of the tendency for any vehicle to oscillate too much, particularly to 'roll' about its longitudinal axis. Thus, by preventing excessive to-and-fro movement and reducing the lateral tendency to oscillate, the buffers of a railway carriage materially assisted the train itself to behave as a unit rather than as a series of independently-minded wayward vehicles! During the early part of this century, this effect could most readily be appreciated by comparing the generally quite stately motion of a passenger train with the 'jack-rabbit' antics of the trucks in a typical loose-coupled goods train. In the latter case, the buffers merely prevented end shocks and were not always particularly successful even in this role.

A further characteristic of the tightly-coupled passenger train was that, if properly assembled, the buffer heads would not even separate when the train started, thus giving even more benefit to the passenger. The smooth starting and stopping of most British passenger trains was an oft-remarked aspect of railway operation in this country, much appreciated by overseas visitors. However, so much was this form of train assembly taken for granted by the British travelling public that should a set of carriages be less than perfectly coupled together the resulting 'snatches' and 'jerks' between carriage ends — not abnormal in other lands — would probably precipitate some sort of adverse comment. Even the *Times* correspondence columns were not free from barbed shafts should the railways thus fall from grace.

With the advent of bogie stock on a more general basis, particularly the longer (60-70 ft) vehicles, the buffer heads became quite large and, viewed end-on, frequently assumed oval form with the major axis horizontal. This was to cope with the mathematical problems caused by long, straight vehicles rounding curves. A study of Figure 9 will reveal that the lateral displacement relative to the track centre-line could be considerable at the vehicle ends, and this was exaggerated if a reverse curve was encountered. If the carriages were being drawn along there would normally be no problem, but when being propelled, in sidings for example, the buffers were in compression and could quite easily slide laterally relative to each other sufficient for one to 'lock' behind the other. This would almost certainly cause derailment when the carriages met the next length of straight track. Larger buffer heads generally resolved this problem, as indeed did an alternative form of carriage coupling — the 'buckeye' type, which will be dealt with later.

The buffer springs themselves were contained behind the headstock or in the buffer housing itself. In earlier days (particularly, but not exclusively, on four-wheel and six-wheel stock), it was quite common to have buffers bearing against a transverse leaf spring, but this gradually gave way to independent springing, generally a longitudinal India rubber or coil spring behind the solebar, and some vehicles had self-contained semi-pneumatic springing within their casings.

Coupling between carriages was made for the most part by a pair of forged links with an adjustable screw

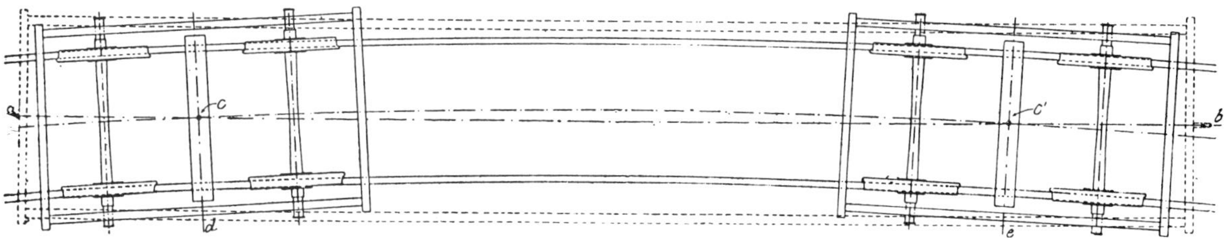

Figure 9 *Diagram showing the geometry of a typical bogie carriage on a curve. The lateral offset of the headstock is shown, dotted, at 'a' and 'b', the bogie pivots are at 'c' and the position of the bogie, relative to the curve centre, is indicated by lines 'd' and 'e'.*

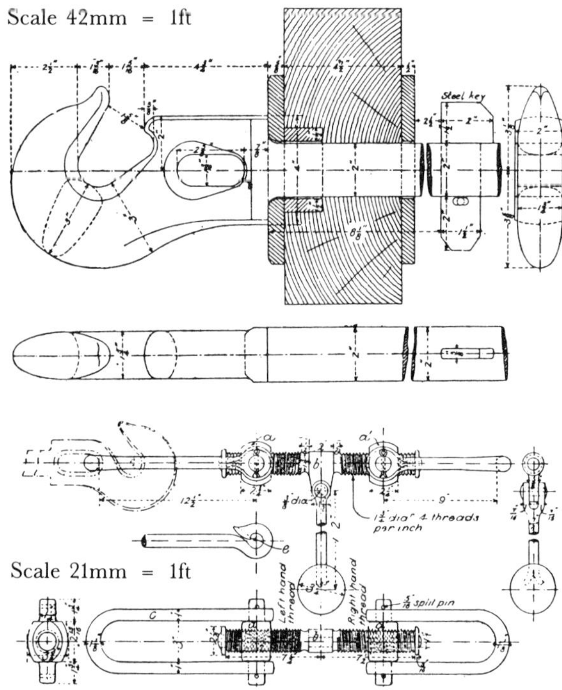

Figure 10 *Typically British pattern draw-hook and adjustable screw coupling.*

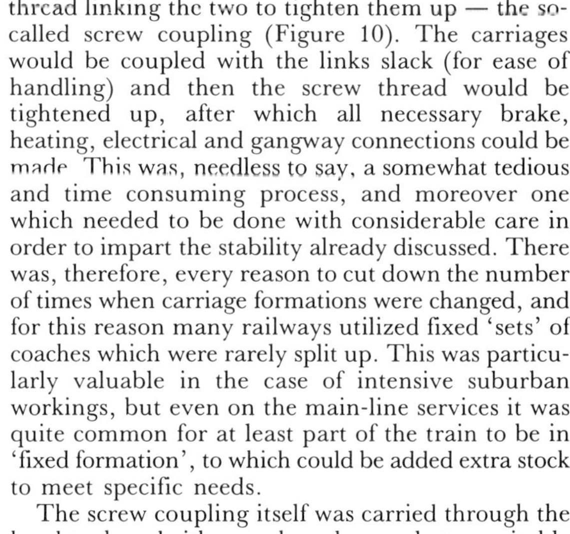

thread linking the two to tighten them up — the so-called screw coupling (Figure 10). The carriages would be coupled with the links slack (for ease of handling) and then the screw thread would be tightened up, after which all necessary brake, heating, electrical and gangway connections could be made. This was, needless to say, a somewhat tedious and time consuming process, and moreover one which needed to be done with considerable care in order to impart the stability already discussed. There was, therefore, every reason to cut down the number of times when carriage formations were changed, and for this reason many railways utilized fixed 'sets' of coaches which were rarely split up. This was particularly valuable in the case of intensive suburban workings, but even on the main-line services it was quite common for at least part of the train to be in 'fixed formation', to which could be added extra stock to meet specific needs.

The screw coupling itself was carried through the headstock and either anchored securely to a suitable part of the underframe or connected with its opposite number at the other end of the carriage, the latter being referred to as 'continuous' drawgear. In either case, the coupling hooks were spring loaded to provide a little 'give' when starting from rest. Several alternative methods were available, well described in numerous technical journals of the day.

With discontinuous drawgear, the front coupling

of the leading carriage had to withstand the whole weight of the train behind it, the progressive strain on each coupling becoming less as the rear of the train was approached. With continuous drawgear, the actual pull was distributed down the train through the various drawbars and each coupling had, in effect, to contend with only the weight of its own coach. Before underframes were made exclusively of steel, the rather more sophisticated continuous pattern drawgrear was preferred, but with the much stronger steel underframe capable of withstanding immense strains this was less critical.

Finally, the screw coupling was sometimes permitted a degree of side to side movement within the headstock. This was to help adjust to line curvature, particularly in the case of long carriages. Typically, for example, the London and North Western Railway permitted some 5 inches of lateral movement of the coupling hook on its long twelve-wheelers.

There was an alternative to the screw coupling/side buffer method and, like the carriage bogie, it was American in its origins. In North America, the Pullman Car Company was probably the principal trend-setter in carriage design and in its carriages it had introduced, from the 1880s, a centre automatic coupling and a new type of gangway — the so-called 'Pullman vestibule' (see page 47). Henry Howard Sessions the superintendent of the Pullman Company in the 1880s, was the leading figure in this improvement, but it was not until the early twentieth century that something similar became widespread in Britain.

This was the so-called Gould or 'buckeye' coupling. It took the form of a movable knuckle-shaped hook in the centre of the headstock, and the mere act of propelling two similarly equipped vehicles together, one of which should have the hook 'open', causes the hooks to spring back behind each other when the joint is made. It can best be envisaged by locking the curled fingers of both hands together. There was, inevitably, a degree of longitudinal tolerance, but most of this was taken up, once the buckeye coupling was 'made', by the compression together of the two Pullman-type gangways. It was in all important respects a better arrangement.

The principal British protagonist of this type of coupling was the celebrated Nigel Gresley (later Sir Nigel) who, when carriage superintendent of the English Great Northern Railway, standardized the Gould coupling on main-line stock. It had, in fact, been used earlier but not universally. It became the standard form on the LNER after grouping and was used exclusively by the English Pullman Company and widely adopted by the English Southern Railway in later years. However, many British companies, notably the Great Western and the principal constituents of what was to become Britain's largest railway, the LMS, remained faithful to the screw coupling and old-style gangway connection.

Far left *Midland Railway corridor carriage No 2845 shows a typical British arrangement of carriage end detail features. Note particularly the screw couplings, large oval-shaped buffer heads, vacuum brake (upper) and steam heat connection hoses and gangway detail — see also Chapters 3 and 4. The coach itself, a brake composite, contained first, third and guard/brake compartments* (BR LMR).

Left *A complete view of the whole buckeye system on GNR twelve-wheel clerestory dining car No 2993, including Pullman-type gangways (see also Chapter 3, page 47). The side buffers themselves, of quasi-oval shape, are extended and the buckeye is dropped for attachment to a conventionally equipped carriage.*

Right *Typical buckeye coupling on a Gresley carriage. The movable hook and the lever to activate it are painted white. Pulling on the lever of the mechanism will open the hook to allow the coupling to be made with a similarly equipped vehicle. Note also the fairly wide slot in the headstock to allow some lateral movement of the drawgear. Buffers and gangway are still to be fitted.*

There were thus two widely disparate standards in use in Britain and they needed to be reconciled in some way for through working if nothing else. This merits clarification, for the two forms of coupling and their associated gangways (where present) were fundamentally incompatible. The gangway aspect is considered in Chapter 3, as part of the discussion of bodywork, but we can conveniently deal with the coupling problem here.

It is a characteristic of the buckeye coupling that it does not actually need corner buffers to stabilize the vehicle. Thus, in an 'all-buckeye' environment, side buffers are not fitted. This has been true for generations past in North America and has become so in Britain in all cases where vehicles can be guaranteed some form of exclusivity in use. However, when it is necessary to couple a buckeyed vehicle to a conventional one, a regular routine throughout much of this century, it is the buckeyed vehicle which needs to be modified. This is done by means of 'unlocking' the centre knuckle coupler and allowing it to hinge down out of the way. This done, there stands revealed a conventional hook to which the adjustable screw link can be attached from the adjacent vehicle.

Additionally, the buckeyed vehicle has to be fitted with side buffers, normally idle and kept retracted close to the headstock and well out of contact range with an adjacent vehicle. To render them operational, the buffer heads are pulled out by some 6-9 inches and a metal collar placed over the exposed shank to prevent it from re-retracting too far. The buffer then functions normally and can be brought into compression with the conventional vehicle.

Somewhat surprisingly, since the buckeye also has considerable advantages in terms of absorbing end impact (eg collision damage), the British did not adopt the system as standard for new construction until well after the railways were nationalized in 1948. Even as these words are written some forty years later still, many vehicles carry the older type of arrangement and it is not possible to predict when, or even if, it will totally vanish. It should, however, be stated that in 1988 no non-buckeyed long-distance passenger-carrying coaches are to be found in regular main-line service in Britain.

Brakes

While no carriages can operate without wheels and drawgear, it is a sad fact that for much of the early phase of nineteenth century history, they managed quite well without any really effective form of braking. However, by the start of the present century, automatic braking became required by law on all passenger trains, and moreover at least one vehicle per train had to be fitted with an auxiliary handbrake. It was in this vehicle that the 'guard' rode. This legal requirement arose from a serious accident at Armagh in 1889, even though the technical problem itself had been addressed some considerable time earlier at the Newark brake trials of 1875.

Although strictly outside the general period of this book, these continuous brake trials merit a brief mention here. They were held on the Midland Railway route between Nottingham and Newark in June 1875 and involved locomotives and trains from six companies. Eight different systems were evaluated, some of more than somewhat dubious merit, and although no very conclusive recommendations came out of the trials, they did serve to demonstrate quite clearly to all save the most partisan the superiority of the Westinghouse air brake over all the others. There were, however, other considerations at work, some of which had little or nothing to do with the relative efficiency of the brakes. Vested interest was also present in such measure that no harmonization was achieved and an opportunity was lost to standardize on an efficient air brake more than a century before it finally came exclusively into its own on BR in the 1980s.

The Newark trials are well recorded elsewhere, but, in spite of the many systems tried, only two forms of braking sufficiently stood the test of time in the twentieth century context to merit our concern here, the vacuum and the air brake; even this was one too many. Inevitably, of course, both existed side by side (as with couplings and gangways) and since they were essentially incompatible, the harmonization of braking systems in Britain was bedevilled for generations. Furthermore, just as with couplings, most British companies adopted the somewhat less effective of the two alternatives, the so-called automatic vacuum brake. Not that there was anything wrong with it *per se* — it was a very good and reliable system, and totally fail safe. It was simply that the air brake was, all round, rather better. The latter type has now become a British standard but it was as recently as 1987 that regular use of the vacuum brake finally terminated. Before describing the systems, it may be helpful to list the conditions, laid down by the Board of Trade, which automatic braking had to fulfil at the end of the Victorian period:

1. In case of accident, the brakes are to be instantaneously self-acting.
2. The brakes are to be capable of being put 'on' and taken 'off' on the engine and every vehicle of the train.
3. The brakes are to be efficient, instantaneous in action and capable of application without difficulty by driver or guard.

Figure 11 *The vacuum brake apparatus. The detail drawings show the 'universal' connecting hose attachment between vehicles (a), the ball valve mechanism (b) and the vacuum cylinder itself (c). The main diagram (d) shows the configuration of the whole system.*

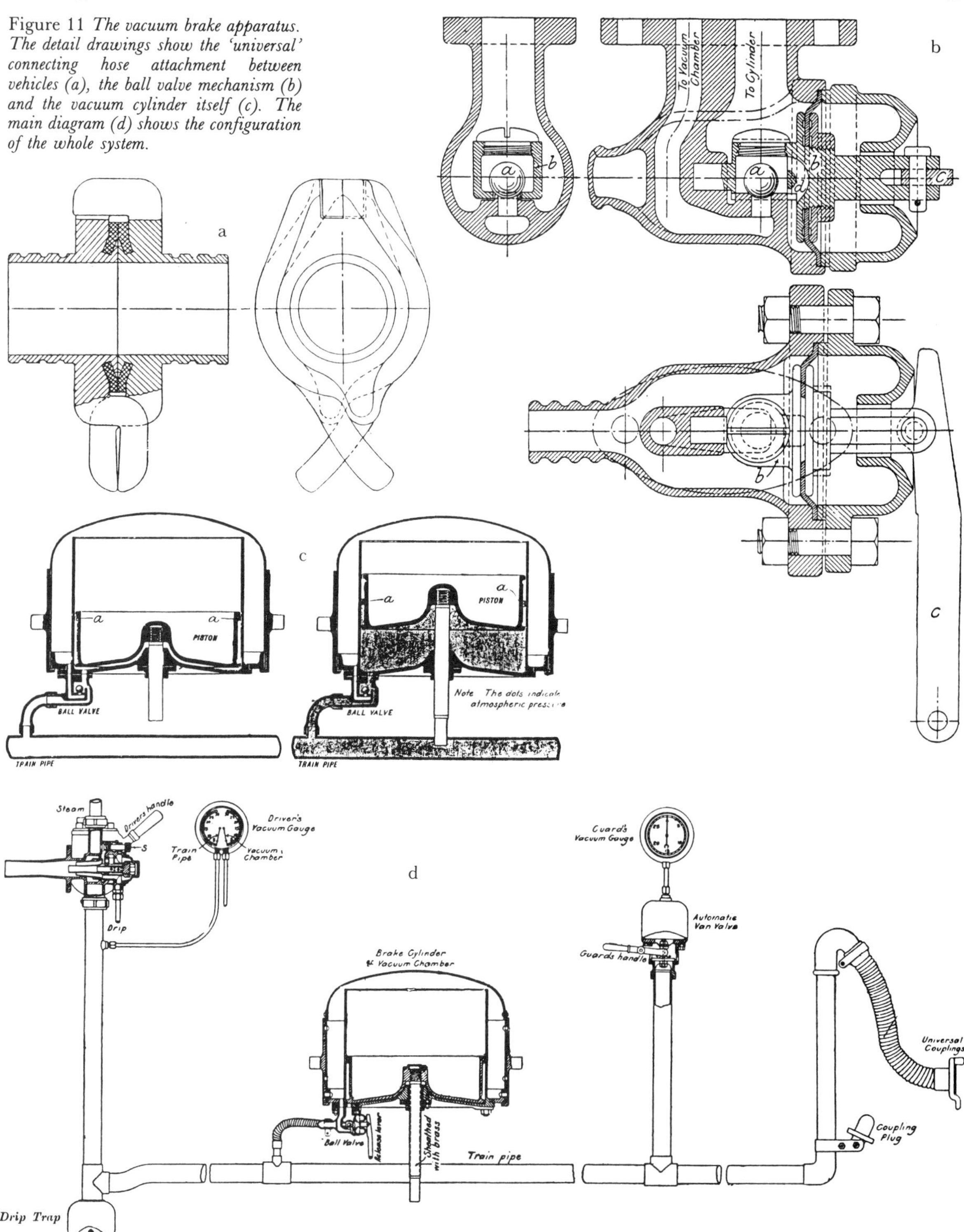

4 The brakes are to be regularly used in daily working.
5 Materials are to be durable and easily maintained in working order.

In both systems, the operation of the brake is brought about by creating a pressure difference on either side of a moving piston enclosed in the brake cylinder. The normal position (ie brakes not applied or 'off') occurs when the pressure (or lack of it) is equal on either side of the piston. Creation of the pressure difference, by accident or design, causes the piston to move, and by means of mechanical linkages (attached to the piston rod(s)) applies the brakes to the wheels. In the vacuum system the pressure difference is, theoretically, that between a perfect vacuum and normal atmospheric pressure (say 1 atmosphere at the very best). In the compressed air system, the pressure difference is between that of the compressed air itself (usually some 80-100 psi) and the atmosphere. This is some 4-6 times more than the pressure of the atmosphere acting against even a perfect vacuum; the air brake therefore possesses intrinsically more power. Indeed, it is a not very dissimilar principle which differentiates the huge and cumbersome low-pressure stationary steam engine from a smaller, but equally powered, high-pressure steam locomotive. The price paid is increased mechanical complexity and the same is true of brakes. It will therefore be helpful to outline some of the processes involved, if only to help explain the reasons for the choice between the two systems.

Dealing first with the vacuum brake, this apparatus works on the basis that a vacuum is created throughout the length of the train braking system from engine to last carriage. This is achieved by means of a continuous tube (or 'train pipe') from one end of the train to the other; vehicles are connected by flexible hoses each of which is equipped with a special connector to avoid ingress of atmospheric air. Below each carriage there is fixed the brake cylinder itself (normally one on a four-wheeler or six-wheeler and two on a bogie coach) which is connected with and 'open' to the train pipe and is thus also maintained in a state of vacuum.

When air enters the train pipe, thus destroying the vacuum, it can only reach one side of the brake piston because inside the brake cylinder is a simple non-return device — typically a ball valve — which only permits the incoming air access to one side of the piston, normally the underside. Thus the pressure difference is created within the brake cylinder which will apply the brakes. This can be achieved either deliberately, by driver or guard by means of a brake control which allows air into the brake pipe, or by accident, should the integrity of the train pipe be destroyed if, for example, two connecting hoses should separate.

This is the essential 'automatic' or 'fail safe' situation. It will be appreciated that a sudden accidental influx of air to the train pipe will apply the brakes more rapidly than the controlled influx by the driver or guard, but this is all to the good, since the train will stop more quickly. It is also possible for the driver to make a firm but controlled 'emergency' application by letting in air more rapidly than he would normally do for a routine stop. Likewise, when a passenger pulls the emergency alarm cord (chain) in a carriage, this has the effect of *partially* destroying the vacuum, thus alerting the driver who will then stop the train at the first safe place, ie within the protection of signals.

To free brakes applied by this system, it is necessary to re-establish the equilibrium in the brake cylinder(s), thus allowing the piston to resume its normal position. This can be done either by re-creating the vacuum in the train pipe or by admitting air to the normally 'vacuum only' side of the brake piston. This latter procedure is normally only carried out after vehicles have finished operating and are safely 'parked' in a siding with a handbrake applied. It is usually achieved by unseating the ball valve from its socket, thus allowing atmospheric air to reach both sides of the piston, and can be speedily effected by pulling a cord release provided for this purpose situated below the carriage floor.

To work the automatic vacuum brake, the only piece of ancillary apparatus other than the brake equipment itself, is a means to create the vacuum. This is normally achieved on the locomotive by means of an 'ejector', a mechanism which, as its name implies, ejects air from the train pipe. Sometimes the ejector was supplemented by a vacuum pump, which could maintain but not create the vacuum.

Turning now to the air brake, its intrinsically quicker-acting nature is obvious from the greater pressure difference already explained, but unlike the vacuum brake, which uses as its operating 'fluid' the universally available atmospheric air, the air-braked train must not only create but also carry with it a supply of compressed air, always available for instant use and readily replenishable. Thus, the first requirement is an air pump or compressor to create and maintain the supply of this working 'fluid'. This is an essentially more bulky and complex mechanism than the vacuum ejector, and when in operation it produces its own distinctly characteristic sounds. These were well in evidence on any steam locomotive to which one was fitted, and, indeed, on modern-day Southern Region electrics and the London Underground trains, to mention but two, the characteristic 'chunk-a-chunk-a-chunk' of the air compressors emanating from somewhere in the bowels of the vehicle is sufficient indication that one is riding an air-braked train!

Having created a supply of compressed air, it must then be stored and made available for use. This is usually achieved by means of a main reservoir on the engine and a series of individual auxiliary reservoirs on each coach, all interconnected. It is the small auxiliaries which actually apply power to the train brakes and they are replenished after a brake application by the compressor via the main reservoir. Already, this is a more complex set of equipment than for vacuum operation and the actuating mechanism itself is also more sophisticated, but again it makes use of the fact that, as with the vacuum brake, should air be allowed into the system (by accident or design), or more correctly should compressed air be allowed *out* of the sytem, the equilibrium is broken within the brake cylinder, the piston within is thereby caused to move and the brakes are applied. In essence, the cycle is as follows:

1 At the start of a journey, the compressed air from the engine's main reservoir is turned into the train pipe and, through branch pipes, 'charges' all the auxiliary reservoirs; but there is at this stage *no compressed air in the brake cylinder itself,* which is separated from both the main pipe and the auxiliary reservoirs by a triple valve (see step 3 below).

2 If the integrity of high pressure within the train pipe is now broken, by brake application or by severance of the flexible hose, the compressed air is released from the system and the state of equilibrium is broken. At this point the triple valve comes into play.

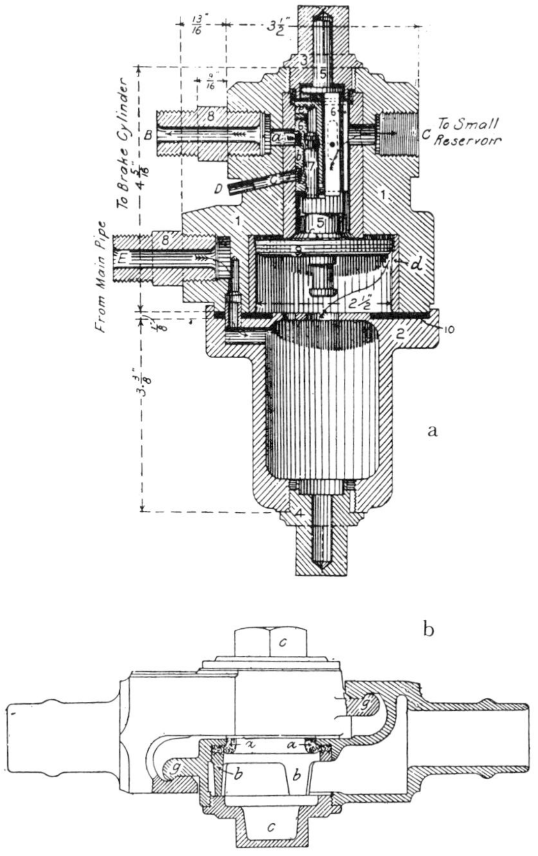

Figure 12 *The air brake apparatus. The detail drawings show the triple valve (a), the hose connection between vehicles (b) and the arrangement of the whole set-up (c).*

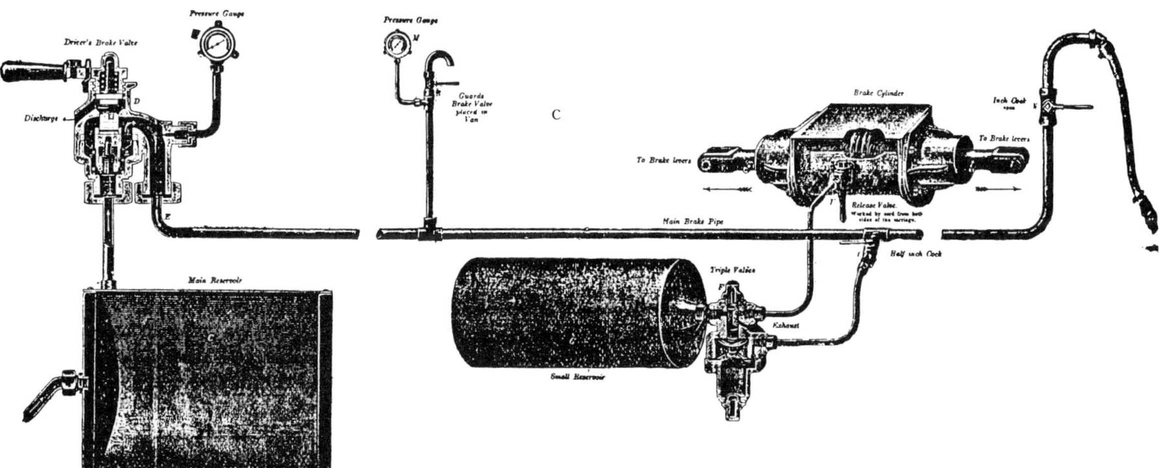

Figure 12

3 Attached to the brake cylinder is a fairly complex triple valve, connected, as its name suggests, to three outlets, the brake cylinder itself, the train pipe and the auxiliary reservoir, only two of which outlets are in mutual contact at any one time. When air is released from the train pipe, the compressed air in the auxiliary reservoir is now at a higher pressure than that in the train pipe, but is prevented from leaving the system by the triple valve. Instead, the air in the reservoir can now react against the lower pressure within the brake cylinder and thus apply the brakes.

Once again, the precise working of the various mechanisms need not concern us, but in essence whereas the vacuum brake works by increasing pressure on the *active* side of the brake cylinder piston, the air brake works by reducing pressure on the *passive* side. To do this requires a much more complicated mechanism to create and maintain the essential compressed air; so it may reasonably be asked why did *any* railway adopt the air brake, a clearly more expensive solution?

The reasons are bound up with train working, for the air brake is essentially quicker acting and this could be an important operational factor. Each auxiliary reservoir functions as an independent power source when the train pipe pressure is reduced, thus producing a well nigh instantaneous reaction down the train. With the vacuum system, the operating medium, air, comes from within the single train pipe and thus takes a measurable, if brief, time to be brought to bear on all vehicles. It is an altogether gentler sort of brake for the passenger and was, for this reason, often preferred. Indeed, when BR finally went over to air braking on most of its hitherto 'vacuum' main lines, many were the jerks and judders to be felt as drivers took time to appreciate the generally fiercer characteristics of the new air brakes compared with the older system.

It was, of course, these very characteristics which caused the air brake to be adopted in Britain by those railways which favoured it. The quick application and quick release offered a much more sensible choice where systems had a high proportion of intensive 'stop and start' suburban operations. Thus, it became an obvious choice for several of the steam railways radiating from London and elsewhere. It was also a natural choice wherever service frequency indicated that the even higher capital cost of electrification was justified, hence the London Underground and Southern Railway examples already mentioned.

The air brake is also advantageous, for reasons already stated, where normal train lengths are considerable and/or where higher speeds are contemplated. Thus, in North America, with its immensely long trains, it has always been favoured (for both passenger and freight), and in Britain its ability to bring a train to a halt from higher speed but at no sacrifice in braking *distance* has been crucial to the speed-up of both passenger and freight operations since the late 1950s and early 1960s.

Before leaving the subject of brakes, one or two more points need making. To expedite through working between vacuum-braked and air-braked railways, it was often necessary for carriages to carry both types of equipment. In this case, the vehicle was said to be 'dual braked' and revealed its status by even more flexible hoses dangling from the carriage ends than either system would require on its own. To avoid wrong hose connections — and this point at least *was* standardized in Britain — the air hoses were normally of smaller diameter than the vacuum hoses, and carried a differently shaped connector.

Finally, for the bulk of the vehicles covered in this survey, the brakes themselves were in the form of friction blocks rubbing against the wheel tread and activated by a series of rods and levers connected to the brake cylinder(s). One set of 'brake rodding' normally sufficed on each carriage, in the case of dual fitted carriages being independently connected to both the vacuum and the air cylinders but, of course, only operated by whichever system was in use at the time.

In the case of so-called 'brake vans', a brake wheel in the guard's compartment could apply the brakes independently, by acting mechanically on the same set of rodding. If this form of handbrake was applied, it could not of course be released by simply pulling an external string, for it had to be physically released from within the vehicle. It was the railway equivalent, if you like, of a parking brake, and was mostly used to hold carriages stationary on gradients or in sidings when not connected to a locomotive. Needless to say, incidences of trains moving off without the handbrake being released were not uncommon and could result, *in extremis*, in the wheels being dragged along the rails for a distance. The resulting 'flat' on the wheel circumference, even if only small, could be disturbing to the passengers and could take several hundreds of miles to be worn away.

3. The carriage body

We must now turn our attention to that part of the carriage which, for most people, gives it character — the main body shell. In Britain, unlike many countries, carriages were usually designed by the railways that operated them rather than being purchased 'off the peg' from a range of manufacturer's standard types. Most were also built by the companies themselves, but even where railways felt the need to go to outside contractors, the carriages were still mostly built to the company's rather than the contractor's design. Of course this was true also for locomotives and as in the latter sphere so too in the carriage field, the British scene was characterized by its infinite variety both in style and decorative treatment. Some railways followed broadly similar lines while others were markedly different, and there were always subtle distinctions to be seen. There was no way, for example, that a London and North Western carriage could be mistaken for a Great Western example, or a Midland one confused with a Great Northern product; and Pullman was different from them all. One suspects that the companies preferred it that way!

Yet within all this manifold variety there was an underlying consistency of approach which this chapter attempts to distil, with the sole exception of the Pullman type, a vehicle of markedly American inspiration in both style and construction which will therefore be considered separately in Chapter 12.

The 'British' carriage made use of a separate body shell, mounted on an appropriate underframe. At the start of the twentieth century, wooden construction was the normal practice and remained the dominant material for most of the period covered by this first volume. Even though certain railways, for example the LNWR, GWR, Midland, Lancashire and Yorkshire and London and South Western, occasionally assayed the use of metal sheeting for parts of the outer 'skin' and added metal reinforcements to the framework, a wooden structure was the basis. After the grouping in 1923, the LMS did not really abandon what was, basically, a wooden-bodied coach until after 1930, while the LNER clung on to solid teak for the vast majority of its coaches until as late as 1941. Even then, both of these great companies still remained faithful to mostly timber frameworks, albeit with metal skins. Nor did techniques vary too much. The late Victorian period had seen the establishment of most of the principles which remained sound for many decades into the new century; they stood the test of time.

The body proper: floors, sides and ends

British carriages at the start of the present century were mostly built on the compartment principle embodying many outside doors. The need to thus interrupt the framing to make way for doorways rather inhibited the more integral type of construction favoured by Pullman (whose carriages generally had end doors only) and was one of the major reasons for the continued use of separate bodies, certainly during the 'wooden' era.

The starting point was the floor itself, a typical form of contemporary turn-of-the-century construction being shown, largely self-explanatory, in Figure 13. The main point to make is that the floor itself was designed to suit the configuration of corridors, partitions, lavatories, etc which were eventually to be erected upon it, and careful marking out and preliminary joinery had to be carried out to make sure that all subsequent components were a precise fit. Most of the actual joinery embodied quite simple forms of construction in order to expedite manufacture by machinery. Normal rules of carpentry applied in terms of the thickness of tenons, depth of mortices and grain direction relative to the joints in question. The aim was to ensure that pieces connected together were weakened as little as possible. The timber most commonly used for floor framing was oak or teak, the floor itself being made of deal, as were the internal partitions. Additionally, metal angle corner brackets (or 'knees') were often used to reinforce right-angle (and other) joints, and many sections were bolted together — indeed, the term 'coach bolt' provides its own explanation.

Above the floor, the side and end framing had to be designed so as to maintain its proper formation as well as support the covering panels. Again, oak or teak was the preferred choice for framing, with some preference for teak which keeps its form better during climatic changes, endemic, of course, as far as British railway carriages were concerned. Typical turn-of-the-century arrangements, giving all the associated nomenclature, are shown in Figure 14.

In general, it was customary to build the side and end frames as a series of sub-assemblies before offering up each completed frame to the floor. The analogy with a modelmaker's 'kit of parts' comes to mind and is a not wholly inappropriate way of visualizing the process. The order of assembly was usually to erect the ends first, followed by the corner panels and all the side sections containing fixed lights. The 'cantrail' was then added along the top of the side sections, thus securing the vertical pillars and forming

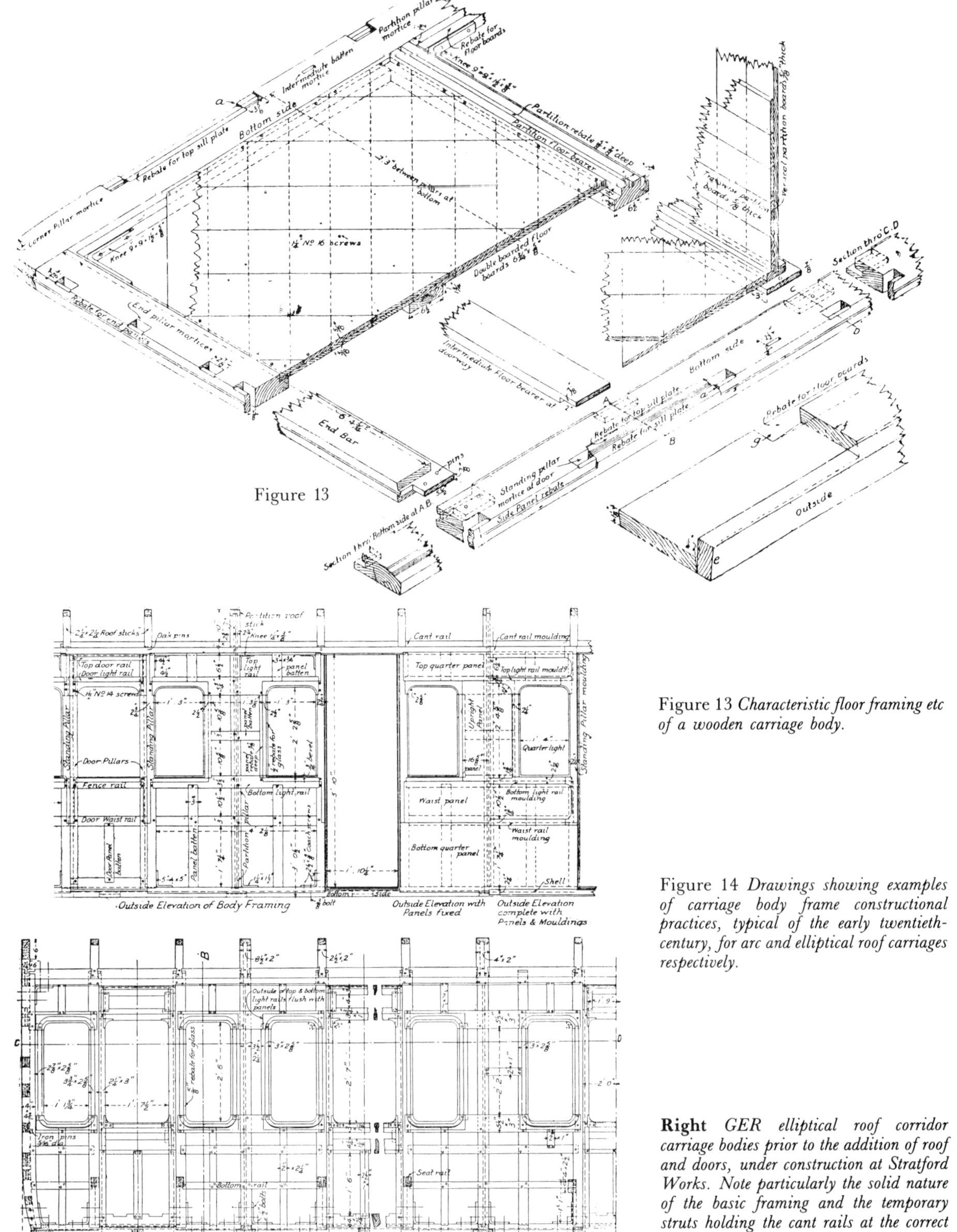

Figure 13

Figure 13 *Characteristic floor framing etc of a wooden carriage body.*

Figure 14 *Drawings showing examples of carriage body frame constructional practices, typical of the early twentieth-century, for arc and elliptical roof carriages respectively.*

Right *GER elliptical roof corridor carriage bodies prior to the addition of roof and doors, under construction at Stratford Works. Note particularly the solid nature of the basic framing and the temporary struts holding the cant rails at the correct distance apart.*

the base of the roof. At this point, and before adding the roof and doors, it was customary practice to 'straighten' the coach body if necessary. If it was found that any part of the framing was bulging outwards or inwards it was either cramped or forced out, and temporary battens or stretchers were fixed across between the side pillars to hold the assembly straight. The datum line for straightness was struck at waist level, for if the body was not straight at this point it would be difficult for the pre-assembled doors to be properly fitted.

At this intermediate stage the body was also kept square by placing temporary struts either between the cantrails or diagonally from the foot of a pillar at one side to the opposite side cantrail. Clearly, once all the internal partitions, seat rails, roof sections and panels had been added, the integrity of the shape would be permanently assured, so it was important to start from a properly 'trued-up' framework. Once a truly square and straight assembly had been achieved, the framing was then cleaned at the joints and tested (with a straight-edge) to ensure that the foundation for the outer panels was level. If not, the panels would twist and possibly split. Moreover, the resultant uneven surface would display itself badly under paint or varnish, and this was most certainly *not* to be desired. This, after all, was the part of the carriage which the customer registered first — its outer 'skin'!

Before the days of the metal-skinned coach, outside panels were usually made of either Moulmein teak or Honduras mahogany. The latter was favoured if a painted finish was desired because it took the paint well, while although the natural oils in teak made it less suitable (when very new) for a paint finish it was an admirable candidate for a varnished finish, its normal treatment. Finally, while it was rare for a new teak-panelled carriage to be *painted*, there were examples of mahogany-panelled carriages being *varnished*, for instance on the London Brighton and South Coast Railway at the turn of the century.

Regardless of timber choice, the selection of the right piece for a particular location was a matter of some skill. Firstly, the correct part of the trunk of the tree had to be used for such panels as needed to be curved (eg the bottom panels below fixed lights and at the bottom of doors). A near-contemporary description states that such panels 'should not be cut from the middle of the tree but from the sides and should have the heart side outwards as the natural law which governs the shrinkage of timber will then tend to keep the panel in the direction in which it is bent'.

Having established the correct shape for the panels

it was then not uncommon, if a varnished finish was to be given, to consider the grain pattern. Builders of wooden-bodied coaches had something of a passion for symmetry, and if grain pattern could enhance such effects it was often felt desirable, especially for the better coaches, to choose and place adjacent panels in harmonizing or matching pairs or triples, depending on the grain pattern.

Before being actually applied to the carriage framing, mahogany and teak panels required rather different treatment. Mahogany is very durable when dry but does not, unless protected by paint or varnish, stand up too well to weather. Moreover, it can become brittle when older, even though retaining its durability. For this reason, mahogany panels had to be additionally treated before fixing to avoid splitting. This was normally achieved by backing them with a canvas layer, thoroughly soaked with hot glue. When this was pressed into the back of the panel it became almost bedded into the wood surface which had been left rough finished just for this very purpose. The outer face of the panel was, of course, scraped or sandpapered.

If the panel was to be one of the curved variety, it was often fixed in position while quite warm, before the glue had set; it bent more readily in this condition and would dry out in the 'curved' configuration. Flat panels were allowed to dry out before fixing, and in either case the body framing was normally treated with white lead paint before the panels were fixed into position. The fixing was done by means of carriage pins set round the edges of the panels (copper was preferred to iron for the best work since it avoided rust). Curved panels were usually fixed from the bottom edge, working upwards.

When positioned, the panels were further stiffened at the back by blocks of wood glued at intervals into the corners formed by the panel and the pillars, rails or battens forming the framework; this was to prevent splitting. Any remaining panel areas unsupported by such blocks were then covered by flat wooden pieces, about 2 inches square, glued in position with their grain running diagonally to that of the panel. When dry, the whole (of the inside surface) was given several coats of protective white lead paint.

All told, it was such an immensely careful procedure as to make one wonder at times why mahogany was used at all compared with teak. The latter wood is much less liable to split and does not necessarily need to be glued; in fact, it was usually so oily when new that contemporary glues would not adhere properly for any length of time anyway. Thus teak panels were often only pinned in position, supported solely by the main framework — a much less time consuming procedure. Again, the inside faces were coated with white lead.

I have been quite unable to determine the reasons why the different railways chose these two disparate

Figure 15 *Typical cross-section of the upper part of a wooden-bodied carriage side showing the framing, panel and window bolection treatment.*

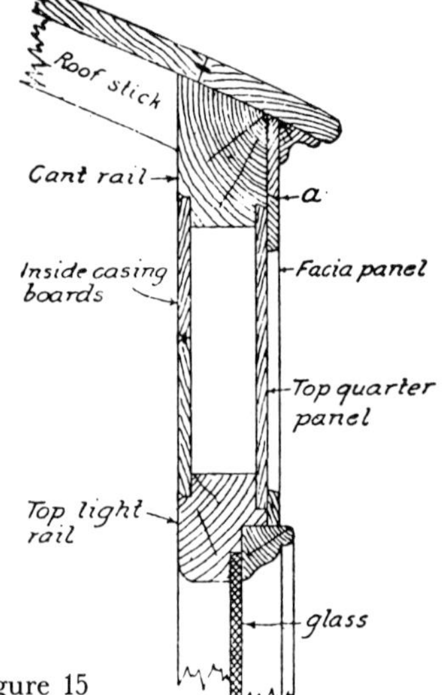

Figure 15

Lower body panel replacement on Queen Alexandra's (ex-LNWR) Royal Saloon at the National Railway Museum during 1981. These curved profile lower panels were always the most difficult to make and, in consequence, often the most likely to need constant attention due to splitting for instance.

The panel beading, window frame and other characteristic details of a typical Edwardian wooden-bodied carriage are well exemplified in this view of London & South Western Railway tri-composite (1st/2nd and 3rd class) brake No 3598 in process of restoration at the National Railway Museum during 1986.

timbers. Economics or merely the desire to have a painted finish may have had something to do with it. Labour, of course, was relatively cheap at the time and even tradition cannot be discounted. Furthermore, mahogany is known to be a lovely wood to work compared with teak, so it may, all in all, have been something of a swings and roundabouts situation.

Once panelled, the outside body (except the doors) could be finished off. This normally took the form of applying outside mouldings (usually of the same ⅜ inch thickness as the panels proper) to cover each of the panel joins, which gave further scope for embellishment. While it may have been necessary to put some sort of moulding on the carriage to protect the panel joins, there were no rules as to the precise shape or profile they should follow. Thus these moulding strips (or 'beading' strips as they were sometimes called) could be round or square cornered, or both in combination; in profile they could be half round, flat or 'D' shaped; and in width could vary from about 1 inch to more than 2 inches. They were pinned into position using pins sufficiently long to penetrate both panel and framework. Each railway adopted somewhat different approaches to set its own hallmark on its carriages (see Chapter 7) and the pictures with this chapter show other possible variations within what was, in all essentials, the same basic process.

The same was true of the fixed quarter lights and other fixed windows. The glass itself was bedded in the aperture on either felt, putty or India rubber and held in position by 'picture frame' type mouldings — sometimes called bolections (Figure 15) — fixed from the outside. In this case, the mouldings were fixed with brass screws so that they could be removed easily when new glass was required. If the screw head was to be left visible (rather than countersunk, filled over and painted), a more decorative screw might be adopted and it was a fair certainty that the craftsmen of the day would then take particular care that all the slots in the screw heads were identically aligned, possibly changing orientation as they went round a corner!

The carriage roof

Yet another distinctive and often distinguishing feature of the railway carriage was its roof. Its purpose was, of course, to protect the interior and its construction was fairly standardized, but its shape was almost as varied as the railways were numerous. So, before going any further this aspect had better be clarified — it will recur regularly in these pages.

Essentially, when discussing roof shape one is referring to its cross-profile, ie viewed from the end. There were two fundamental sorts, the plain roof profile and the clerestory section. Both could exhibit several variations in curvature, but the essential difference was that the clerestory roof had a raised centre section and its employment forced a change in constructional technique.

Taking the plain roof first, this could vary from being almost flat (the British carriage never, as far as is known, employed a flat roof) to a deep, almost (but not quite) semi-circular profile. Generally, the plain roof could be grouped into three broad families, whose characteristics are summarized below:

1 *The 'arc' or 'compass' roof* (Figure 16) This roof shape usually displayed a perfect arc of a circle, of differing radii depending on the individual company. In some cases, the curvature sharpened a little as it approached the carriage side, but the genuine arc roof was always characterized by meeting the side proper at a quite definite angle. The arc roof was essentially a nineteenth-century style, but some coaches were built to this profile in the twentieth.
2 *The 'low elliptical' or 'cove' roof* (Figure 17) This roof shape had an 'arc' type centre section (again of varying radius depending on the company), but the junction between the main roof curve and the top of the cantrail was in the form of a radius of

Scale 7mm = 1ft

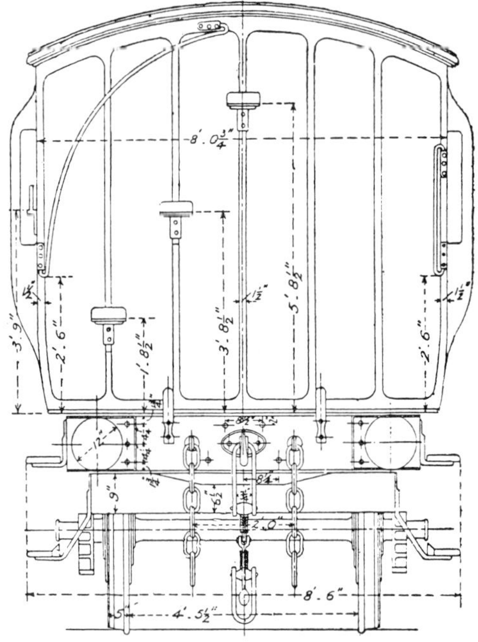

Figure 16 *Typical arc roof profile displayed on a Caledonian Railway brake-ended carriage.*

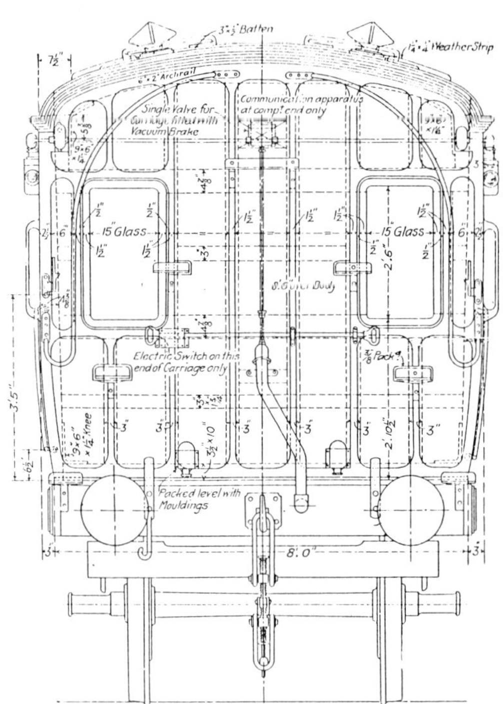

Figure 17 *A turn of the century 'cove' or low-elliptical roof profile as adopted by the Great Central Railway.*

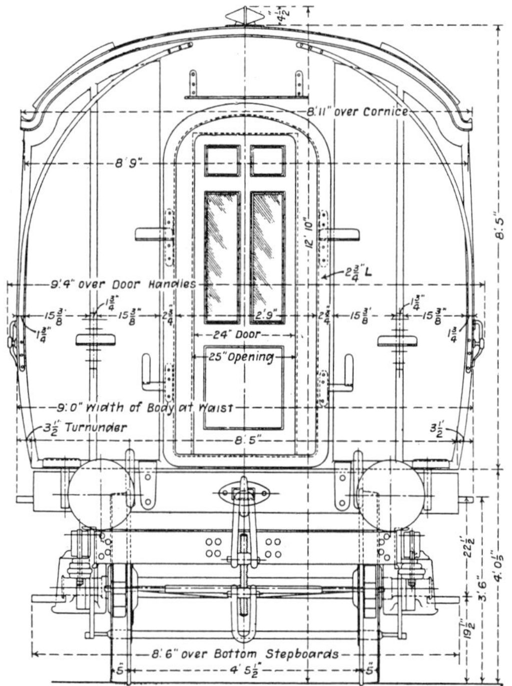

Figure 18 *The most typically twentieth-century roof shape was the fully elliptical form, as characterized here by an LNWR example.*

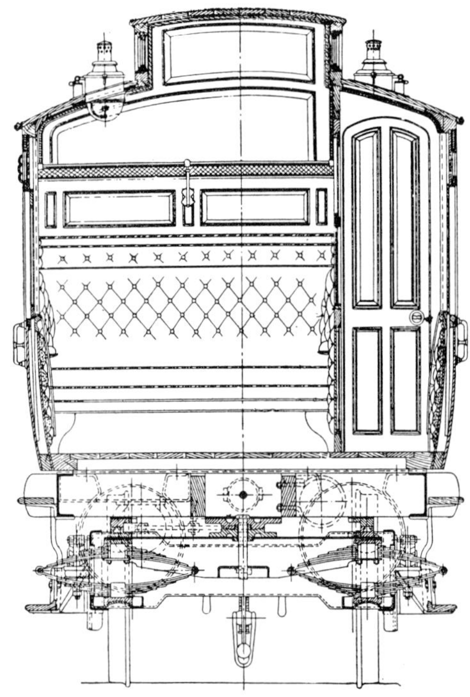

Figure 19 *Cross-sectional drawing of a typical British 'add-on' clerestory roof, in this case a late-nineteenth-century NER example. Further drawings of this particular type are shown in Figure 32 (page 66).*

a circle (often quite small) which was actually directed almost vertically where the roof met the side. This style also dated back to the nineteenth century but remained in use for new construction for some little time after 1900.

3 *The 'high-elliptical' or 'full elliptical' roof* (Figure 18) This section was, in all its subtle variations, by far the most typical British twentieth-century roof shape and after the railway grouping of 1923 no other type was built. Indeed, many companies had adopted it much earlier in the century.

The word 'elliptical' is something of a misnomer. For a start, it was, in fact, only at best a semi-elliptical of linguistic impurity it is doubtful if the so-called 'elliptical' roof ever bore much more than a passing resemblance to the pure mathematical form from which it took its name. It was, of course, a sort of 'half oval', but the actual shape was usually derived by setting out a series of genuine circular arcs linked together.

If to these three categories one adds various other qualifying adjectives, one can readily imagine the descriptive situation quickly getting out of hand, but oddly enough this does not seem to have caused too much actual confusion — so this book will continue the tradition.

The 'add-on' clerestory style is well exemplified by NER composite (first/third) No 3414. This was a particularly opulent vehicle for its time, having lavatories for both classes but no draughty outside doors for either category. The carriage displays typical David Bain panelling — see page 110 — and its stylistic similarity, roof excepted, to the picture on page 40 is readily apparent.

Turning now to the clerestory roof (Figure 19), its ecclesiastical nomenclature is obvious. The raised centre section, ie the clerestory proper, had vertical sides, sometimes fitted with windows known as 'deck lights'. Two main forms of clerestory were to be seen in Britain, once again with considerable subtle variations within each. The older type simply added the clerestory to the top of an arc roof section, the clerestory roof itself also displaying an arc profile. The North Eastern Railway was rather fond of this shape, as was the nineteenth-century Midland (in small doses).

Later clerestories were often of much more subtle contour, generally employing a more rounded (or 'shouldered') lower roof profile together with a clerestory top which could either be a perfect arc or, as in the case of the later Midland examples, of more subtle compound curvature. The London and North Western and Great Northern Railways produced some particularly nice examples, while the Great Western entered the twentieth century with its own distinctive form which did not quite fit either category.

On most British carriages until quite modern times, the roof cross-profile continued to the carriage end unmodified and was reflected in the detail treatment given to this part of the vehicle. However, some railways adopted a down-curved roof at the ends of the coach (viewed from the side). This is usually referred to as a 'domed' roof, once again employing a not wholly accurate descriptive word. Some particularly beautiful effects were often created, both with plain and clerestory profiles, possibly the most celebrated examples of which on a plain roof were the many teak-bodied coaches built for the GNR and

MIDLAND
THIRD
THIRD
2951
FIRST
FIRST
THIRD
2951
THIRD

N.E.R.
THIRD

45022

Left *The MR clerestory shape, introduced in 1897, has often been described as an 'organic' style, partly because the end panelling continued without interruption into the clerestory itself but also because the roof profile itself employed subtle forms of curvature. This example, No 2951, is a lavatory brake composite (ie first and third class) designed and built by David Bain in 1905. The NER stylistic influence — see the picture on page 39 — is obvious* (BR LMR).

LNER by Nigel Gresley in the pre-grouping and post-grouping period, which became a real hallmark of the LNER main lines in the 1920s and 1930s. The North Eastern also produced a rather similar roof, as did the GWR in the 1940s.

On the clerestory side, the 'doming' could be either on both the lower roof *and* the clerestory, or on the clerestory roof only. In the former category, outstanding examples were the LNWR dining and sleeping cars whose construction just extended into the twentieth century, while in the second category the later LNWR clerestories and those of the East Coast Joint Stock were as good as any to serve as quick examples at this point in the narrative.

So to the building of the roof itself. For a plain roof without a domed end, the essential requirement was to establish the correct profile at the carriage end and then repeat it at intervals throughout the length of the vehicle, thus establishing the basic skeletal shape on to which the roof covering was to be fixed. Starting with the carriage end framing, the top member known as the 'arch rail' was the key. It was a substantial component, often sawn out of a single piece of wood. Sometimes, for economy, particularly with more curvaceous roof sections, several pieces of wood were employed, carefully jointed together. Like all other members of the carriage framework it could be — and usually was — rebated at the lower edge to accept the various pieces of panel timber and, as with the sides, joints were covered with beading strips.

Between the two end arch rails were situated a series of 'roof sticks' across the carriage, fixed to the tops of the cantrails. These copied exactly the curve of the arch rail and were rarely more than 2 or 3 feet apart. For example, above a typical compartment of say 6 feet between partitions, each partition would be surmounted by a roof stick and there would be at least one and commonly two sticks between the partitions. Roof sticks were sometimes made of ash, sawn to the curve of the roof, but this was rather wasteful of timber so a common solution was to bend roof sticks on a machine.

The machine itself was a device rather resembling a longitudinal slice from the outside of a cylinder whose radius was somewhat less than that of the roof. The roof sticks were placed on top of this curved surface and then bent down to meet the curve, being held in position by rollers which were screwed down from above. To provide the right conditions for bending, the roof sticks, before being put on the machine, were place in a closed steam chamber for about 2 hours at some 50 psi. They were then clamped to the machine and left for at least 6 hours to cool down. Even so, there was still a natural tendency for them to straighten partially as the drying out continued. In part this was allowed for by making the radius of the bending machine smaller than that of the coach roof, but just to make sure a straight lath was placed across the ends of the roof sticks and pinned to them to prevent further straightening. They were then allowed to dry completely and only at this point were they cut to finished section with all necessary grooving or shaping.

When fixing the roof sticks to the cantrails, it was common to make a slight modification to the usual rectilinear framing joints. The natural tendency of the roof stick would still be to push the cantrails away from each other, so the joint was often made in the form of a dovetail whose shape, acting as a wedge, would serve to prevent the sides from spreading.

Middle left *The domed-end elliptical roof was very much a Gresley (GNR) idea, but the NER also adopted it with some enthusiasm during Edwardian days. The example illustrated is gangwayed open third class No 3750, a particularly neat design.*

Left *Early LNWR clerestories often had doming at the ends of both the lower and clerestory roof. Most of them were twelve-wheel sleeping or dining cars, but No 45022 seen in LMS days* circa *1937, some forty years after building, was an eight-wheel railway officers' inspection saloon and enjoyed a more than normally long life* (BR LMR).

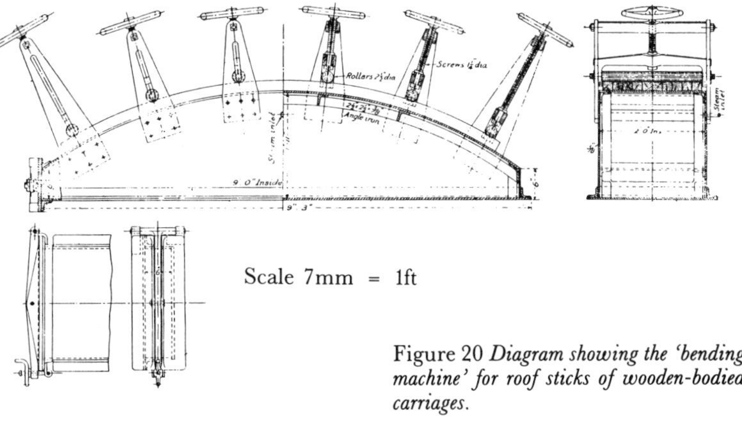

Figure 20 *Diagram showing the 'bending machine' for roof sticks of wooden-bodied carriages.*

Ready for canvassing — the NRM's LSWR tri-composite No 3598 (see the picture on page 37). Again note the variable width roof boards.

Interior view of an elliptical roof carriage before the addition of interior fittings. Note the metal reinforced roof sticks and the variable width roof boards, narrower at the more curved portion, wider in the centre. The carriage is an MR-design gangwayed open third class of the type shown in the picture on page 191.

Roof sticks were, quite clearly, not the easiest of components to make, particularly as the demand arose for deeper and more curvaceous roofs. They were at their simplest in the pure arc roof form and it is not without significance that even before the end of the nineteenth century, several railways had begun to use rolled metal bars of angle, 'T' or channel section to support the roof, and this ability to use an alternative material may have helped the move to the semi-elliptical roof. Certainly this was one of the first areas where an alternative to wood was used as part of the basic constructional framework of the vehicle. Even where a fully metal roof stick was not employed, it became increasingly common to reinforce the conventional wooden version with a flat metal plate along the whole length.

For a domed roof, it was the roof sticks only which established the cross-profile, since the arch rail followed the contour of the lowered outer end. In these cases, the normal procedure was to fill in the space between the last proper roof stick and the arch rail with a series of shorter curved pieces (at right angles to the roof stick and arch rail) whose curvature matched the desired shape at the point on the roof.

The roof was normally covered with tongue and groove boarding, fixed longitudinally between the roof sticks, utilizing the latter as formers. The width of the boarding varied according to the curvature of the roof; for instance, a coved roof would have quite narrow boards round the sharper curve of the roof edge and considerably wider ones at the more gently curved centre section. When the roof was boarded over, the gaps between the boards were stopped up and then the whole roof was covered in canvas, well impregnated with a fairly gruesome and messy mixture of linseed oil, white lead and putty. This substance oozed into all the crevices and through the canvas itself to form a waterproof seal. Further layers were added on top of the fixed canvas and a study of preserved coaches reveals that this was one area where perfection of appearance was often sacrificed to expediency. Perhaps it was the unpleasant nature of the work or maybe simply 'out of sight, out of mind'.

As a general rule the roof edge along the cantrail was finished off in one of two ways. The edge of an arc roof overhung the cantrail and the canvas went round to the underside. This sort of overhanging eaves effect was normally considered sufficient to protect the side panelling, and no separate gutter was provided by most companies. However, the LNWR (and a few others) did fix a moulding along the outer edge which in part prevented water from dripping on to passengers' heads in wet weather.

On a cove or elliptical roof coach, the lower edge of the canvas where it met the cantrail was trapped in position by a longitudinal gutter moulding, often of quite generous proportions and sometimes given quite a decorative cross-sectional shape. Such gutters

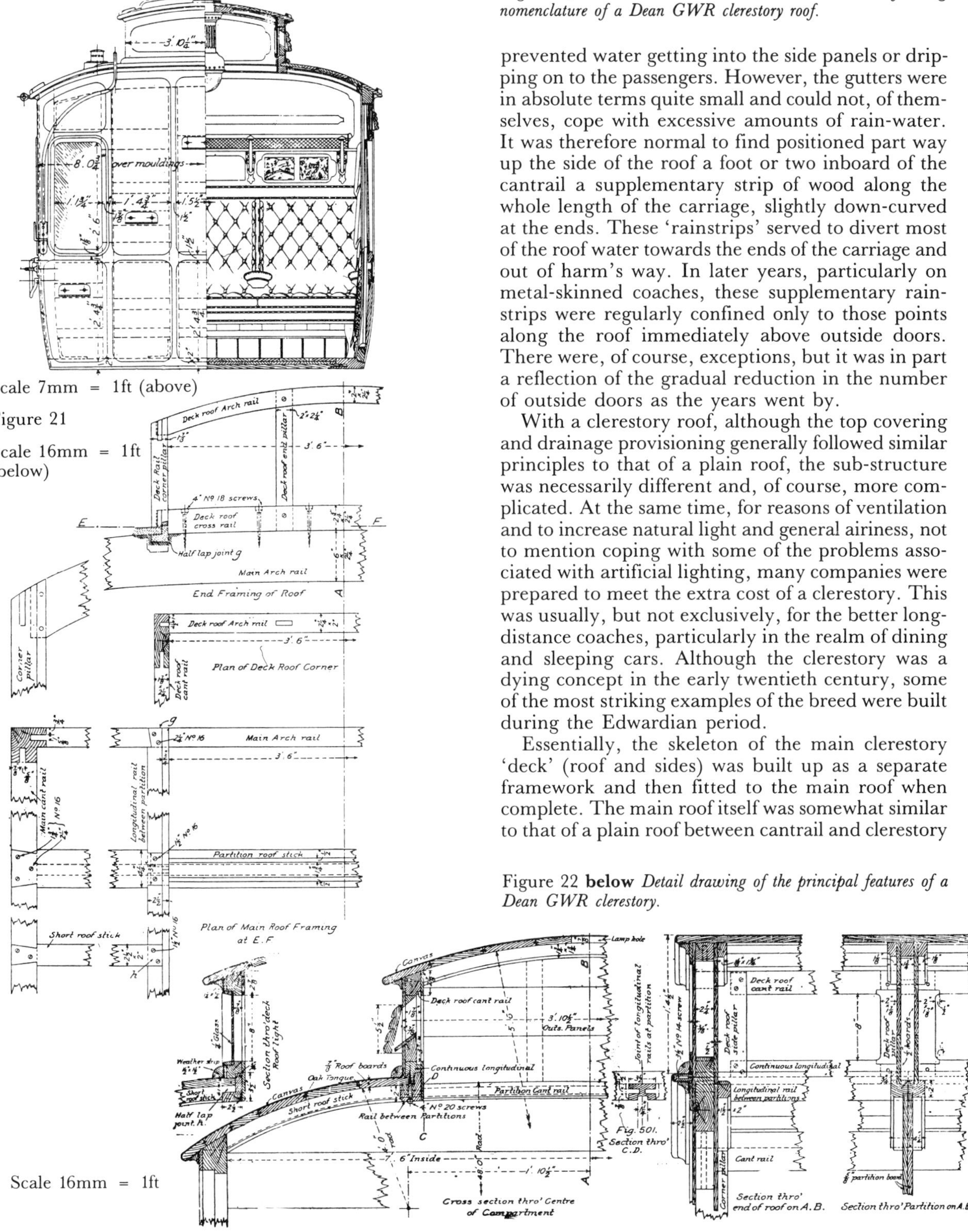

Scale 7mm = 1ft (above)

Figure 21

Scale 16mm = 1ft (below)

Figure 21 **left** *Cross-sectional elevation and basic framing nomenclature of a Dean GWR clerestory roof.*

prevented water getting into the side panels or dripping on to the passengers. However, the gutters were in absolute terms quite small and could not, of themselves, cope with excessive amounts of rain-water. It was therefore normal to find positioned part way up the side of the roof a foot or two inboard of the cantrail a supplementary strip of wood along the whole length of the carriage, slightly down-curved at the ends. These 'rainstrips' served to divert most of the roof water towards the ends of the carriage and out of harm's way. In later years, particularly on metal-skinned coaches, these supplementary rainstrips were regularly confined only to those points along the roof immediately above outside doors. There were, of course, exceptions, but it was in part a reflection of the gradual reduction in the number of outside doors as the years went by.

With a clerestory roof, although the top covering and drainage provisioning generally followed similar principles to that of a plain roof, the sub-structure was necessarily different and, of course, more complicated. At the same time, for reasons of ventilation and to increase natural light and general airiness, not to mention coping with some of the problems associated with artificial lighting, many companies were prepared to meet the extra cost of a clerestory. This was usually, but not exclusively, for the better long-distance coaches, particularly in the realm of dining and sleeping cars. Although the clerestory was a dying concept in the early twentieth century, some of the most striking examples of the breed were built during the Edwardian period.

Essentially, the skeleton of the main clerestory 'deck' (roof and sides) was built up as a separate framework and then fitted to the main roof when complete. The main roof itself was somewhat similar to that of a plain roof between cantrail and clerestory

Figure 22 **below** *Detail drawing of the principal features of a Dean GWR clerestory.*

Scale 16mm = 1ft

deck, but obviously there could be no series of continuous roof sticks in the conventional sense spanning the carriage at the lower level of the main roof between cantrails — it would have negated the whole purpose of adopting the clerestory in the first place. Clearly there would be some degree of transverse support for the clerestory deck wherever there were partitions, but this was not sufficient; in any case, many clerestory coaches had large open saloons, so further strengthening was always essential. This took the form of a substantial and continuous longitudinal rail where the main roof met the clerestory deck, usually supplemented by a second longitudinal immediately below it and fixed between the partitions. Straight-grained pitch-pine was preferred for this continuous longitudinal since it not only had the desired grain structure but the length of available logs also regularly made it possible for there to be no need to splice two pieces together to span the whole of the carriage from one end to the other.

Additionally, where clerestory carriages had very long open saloon interiors, it was common to incorporate what were known as 'carlines' made of iron and fixed at roughly 6 feet intervals to hold the sides together. These carlines were bent to conform with the shape of the main and deck roofs from side to side of the carriage, the outer ends being bolted to the cantrail. This added to the rigidity of the structure, but even so there was always the risk of a sagging roof on a clerestory coach with the passage of time, as study of the preserved Midland dining car (built in 1914) at the National Railway Museum will reveal.

This view of a Dean GWR family saloon gives a very clear impression of the roof structure of a typical open clerestory interior. The noticeably more substantial profile piece spanning the vehicle from side to side some three windows from the extreme end was known as a 'carline'.

Doors and other external fittings

Even a cursory glance at a typical railway carriage by a non expert will reveal the numerous 'bits and pieces' which are regularly carried on the outside of the vehicle. Many of these are quite simple fittings whose purpose was self evident. Amongst these can be included footstep boards, end steps (to enable railwaymen to gain access to the roof top), handrails and door handles, door stops, brackets for destination boards, external lighting control gear (including electrical connections to the next carriage if required and relevant) and so forth. Their purpose was self evident and need not take any further explanatory space. Neither, for that matter, need the rather more subtle variations which were used from time to time, to provide a better 'look out' for the guard or, in their outward appearance, to hint at other semi-specialized functions for the vehicle in question. These will be dealt with as they become relevant in context.

However, two external features of the carriage do need a little more amplification: the outside doors (for all vehicles) and the gangway connection (for those vehicles offering inter-vehicle communication).

Starting with the doors, these components were not normally fitted until almost the end of the body construction process. In part this was to enable the craftsmen to move more readily between the inside and outside of the vehicle as construction continued, but it was also because the door itself, along with its fittings, was quite a complex component involving, relative to its size, considerably more work than the plainer parts of the carriage. It was in fact easier to make the doors separately, virtually to completion apart from painting, and then fit them late in the building phase.

A fairly typical turn-of-the-century pattern of wooden door is shown in Figure 23, and the basic style hardly changed, save for the outer skin, for the first half of the century — or even longer. Quite apart from its obvious function, the door was also used (when closed) as a prime means of increasing ventilation. It always carried a 'drop light' and regularly a ventilator at the top as well. These features are both shown on the drawing. Additionally, the door had to be immensely strong to withstand hard usage. During most of the twentieth century, the carriage door was fitted with a 'slam lock' mechanism for safety, but this meant that the doors experienced little in the way of gentle handling when they were closed. Even in the 1980s, many suburban and cross-country trains have this type of door and there can be few rail travellers, particularly through London, who have not heard the fusillade of slamming doors which was and often still is the almost mandatory sound accompanying a train of workbound commuters on arrival at places like Waterloo, Charing Cross, Victoria and elsewhere!

Perhaps the most characteristic yet at times bewildering feature of the carriage door is the drop light — characteristic because it is always there but bewildering to many people because of its mode of operation. The drop light derives from the door of the old stagecoach, and although one of its functions is to allow fresh air inside the vehicle, an important secondary function is to allow the door to be opened from within. For safety reasons, many British carriage doors could only be opened by using the outside handle (and this is as true on the HSTs of the 1980s as it was on an Edwardian express, in both cases it being almost impossible to open a door accidentally

Figure 23 *Carriage door detail.*

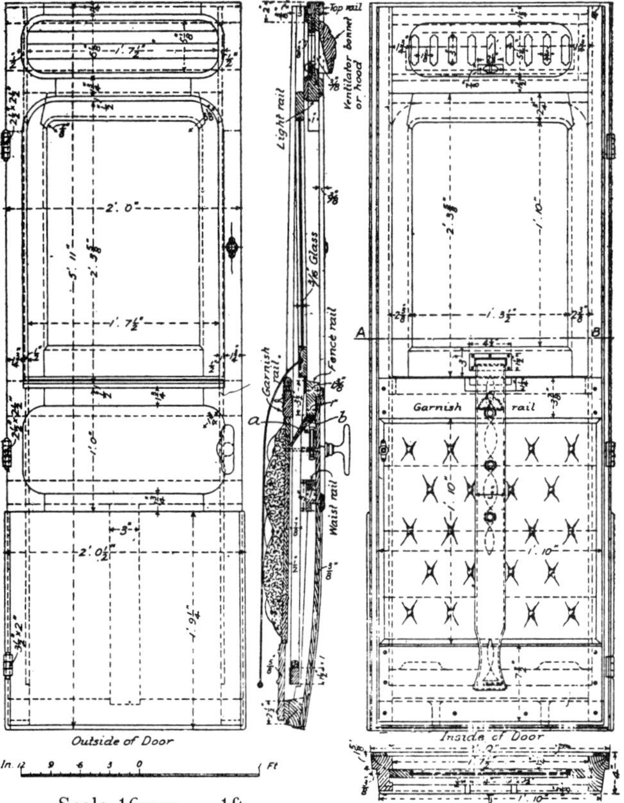

Scale 16mm = 1ft

from inside). It was and is, therefore, necessary to lower the drop light from within to allow the outer handle to be reached.

As a slight aside, this configuration, while not exclusively British, was typically so and can still cause confusion, especially to overseas visitors or those who use trains but rarely. Many are the puzzled looks on the faces of inexperienced passengers when faced at a station stop with an apparently handleless door! Moreover, the lack of an inside handle also carries with it a strong likelihood that an embarking passenger will either fail to close the door behind him or do so incompletely. For this reason, the slam lock is almost universal and has been so on most British carriages this century. It is nothing more than a spring loaded conventional latch arrangement which, if the door is slammed, automatically springs into its final resting place. It is connected directly with the outer handle, and a quick visual check by the station staff of the handle position can readily reveal an improperly closed door. Unless the handle is horizontal, the door latch is not properly engaged.

However, back to the drop light. Traditionally this was a wood-framed sliding window fitted at the bottom with a strong strap. In the fully closed position it was normally held in position by its lower edge resting on a ledge in the window frame often assisted by a spring mechanism. To lower the drop light it had first to be lifted off its ledge, pulled slightly towards the inside of the door and then lowered by the strap, the latter being sufficiently long that its free end was still accessible even with the drop light fully lowered. The strap had large holes at intervals which could be located over a brass pin on the garnish rail to hold the drop light in one of several intermediate positions. Should the drop light lose its strap (and they did make very good honing strops for cut-throat razors!), life became difficult although not necessarily impossible, especially if, as was often the case, an auxiliary 'finger pull' was affixed to the top of the drop light frame.

There were several slight variations within this general principle, and, as years went by, some railways introduced spring-loaded drop lights which would 'stay' in any given position and employed a finger pull at the top. Wooden frames sometimes gave way to metal and, later, a 'frameless' drop light of strong plate glass made its appearance. This latter is the common type to be found on the doors of modern BR stock. The drop light principle was not confined to the door, and many railways used them in other parts of the carriage for enhanced ventilation, sometimes with various additional operational subtleties.

The door top ventilator was often a characteristic stylistic feature. As with external beading, its basic structure and function was virtually the same wherever it appeared — essentially, a moving 'hit and miss' wooden slide, protected on the outside by a bonnet or hood. The physical appearance of this bonnet could, however, be anything within reason provided it functioned properly and was of a size appropriate to the door. It thus gave scope for considerable stylistic variation. Not all railways used them, and with some railways they tended to be either removed or blanked off in later years or even not fitted at all.

Finally, before leaving the door, it should be mentioned that the lack of internal door handles was not universal. Several railways employed a spring loaded internal sliding door catch which, with some effort, could be used to open the door. It connected directly with the door latch and was virtually impossible to make work, except deliberately, so was not really a safety hazard. These door catches were, and still are, commonly fitted to suburban and commuter trains since they do materially speed up the door opening procedure, an important aspect of operation when a 'high frequency, short station stop' service is desired.

The last principal feature to be mentioned in this section is the end gangway. It has already been mentioned in Chapter 2 that two incompatible styles were adopted in Britain, the so-called and traditional 'British Standard' and the more effective 'Pullman' type. In either case, there had, of course, to be a door frame put into the end of the carriage and this would normally be closed from within the vehicle by means of either a conventional hinged or sliding door. These doors were lockable, a very essential feature when a vehicle formed the last coach of the train, even if an 'end board' was fitted (see below).

GER third class carriage door showing the drop light strap and the internal spring-loaded door opening catch. The semi-circular door top was a feature of much GER suburban stock.

The external gangway structure was, however, markedly different and somewhat easier to visualize than actually to describe. In essence, however, the British Standard type was pulled out to meet its opposite number on an adjacent coach whereas the Pullman type projected slightly beyond the centre buckeye coupling and was compressed when two vehicles were connected together. This fundamental operational difference was reflected in the outside structural framework.

The British Standard gangway was supported by a massive metal 'housing' — almost a shallow box — mounted on the carriage end and around the door frame. It was about 3 feet wide, 7 feet high and had an almost semi-circular top. It projected anything from about 9 inches to almost 2 feet from the carriage end. Connected to this fixed housing was a movable outer frame, made of 'T' or 'L' section, whose elevation matched that of the housing. The connection was made by means of 'scissor' irons, sometimes called 'lazy tongs', whose nomenclature, for once, is descriptively apt. This allowed the outer frame to be moved outwards from the carriage end to meet the next vehicle, the two movable frames being held together by 'side' or 'gangway' clips, one being fitted permanently to the right hand edge of each frame when looking at the carriage end.

The movable frame carried a stiff horizontal metal plate at the bottom, at right angles to the frame itself and projecting back towards the fixed housing. This formed the floor of the gangway and slid over the top of the floor of the housing. Its length was such that even at maximum extension there was always an overlap between the moving and fixed parts, although accidents could (and did) happen, sometimes with interesting consequences to the three-dimensional geometry of the whole set-up! The floor was normally covered by a loose carpet or mat, to give some sort of additional protection to the customers passing through.

To those who have never encountered such a feature, it must sound a mite hazardous but was not, in fact, anything like as risky a business as it might seem. Once the train was assembled, the tight screw coupling and the side buffers imparted considerable

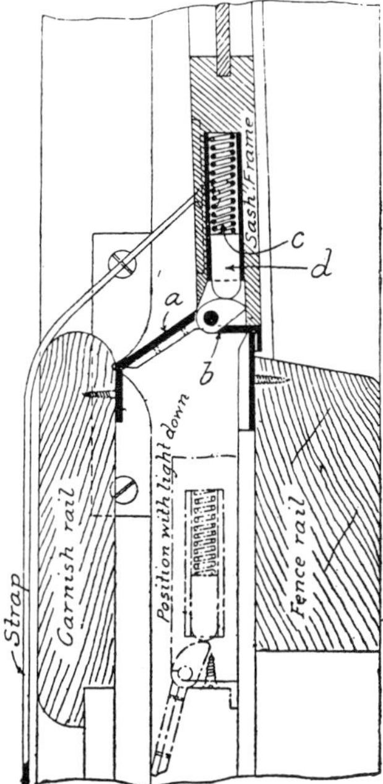

Figure 24 *A typical late-nineteenth-century carriage door dust and draught excluder to Telling's patent. When the drop light was closed, spring 'c' held the closing plate 'a' (pivoted on hinge 'b') in contact with the garnish rail by means of pin 'd'. This idea was used on carriage doors of* inter alia *the GWR, LNWR and LB & SCR.*

British Standard gangway components under construction at the Wolverton works of the LNWR, later LMS. Prominent in the foreground is the housing which will later be affixed to the carriage end.

stability, and although there was movement it was rarely excessive enough to cause alarm. In this respect it was considerably better than some of the abominable contraptions to be found on some continental coaches which not only moved about a great deal more but which also forced the passenger to walk, as it were, up, through and down the other side!

Weather protection for the gangway itself was formed by a flexible 'bellows' connection, made of leather and fitted between the fixed housing and movable frame, *inside* the lazy tongs. The whole was surmounted on top by a second cover sheet which gave double weather protection at the most vulnerable part. The only significant change to this style of gangway was introduced by the GWR (later copied by the LMS) in the early part of the post-grouping period. This replaced the scissors type extension by a spring suspension mounted at the top of the gangway frame. These were sometimes known as 'suspended' gangways but otherwise functioned much as before. When not actually in use, the British Standard gangway was pushed fully 'home' towards the housing and the movable frame was held in position against the fixed housing by retaining hooks on each side. At the outer ends of a set of gangwayed carriages an 'end board' would be fitted, completely covering the full area of the outer frame.

By contrast with all this, the Pullman gangway was amazingly simple. It too had a metal housing on the carriage end and a movable frame connected to the housing by means of leather with additional top weather protection. At its base it was supported by a spring loaded platform and by additional springs at the top. These springs were set so as to allow the gangway to project in front of the coupler. When two such coaches were buckeyed together, the gangway springs went into slight compression and no gangway clips or other restraints were required.

The real fun began when examples of each of these two types of gangways were to be put together in a train. The previous chapter explained the dropping of the buckeye and the extending of the buffers, but the gangway connection could also cause problems. For one thing, the Pullman type gangway was generally wider than the BS type — and often taller too. Its outer frame was generally more substantial so there was a total mis-match as far as shape was concerned, and this meant that the BS gangway had to be adapted to suit the Pullman type. This was

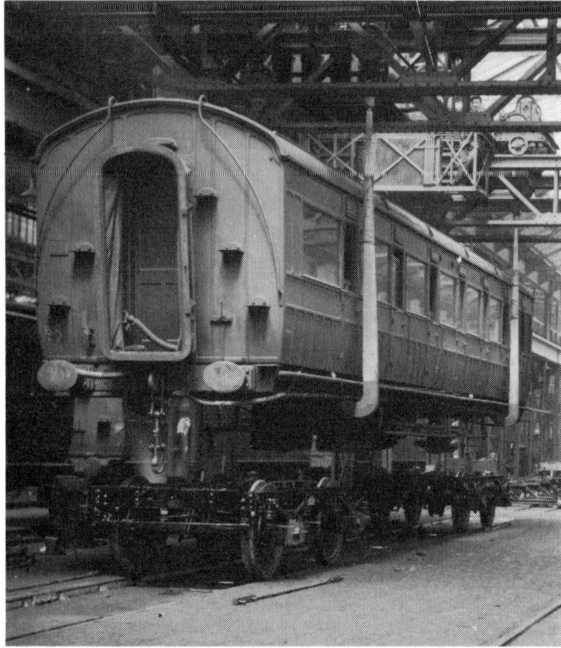

A virtually complete corridor carriage body and underframe about to be lowered on to its bogies at the Stratford works of the old GER; the gangway apparatus is prominent. Although the underframe was built separately from the body proper, it was common practice at British carriage works for these two components to be kept fixed together after finishing and be lifted as a unit whenever it was necessary to attend to the bogies themselves. This particular process survives to the present day, even though integral carriage construction is now normal practice.

British Standard gangway connections between two corridor carriages of the LNWR. There is added interest in this picture in that the vehicle on the left is equipped for slip working and has a raised 'birdcage' guard's lookout for this purpose — see page 166 (BR LMR).

achieved firstly by welding an extra horse-shoe shape to the top of the BS gangway moving frame which effectively increased its height and top width closer to that of the Pullman version. Secondly, extension pieces were welded or bolted to each side of the BS gangway to increase the width at that point to that of the Pullman gangway. This was because these extensions each had to carry additional gangway clips in order to hold the BS gangway firmly against its non-compatible partner. Without the stabilising effect of the centre buckeye coupler, and given the total disparity of shape between the two gangways, there could easily be too much side play to allow 'unclipped' gangways to be used.

This somewhat extraordinary situation held sway in Britain well into the modern period and had some interesting consequences. For one thing, it was obviously uneconomical to adapt all the BS gangways in existence, so those railways which used them had to maintain a sort of pool of gangway-adapted vehicles for use with buckeyed stock. This must have had some element of economic disadvantage in terms of lack of overall flexibility of use. Secondly, although strictly outside the timespan of this first volume, as the years went by and more and more buckeyed coaches came into use, it became more probable that some of the newer recruits in the carriage sidings would not be aware of the need to 'clip and adapt'! Thus, when uncoupling trains it was increasingly likely that the gangway clips would be forgotten, and should this happen, even though the carriages were *uncoupled*, the gangways were still connected. The next move of the shunting engine would almost inevitably pull the BS gangway clean off the end of its coach and dump it unceremoniously on to the ballast! It was, however, all very British.

Overall dimensions

Before leaving the question of carriage bodies, it should be pointed out that there were certain overall dimensional constraints to which every carriage had to conform. In Britain, by comparison with most overseas countries, these were relatively modest, although they grew a little more tolerant as the twentieth century progressed. Each railway therefore imposed its own 'loading gauge', as it was called.

Setting aside the few rather more generous and the few somewhat more restricted loading gauges imposed by a handful of companies, a typical British figure would be to permit an absolute maximum width of some 9 feet (or a little more) and a height of about 13 feet. However, these figures did not refer to a rectangular cross-section. The maximum height was only permissible close to the centre-line and the maximum width rarely applied much above 10 feet from the rail top or much below about 5-6 feet either for that matter. Over the years, attempts were made to harmonize between various parts of the system but there were always some exceptions.

In consequence, the end elevation of a typical British coach — again with some exceptions — showed certain characteristic features. It was normal for the carriage body to 'narrow' from the waist downwards — this feature, necessitating the curved panelling mentioned above, was either known as 'turn-under' or 'tumblehome'. Similarly, if a carriage was built to the full 9 feet waist width, it was common for the cantrail width to be a few inches less, typically about 8 ft 9 in. Thus the sides, above the waist, were often 'battered' (ie inclined inwards). A combination of inward batter plus marked tumblehome was often, in some descriptions, called 'clipper' shaped, presumably because it was vaguely reminiscent of the hull profile of a clipper ship.

At the turn of the century, vertically sided coaches were normal but, for structure gauge reasons, were generally confined to a maximum of 8 ft 6 in wide (8 feet being a particularly common figure). Virtually all had turned-under lower bodyside panels, but the true clipper shape was largely a twentieth-century feature. It was found that by increasing the waist width to a full 9 feet over the panels that an extra seat per side could often be incorporated and the slight reduction of width at the roof made little or no difference in this respect.

Because of the geometry of a vehicle on a curve, the dimensions quoted also allowed for a degree of lateral offset or 'throwover' at the vehicle ends (see Figure 9, page 25) and at the middle. This, in turn, imposed length limitations. Once again, a typical turn-of-the-century bogie vehicle would normally be within the 45-60 feet bracket, with a few pushing to 65 or 70 feet where either more specialized usage or limited spheres of operation thus allowed. This 65-70 feet length remained a *de rigueur* maximum until well into the 1970s, and it was only well into BR days that the somewhat longer MkIII coach could be accepted. Even so, there still has to be a modest inward taper at the carriage end to make allowances for the very long length (by British standards) of the MkIII carriage.

Above *This extraordinary cornucopia was the East Coast Joint Stock solution to the* third *class dining car challenge of its rivals at the turn of the century in 1900. It was built at Doncaster, and whatever one might think of the stylistic mishmash no one could seriously accuse the railways of not trying when the twentieth-century began. This design was surely one of the most comprehensive vehicles ever offered to third class passengers at this time — just look at those gas lamps!*

Left *The 'somewhat uneasy mixture of Victorian rectitude and art nouveau' is well exemplified by this interior view of the smoking compartment of an LNWR first class clerestory sleeping car of 1905. The cane chairs are very much à la mode as is some detail of the raised border patterns on the otherwise plain Lincrusta ceiling and wall panels, although the dark mahogany woodwork, the symmetry of the panel treatment and the fussy floor covering all betoken an earlier era. However, it seems to have worked — this was undoubtedly a pleasant room in which to linger over a malt whisky and a good cigar, watching the sun go down on a summer evening before turning in for the night!* (BR LMR).

4. Interior finishing and passenger amenities

If it is the exterior bodywork of the carriage which gives it character, distinction and, possibly, any aesthetic virtues it may have on first acquaintance, this appeal can only be 'skin deep' at the final analysis, for it is the interior arrangement which will create the most profound and long-lasting effect on its potential customer. Even speaking from a purely personal standpoint. I can remember the carriage *interiors* of my youth long after I have forgotten some of the more esoteric aspects of their exterior elevation. Moreover, beauty of exterior aspect can at times be utterly misleading. The sublime exterior elegance and symmetry of the Gresley LNER open thirds may be remembered, married to a quite diabolical degree of discomfort in their atrocious 'bucket' seats; the aesthetic pleasures of the ex-NER clerestories with their hard, horsehair benches; the often quite unharmonious 'look' of many GWR and LMS carriages which often belied a rather better interior and even, in much more modern days, the sleek, elegant style of the BR Blue Pullmans of the 1960s (both inside and out) but the more than adventurous nature of their suspension system!

Happy indeed was the traveller who could feast his aesthetic sensitivity as he boarded his carriage and have his delight further enhanced from within when the journey commenced. Fortunately, at least on their better trains, the British were rather good at satisfying both criteria, even for the third class passenger; it did not happen by accident.

The carriage interior must inevitably be a subtle combination of visual elements and practical provisioning, both being measured against a whole series of constraints covering such things as dimensional restrictions, weight limitation, seating capacity, envisaged usage, durability, economy or manufacture and so forth. It is always and quite inescapably a compromise between often contrary elements and can never be wholly perfect. Sometimes the constraints are few, sometimes many, and it is no small tribute to the designers — rarely even distinguished by name in contemporary accounts, unlike their privileged locomotive counterparts — that they so often managed to produce not only vehicles of great intrinsic beauty but also great practical virtue as well.

The story, as always, is one of continuous evolution both in style and technology, so yet again the starting point must be the situation broadly as it stood at the turn of the century. As with most aspects of the carriage, a basic understanding of the various practices which had developed by the end of Victoria's reign enables most of the rest of the story to be understood quite readily until well into the BR period.

Interior partitions and doors

The purpose for which the carriage was designed determined the exact layout of the interior partitions and doors, and these had to be pre-planned into the floor structure. Thereafter, partition framing was erected much as for the exterior, and both sides of the partition were then covered in by 'casing boards', often quite basic in their material, on top of which were then applied the visible decorative finishes. Interior doors were made in much the same fashion as for any domestic interior and arranged either to hinge or slide according to need. Naturally, the surface finishings of doors and interior walls were designed to harmonize.

In terms of wall finishes, most carriages reflected the fact that much of the furniture, paticularly the seating, was 'built in'. As a consequence, if one removed a complete seating unit there often stood revealed bare casing boards without the semblance of a finishing layer. However, where the walls revealed themselves above the seats, round the windows and in corridors and passageways, much flamboyance could be seen. It generally reflected the class of the carriage or compartment but was almost always done with care and, on the best carriages, with an astonishing attention to detail.

The favourite material was always wood, whether inlaid, panelled, veneered or, in later days, left relatively plain and simply polished to enhance its colour and/or grain pattern. It was not until well into the 1950s that extensive use was made of alternative materials to any great extent, and only in the 1970s and 1980s did one see any real diminution of the traditional wood finishes. Thus, during the period covering the first two of these three volumes, wood was king and the techniques of handling it hardly changed — only the design altered. Throughout this survey, examples of fine craftsmanship, even in the humblest of coaches, will regularly reappear, so there is no need to dwell too long at this point; but there are a few other preliminary remarks worth making.

The decorative wood treatment generally stopped at about cantrail or head height, above which it was customary practice to paint, in white or cream, the

'All-over-patterned' Lincrusta seems to have been just about the only wall and ceiling finish for everything but the wood framing in this Edwardian vintage LSWR corridor coach.

Austere finish in a GER third class suburban carriage. Even the partitions scarcely reached to mid-window height and the less said about those seats the better. Even so, however, the grain finish of the plain tongue and groove casing boards is likely to have been put there in paint — a small concession, but at least it was something.

upper wall sides (sometimes) and the ceilings (almost always). In this respect there was a conscious imitation of domestic interiors above and below the picture rail, so to speak. Not that there were hanging pictures or even a picture rail as such; but there *were* pictures and mirrors, often in abundance, whose fixed frames were often part of the panelling. These pictures could range from sepia-toned photographs of places served by the railway or specially made prints of original paintings, via colourful poster-type notices with an advertising flavour, to stark printed statements as to the policy of the railway itself. I feel that it is one of the more regrettable aspects of modern rolling-stock — which has many virtues not possessed by its ancestors — that pictorial decoration of the interior generally seems 'out' and that the railway's own 'in house' material is frequently applied by the cheap and nasty method of pasting an appropriate notice directly on to wall or window. It would cost so little and look so much better to do it properly.

Returning to wall finishes, a particularly popular alternative to wood — especially during the period covered by this first volume — was the use of textured Lincrusta, particularly on ceilings and top wall panels of compartments and on the dado (ie the area between waist and floor) of corridors and passageways. Like many things, it drew its basic inspiration from contemporary domestic interiors, and the new century dawned with a sort of mixed stylistic treatment best described as a somewhat uneasy mixture of Victorian rectitude and art nouveau. Oddly enough, it generally worked rather well, even when to it was added the occasional Edwardian revival of Adam style decorative motifs in some of the best carriages. Stylistic purity of concept was never at the heart of railway carriage interior design but somehow it did not seem to matter too much. Symmetry of design pattern was, however, a well nigh universal feature if permitted by the carriage 'geometry'.

At the heart of it all was, in addition to wood, that wonderfully versatile material 'Lincrusta-Walton'. Unlike wood finishes, which are still very much a part of general interior design in the late twentieth century (even if not so prevalent in carriages), figured Lincrusta is a substance rarely met these days. In fact, and risking a somewhat irrelevant aside, it has proved to be quite a problem, when trying to restore vintage carriages at the National Railway Museum, to find anything which really encapsulates the character of Lincrusta, and the more modern and not quite so appropriate Anaglypta has had to be accepted. It therefore seems worthwhile to devote a few lines to the subject.*

Lincrusta-Walton was introduced in later Victorian days as a replacement for figured waxcloth.

**Since writing the above, genuine Lincrusta has come back on to the market!*

It was just as readily fixed but rather more durable and its nature made it rather more versatile in terms of decorative possibilities. Essentially it was a heavy compressed composition paper, moulded (under pressure) to give the desired patterns. These could be either raised, the usual approach, or embossed. The non-textured part of the Lincrusta was known as the 'ground' and it was common to pick out the textured pattern in a different colour, or even gilt. Thus 'gilt on cream ground Lincrusta' inferred gilt patterns (raised or embossed) on a cream background.

It was supplied mounted on stout millboard and cut out to fit the various areas to which it was applied. It was treated very much like wood interior panelling — ie pinned in position on casing boards or under the roof framing — and the areas to which it was applied had to offer an even surface before the Lincrusta was added. There were other similar materials with their own brand names, but 'Lincrusta' became a sort of generic term to describe a process — much in the manner of 'Hoover' in our present day.

As a 'standard' treatment it had a pretty good run during the first twenty years or so of the century but tended to die out, following currently fashionable trends, during the 1920s. Of course, such was the longevity of carriages that quite a few Lincrusta-panelled coaches ran in service until after the Second World War — principally dining and sleeping cars and other more specialized vehicles.

Before completing this basic review of wall finishes it is also worth mentioning that in humbler coaches plain tongue and groove boarding was often used on top of the casing boards, sometimes grain painted to simulate something better. Plain boarding was equally often applied to the undersides of ceilings. There were no hard and fast rules, but there was plenty of scope for individual company variety.

Seat construction, trimming and other interior decoration

Save for those relatively rare cases where 'loose' furniture, of typical domestic kind, was incorporated in a carriage, the seats themselves were permanently fixed in place and were usually of a built-in nature. They were not, however, made *in situ*. Like many parts of the carriages, as much as possible of the seating was fabricated as a separate process and the finished unit added to the structure quite late in the assembly. In general, the backs and seat cushions were separate loose items and the seat base, although made outside the body, became a semi-permanent fixture once offered up to the carriage.

The seat base, frequently sprung, was anchored to the wall of the carriage by means of a rear seat rail — a substantial timber section fixed to the wall. The front seat rail was a similar strong member, anchored to the sides of the compartment and sometimes supported, intermediately, by one or two legs to the floor. The seat back unit — sometimes called a back 'squab' — was a separate item which, unlike the seat base, usually carried the finishing material. It was designed so as to be able to be lifted clear of the wall in one piece without disturbing the trim.

Although earlier than the two dining carriages pictured on page 56, this turn-of-the-century LNWR first class interior shows an altogether more enterprising use of trimming material. It could well have been the famous green Blenheim moquette, much quoted in contemporary accounts. Regardless of precise colour, however, the attention to detail was formidable (BR LMR).

On most first and many second class seats, the actual cushion on which the passengers sat was made up as a separate loose item, sometimes with its own interior springing and was removable for cleaning.

By contrast, third class seating units were often single-piece structures containing all the springs, and the seat base in these cases was merely a framework on which the whole seat unit rested. This sort of fixed seating was the normal practice in compartment and side corridor stock. Where a centre aisle was used, in the open interior configuration of a dining car for example, the seat units adjacent to the transverse partition walls were much as described, but the intermediate 'double-sided' units were slightly different. A fixed timber framework, with seat bases on both sides of a central vertical back-board, was installed on to which the seats and back squabs were fixed as for a conventional compartment. The inner end of

this unit (adjacent to the carriage side) was anchored to a seat rail, but the outer end, adjacent to the aisle, was a decorative member carrying legs, the whole being used as a principal design feature of the carriage interior.

A similar solution was also adopted in non-corridor compartment stock where a seat unit did not stretch from side to side of the compartment, for example in those cases where a break had to be made for an access door to a lavatory, for example.

The most obvious aspect of the seating was, of course, its upholstery, or 'trimming' to use the more common railway term. During most of the nineteenth century, railways had been somewhat unenterprising in this area and had employed relatively few different finishes. For example, 'blue cloth' was the most common first class trimming used by nearly all companies. It was quite plain with a sort of velour type finish and remained popular well into the present century. In fact, when the NRM was restoring its Midland six-wheeler of 1883, a suitable length of blue cloth was, happily, exhumed by Wolverton Works as late as 1974! The lower orders had to make do with plainer materials such as plush or rep, but sometimes velvet was used. Plain colours — usually brown or red — were most common.

This somewhat austere situation began to change in late Victorian days and the twentieth century dawned with a much more enterprising attitude to interior finishes, both in terms of quality and variety. Typical first class materials, in addition to the familiar blue cloth, could now embrace velvet, morocco and buffalo leather, moquette and sometimes even brocade. Floral and other patterns began to appear and the decorative braiding round seat cushions and seat supports was often supplemented by decorative fringes, tassels or whatever.

An equal variety also began to appear in second and third class compartments, often of very high quality and regularly of some considerable variety. Regrettably, little dedicated research has been carried out on carriage interior materials and it is very difficult — save by means of the often fallible human memory — to establish precisely what materials were used. The situation has become progressively more bewildering during the subsequent decades and it is rarely possible to do more than generalize or try to make an intelligent guess as to colour from a black and white photograph.

However, regardless of precise pattern or type, carriage upholstery cloth had to fulfil certain fundamental criteria. It was originally some 60 inches wide — more recently 48 inches — and of durable weight per yard, about 24 oz being typical for the 60 inch width. Its strength was such that a strip of the weft, or cross threads (edge to edge), should not tear with a pull of less than 55 lbs, while a strip of the warp (longitudinal threads) had to withstand a 75 lb pull. This was to ensure, as far as possible, resistance to rough usage and also the inevitable strain when cloth was drawn down by button finishing or at cushion and seat edges. Woollen cloth was considered to be the most suitable and, in addition to strength, the cloth should have a clean, even surface well covered with nap, short and cleanly cut. Finally, the cloth should be evenly coloured throughout.

Leather, sometimes used for complete seats and regularly for armrests and other features, had to be of even thickness, free from cuts or cracks, and be able to withstanding bending or pleating without

Above left *This pair of views shows comparisons between the second and third class in an LSWR non-corridor lavatory-equipped carriage. One or two obvious differences are evident, but most are rather subtle; there was probably little to choose in terms of real comfort.*

Above *First and third class on the Cheshire Lines Committee. This agreeable design emerged from Doncaster in 1911, essentially to Gresley's GNR style of construction although vastly better than anything Doncaster ever built for the harassed King's Cross commuters. The lack of outer armrest in the third class is a bit unusual.*

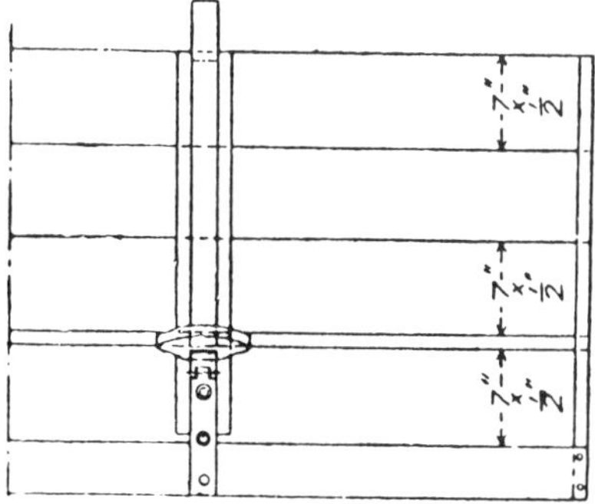

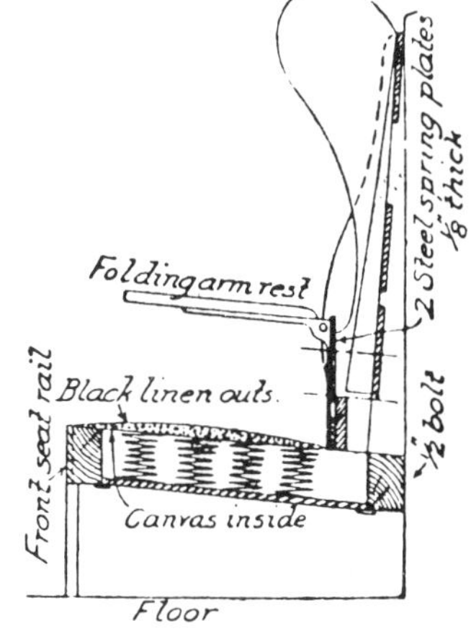

Figure 25 Scale 16mm = 1ft

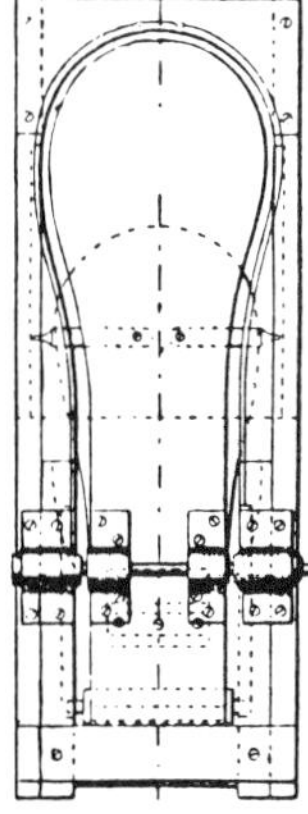

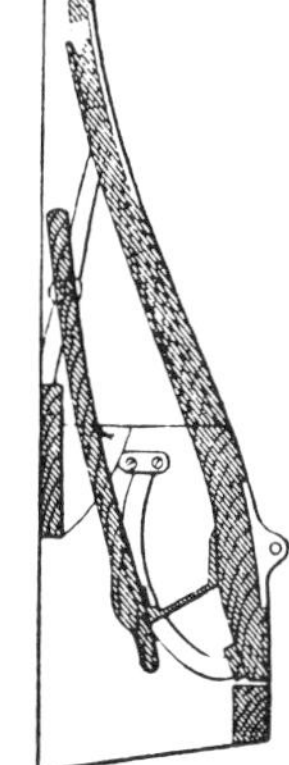

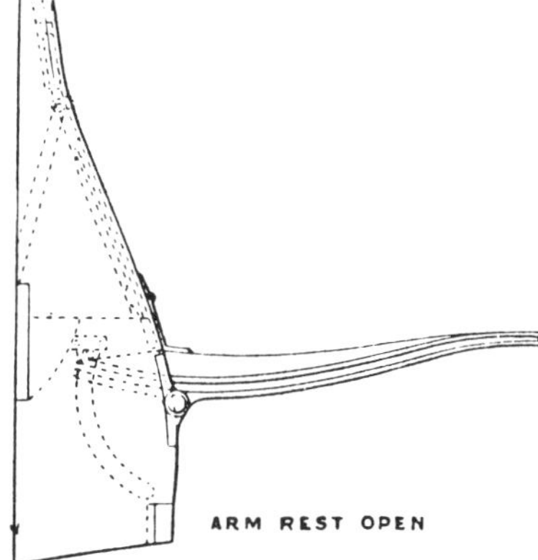

Figure 25 *General construction of a first class seat unit (with simple folding arms and a sprung permanent base) and, in enlarged detail, Attock's LYR pattern folding armrest. In this fitment, raising the arm caused part of the seat back to retract, leaving a space into which the arm could fit flush with the seat back, thus allowing more passengers to be seated at busy times. This, in one form or another became the normal British arrangement, especially in third class carriages during and after the 1930s.*

cracking. Laces and braid for finishing had to be perfect and straight to pattern, be of firm quality, even finish and good clean colour. Wool or silk were the customary materials.

The cushions and back squabs, in addition to the springing if present, were stuffed with best quality curled horsehair which, when uncurled for stuffing, retained its elasticity, sometimes too much so, as those of us who recall sitting on horsehair seats in short trousers remember only too clearly — the backs of the knees were distinctly vulnerable! A contemporary description states of horsehair that 'Inferior hair is knotty, dull, short and the ends are frequently split, indicating that the hair has not been obtained from the horse, but probably from the hog or some other unsuitable animal'! On a fair number of carriages, horsehair stuffing without springs could often be considered adequate, particularly on seat backs. This practice was not customary in first class carriages, save in some cases for the loose cushions which sat on top of the sprung base, but third class seat backs were regularly stuffed only! It was comparatively rare in the twentieth century, however, to find a third class carriage without at least some form of springing in the seat itself.

This basic form of carriage seat construction stood the test of time well into the modern (post-nationalization) era and it was not really until the BR MkII

Left *Typical 'blue-cloth' seat trimming in a first class dining carriage of the Midland Railway, along with many other characteristic interior detail features, most of which were also offered to third class diners too — see the picture on page 50* (BR LMR).

Below left *The 'Edwardian Adam' design influence may have been at work in this first class open carriage of the North Eastern Railway which conveys a somewhat less fussy impression than the previous MR example; both are good. Blue cloth is again the trim material, but the seats have loose cushions, the rather more customary practice in first class carriages. The dark mahogany is still there, however.*

Above right *This 1914 lavatory compartment in an East Coast corridor carriage is rather more spacious than most and features a fixed ceramic wash basin rather than the more common folding type.*

Above far right *This well-appointed first class lavatory compartment of LYR non-corridor composite No 1085 as well as showing a cased in wash basin also features a drinking water filtration system.*

period (1960s onwards) that any significant structural changes were made — and then only slowly. Fashions changed, of course, as did the actual shapes and layouts of seats, but the interiors of BR MkI coaches almost always revealed their traditional origins — and there are still those of us who reckon that nothing subsequently has bettered the traditional first class compartments last employed for all practical purposes in the late MkI and early MkII BR stock.

In addition to the seats, armrests and other basic items of the carriage interior, there were numerous small fittings which could enhance the pleasure of the traveller. These could range from such vital components as window blinds for use in sunny weather to such pleasant touches as small courtesy shelves for the odd cup or glass, ashtrays for the smoker, folding tables — or even permanent ones — for more substantial use, luggage and parcel racks or shelves, coat-hooks (or even coat-hangers), luggage compartments and, very occasionally, even fold-away seats in the corridors. These latter were for use either at times of overcrowding or, more amenably, as a means of parking the derrière when the scenery on the corridor side was deemed more pleasant than that opposite! The railways seemed to think of most things which people might want and occasionally a few which were of less obvious practical value. There were, however, amongst all these items a few rather more general amenities which merit a little more detailed consideration.

Lavatories and toilets

Amongst all the vulgarities of humour contained in the British make-up — and one has only to read a few words of Shakespeare to realize how long-standing this has been — the subject of the toilet and its trappings has always been firmly at the top of the list for a spontaneous giggle; yet the start of the heyday of the railway carriage actually coincided with the curious period in history where one did not mention such things in polite society. Consequently, the providing of a lavatory in a train was fraught with social as well as practical problems in the early days.

It had largely been solved by the end of the Victorian period and Hamilton Ellis has virtually said all that needs to be stated of the pioneer developments*. By the twentieth century, the position of the lavatory had taken one of two basic arrangements. It was either located off the corridor at one or both ends of the carriage (sometimes intermediately as well) or, in the case of non-corridor stock, an individual compartment had its own provisioning, leading directly off the compartment. Centre-aisled carriages tended to follow the corridor style with lavatories at the coach ends.

Within the toilet compartment itself there would normally be found the usual pedestal fitting and some sort of washbasin facility, along with a towel and soap, provided that someone had not removed the

* Railway Carriages in the British Isles from 1830-1914

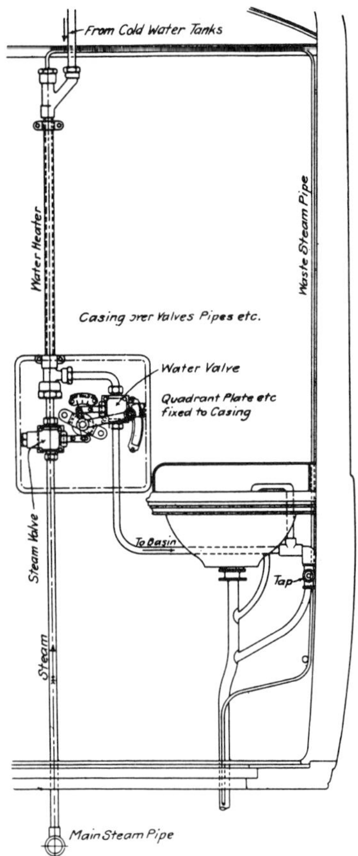

Figure 26 *Hot water heating system of the type fitted to East Coast carriages such as depicted in the picture on the previous page.*

Above *This interior view of an LNWR kitchen car for the American boat trains — see Chapter 13 — clearly shows the supplementary drinking water tanks suspended below the ceiling (BR LMR).*

latter pair of items. Since the lavatory compartment took up floor space for essentially non-revenue-earning use, it was normally very cramped and folding washbasin units were commonplace. Especially typical, until very recent years, were those made by Beresford of Birmingham. They were usually of nickel-plated brass and they folded away against the wall when not in use, projecting only a few inches from the partition. The action of folding them away discharged the water from the back of the basin into a sort of reception chute and hence to the outside of the carriage below the floor. The basins had a deep lip round the rim to prevent spillage of water when the train was in motion.

Until quite recent days, generally post-nationalization, the fixed handbasin was a somewhat less common feature than a folding one. Where used, however, it was commonly placed in a corner angle of the toilet compartment and shaped to suit this location. It could be made either from metal or, more likely, a ceramic material. Regardless of washbasin type, however, only a cold water supply was provided at the start of the century in most cases. In later years, some carriages were given a hot water supply as well, the heat being derived from the carriage steam heating system (see below).

The pedestal fitting — which doubled as a urinal — was generally earthenware, usually white glazed and, especially in earlier days, often of quite florid and spectacular vulgarity. Sometimes the whole was encased in a wooden housing.

The water supply for both fittings was gravity fed from tanks housed in the roof and was most certainly of non-drinking quality. The tanks were filled from the outside by hoses either directly into the top of the tank itself via an aperture in the roof (which had a detachable cover) or, later, by attaching the hose to a filler pipe which was fixed to the carriage end and went up the end and over the top of the roof to the water tank location(s). 'Carriage watering', as it was known, was and is an essential accompaniment to the operation of the railway, since water storage capacity is always limited.

Discharge (solid and liquid) from the toilet compartment, whether from washbasin or toilet, was always direct to the ballast of the track (below the carriage) which acted as a natural filter bed. The effluent was inevitably spread quite hygenically over many yards of track as the carriage moved along, but the nature of the effluent was, of course, such as to make immediately obvious the reasons for the familiar exhortation inside the vehicle not to use the facilities while the train was standing in the station! Amazingly, it was not until well into the MkIII era· that BR began to use self-contained, below floor discharge tanks for lavatories, but in this respect it was and is no different from anywhere else in the world.

A somewhat less savoury sanitary fitting was the 'dry closet' which was more prevalent in countries with poor supplies of water. In these instances, discharge to the ground was achieved merely by opening a valve or hinged flap at the base of the pan (usually by foot treadle or hand lever) and allowing gravity to take over. In essence this was not too different in its mechanical operation from that of the water closet, but the lack of sluice water could cause it to be anything but pleasant. Happily, this sort of apparatus was considerably less common in Britain than elsewhere. It should be appreciated, of course, that the 'S'-bend trap at the base of the pedestal was not normally used in a train even if it was of the water closet variety.

The flushing mechanism itself was operated by foot treadle, lever or chain and, in some cases, by raising the seat of the pan to the upright position — a baffling situation to encounter for anyone with no experience of the process since there were no operating instructions! In general, however, during the twentieth century the British railway lavatory managed to get by better than most after its appallingly slow Victorian start, and it was only in the more modern era that major changes were made.

The actual position of the roof tanks was variable. They were often purpose-built in shape, to match the roof profile, and were incorporated in the roof structure. An alternative method, also used in a supplementary way if extra water capacity was needed, was to fit tanks inside the carriage, below the roof boards and covered with casing boards. In this position there was less likelihood of freezing in cold weather. Galvanized steel or iron, or sometimes copper, were the common materials, and in dining cars even more water provisioning was often provided by cylindrical tanks hanging from the kitchen and pantry ceilings. In these cases, some of the water supply was led through water filters to purify it and make it fit for drinking, and this practice could be found in some of the better quality ordinary stock as well, including sleeping cars.

Mention of the latter serves as a reminder that in this specific category of vehicle, the plumbing arrangements were normally much more sophisticated. These mobile 'hotels' were and are the most opulent general service vehicles built by the railways and are considered in more detail in Chapter 11.

Carriage heating

A particular problem which affected British carriages in the nineteenth century was the difficulty of heating an interior which, in almost all cases, was constructed on the compartment principle. An open saloon interior could be warmed by a stove, and this method was commonplace overseas. The problem in Britain was only solved in a satisfactory manner at the end of Victoria's reign and fully effective carriage heating is thus, in British terms, very much a twentieth-century development. However, since it took time to be fully developed, the older methods remained in use during the earlier part of the period under survey and warrant a brief word.

Firstly was the so-called 'foot warmer', an individual flat metal cannister of quite substantial size and vast inconvenience. Originally they were filled with hot water by means of a screw top aperture, much in the manner of a hot water bottle; by 1900, they had developed to a sealed form containing soda acetate crystals. These were pre-heated before being distributed to the passengers and continued to give out heat as the solution re-crystallized. By giving them a good shake from time to time they could, to some extent, be made to give warmth for several

Figure 27 *Typical arrangement of the steam heating system in a compartment carriage. The two main steam pipes 'a' and 'd' are connected by individual valves 'b' to the heaters 'c'. The whole system can be drained by valves 'e' and 'f', one for each of the main feed pipes.*

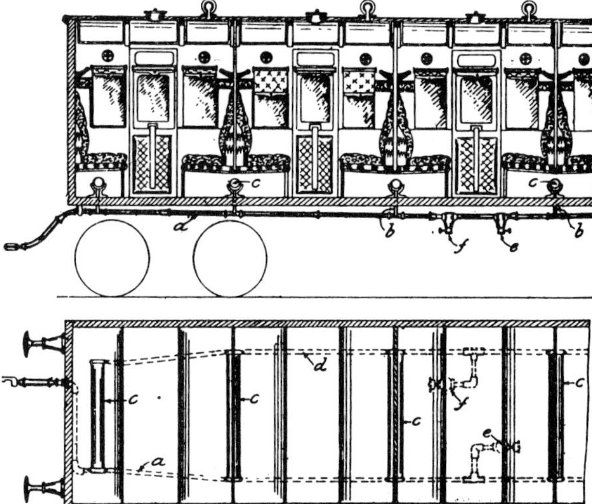

hours. They did not long survive the introduction of steam heating. The alternative older method, used in a few carriages, was some form of circulating hot water system fed by a small boiler. Pullmans were often equipped with this system — of essentially American origin — as were some of the better late Victorian sleeping cars. It, too, was superseded by the steam heating method. Rarely if ever did a British passenger-carrying vehicle make use of the iron stove, radiating its heat directly to the interior, which was so popular elsewhere, not least on the brake vans of British goods trains.

A variant of the circulating hot water system was tried out, experimentally, by the Midland Railway late in the nineteenth century using hot water from the locomotive, but the best solution was that of feeding a supply of steam to the train. Several systems were developed late in Victorian days and all were very similar in principle. Steam from the locomotive was passed through a pressure reducing valve to a continuous pipe below the carriages, the linkage between each carriage being by means of flexible hose couplings similar to the brake connections (see Chapter 2). From each pipe, a feeder led to a radiator inside the compartment. These were usually located either below the seats or, in some open stock, were located in the angle between the floor and the side of the carriage. In this variation, the radiators were generally covered by means of a pierced metal grille which served both as a decorative feature in its own right and as a protection both for the radiator itself and the feet of the passenger.

The radiator itself could sometimes be of the storage type and filled with a soda acetate solution working in much the same way as a foot warmer, ie absorbing heat from the steam supply and then giving it off as it cooled. Fresh steam was automatically admitted when the cooling reached a predetermined point. More often, however, the system was non-storage with live steam in the radiator itself. Supplementing these radiators many railways also used the steam pipe itself — along corridors for example — protecting it, and the passengers, by means of covers or grilles.

In many carriages, the supply of steam to the radiators could be adjusted by the passenger by means of a control knob or lever and this method of heating remained standard throughout the steam period. Indeed, the first generation diesel locomotives in Britain were often equipped with auxiliary boilers to provide a supply of steam for the heating system. In all cases, drain cocks were provided in every carriage to avoid condensing steam freezing solid in the pipes during cold weather, especially when standing in the sidings.

The principal exception to steam heating during the early days was to be found in electrically-propelled stock which, not surprisingly, was also electrically heated; this has now become the accepted modern method for almost all trains in Britain.

Ventilation

The object of carriage ventilation is to get a free circulation of air without either draught or dust. This was not really possible with the traditional drop light type of opening window, or indeed some of the later styles of opening window. Any form of opening window was bound at some stage to admit not only draughts and dust but also rain, and was often a frequent cause of argument between passengers who wanted it open and those who preferred it closed. The matter was never really settled and only became a dead issue with the introduction of permanently sealed windows, allied with air-conditioning, in more recent times, although there are still many who yearn for an openable window in those coaches which have none.

There were, however, other forms of carriage ventilation. The door top version with its sliding 'hit and miss' shutter has already been mentioned in connection with body construction. It had a series of holes or slots in a sliding panel which, when open, coincided with similar apertures in the door top panel. On the outside these ventilators were covered by decorative hoods, and could also be found over many of the fixed lights. There was, however, no special device for extracting stale air.

A variation of this type was the Anderson ventilator which did have extractor capability — see Figure 28. From the outside, the hood (or 'bonnet') looked much the same but, be it metal or wood, was open at both ends. Behind the hood there was a flattened suction tube of a kind of double conical shape rather like a semi-collapsed diabolo, while inside the carriage a deflector tube, which prevented the incoming fresh air mixing with the outgoing stale air, was sometimes fitted. When the carriage was moving, the outer suction tube created a partial vacuum at the rear end which sucked out the stale air as the fresh air entered the carriage. The arrows on the diagram show the various directions of movement.

Another quite popular form of carriage side ventilator was the glass vane type (see Figure 29), particularly favoured by the LMS in the 1920s but which actually came into use during pre-grouping days on several railways. These units were mounted above some of the windows in the eaves panel and had a series of vertical glass vanes, all held in place at the top and bottom by individual brass castings which could pivot in a common frame. All the vanes

This pair of glass vane ventilators surmounting the large picture window of a North Eastern first class open carriage were described, somewhat puzzlingly, as 'Patent louvre ball-bearing hit and miss ventilators'!

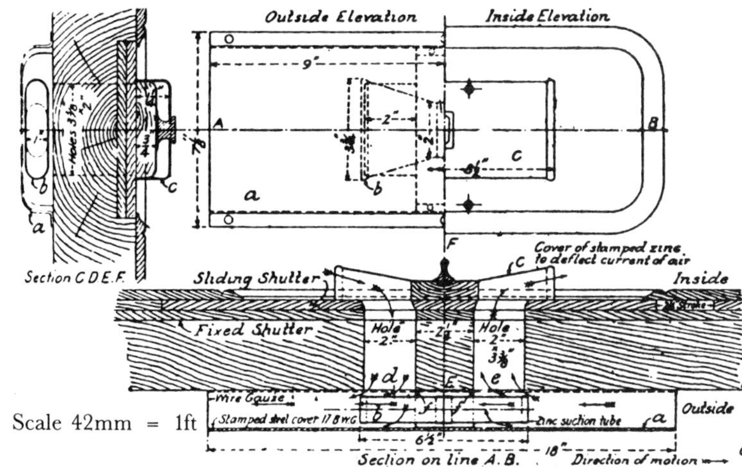

Figure 28 *Diagram of the Anderson extractor ventilator.*

Scale 42mm = 1ft

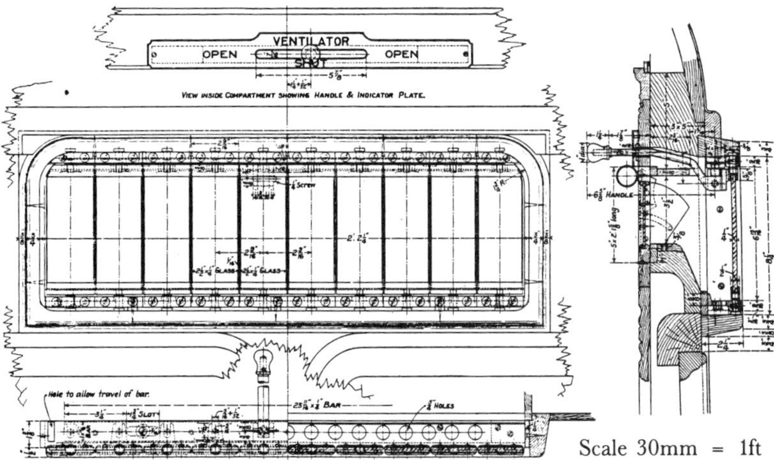

Figure 29 *Diagram of Great Eastern Railway pattern glass vane ventilator.*

Scale 30mm = 1ft

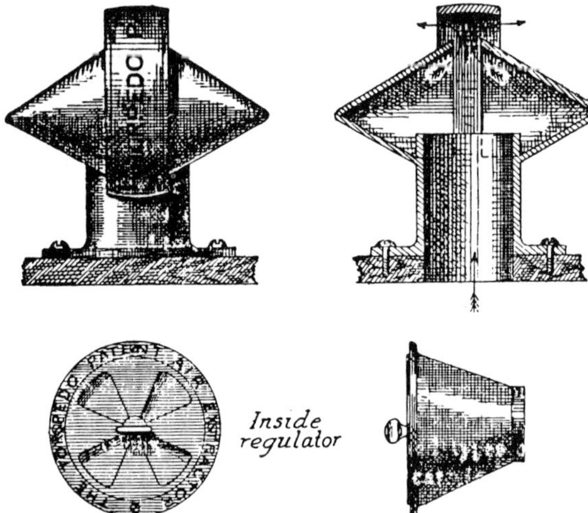

Figure 30 *The original Laycock's patent 'Torpedo' roof ventilator.*

were arranged to move simultaneously by means of a linkage attached to an interior handle, so that they could be set either flush with the carriage side, in which position the edges of the vanes almost touched and admitted but little air, or they could be swivelled to either face or trail the airstream at an angle, thus producing either an incoming or outgoing air current. Inside the carriage, the ventilator aperture was oten fitted with a small secondary window, hinged at the lower edge, which could be kept closed by a catch at the top edge. To make use of the glass vane facility, this inner window had first to be opened.

Further forms of carriage side ventilation appeared down the years and will be considered in their proper chronology, but one final and almost universal form which lasted throughout the century (save in air-conditioned stock) must be mentioned here. It was perhaps the most characteristic of them all and was fitted to the top of the roof, often to the sides of clerestories if present, and was generally known as the 'Torpedo' ventilator.

There were, in fact, many subtle variations on the theme both in shape and size, and the shape, disposition and number of roof ventilators could be just as distinctive a visual characteristic of a particular railway as its panelling style or carriage livery. All the varieties worked in much the same way, but strictly speaking the 'Torpedo' name is properly applied only to that type invented and patented by Laycock in the nineteenth century.

Essentially, the 'Torpedo' was an extractor unit and worked by the creation of a partial vacuum between the outer band and the inner cones when the train was moving. To close it, an interior 'hit and miss' revolving shutter was fitted, yet another gadget which could give an imaginative carriage builder some scope for decorative innovation. The shutters were normally finished in brass or bronze but some were wood and other materials could also be found. The outer unit was normally cast iron.

Lighting

At the start of the present century, carriage lighting for new construction had settled down to one of two main alternatives, gas or electricity. There were still surviving examples of the older oil lamps in use, but many formerly oil-lit carriages had been converted to the more modern form by the start of the period, and this obsolete form need not concern us save to note its occasional continuance. Of the two more recent methods, gas was the older. During the last quarter of the nineteenth century, several experiments in gas lighting were conducted, some involving coal gas carried in a separate vehicle, but by 1900 the railways had pretty well standardized on compressed oil gas if they had not moved over to electricity. Compressed oil gas as a method of lighting was first introduced to Britain in 1876 on the Metropolitan Railway which adopted a system developed by Julius Pintsch. This and the contemporary Pope's system differed only in a few details at the distillation stage and a general outline of the basic principles should suffice for both.

Oil gas was made in a separate gas plant by means of distillation, and the railways often built their own gasworks for this purpose. Various heavier tars and impurities were removed during the distillation process and the 'cleaned' gas was then passed to a gasholder prior to its transfer to the carriages. In order not to take up too much space on the carriages and to enable the supply to last for a considerable time, the gas was compressed into cylindrical holders at a pressure of some 10 atmospheres (about 140-150 psi).

Transfer to the gas reservoirs of the carriages themselves was by one of two methods. When a major carriage servicing depot was close to the gas plant, a direct pipeline supply was laid to the depot terminating in gas charging standards which could be connected directly to the carriages. Equally common, however, were the travelling gasholders (gas wagons) which were positioned up and down the railway system wherever carriages may have need to be 'topped up'. Clearly, more remote locations were served exclusively by such wagons, but at many busy stations it was normal to have a few gas wagons at strategic locations in order to avoid wasting time by sending stock to the depot, even if the latter was only a mile or two away. Needless to say, the tanks of these wagons had to be strong enough to withstand the high pressure; some railways favoured a single tank on the

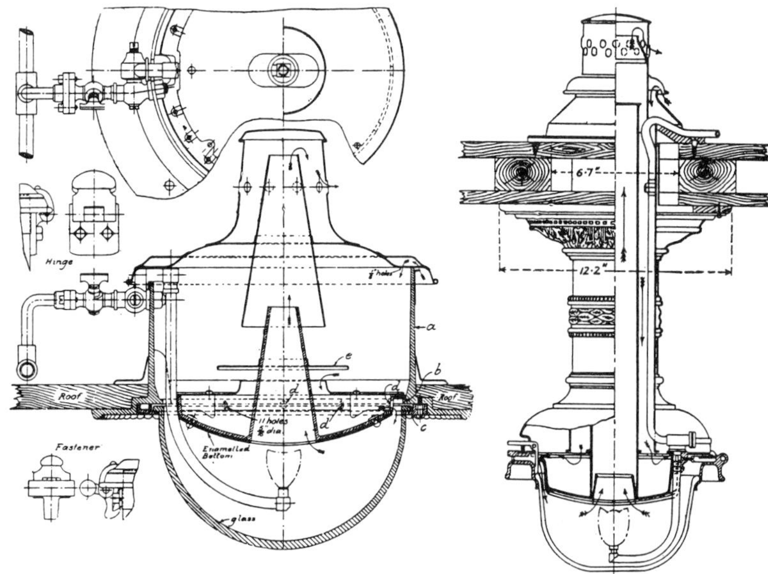

Figure 31 *These drawings show (right) the Pope's and (far right) the Pintsch's form of 'butterfly burner' gas lamp. The arrows indicate the general direction of air circulation. The Pintsch lamp also shows the form of construction adopted when such lamps were fitted in the elevated centre roof section of a clerestory carriage.*

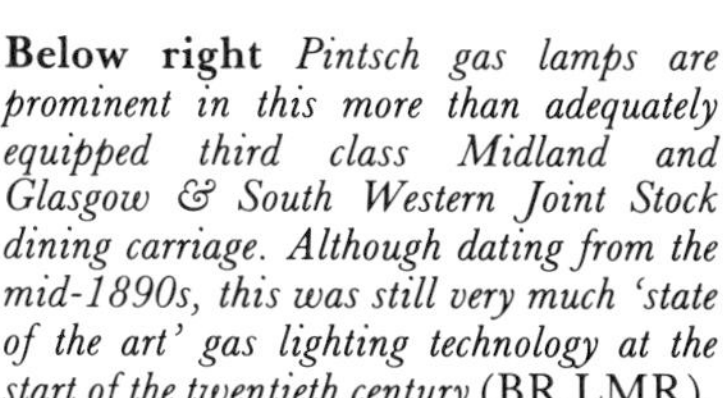

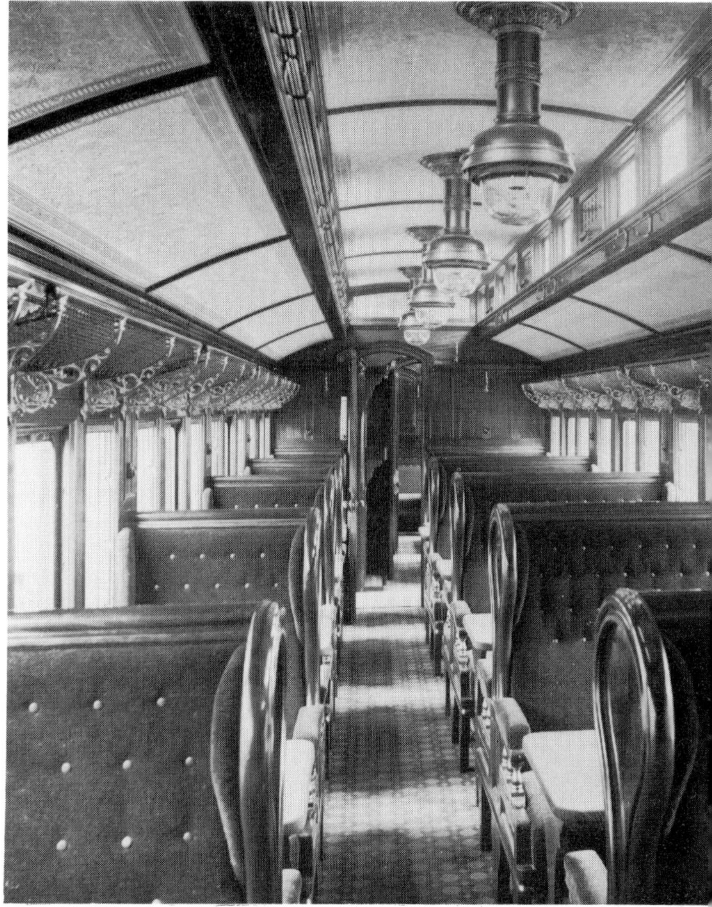

Below right *Pintsch gas lamps are prominent in this more than adequately equipped third class Midland and Glasgow & South Western Joint Stock dining carriage. Although dating from the mid-1890s, this was still very much 'state of the art' gas lighting technology at the start of the twentieth century* (BR LMR).

wagon, others opted for two or more smaller ones.

On the carriage itself, there were reservoirs suspended from the underframe, the size of which depended on the number of gas appliances to be served and the desired time between 'refills'. If more than one gas reservoir was carried, they were interconnected. It would be normal to carry sufficient supplies for at least one or two days of the darkest possible conditions, ie midwinter. For example, a fairly typical reservoir some 6 ft long by 1 ft 9 in diameter would contain about 12 cubic feet which, at the designed pressure, could supply three 8-candle-power burners for some 36-40 hours at full gas pressure (the gas pressure in the carriage reservoirs was somewhat less than that of the main storage tanks, typically about 60-70%, ie about 80-100 psi). The carriage reservoirs were charged from the tank wagons or depot pipelines through valves and hose-pipes and a pressure gauge was placed close to the inlet valve to show when the required pressure had been reached, at which point the valve was closed. Once again, the Pintsch and Pope systems varied only slightly, mainly in the design of the valves.

From the reservoirs, the gas was taken to the lamps in small-bore piping, usually externally mounted on the roof. A regulating valve kept the supply pressure constant and a pull-out handle at the carriage end enabled platform staff to turn on or off the main gas supply to the interior. This action controlled all the lamps simultaneously, since they usually had small permanently lit pilot flames fed by a secondary supply. Without pilot flames, lamps had to be individually turned on and lit from within the compartment; this cumbersome and time-wasting process

was virtually obsolete by the end of the nineteenth century.

The lamps themselves were relatively simple, comprising a pipe and burner below a chimney. The burners were initially of the 'butterfly' type, so-called because the shape of the flame was somewhat like a butterfly's wing. One of these burners gave about 7 candlepower, but many lamps were fitted with duplex burners — one pipe fed two 'butterfly' flames and this doubled the light intensity. There was usually a pivot mechanism allowing the whole of the pipe/burner apparatus to be hinged out of the way to allow for cleaning the lamp and also, in the days before pilot lights, for easier lighting as well. From about 1905 onwards, gas mantles often replaced the open flame burners to give a further improvement in light intensity.

Inside the carriage, it was not always possible for the flame size to be adjusted — save by railway staff — or for the light to be extinguished, so hinged cloth covers were often provided to shroud the gas globe and dim the compartment. Another interesting aspect of gas lighting was its ability to augment the warmth of the carriage, not to mention the scope it gave for exuberant decorative treatment of the light fittings themselves.

The basic simplicity of the gas lighting system, together with its ability to produce quite bright light, especially after the introduction of gas mantles, gave it a long life, even in the twentieth century. Some railways were particularly wedded to gas lighting, even after electric light systems had become more reliable, noteworthy being the GWR and Midland; and this, in spite of the considerable fire risk which several railways, particularly the Midland, had good cause to appreciate. Grantham on the GNR (1906), together with Hawes Junction (1910) and Ais Gill (1913), both Midland, were three thoroughly embarrassing 'mishaps', to use the typically understated and favourite railway euphemism for what was often a cataclysmic accident, and did not enhance the reputation of gas. But the LYR in 1913, rather than go all-electric, persevered with a 'fireproof' gaslit train — see page 190 — and repeated the exercise in 1917.

In part, the reason was the lighter weight of the gas equipment compared with electric, not to mention the considerable capital investment made by many railways in their gas-producing plants. Moreover, in spite of several possible alternatives, compressed oil gas was still far and away the best solution to on-train cooking. Consequently, the death throes of oil gas were drawn out, extending well beyond the period of this first book. The LMS was still installing gas lights in its otherwise thoroughly modern flush-sided kitchen cars in the 1930s and as a cooking medium oil gas did not actually vanish until the much more recent introduction of bottled gas. Moreover, many gaslit coaches remained thus to the end — well into the 1930s and 1940s.

In this context, although a bit outside the immediate period of this survey, it might be worth pointing out the fundamental difference between compressed oil gas and bottled gas as applied to railways. Both types were petroleum based, but whereas compressed oil gas was carried on the vehicles in *gaseous* form under pressure, modern bottled gas, be it propane, butane or merely described as lpg (liquefied petroleum gas), is actually stored as a liquid until it passes from its pressurized container to the 'user' end.

In the latter part of the twentieth century, we are accustomed to constant media exhortations as to the virtues of electricity and take it for granted, but there was still a sort of 'magical mystery' surrounding the subject at the start of our survey and, yet again, the seminal period was late Victorian. Hamilton Ellis has, as usual, reviewed the ground most thoroughly in his work so there is no need for undue repetition here. Suffice it to say that by the start of our period, most experiments were over and a fairly standardized system patented by J. Stone in the 1890s became by far the most widely used.

Setting aside for the moment the sheer convenience factor of electric lighting, the main problem with using it on a moving vehicle is that of current storage, in the absence of a regular outside supply such as that provided to our homes and workplaces. Even if the railway is itself electrified, this does not really solve the problem of supply since a typical locomotive-

Left *This Midland picnic saloon of 1907 displays gas lamps with mantles, now fitted to the main roof and almost flush with the ceiling, thus leaving the clerestory itself free to provide perhaps better ventilation than when the lamps were mounted there* (BR LMR).

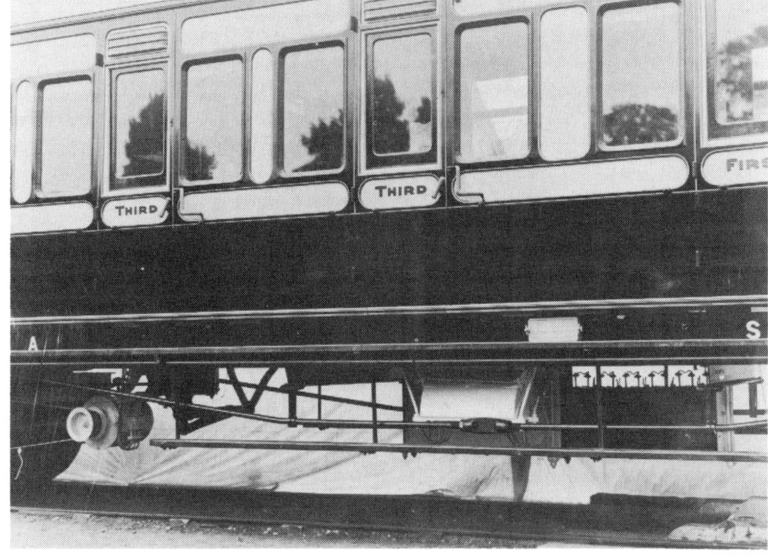

Right *This LNWR corridor carriage of* circa *1913 displays, below its floor, the full electrical apparatus for carriage lighting. To the left is the dynamo, right centre is the regulator and fusebox, the latter fixed to the solebar, while on the far right the cell box has had its top cover removed to reveal the battery connection wires* (BR LMR).

hauled railway carriage could well find itself operating in all parts of the system, whether it be electrified or not. It is therefore not a totally practical proposition for a locomotive-hauled railway carriage to pick up current from outside. The system must be self-contained and therein lies the basic problem. The fact that it still bedevils the road vehicle industry's attempts to harness electric power for traction purposes is sufficient proof of this.

If there is no 'mains supply', electricity can only be stored in some form of accumulator or battery and these things take up much space and contribute considerable weight if they are to have any reasonable storage potential. Indeed, one of the more noteworthy nineteenth-century efforts — Stroudley's on the LB & SCR — realized this problem and made a valiant attempt to solve it by putting a generator in the guard's van. This was the key.

The best way to reduce the need for battery storage of electricity is to generate it as you go along. This can be done by means of a completely self-contained unit (eg the diesel-powered generators in modern diesel-electric locomotives) or by harnessing the motion of the train itself. In the former case, the electricity generation is independent of the movement of the train but incurs a severe weight penalty by the need to have a separate 'engine' to drive the generator. If on the other hand one drives a generator by harnessing the rotary motion of the wheels and axles, the generation stops when the vehicle is not moving. Nevertheless, it was the latter mode which Stone developed in the 1890s and which became standard until well into BR days.

In Stone's system, a generator (dynamo) was mounted beneath the carriage and the moving parts given rotary motion by connecting them via pulleys and a belt to the nearest axle. The dynamo had to be manufactured in such a way that it functioned properly regardless of the direction of travel which, of course, would determine whether the rotation was clockwise or anticlockwise.

The rate of electricity generation was, of course, determined by the speed of the rotation of the wheels, so there was an undesirable variation in the rate. Thus, before the current was fed to the lights a voltage regulator was inserted — in effect a variable resistance — so that the supply to the lights was kept constant. Now this arrangement was fine so long as the vehicles were moving fast enough for current to be generated, but there comes a point (when either the vehicle speed is too low or the carriage is stationary) at which the dynamo ceases to provide enough current to keep the lights going. To overcome this, a battery supply was still needed, albeit nothing like as large as it would have been if there was no generator capacity. Thus, the complete Stone's system embodied dynamo, regulator *and* batteries, the latter being housed in one or more 'cell boxes' fixed below the underframe. The lights took their current either from the dynamo via the cells (when moving normally) or the cells alone (when moving slowly or stationary). The generating capacity of the dynamo had of course to *exceed* the demands of the lights when running at normal speeds so that the excess generating capacity could be diverted into the important business of re-charging the batteries in the

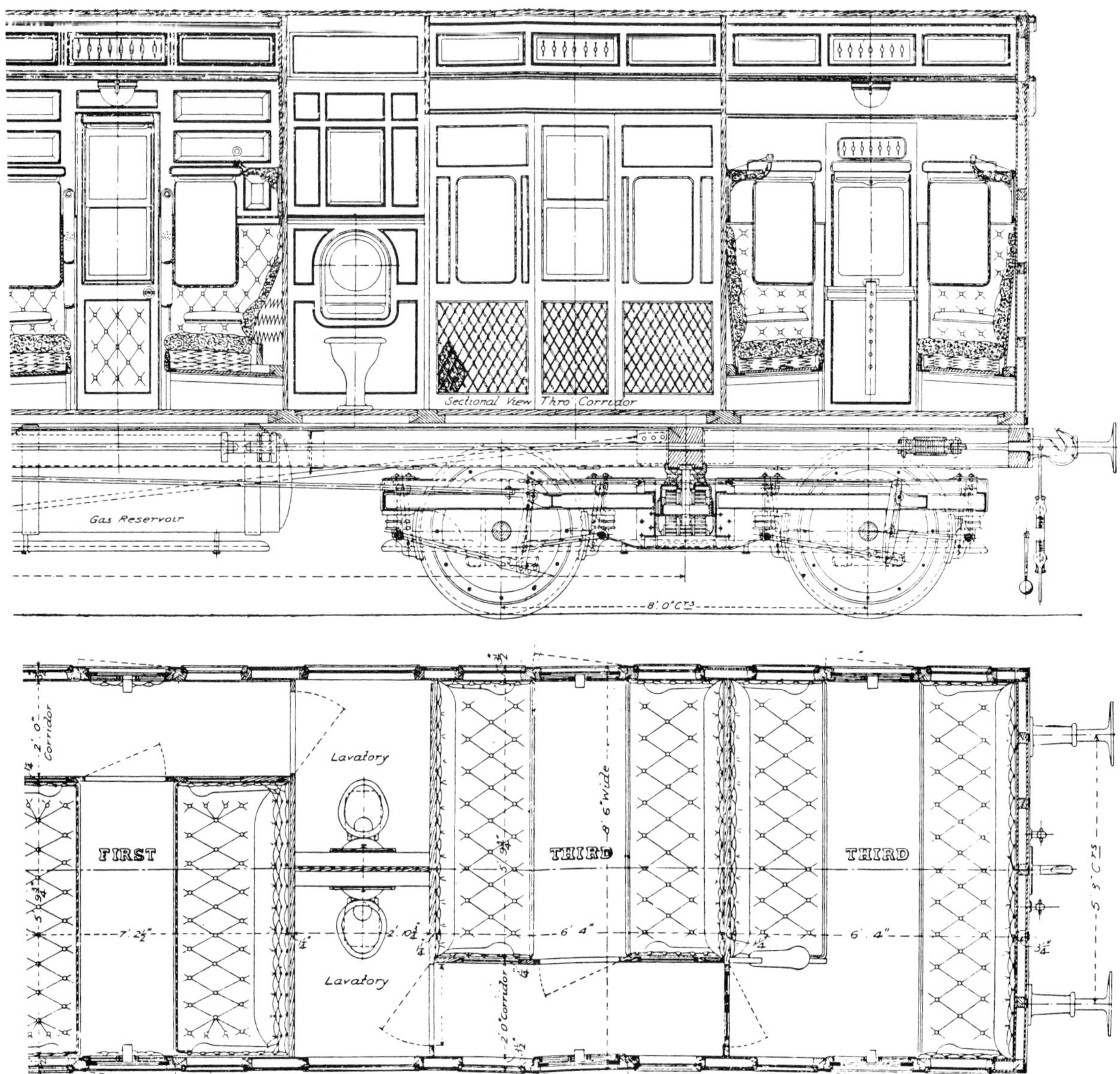

Scale 6.5mm = 1ft

Figure 32 *This and the next two drawings show something of the total design integration achieved by British carriage builders at their best. This one is a very late Victorian NER clerestory non-corridor with lavatories, a type which set standards for many decades both on the NER and elsewhere. An end elevation can also be found in Figure 19.*

cell boxes. The dynamo capacity varied, according to need, and sometimes (for instance in suburban trains), one dynamo could serve two coaches.

The batteries themselves were conventional lead-acid accumulators and were quite heavy, especially if the demands of the carriage itself were greater than normal due to extra lights, electric fans and so on. Nevertheless, the system stood the test of time, although it did add more weight to the carriage than the gas lighting apparatus already considered. It began to run into trouble when the demand for electricity exceeded its intrinsic capability, such as when all-electric cooking was adopted to some extent in the 1930s.

So successful was the basic Stone's principle,

Figure 33 *Right at the turn of the century, the GCR produced some small but stylish side-corridors of somewhat 'continental' aspect for the London Extension. These cross-sections show something of the detail which went into them. The seat design and toilet fittings encapsulate most of the issues discussed in this chapter. For plans, see Figure 44 (page 168).*

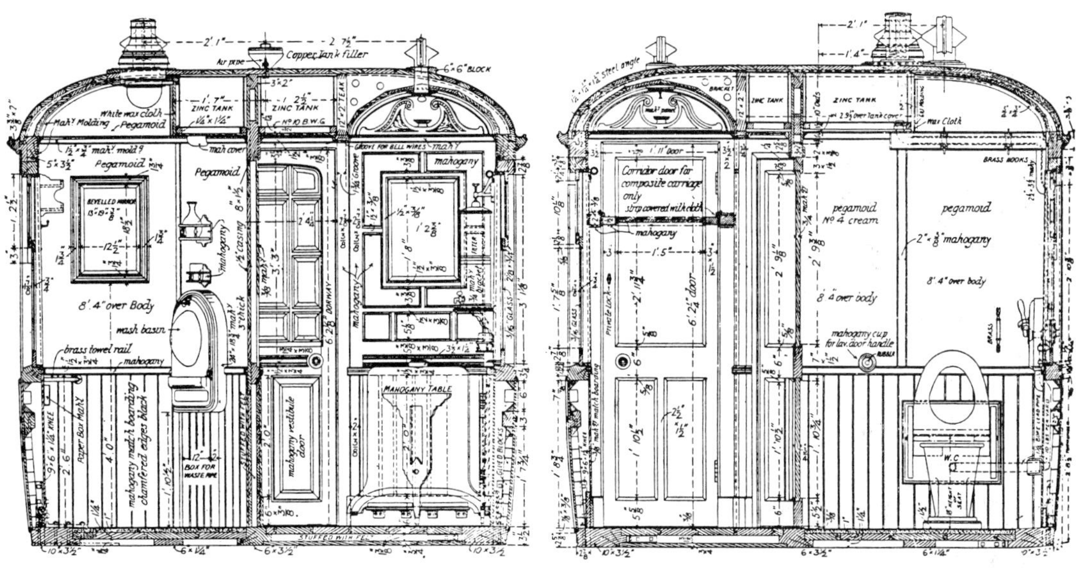

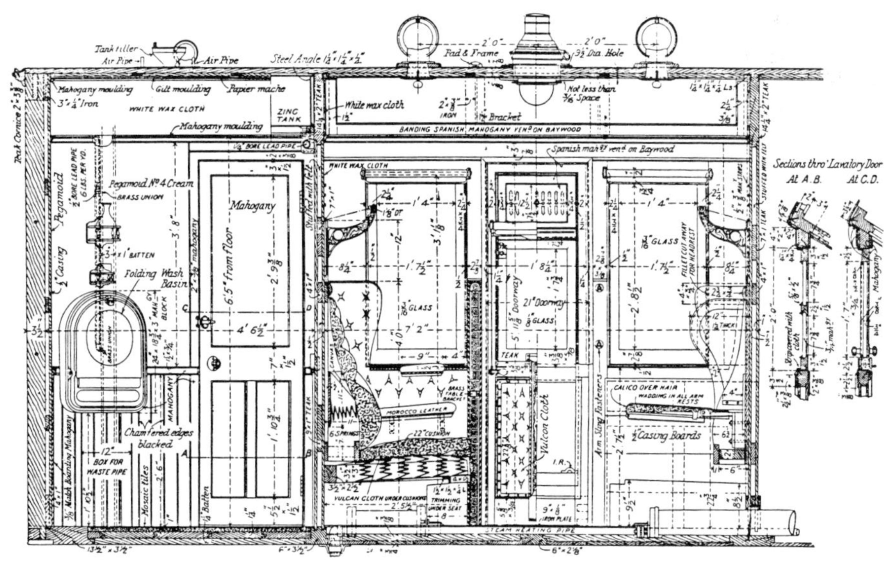

Scale 8mm = 1ft

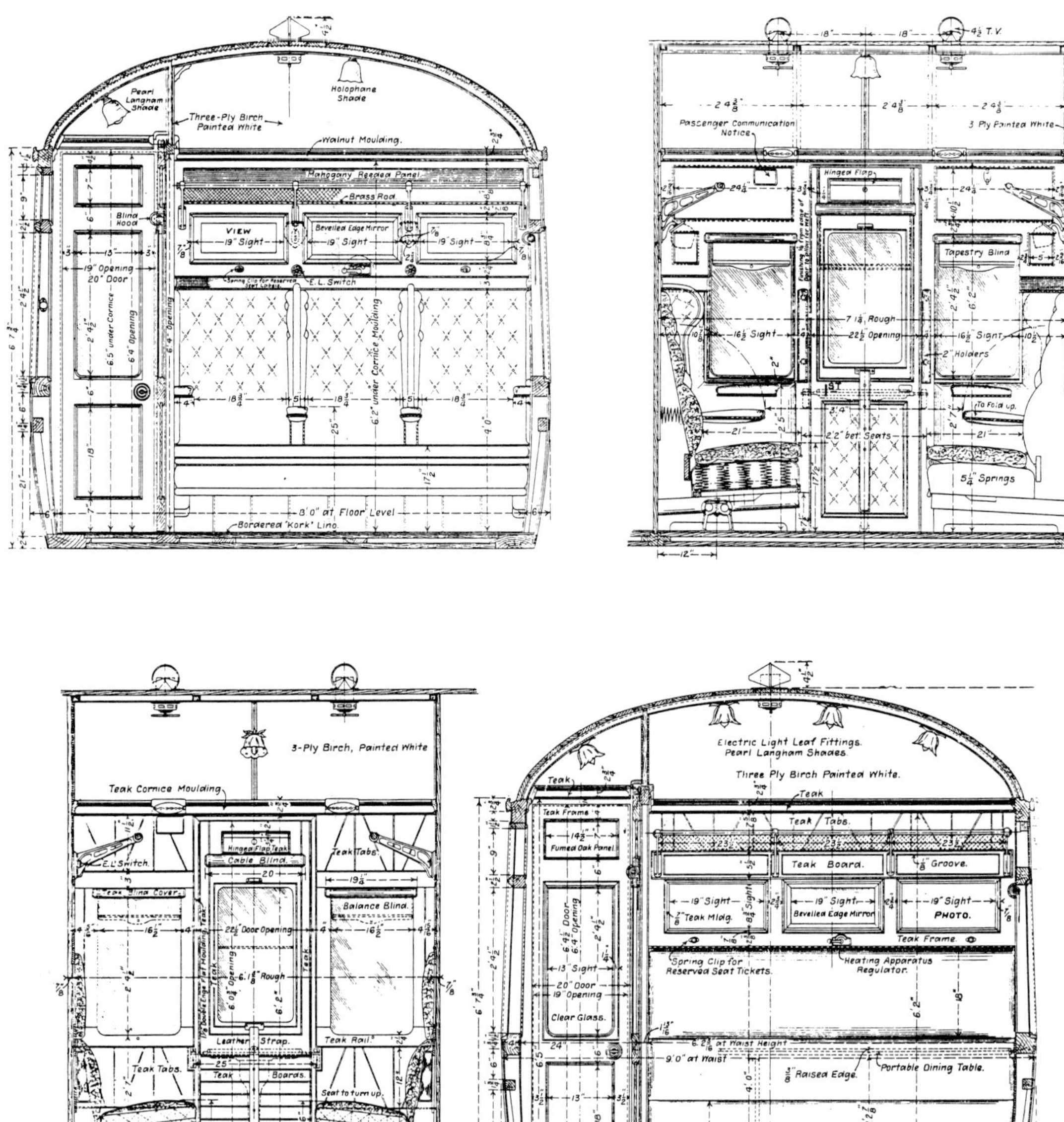

Scale 8mm = 1ft

Figure 34 *Compartment details of a West Coast Joint Stock corridor carriage of 1913. These and dozens more like them from many railways established standards which were not significantly bettered until the 1930s. Indeed, most better carriages of this period were not scrapped until well into BR days, surely adequate testimony to the essential quality of their original design.*

whether in its original form or as somewhat modified in later years by the LMS into what was known as the 'Wolverton' system, that there was no need to make any really fundamental changes for decades. In fact, the BR MkI period still utilized an essentially similar method during the 1950s and early 1960s to that which had existed since the turn of the century.

The carriage itself carried its electric supply cables either concealed beneath the inside panelling or sometimes in conduits on the roof top, and the 'supply side' voltage was normally quite low (24-28 volts) compared with domestic electric equipment. Light bulbs were normally about 25 watts with a pearl finish but they could be found in light fittings of infinite variety and style.

One particular advantage of electric lighting as compared with gas was the much simpler process of turning it on or off by means of a simple switch. It is therefore not at all surprising that the onset of electrically-lit coaches pretty well coincided with the increasing use of auxiliary optional (or 'courtesy') lights. These might be individual wall lights, separate table lamps, bedhead lights in sleeping cars and so forth, all under passenger control. It became possible to dim the lights at night or take the option between full or partial lighting, and there were few more pleasurable experiences than to ride in an electrically-lit Pullman or dining car with all the lights extinguished save for the cosy table lamp. The modern BR coaches do not offer this option — more's the pity!

The really significant changes in carriage electrics did not generally appear until the 1960s and 1970s with the onset of fluorescent lighting, air-conditioning and so on which also demanded changed methods of power generation. They will not, therefore, be considered further until Volume 3.

It should perhaps be repeated that the above account of electric lighting applies only to locomotive-hauled stock. Where carriages formed a permanent part of electrically-propelled multiple unit formations (EMUs), their lighting current could, of course, be supplied from the conductor rail (or wire). Although this supplied traction current at high voltage, by means of suitable voltage reduction apparatus it could also be used to light the train, hence the occasional momentary 'dimming or blacking out' sometimes experienced when EMUs negotiate a break between two electrical supply sections.

Before concluding this review of interior amenities, it is worth adding a short note simply to point out that certain types of vehicle, by virtue of their specialized nature, regularly carried more interior fittings — both in terms of quantity and variety — than did ordinary day coaches. Dining cars, for example, had to carry extra water supplies and extra gas cylinders for the kitchen, while the latter itself often added weight to the carriage by virtue of its heavy equipment. Sleeping cars had a plethora of partitions and cupboards, not to mention extra water, lavatory and lighting facilities, and so forth. In consequence, the need to contain elaborate interior equipment could spill over into the basic design of the vehicle itself, thus explaining the larger and heavier characteristics of many specialized carriages (12 rather than 8 wheels, for example).

There was, in fact, a tremendous degree of integration between all the three aspects of vehicle design (chassis, body and interior) which have been for convenience sake separated for analysis in this and the previous two chapters. The complete vehicle was a total synthesis of many differing requirements, and at times a compromise between disparate sets of conditions — and it does no harm to be reminded of this point from time to time if only more fully to appreciate the ingenuity with which the railways regularly solved the problems.

5. Livery, painting and decoration

Throughout most of their history the railways of Britain have been quite notably colourful, in the literal sense of the word, and happily, as these words are written in the later 1980s, there are many encouraging signs of a rebirth on the railways of something of the colourful variety which was once so characteristic of the company era. Nowhere was the use of colour more strikingly manifest than in the liveries adopted for the adornment of carriages, whether it be the humblest of suburban conveyances or the most grandly finished special saloons.

The tradition undoubtedly goes back to the horse-drawn road-coach era where rival coach operators often decorated their vehicles with a high degree of flamboyance. In part this was an expression of pride but it also had the practical virtue of identification, whether it be for the company in question or the service which was operated. Since they drew much of their early carriage inspiration from the road-coach business, the railways, not surprisingly, copied the ideas with a considerable degree of fidelity, even to the extent of giving names to some of their carriages. By the start of the twentieth century, although the practice of naming had become all but exclusive to Pullman cars, the distinctively different basic liveries remained as prevalent as ever.

By this time, livery was most definitely associated with specific companies rather than particular types of vehicles or services. With relatively few exceptions which can, realistically, be ignored, there was no longer a significant livery differentiation between, say, first and second class vehicles, but there was considerable variation between the colour schemes adopted by the individual private systems. In modern jargon it would be called 'house style'; in those days it was sufficient simply to refer to 'Midland red'. 'Great Western chocolate and cream', Great Northern teak', or whatever, to establish, beyond peradventure, the system on which one was travelling.

As an aside, it is interesting to note that the modern (ie 1985 onwards) re-introduction of colourful variety in carriage livery is almost a

Furness Railway six-wheel composite No 57 shows the customary method of applying a two-colour livery, in this case blue and white, to a wooden-panelled coach. Most companies put fine lining round almost every piece of panel moulding, and the main point of variation, colours apart, was whether or not the waist panel was painted the darker or lighter of the two shades. This picture represents the slightly more common approach, but some very famous railways, for example the GWR with its famous chocolate and cream, adopted the alternative course, ie with a dark waist panel. This FR carriage has a very long wheelbase for a rigid six-wheeler; secondly, and unusually for an English railway, it features what I have called the 'Scottish' style of twin-layer body panelling — see page 103 (Author's collection).

On LNWR tri-composite (three-class) corridor brake carriage No 900, the two-colour livery (carmine lake and white) also confined the darker shade to the bottom panels only but the Wolverton panelling (see page 103) gives it quite a different look. Because there was relatively little panel beading carrying a darker shade above the waist, LNWR carriages were often called 'white' trains, exaggerated if, as was often the case, the roof was also painted white (BR LMR).

Top *The LYR adopted a two-colour system which took its darker livery colour to window level. For photographic purposes, it also painted the odd carriage in various shades of 'works grey' to display more clearly the details and livery style, the 'Lanky' carriage colours, carmine lake and dark tan, being hard for contemporary photographic emulsions to separate. This produced a very clear impression of the character of the carriage, in this case tri-composite corridor brake No 1061. It would have received the proper livery before entering service.*

Above *A less common variant of the two-colour style was adopted by the LSWR, represented by arc roof bogie first class non-corridor No 175. Not only were the colours unusual (salmon pink and dark brown), but the practice of painting the upper panel beading the same colour as the panels themselves, rather than the darker body colour, was comparatively rare and followed by few other railways.*

reversion to a very early form of vehicle identification by service or carriage type, rather than to identify the company itself. There is thus no longer a universal BR carriage livery *as such,* but we now have 'Network SouthEast', 'ScotRail', 'InterCity' and many other similar terms, all serving as justification for the various colour schemes currently adopted by the unified BR system. Whatever the reasoning, it is a very welcome change.

Until recently, this colourful variety of exterior treatment was a somewhat peculiarly British manifestation of train travel. It was not that other countries never employed colourful styles, but they rarely went to such extravagant extremes as did the British companies, and this characteristically 'British' approach to carriage decoration was very much in evidence during and very typical of the first few decades of the present century.

Essentially, of course, the primary object of painting a carriage is to preserve the material so painted from climatic and other deterioration as a result of prolonged exposure to open-air conditions. Therefore, the first property of a carriage livery was to be of sufficient substance to protect and seal the structure of the vehicle. In Britain, the two most favoured approaches were to use either a colour base or a varnished wood treatment and the decorative possibilities were very much secondary, yet they inevitably achieved more public attention simply because of their nature. By the start of the twentieth century, fairly standardized methods of treatment had been established by the railway industry, regardless of specific livery style, and these painting and varnishing methods lasted throughout the first half of the century, largely unchanged, right into early BR days. They were slow to change even after the 1950s and, in certain particulars, have continued in use to the present days; needless to say, the origins were firmly Victorian.

The traditional method of coach painting as practised by the railways is as much art as science and its full appreciation by the onlooker can be much enhanced by a basic understanding of two fundamental and closely related aspects of the subject, namely the materials themselves and their method of application. This, therefore, will be the starting point.

Carriage painting materials

The basic ingredients

From the outset it should be understood that unlike modern paints, which make extensive use of synthetic chemical constituents, the materials used by coach painters during the first half of the century were based on naturally occurring substances falling into three broad categories. These gave way but slowly to the modern materials and, in some cases, what might be termed 'older fashioned' paint, provided it does not offend some modern 'health and safety' regulation, is still preferred by a real craftsman.

1 *Basic pigments* These constituents, which imparted colour and covering power to the finished product, were the fundamentals of paint. Indeed, they were often called 'bases', the term 'pigment' being reserved to designate those which actually imparted the finished colour. The commonly used bases were such as white and red lead, oxide of iron, zinc white, various blacks and the umbers. A more detailed analysis of the various bases and their colours is given below. They were often supplied in non-liquid form — solid, paste or powder being characteristic.
2 *Vehicles, mixes and solvents* These were the substances which, when mixed with the chosen basic pigment(s), turned them into a consistency which was recognizably 'paint', Various oils or spirits of turpentine were the norm.
3 *Driers* These, as the name implies, were substances added to the paint to hasten the drying or hardening process. Such materials as litharge, zinc sulphate or lead acetate were commonly used.
4 *Stoppers and fillers* Prior to application of any paint or varnish finishes, much less the final decorative embellishments, blemishes on the carriage surface had to be stopped or filled to give a smooth surface. The materials used were closely allied to the paints themselves and three sub-categories can be identified.
a) *Putty* This was a substance formed by mixing dried 'whiting' (fine powder produced from pure white chalk) into a stiff paste with raw linseed oil and then kneading well. A little white lead added prior to kneading improved matters and the putty could be tinted by adding colouring pigments if required. It was, of course, principally used for glazing purposes. Whiting on its own, incidentally, when rubbed on to a surface, could be used to prepare it for gilding or varnishing, having the interesting property of imparting a texture to the surface which allowed the varnish, gold size or whatever to 'lay' properly; it did not affect the finished texture and/or colour of the top coating.
b) *'Hard stopping'* This was the form of hard-drying putty, made from dry white lead mixed with gold size or varnish, and used to fill cracks, crevices and so forth. When dry, it could be smoothed down ('faced down') with pumice stone prior to painting. If a little turpentine and whiting were added, it was possible to face down the stopping with sandpaper rather than pumice stone and in this form it was called 'sandpaper stopping'. In general, hard stopping was preferred for rectifying blemishes in panels and the like because of its ability to be rubbed down to a very smooth finish. However, most carriage painters would choose to use a normal putty for major defects in joints, since this material was far less likely to become completely brittle and fall out of the crevice when subjected to the vibrations of the carriage in traffic.
c) *'Knotting'* The third filling material — something of a misnomer in this case — was used only on wooden components. The object of this substance was to 'kill' any knots in the wood (ie prevent any subsequent exudation of turpentine or resin) and also to prevent the knots absorbing paint or causing discoloration on the surface when painted. The first application was made from a mixture prepared by grinding red lead in water, mixing with glue size and applying when hot; it dried in about ten minutes. The second application was of red lead ground in oil and thinned with either boiled linseed oil or turpentine. There was also a patent form of knotting consisting of shellac dissolved in naphtha. In all its forms, knotting had no real filling power; it merely served as protection.

The art of the coach painter, in every sense, was a combination of his ability to mix these materials properly for the required purpose and his skill in applying effectively 'his' mixes to the surface in question. Used in various combinations, the above materials could provide not only the means whereby the final finish was obtained but they could also assist in the preparation process. The coach painter had to master it all.

The bases and pigments

The most commonly occurring constituent of traditional coach painting was white lead, a mixture of lead hydrate and lead carbonate. This was an extensively used substance, whether as base or pigment. When combined with oil it possessed great permanency and covering power as a base and it was unequalled amongst the various available whites as a pigment. In dry form, it could be used for stopping up cracks in the woodwork, and in any form it could be tinted with other pigments to provide many desired finishing colours. Used in small quantities, it tended to make paint somewhat easier to work with the brush and it is said that the Caledonian Railway locomotive painters at Perth were more than adept at using it in this mode. As a result they went to such extremes that, over the years, they managed to produce a somewhat lighter shade of Prussian blue than the official version — 'Perth blue' as it was sometimes called. It later became the recognized Caledonian locomotive colour, or so it is said... At the same time, however, who is to say that painters in the carriage works did not resort to the same trick with official carriage colours as well? For painting use, white lead was normally provided in 'tub' form (ie mixed with some 8-15% oil in the form of a paste).

Lead-based paint, as it was often called when white lead was a principal constituent, was poisonous and its manufacture is no longer permitted, but it had a long run as an essential basis for exterior painting. Its toxic properties were known, if not quite so feared as in our often over-sensitive modern era, and for interior use a common, non-poisonous alternative was based on zinc sulphide, frequently known as 'enamel' white. There was also a non-poisonous lead white (lead sulphate) but neither of these non-toxic white bases was quite as good as the traditional white lead, always the favoured choice of the best coach painters.

The second very common base was red lead, this time an oxide of the metal. Like white lead, it mixed well with oil, had good covering power and dried quickly. For these reasons it was a popular undercoat or primer and was particularly suited to metal components. However, unlike white lead, it could only be mixed safely (in regard to permanence of colour) with ochres, earths and blacks. Mixed with other pigments (including white lead), it went 'fugitive' — in other words, it lost colour permanence.

To obtain the vast range of different colour shades so characteristic of railway liveries, other pigments had to be added, and although this survey is not meant to be a paint manufacturing manual, a brief summary of the more common colour pigments will not be out of place. For one thing, even a slight knowledge of the considerable complexity of the pigments employed can only serve to enhance the appreciation of the skills applied by those really competent coach painters who knew how to use them properly. The various pigments group themselves into broad colour categories, in each of which such qualities as beauty and depth of colour, 'body' (ie covering power), ease of application, durability and permanence were all sought-after characteristics.

Blacks

Several kinds of black pigment were used by the railway painters. 'Lamp' and 'vegetable' black, usually containing 98% or more carbon, were obtained from the soot formed by burning various substances such as coal, tar, oil or tallow. The superior version (vegetable black) was that obtained from the burning of pure vegetable oil. Another common type was 'ivory' or 'bone' black obtained by burning (calcining) ivory or bone in closed vessels and then grinding it to a fine powder. Ivory was considered superior to other bone and produced an intense black pigment. A description often encountered was 'drop black', referring to the practice of selling the black pigment in pear-shaped drops of exceedingly fine quality, easily fractured prior to grinding and mixing with the appropriate 'vehicle'.

Browns and yellows

These pigments came in a variety of forms, mostly derived from natural earths and clays whose colours were mainly due to the presence of oxides of iron and manganese. Common names found in this category were the 'umbers', a large class of natural dark earths found in many places, particularly Turkey; the 'ochres', somewhat similar natural clays of rather lighter tone, often used as a basis for a yellow colour; and the 'siennas', close allies of both, a warmer shade lying somewhere between them in tone. 'Burnt' as opposed to 'raw' umbers and siennas were produced by burning to give a darker colour, while 'Vandyke brown' was a naturally occurring dark brown mineral pigment.

The brown family in its more or less natural state graded at one end into a sort of yellow and at the other end into red, while the darkest browns could be given all manner of subtle hues by amalgamation with blacks or greens. The permutations were infinite but a particularly good example of what could be achieved is the elusive and indescribable shade used for the lower panels in the distinctive two-tone carriage livery adopted by the London and South Western Railway. To call it 'dark brown' begs the question. In some conditions it could seem almost black, while in others, by all accounts, it took on a sort of greenish hue. It has proved a very difficult colour to reproduce with modern synthetics at the National Railway Museum.

The other principal source of yellow pigmentation was from chromate of lead (chrome yellow), much used in the preparation of green shades (see below).

Reds

Red, together with blue and yellow, is one of the three primary colours and, along with green in some form or another, was probably the most common railway livery colour. Even those railways which never adopted it as a basic livery tone always used some form of red for items such as locomotive buffer planks, signals and so on, and also quite regularly for lining out an otherwise 'red-free' colour scheme. Reds varied from the near-brown to a bright vermilion bordering on orange, and in the darker part of the spectrum some singularly beautiful and rich shades were to be seen.

At the 'red/brown' end were to be found a series of fine powders prepared from antimony sulphide which required little or no grinding and mixed readily with oil. They had great covering power as did the reds obtained from iron oxides. They were also very durable, hence the common use of red oxide as suitable finish for tens of thousands of humble goods wagons. Red/brown in its most celebrated form was often known as 'Indian red', a name which in theory should only be applied to those red pigments obtained by grinding Bengalese haematite ore to a fine powder. There were, however, many substitutes to be found, possibly the best of them being calcined sulphate of iron. The red/browns were rarely used as a basic livery colour for carriages, save perhaps for picking out window frames and other details, but were a common form of undercoat, particularly for the rich, dark shades of red wherein the warmth of the red/brown undercoat would transmit its richness through the final, almost semi-translucent quality of the top coat.

The brightest of the reds was vermilion, a naturally occurring sulphide of mercury known as cinnabar, and the best came from China. When prepared with sulphide of potassium, it could rarely be bettered for sheer brilliance of colour. Once again, it was rarely a basic livery colour, but applied in the form of fine lining at the edge of gilt-embellished panel beading, it imparted an unparalleled opulence to the finished carriage. Not surprisingly, many railways used it for just this purpose.

The 'real' railway reds (ie those used as basic colours for the final liveries) were usually classified as 'lakes'. The word really describes a process rather than a substance and was used to denote the method whereby organic colouring substances were precipitated by potassium carbonate or a solution of alum from a variety of raw materials, the nature of which gave the lake its essential colour. Thus, such sources as the 'coccus cacti' insect would produce carmine, cochineal would produce crimson, the madder plant would produce the lake of the same name, and so on. Several other lakes could be manufactured from coal tar colours and, again, the varieties and their descriptions were endless.

In purely British railway carriage terms, the most commonly found lakes were the famous crimson, particularly associated with the Midland Railway and, later, the LMS, but also used in near identical shade by the North British, North Eastern and Glasgow and South Western Railways, to mention but three. A very dark lake — almost purple-brown — was carmine, particularly associated with the London and North Western and Lancashire and Yorkshire companies, but also used in a slightly lighter form by the Caledonian Railway. Lying somewhat between these two colours in the spectrum was a third basic dark shade of red, described, probably correctly, as madder lake on the North Staffordshire system but also used in near identical shade on the

Liveries involving dark red and black, especially those using a single basic colour, were difficult to photograph before colour sensitive photographic emulsions came to the rescue. However, when the odd picture was taken using material which could differentiate the shades, the result could give a crystal clear indication of the disposition of both main colour and lining. This is clearly shown on Midland Railway corridor third class brake No 1617 in 1916. Even the two-colour roof (black and grey) is differentiated (BR LMR).

South Eastern and Chatham Railway and even, for a short time between 1913 and 1922, on the Great Western in replacement of the famous 'chocolate and cream'. The latter, of course, came back at the 1923 grouping of the railways.

We are now, of course, in the highly subjective area of colour description, a topic pretty well guaranteed to cause argument and controversy. It is, in fact, well-nigh impossible to describe colours in words with any real precision, but the mere fact that even in the 1980s the topic of Edwardian liveries still causes such endless debate merely reinforces the fact that railway colour schemes were and are a prime aspect of the railway scene in Britain. The next group of colours was no different from the reds in this respect.

Greens

In theoretical colour terms, green, although the most widely occurring colour in nature, is not a primary shade and is in fact composed of a mixture of blue and yellow in various proportions. The natural green sources for paint pigments reflected this situation, being classified in two main groups. Those manufactured from sulphates were generally classed as 'Brunswick' greens and originated from barytes, gypsum or lead sulphates, acted upon by Prussian blue (see below) or chrome yellow. Those derived from chrome oxide, were unsurprisingly, classified as the 'chrome' greens. For the most part, and accepting the subjective and somewhat sweeping nature of the comment, Brunswick greens often seemed to possess a slightly colder quality than chrome greens, the latter tending rather more towards the yellow end of the spectrum.

Green was much more a locomotive than a carriage colour and many were and are the arguments surrounding the precise shades used. Indeed, I cannot resist commenting that the famous GWR locomotive green was of the chrome variety rather than oft-quoted Brunswick version! In the context of this book, however, its more subtle nuances need rarely concern us since few railways used green either as a basic carriage colour or even for decoration.

Prior to the grouping, the only major railways which adopted the shade were the Cambrian, Highland, Maryport & Carlisle, and (for some stock only) the London and South Western. After 1922, the Southern Railway, in succession to the LSWR, was the only major user of green for carriages, by which time the whole issue was further confused by the insertion of additional adjectives such as 'olive', 'malachite' and so forth.

Blues

Blue is one of the three primary colours but until fairly recent BR days (1965 onwards) it did not find too much favour as a carriage colour. In fact, it was even less popular than green. Before 1923 only the Furness Railway and the Somerset and Dorset Joint Railway used it to any great extent for carriages and, prior to 1965, its only other significant appearance was in the form of the somewhat specialized liveries adopted by the LMS and LNER for their streamlined trains of the 1930s, neither of which had any great claim to aesthetic distinction. Even as a locomotive colour, blue was not much more widespread and, risking a personal opinion, I find blue to be a somewhat less attractive shade than most for railway use, its only redeeming manifestations being perhaps the locomotive liveries of the Great Eastern and Caledonian Railways. It nearly always has a 'cold' quality to it.

At the same time, when added to other pigments blue can impart real quality to the end product. The famous LNWR 'white', for example, used on the upper panels of its carriages, could never have achieved its fame but for the addition of a mere pound weight of ultramarine to each hundredweight (112 lb) of white tub lead.

In natural form, blue pigments were most commonly (in railway usage) of either 'Prussian' or 'ultramarine' type. Prussian blue was the complex chemical result of adding proto-sulphate of iron to a solution of potassium ferro-cyanide to which, when precipitated, was further added a small amount of a solution of bichromate of potash and sulphuric acid, the whole process resulting in the familiar deep blue shade. Ultramarine, on the other hand, was prepared from alum, sulphur, soda and silica, acids being used to completely deodorize the end product. A third natural blue, known as 'Brunswick' blue and, of course, used in preparation of the green bearing the same prefix, was made from barytes, green copperas, china clay and yellow prussiate.

These, then, were some of the natural sources of the various colours used by the railways. Many of them were mixed by the paint manufacturers before being supplied to the users, but within the railway paintshop itself the painters too had to be well versed in the art of paint mixing, partly for matching purposes when rectifying worn or damaged paintwork, or possibly even to get a more precise match between two separate batches of a nominally identical colour. It should be appreciated that it was much more difficult to fix a precise shade using natural sources, however carefully prepared, than it is to do so with modern synthetic chemicals.

Vehicles, mixes and solvents

Most of the real skill of the painter was bound up closely with his knowledge and appreciation of the various oils, solvents and driers, the vehicles used for rendering the various paints workable. Most of them were either fixed or volatile oils of either the linseed or turpentine families. They came in varying properties and qualities and were chosen according to precise needs. However, they all had to work freely, display drying power and be transparent, preferably as near colourless as possible.

Linseed oils

Linseed oil is obtained from flax seed and was traditionally imported from the Baltic and Black Sea areas and also from India, the latter source generally being regarded as somewhat inferior. It could be processed in various different ways to produce three main sub-forms:

1 *Raw linseed oil (cold drawn oil)* This variety, the best quality, was obtained by crushing, grinding and pressing the oil from the seed *without heat.* It was pale, transparent, viscous and almost odourless. It did not keep as well as oil produced by heating, nor did it yield much more than 20% oil, but it was the preferred choice for the best work, although somewhat slow drying by nature.

2 *Ordinary linseed oil* This was a similar product but the seed was steam heated to about 200° F. The yield was better at some 25-30%, but the oil was less viscous and had a much darker colour — a sort of amber shade.

3 *Boiled linseed oil* This was obtained by mixing linseed oil with lead oxide (litharge) or other additives and heating to about 400° F, a process which drove off those substances which impeded oxidation, thus improving the drying powers. Even without additives, boiled linseed oil would dry more rapidly and was sometimes called 'drying oil', but the additives made the drying process even quicker and some of them altered the oil's consistency in important ways. Lead acetate, for example, would produce a lighter shade than litharge, while for use with zinc-based paints the oil had to be free from lead oxide altogether and was boiled instead with about 5% manganese peroxide.

In any form, linseed oil, although it would not keep for ever, had to be at least six months old before it was fit for use with paint, during which time it was stored in tanks to allow it to purify and mature, so to speak. Any residual water or impurities would settle as a precipitate, a sort of gooey mass called 'foots'. Sometimes white lead (about 1 lb per gallon) was also added and allowed to settle out. This improved the colour and also the drying properties of the oil and the white lead 'foots' could later be used for rough work. Oil could even be bleached by putting it in shallow, lead-lined troughs and covering it with glass, the lead aiding the bleaching process.

Linseed oil, on final exposure to the air, oxidizes and becomes thicker. In its purest form it is quite slow to dry, but even the best quality, when used in paint, should have dried out within two or three days. Anything longer was an indication of poor quality, as was too dark a colour.

Of the three varieties, raw and ordinary linseed oils, preferably the former, were, of course, the obvious choice for the main colour pigments, while the boiled variety was confined to paint destined for carriage roofs or any other areas which received 'rougher' preparation. In addition to helping make paint pigments, linseed oil was also used in manufacture of putty and other fillers (see page 72).

Oil of turpentine

Turpentine, or 'turps', is a volatile oil obtained by tapping pine and larch trees — much in the manner of tapping rubber trees — and then distilling the raw turpentine. The residue after distillation is common resin and traditionally the best quality came from America.

Turpentine is used as a solvent in painting and in the manufacture of varnish; it also has a slight bleaching quality which, to some extent, tends to correct the colouring effect of the linseed oil with which it is mixed. It is used to 'flatten' white and make quicker drying paints, but it is merely a solvent to enable paint to work more freely and is no use on its own. Since in due course it will evaporate, it actually weakens the paint pigment, hence its best-known everyday function — cleaning brushes. However, it also has an interesting property of preventing the blistering of paint so, used in the correct quantity, it was an obvious valuable ingredient of those paints and varnishes which were exposed to the sun — hence its value in carriage painting.

Paint driers

These have already been mentioned, and they worked on the principle that the maximum drying power in oils is achieved by adding atmospheric oxygen to them. This was best done by using metallic substances which acted as 'carriers' of atmospheric oxygen and if, in addition, these substances themselves contained oxygen, so much the better. The best were therefore the metallic oxides such as the above-mentioned litharge (lead oxide), the most common single variety. Other driers in the traditional paint business included lead acetate, zinc sulphate, manganese sulphate and manganese oxide. As already mentioned, *lead* oxides were not used for zinc-based paint. Some driers, like manganese oxide, although quick in effect, were dark tones and could only be

This is pure 'signwriting'. On the original print, the brush marks can be seen as can the variations in the hand-applied gold leaf. The picture was taken to illustrate the GNR's new-style elongated insignia introduced in 1906 — see the picture on page 82. Later, of course, transfers would be made, but it was normal and cheaper to use the signwriter when new styles were first evaluated.

used for dark-coloured paints. Paint dryers were often supplied ready for use, ground and mixed in oil.

Regardless of type, driers had to be handled carefully. Only the absolute minimum quantity was needed since, paradoxically, if used in too great amounts, in spite of their name they actually slowed down the drying process! With finishing coats, little or any was used, especially if the tint might be affected, and in all cases driers were mixed into the colour at the very last moment prior to use. There were several different kinds of driers, most of which could not be used together and amongst the best known varieties were 'japan' and 'gold size'. The former was much used for tinting greens and browns but was particularly associated with black whenever a good high finish was required. Gold size, as its name implies, was used for picking out gilded areas, where its particular ability to become tacky quite speedily was of value in laying on the subsequent gold leaf (see below). Used on its own as a drier, gold size blended well with varnish, did not affect the brilliancy of the finished coat and did not become brittle with weathering. There were various types of gold size according to specific needs.

Gold leaf and transfers, and their application

Gold leaf, and its close ally the 'varnish fix' transfer, were used quite regularly in the process of gilding and decorating carriages. Gold leaf itself is beaten out of a thin sheet of pure gold until it is only a few thousandths of an inch thick and is normally supplied in books containing individual leaves some 3-4 inches square, each placed between a tissue layer coated with chalk to prevent the gold itself sticking to the paper.

The precise shade could vary from very pale to almost an orange-red. Some suppliers offered 'ribbon' gold, a long roll of gold leaf some 3/8-1/2 inch wide, ideally suited to carriage lining. Application to the carriage was by means of gold size. The area to be gilded was treated with gold size and, while the size was still tacky, the gold leaf was rubbed into place through the carrying tissue, the size acting as an adhesive. It demanded skilful judgement on the part of the painter to know precisely the right moment at which to apply the gilding. Gold leaf was easier to apply if it was slightly warmed so as to be perfectly dry and when the process was completed, a gentle wipe down was all that was normally required prior to covering with varnish.

It is surprising how often gold leaf was used for picking out lining, even on quite humble carriages, at the start of the century. Although many railways used yellow painted lines for their vehicles, many others preferred gilt lining throughout. Other systems reserved gilding for their particularly important special vehicles while some railways used gold for their corridor coaches but not for their shorter-distance stock, rather than waste any. Although gilding was durable it was undoubtedly expensive

This close-up view of a well-weathered NER carriage clearly shows the use of transfer insignia, the texture of the letters RAI being particularly clear. The lining, however, can scarcely be distinguished; it was *there! This view also gives good detail of typical carriage bodyside features — see Chapter 3. Note particularly the 'frameless' drop light in the door.*

and painters, rather than waste any, would save the 'scrapings' from the gold sheets for touching up purposes elsewhere.

That said, however, gilding as a *routine* decorative procedure began to decline quite early in the century — largely because of the expense — but it continued to be quite common on the better stock throughout the period of this first volume. In fact, it was not really until the later 1930s that it became a particularly rare process in the carriage works. It has not been possible to discover the precise cost of gilding a typical carriage of the Edwardian period, but it might be of interest to reveal that in the 1980s the cost of re-gilding a historic twelve-wheel bogie vehicle of that same Edwardian period using the traditional techniques and materials can be some £1,000-£1,500 *more* than for plain painted lining!

Gold leaf was also used to a very considerable extent in the manufacture of the characteristic transfer emblems, heraldic devices and carriage insignia, once so common. This form of establishing company identity and the like was a far less time-consuming process than hand lettering, but needed economies of scale to make the often high cost of the transfers themselves justifiable. For this reason, in our modern age the old insignia which increasingly appear on vintage vehicles have to be put there by hand, thus keeping alive yet another of the sub-skills of the traditional carriage painter, that of signwriting. As the years went by, the use of gold leaf in the transfers inevitably gave way, through rising costs of material, to the use of gold powder (a rather inferior substitute) and eventually yellow pigments, but it was not until very recently that BR abandoned the traditional type of transfer insignia. There are still quite a few practitioners around in the preservation movement and the 'old-fashioned' transfers are still made from time to time.

Transfer manufacture, an art in itself, is usually carried out by specialist firms. The transfer itself consists of multiple layers of coloured pigments, one each for *every single* colour called for by the finished device. These are laid down in careful register in reverse order and mirror-image configuration so that the first layer to go on the carrying paper is that which will eventually form the outer side of whatever emblem is represented. The transfer is actually 'printed' on to a quite thin tissue backing layer to which is bonded a thicker protective layer for ease of preliminary handling. As with gold leaf, the face of the transfer which will be applied to the carriage side is normally protected with a loose sheet of tissue to avoid the delicate detail being damaged. Transfers made in this way are normally called 'varnish fixing' and they are applied to the carriage in much the same way as gold leaf.

Transfers were not always easy to distinguish from the hand-written equivalent on a well-finished vehicle, but if something went wrong in the paintshop it could sometimes be revealed by accident. On this LYR steam railmotor, the misalignment between the 'Luggage' and 'Compartment' wording suggests that someone got the transfers in the wrong position and did not discover it until too late! The picture also shows excellent detail of a typical fully panelled carriage body; note particularly the substantial hinges and door stops.

The first process is to partially separate the heavier protective paper layer from the transfer-carrying tissue layer by gently teasing one corner free, the full separation of carrying tissue from protective layer coming later. The transfer is then attached to the carriage by applying varnish or gold size to the transfer itself and waiting for it to become tacky, a process, as with gold leaf application, requiring some considerable judgement on the part of the painter. When reckoned to be ready, the transfer is then pressed into position on the correct part of the carriage side and pressed down firmly, taking particular care to expel any air bubbles which might be trapped between transfer and panel. Sometimes a particularly recalcitrant air bubble could be persuaded to vanish by pricking a hole through the backing paper. The heavy supporting paper layer is then carefully peeled from the tissue-carrying layer, leaving the latter, with its transfer , on the coach side. When properly dry, the tissue layer can then be swabbed down with a damp cloth impregnated with turpentine so as to soak it thoroughly, thus rendering it capable of easy removal. A gentle wipe down with the same or a similar damp cloth would normally remove any vestiges of gum or varnish.

It sounds tedious and certainly took time, but to watch a real expert carry out the process was to marvel at the sheer skill and dexterity with which it could be carried out. Normally, some sort of 'production line' procedure would be adopted so as not to waste too much time waiting for things to be right. It would thus be normal, for example, to apply the whole of the required transfers to one coach, or even several coaches, in sequence, starting at one end of the vehicles and progressing down the line.

Varnishes

Varnishes imparted the final finish, whether on unpainted or painted material, and served to protect surfaces from atmospheric weathering. They also required to be such that the surface can be cleaned or washed without damage. Such was their importance in the paint-makers' repertoire that their precise preparation was not always specified. In fact, a contemporary description states: 'The manufacture of varnishes is more or less a complicated and to some extent a secret process, which cannot be dealt with...'!

The principle constituent of varnish in its natural form was 'gum', the fossil exudation of certain trees. When a surface was varnished, the solvents eventually evaporated from the mixture leaving the gum as a thin transparent film of resin-like quality. Varnishes were named according to their gum (eg amber, copal, etc), their usage (finishing, fine-coating, etc), the solvent which held the gum in solution (oil, spirit, etc) or even by their brand names.

The best suited for outside work and for areas needing frequent cleaning and polishing were the oil varnishes made from the hardest gums; they took time to dry but were the most durable in service. They were best for being kept as long as possible before use and were never less than three months old. In carriage terms, two main qualities prevailed, known as 'first coat' (or 'rubbing') varnishes and 'second coat' (or 'finishing') varnishes. The former had a greater proportion of gum to aid drying and hardening, while the latter were paler and more brilliant in gloss, giving a durable top surface.

Spirit varnishes (or lacquers) were made by dissolving softer gums in spirit and they dried through evaporation rather than by oxidation. They were more brilliant than oil and turpentine varnishes and had a harder surface. However, being more brittle and liable to crack or break off the surface, they were only really suited to inside work.

The move towards synthetic materials

Progressively through the century, and particularly since the Second World War, the natural materials from which traditional coach paints were made have given way to purely chemically prepared synthetic substances, and modern paint technology is vastly different from that of a century ago. In particular, the ability of the modern paint technologist to fix a shade and then specify its precise formulation so as to be capable of repetition time after time has much reduced the individual painter's need to be able to 'mix and match' his own materials. Of course, the art of the colour mixer in the first stage is much as it always was, but the vastly increased range of both paint shades and varnishes (for all manner of purposes) has undoubtedly reduced the need for the individual craftsman to have the deep knowledge of materials and their properties which his early twentieth-century predecessor had to have. There is nowadays probably a whole generation of painters which knows not the virtues of lead-based paint, having been thoroughly brainwashed by our frequently over-neurotic society into an attitude conditioned solely by its admittedly toxic qualities! Furthermore, changes in livery styles themselves have also reduced the need for mastery of the skills of lettering and lining to not much more than a pale shadow of that which was needed in former times.

These two factors accepted, however, the painting of a railway carriage, even in the modern era, is not the same sort of business as that of spraying or dipping a car body. Although the paints themselves may have changed and the styles of decoration have become simpler, the actual process of putting the paint on to the vehicle was and still is a skilled and specialized matter, for the railway carriage has to withstand a pretty tough life. For one thing, it is not cossetted and coddled like the domestic motor car, nor does it live most of its life sheltered in a nice garage. It is expected to be able to run almost as many millions of miles as the car will run thousands and is considered something of a failure if its useful lifespan is not twice or three times that of a road vehicle.

To enable it to do this, it needs regularly to be fully repainted, a typical interval being about five to seven years; between these full repaints, an intermediate touch up and re-varnish would be normal. This aspect of the subject must now be considered, concentrating as before on the traditional early twentieth century way of doing things. Sadly, it has to be said that the demands for cost-effectiveness by the modern railway do not permit of quite the same degree of thoroughness, nor do modern synthetics wholly compensate for its absence.

The paintshop at York carriage works during NER days. On the left, a humble six-wheel brake van is receiving the full treatment — note the chalk marks indicating where further attention is needed. On the right, another similar vehicle is almost finished. The gloss is such that one can almost use the carriage side as a mirror.

Carriage painting methods

The painting of a railway carriage may be divided into three categories, of which the third, interior painting, was so indistinguishable from conventional interior decorating as to concern us not at all, save to record that it took place during the interior finishing stages already described. The other two categories were concerned with the exterior finishing of the carriage and came in two quite specific stages, perhaps best summarized by the words 'preparation' and 'finishing'.

Preparation

The preparatory, preliminary or plain painting (all three descriptions were used) was relatively straightforward, consisting mainly of the application of various primers — usually lead-based — to act as protection for framework, insides of panels, ironwork and so on. Much of this work was carried out as construction took place and the general aim was to ensure that *no* materials or surfaces, however difficult of access, remained unprotected. This made sound economic sense in that any protective coating, be it on metal or wood, kept out the air and prevented, or at least delayed, the onset of decay, rot and rust.

A typical process would be to thoroughly clean all grease, oil, rust, scale, glue and so forth from the bodywork and then treat any appropriate areas with knotting, followed by overall coats of a lead based primer. For any ferrous surfaces, red lead mixed with linseed oil gave a good protection and for wood a grey base was fairly common. Quite often, these priming paints were mixed in the paintshop from left overs and 'foots' from other purposes, provided they were of the right constituency. Their colour was less critical than their purpose (protection) and generalization would be pointless save to say that a typical body primer would be about 3½ lbs of tub lead with one pint of linseed oil and relatively little drier. Mixed into a stiff paste, it would be thinned with turpentine to help it penetrate the joints. The only exception to this basic priming process was of course on the *visible* surfaces of any carriage which was to receive a natural varnished wood finish. The special circumstances of this type of finish will be considered after the analysis of the methods used to apply a fully painted livery.

Finishing

In a curious way, the actual process of 'finishing', in coach painting terms, was, in fact, a series of preparation processes carried out with the next stage in mind and generally obscured by it. The only finish one saw was the very last coat of paint (as well as varnish, of course) and anything up to 90% or more of the effort which went before was buried below; but this was the nature of coach painting — and woe betide the painter who did not tackle the job thoroughly and properly, for the eventual finish would all too easily reveal any poorly executed preliminaries.

It is probable that no two railways followed precisely the same processes of painting their carriages in every detail, but they all adopted very similar principles and it is these which guaranteed the end product.

After the first primer coat, one or two more coats of similar colour would be applied, properly brushed out and 'laid off' (that is *across* the grain of the timber areas, if present), free from heavy brush marks. At this point, all holes, blemishes and the like would be filled with hard stopping applied with a sort of palette-knife. Sometimes, several more coats of 'brush filler' would be applied. This was basically the same as normal filler save for being thinned to allow it to be brushed rather than spread with a knife. When the supervisor judged that the stopping and filling process had gone far enough, the filler would be allowed to harden, at which point the surfaces were faced down with pumice stone and water and dried off with chamois leather. The modern substitute is, of course, 'wet and dry' abrasive paper, but the process is much the same.

Next came the 'guide' or 'disguise' coat — again usually of lead colour — and this gave the final opportunity to examine the surface for any uneven parts which may have been overlooked. Further stopping (if need be) and rubbing down (always) was followed by a final lead colour coat and a last rub down.

In this view at Eastleigh, LSWR-pattern 1st/3rd non-corridor carriage No 7627 is being finished off with lining pencils by two craftsmen prior to the final varnishing. It now carries the all-green livery which, although adopted by the Southern Railway in 1923, was introduced by the LSWR in 1915 when many former non-corridor coaches were converted or rebuilt to electric multiple unit form. No 7627 was one such — note the modified headstock for close coupling.

SMOKING
SMOKING

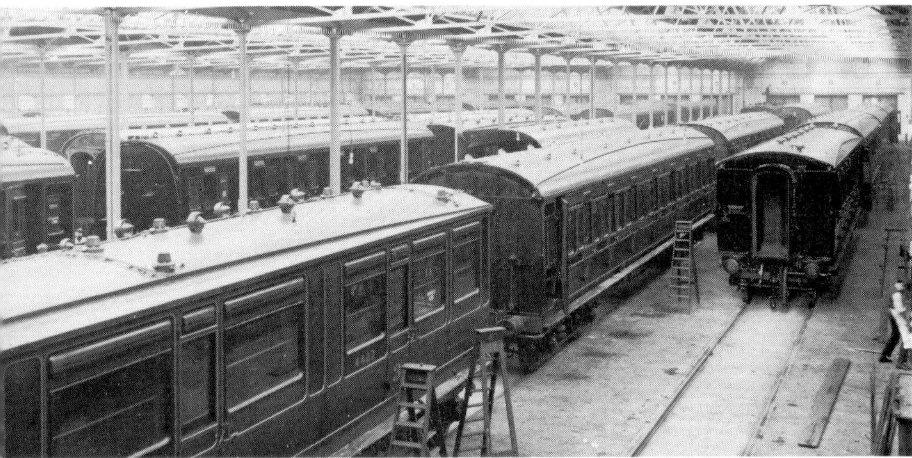

Although taken in 1933, this view of carriages 'hardening off' prior to re-entering service would not have been much different, save for changed livery styles, at any time in the first half of the twentieth-century. They are in fact mostly LNWR coaches at Wolverton, all now wearing the fully-lined LMS standard livery. Note, cf the picture on page 74, the lack of resolution between the crimson bodies and the black beading.

By now, counting in the preparation phase, a typical carriage would have from five to seven layers of paint on its surface, and it was only at this point that any real thought was given to the final body colour. The appropriate undercoat would go on first, followed by two or more coats of the final colour (it was usually more than two!). Between each coat it was customary to 'flat down' the surface to remove minor inperfections. This was a similar if rather less aggressive process to facing down and produced a nice matt surface for the next layer. It was common practice for the very last layer of finish coat to be mixed with varnish and if so, to be referred to as a 'glaze coat'.

There would now be at least ten layers of paint on the carriage and only then did the final decoration begin. The final body coat would again be flatted down and the lettering, lining and other decoration applied, including gilding and transfers if called for, as already described. Lining was invariably hand applied, whether in paint or gilt, and for this purpose special brushes known as 'lining pencils' were used; the length of the bristles could be anything up to 3 inches long and their number depended upon the thickness of the desired line. Many carriages carried what were known as 'picking-out' lines at the edge of the main lining, the width of which was only 1/8 inch or less, and for these lines the pencils had very few bristles indeed. The paint for lining was usually

The full treatment has been given to the pioneer GNR carriage to receive the new type of insignia in 1906, first and third class dining saloon No 3039. The GNR (and later the LNER) standardized this attractive style of lettering, but in this particular instance it was probably a bit 'over-the-top'. The carriage itself is very stylish but a little more decorative restraint might have been beneficial.

mixed by the individual painter on a palette and the pencil drawn across the palette to charge it with paint. If lining was to be of the gold leaf variety, the gold size was applied using the lining pencil technique. Once again, to watch the real expert at work on this kind of process is an education in itself.

When all lining and decoration was dry, all was dusted off and preparation for final varnishing begun. This would normally involve a re-washing of the carriage which was also commonly rubbed with fine pumice dust or a whiting rag as well in order to provide an absolutely clean, dry surface for the varnish, but taking great care not to damage the decorative embellishments.

The first varnish coat was applied thinly to prevent ridges, stains or 'tear drops' and was allowed to dry thoroughly before the next coat was applied. Only after the second varnish coat was it safe to rub down again — any earlier rubbing down might damage the lining and other decoration. Once protected with two layers of varnish, however, the carriage received its most thorough rub down since the pre-guide-coat stage, using ground pumice dust and water applied by cloth or pad, the aim being to produce an impeccably smooth and clean surface for the final varnish coat(s). A total of three or four further coats of finishing varnish was then normal for all railways, after which the carriage was allowed to harden off before going into traffic.

Roof tops, after canvassing if applicable (see Chapter 3), were generally finished with white or grey lead paint, the final coat being mixed with varnish. External underframe surfaces after priming, were usually painted with two or three coats of black. Sometimes parts of the underframe (eg solebar faces and headstocks) would be given a colour to harmonize with the main body shade.

A fully-varnished exterior, such as found on the characteristic East Coast teak carriages, was dealt with in a somewhat similar way to that of painted carriages save that varnish was used at all stages rather than the primers, guide coats and top coats. Stopping and filling was, naturally, tinted to match the colour of the wood. Typically, after the first varnish coat and any stopping and filling, anything up to six coats of hard drying varnish would be applied and individually rubbed down *before* the lining and lettering was added. The paint for any ironwork and so on was tinted to match the basic wood shade and sometimes referred to as 'teak' or 'mahogany' colour. After the decorative phase, much the same procedure was followed as for a painted carriage.

Either way, the end result was usually a mirror-like finish of great beauty and high durability, perhaps the most revealing point being that it was given to all carriages from the most humble to the most mighty. The secret was not to hurry the work and to allow ample time for drying out — normally at least a day between each process. It was especially necessary for the last coat of varnish to harden thoroughly before the carriage was sent into traffic. Even in the 1930s, a typical new carriage would be allotted some three weeks to go through the paint-shop, and this was little changed when the first metal-panelled vehicles began to replace their wooden-bodied forebears.

Repainted carriages were normally treated in much the same way as new work. Quite regularly, the new coat would be applied over the remains of the old one which formed a sound base from which to start and avoided much stopping and filling. It did, of course, need to be well rubbed down first to get back to the desired smooth surface, and it was not unusual for the top layers of the old paint to be burned before starting the whole process again. Sometimes it was necessary to go to bare timber or metal, especially if structural repairs were called for. The state and, indeed, the status of the vehicle would also come into play in this respect. A fairly new, or, if not fairly new, then a more important vehicle, would obviously rate more attention than one which was near the end of its life or only destined for limited or relatively 'down market' usage. Considerable discretion was allowed to the paintshop foreman in this respect, but such was the pride in their job that few of them would permit even the humblest of carriages to leave 'their' shop in a form which reflected adversely upon either them or their painters.

That then was coach painting. It was a technique which had developed over a long period of time and had withstood the test of many changes both in paint technology and livery styles. The full procedure remained normal in railway workshops until well into the BR period and although today it is not practised to the full degree, a railway paintshop still reveals evidence of the long-standing traditions which it has inherited. Furthermore, that the techniques can still be practised to the full when and if called for is only too apparent by even the most cursory glance at some of the restored carriages in such places as the National Railway Museum. Even though the painter of today has to use modern synthetic materials, the old techniques of application have well and truly stood the test of time and probably always will.

6. Patterns of passenger traffic 1901-21

It should be something of a *non sequitur* that since most carriages are meant to carry people, their design should reflect the patterns of traffic which the passenger generates. Yet rarely in any books on historic railway carriages does one see more than passing mention of the subject and I find this surprising. After all, there is little point in building exotic and expensive dining and sleeping cars if one's business is mainly in the field of conveying thousands of home-to-work travellers over distances of less than ten miles. Likewise, if one's business lies mainly in the long-distance field, there may be less financial necessity, or even generated demand, for the high-capacity 'maximum seating at all costs' type of vehicle. Now there can be no doubt that the different private railways realized this and adopted very different approaches to their carriage provisioning. This inevitably affected the *sort* and quantities of carriages they built, so it will be the purpose of this chapter to analyse the traffic itself in order to set the background against which this carriage building took place.

We shall, of course, have to resort to statistics to reveal the story, and the British scene is particularly well served by the surviving records kept (as a requirement by Parliament) in the form of Board of Trade and other statutory returns. At the turn of the century, every railway was required by law to submit at *yearly* intervals a mass of data to the Board of Trade. At first glance, these masses of data can seem indigestible, but, given the effort, they are wonderfully revealing. For this analysis, I have taken all those railways which had a route mileage greater than 100 in 1901 and 1911, and these are summarized at Table 1, taking ten-year intervals. This chosen interval and the 100 route mile rule are slightly arbitrary and may conceal some subtle changes, but the main pattern is clear.

The country was dominated by nine companies whose individual route mileage was some 800 or more, and their 'pecking order' never changed in twenty years. Following these was a second tier of more or less 400-800-mile companies whose order of mileage tended to fluctuate a little, while bringing up the rear was a third group of eight, under-400-mile railways which again showed a remarkable consistency in their relative rankings.

It might be supposed at first glance that this classification of the railways might be reflected in the carriage situation, but Table 2 reveals a slightly different story. In terms of vehicle fleets, one of the second group of companies, the LYR, comes well up on the list, while the two biggest Scottish companies drop from fifth and seventh to eleventh and twelfth overall. The bottom group, however, is identifiably much the same set of companies whether by route mileage or carriage fleet.

Other railways showing well in this second analysis relative to route mileage include the SE & CR and the LB & SCR, and this is further reinforced by Table 3 wherein the volume of passenger traffic is analysed. Only four of the top seven route mileage companies now qualify for a high ranking, but the three middle-sized concerns already mentioned are all performing well relative to the bigger companies. The Caledonian and the NBR are still well down the list and the famous Midland does not get above ninth place until 1921 when it suddenly comes third behind the GWR and LNWR. This is almost certainly explained by its absorption in 1912 of the London Tilbury and Southend Railway (LT & SR), a system which was not in the '100-plus' route mile category but which contributed a considerable volume of short-range commuter type traffic.

In this context, it should be pointed out that the LT & SR was one of a few companies excluded from this survey which, proportional to length, added quite substantially to the stock of carriages and particularly to the total number of passengers carried. The excluded companies were mostly of an urban nature and, apart from the LT & SR, perhaps the most important were the various 'underground' systems in and around London, both the surface and 'tube' construction. The nearest to a main line system of any of these railways was probably the Metropolitan,

Above left *Vintage North Western — a typical array of gangwayed carriage styles is presented by the first four vehicles of the 'Sunny South Special', a through working to the south coast from Manchester, at Rugby* circa *1912. Arc, elliptical and clerestory roof profiles, along with 50-foot, 57-foot and 65 ft 6 in lengths and either eight or twelve wheels are all seen, a sort of mixture characteristic of many British main-line railways in the first half of the century* (BR LMR).

Left *This view of a southbound Midland train in 1910 near Cotehill on the Settle and Carlisle line is of interest both for the variety and number of vehicles present in what was, after all, a mere stopping train through a sparsely populated area. There are two quite new horseboxes, a less than five-years-old 1st/3rd* corridor *clerestory, two 20-30-year-old arc roof bogie non-corridors, two ten-year-old clerestories (six-wheel luggage/brake van and bogie non-corridor with lavatories) and three more nineteenth-century arc roof carriages with, respectively, six, eight and four wheels. It is quite possible that the load would not have taxed the capacity of the first three passenger-carrying vehicles!* (BR LMR).

Table 1 Railways by route mileage 1901-1911-1921

Notes:
1. This table includes only those railways (including joint lines) whose route mileage was 100 or more in both 1901 and 1911 and is confined to the mainland of Great Britain.
2. Railways are listed in 1901 order of route mileage.

Company	1901 order	1901	1911	Change (%) (1901-1911)	1911 order	1921	Change (%) (1911-1921)	1921 order
		Route miles and changes						
GWR	1	2627	3006	+ 379 (14.4)	1	3005	− 1 (.03)	1
LNWR	2	1937	1966	+ 29 (1.5)	2	2045	+ 79 (4)	2
NER	3	1654	1728	+ 74 (4.5)	3	1757	+ 29 (1.7)	3
MR	4	1437	1532	+ 95 (6.6)	4	1731	+ 199 (13)	4
NBR	5	1242	1339	+ 97 (7.8)	5	1376	+ 37 (2.8)	5
GER	6	1110	1133	+ 23 (2.1)	6	1187	+ 54 (4.8)	6
CR	7	939	1072	+ 133 (14.1)	7	1114	+ 42 (3.9)	7
LSWR	8	898	964	+ 66 (7.3)	8	965	+ 1 (0.1)	8
GNR	9	825	856	+ 31 (3.8)	9	905	+ 49 (5.7)	9
SE & CR	10	609	629	+ 20 (3.3)	11	638	+ 9 (1.4)	11
LYR	11	556	591	+ 25 (6.3)	12	601	+ 10 (1.7)	12
GCR	12	494	757	+ 263 (53.2)	10	804	+ 47 (6.2)	10
HR	13	485	485	—	13	506	+ 21 (4.3)	13
LB & SCR	14	448	454	+ 6 (1.3)	15	457	+ 3 (0.7)	15
GSWR	15	399	466	+ 67 (16.18)	14	493	+ 27 (5.8)	14
GNSR	16	331	333	+ 2 (0.6)	16	335	+ 2 (0.6)	16
Cambrian	17	252	283	+ 31 (12.3)	17	296	+ 13 (4.6)	17
NSR	18	193	216	+ 23 (11.9)	18	212	− 4 (2)	18
M & GN*	19	182	194	+ 12 (6.6)	19	194	—	19
CLC*	20	140	142	+ 2 (1.4)	20	143	+ 1 (0.7)	21
FR	21	134	134	—	21	158	+ 24 (17.9)	20
TVR	22	124	124	—	22	125	− 1 (0.7)	22
S & DJR*	23	101	106	+ 5 (5)	23	106	—	23

Totals:

	1901	1911		1921	
Lines listed					
England & Wales	13721	14815	+ 1094 (8%)	15329	+ 514 (3.5%)
Scotland	3396	3695	+ 299 (8.8%)	3824	+ 129 (3.5%)
Great Britain	17117	18510	+ 1393 (8.1%)	19153	+ 643 (3.5%)
All lines					
England & Wales	15187	16200	+ 1013 (6.7%)	16401	+ 201 (1.2%)
Scotland	3485	3815	+ 330 (9.5%)	3880	+ 65 (1.7%)
Great Britain	18672	20015	+ 1343 (7.2%)	20281	+ 266 (1.3%)

* denotes a jointly-owned line.

but the circumstances of operation of most of these urban lines, and their regular early involvement with electrification, makes their nature somewhat untypical of the nation as a whole and they will be dealt with later. Interestingly, however, in view of the above comment, the middle-ranking main-line systems mentioned in the previous paragraphs (LB & SCR, LYR and SE & CR), along with the LSWR (almost middle rank!) represented the main areas in which suburban electrification was seriously entertained in the pre-BR period. Tables 2 and 3 certainly help to explain why.

Before leaving this particular point, it is interesting to compare the total figures in Table 3 for the 23 listed railways with the totals for the country as a whole. Whereas in most of the summaries in this chapter,

Table 2 Passenger rated rolling-stock 1901-1911-1921

Note: Companies are listed in 1901 order of ranking in *each* category.

1901 order	Company	Passenger carriages 1901	1911[1]	1911 order	1921[2]	1921 order	Company	Other coaching stock 1901	1911	1911 order	1921	1921 order	Company	Total coaching stock 1901	1911[1]	1911 order	1921[2]	1921 order
1	LNWR	6092	5880	1	6239	1	LNWR	3455	3503	1	3320	1	LNWR	9547	9383	1	9559	1
2	GWR	4495	5321	2	5646	2	GWR	2103	2524	2	3100	2	GWR	6599	7845	2	8746	2
3	LYR	3950	4181	3	3749	5	MR	1863	1849	3	1790	3	MR	5374	5486	3	6121	3
4	GER	3685	3829	4	3970	4	LSWR	1470	1383	5	1416	5	GER	5063	5297	4	5653	4
5	MR	3511	3637	6	4331	3	GER	1378	1468	4	1683	4	LYR	4513	4738	5	4328	5
6	SE & CR	3286	2961	7	2766	7	SE & CR	1059	1090	7	1047	7	SE & CR	4345	4051	8	3813	8
7	NER	2997	3675	5	3106	6	NBR	1008	1170	6	1277	6	LSWR	3985	4224	7	4065	7
8	GNR	2559	2508	9	2639	9	NER	982	985	8	1012	9	NER	3979	4660	6	4118	6
9	LSWR	2515	2841	8	2649	8	GNR	804	733	10	868	10	GNR	3363	3241	10	3507	10
10	LB & SCR	2398	2313	10	1871	12	LB & SCR	777	806	9	734	11	LB & SCR	3175	3119	11	2605	13
11	NBR	1995	2301	11	2424	10	LYR	563	557	11	579	13	NBR	3003	3471	9	3701	9
12	CR	1796	1925	12	2290	11	CR	474	515	12	732	12	CR	2270	2440	12	3022	11
13	GCR	998	1489	13	1694	13	GSWR	340	320	14	421	15	GSWR	1275	1360	14	1608	14
14	GSWR	935	990	14	1187	14	GNSR	306	309	15	319	16	GCR	1170	1831	13	2725	12
15	GNSR	423	427	15	454	16	GCR	172	342	13	1031	8	GNSR	729	736	15	773	16
16	CLC	345	345	16	462	15	NSR	141	149	17	193	17	CLC	467	447	17	553	17
17	HR	295	324	17	303	19	HR	127	160	16	496	14	HR	422	484	16	799	15
18	NSR	281	287	18	341	17	CLC	122	102	19	91	21	NSR	422	436	18	534	18
19	FR	277	249	20	269	20	FR	99	99	20	93	20	FR	376	348	20	362	20
20	Cambrian	201	225	21	221	21	Cambrian	83	116	18	116	18	Cambrian	284	341	21	337	21
21	TVR	198	285	19	316	18	TVR	68	78	21	96	19	TVR	266	363	19	412	19
22	S & DJR	127	127	23	131	23	S & DJR	52	65	22	70	22	S & DJR	179	192	23	201	23
23	M & GN	33	173	22	173	22	M & GN	24	53	23	49	23	M & GN	57	226	22	222	22

Totals:	Passenger carriages 1901	1911	1921	Other coaching stock 1901	1911	1921	Total coaching stock 1901	1911	1921
Lines listed									
England & Wales	37948	40325	40573	15216	15902	17288	53164	56227	57861
Scotland	5444	5967	6658	2255	2524	3245	7699	8491	9903
Great Britain	43392	46292	47181	17471	18426	20533	60683	64718	67764
All lines									
England & Wales	41431	43916	42232	15648	16371	17661	57079	60287	59893
Scotland	5503	6028	6714	2256	2525	3246	7759	8553	9960
Great Britain	46934	49944	48946	17904	18896	20907	64838	68840	69853

1 Including steam railmotor carriages.
2 Including steam railmotors, but *excluding* electrical multiple unit stock.

Table 3 Passenger bookings by class 1901-1911-1921

Note: Companies are listed in 1901 order of ranking of *total* number of passengers.

1901 order	Company	1901 (1000's) 1st	2nd	3rd	Total	1911 (1000's) 1st	2nd	3rd	Total	1911 order	1921 (1000's) 1st	2nd	3rd	Total	1921 order
1	GER	2040	4868	113810	120718	1548	2229	94554	98331	2	1444	1471	75719	78634	4
2	LNWR	1912	5369	74231	81512	1245	3391	69917	74553	3	1158	—	82301	83459	2
3	GWR	1406	6103	72664	80173	1749	439	100335	102523	1	1081	—	89863	90944	1
4	SE & CR	2343	5263	65505	73111	1676	3942	54291	59909	6	1174	1572	46965	49711	9
5	LSWR	2292	4754	54887	61933	2011	2544	63516	68071	4	1458	—	63536	64994	6
6	NER	1566	—	58833	60339	1202	—	59771	60973	5	796	—	60488	61284	7
7	LYR	908	4213	54386	59507	1129	3287	54540	58956	7	1897	—	69886	71783	5
8	LB & SCR	1920	4402	50349	56671	1628	2373	52997	56998	8	1328	100	55092	56520	8
9	MR	1370	—	50737	52107	900	—	49640	50540	9	907	—	80952	81859	3
10	CR	3137	—	41685	44822	2502	—	30732	33234	12	2487	—	33370	35857	10
11	NBR	1845	—	38362	40207	1354	—	34323	35677	10	1791	—	32827	34618	11
12	GNR	924	1261	35376	37561	753	510	34408	35671	11	563	209	27057	27829	12
13	GCR	372	—	18803	19175	453	—	24563	25016	13	294	—	20805	21099	13
14	GSWR	738	—	17680	18418	509	—	16232	16741	14	357	—	14649	15006	14
15	CLC	615	—	10014	10629	451	—	9934	10385	15	426	—	9732	10158	15
16	TVR	67	320	7497	7884	61	202	8105	8368	16	57	173	7792	8022	17
17	NSR	118	562	6442	7122	72	445	6485	7002	17	84	—	10058	10142	16
18	GNSR	102	—	3346	3448	99	—	3253	3352	18	101	—	3572	3673	18
19	FR	55	15	2615	2685	45	22	2906	2973	19	18	—	3415	3433	19
20	Cambrian	45	88	2295	2428	41	69	2634	2744	20	17	—	2134	2151	20
21	HR	92	—	2236	2328	75	—	2053	2128	21	38	—	1482	1520	21
22	M & GN	26	—	1584	1610	25	—	1871	1896	22	10	—	1218	1228	22
23	S & DJR	26	—	1150	1176	20	—	1327	1347	23	5	—	870	875	23

Totals:	1901 1st	2nd	3rd	Total	1911 1st	2nd	3rd	Total	1921 1st	2nd	3rd	Total
Lines listed												
England + Wales	18005	37218	681178	736401	15009	19453	691794	726256	12717	3525	707883	724125
Scotland	5914	—	103309	109223	4539	—	86593	91132	4774	—	85900	90674
Great Britain	23919	37218	784487	845624	19548	19453	778387	817388	17491	3525	793783	814799
All lines												
England + Wales	27263	65227	1021179	1113669	24199	22573	141432	1188204	19871	4546	1102679	1127096
Scotland	5937	—	118427	124364	4635	—	102663	107298	4777	—	97551	102328
Great Britain	33200	65227	1139606	1238033	28834	22573	1244095	1295502	24648	4546	1200230	1229424

This particularly neat assembly on the SE & CR, circa *1908, pulled by one of his celebrated Class 'E' locomotives, is one of Harry Wainwright's stylish boat trains, composed entirely of matching non-corridor stock amply provided with lavatories, luggage space and comfortable seats — see also page 162.*

Standing in marked contrast to its SE & CR equivalent of some ten years earlier is this equally neat 11-coach set of LYR gangwayed carriages of open interior rather than side-corridor configuration. Like the SE & CR, the LYR provided plenty of vehicles for its patrons and was justly proud of its best stock. This is a posed view, taken in 1921, of a new batch of so-called 'fireproof' coaches (see page 190), most of which were destined, initially, for boat train service.

the '100-plus' route mile railways accounted for some 90% or more of British activity, in terms of numbers of passengers the proportion was only some two-thirds. This rather suggests that further analysis is needed before firm conclusions can be drawn, and to this end Table 4 has been compiled.

In the first two categories, the dominance of what might be called the urban-based systems is clear. In the first summary, only the GER and LNWR of the 'big seven' by mileage manage to get into the top one-third while when it comes to passengers per route mile the GER alone retains its top ranking status. One of the most startling leaders now turns out to be the Cheshire Lines Committee along with the Taff Vale Railway, and these two are even higher when it comes to vehicle loading levels. This latter comparison is at first a little surprising since one might expect the railways with high 'per route mile' figures to maintain a high level of loading, but this did not always happen.

Take the LYR, for example, (in both 1901 and 1911) or the SE & CR in 1921. These lines always made generous carriage provisioning in terms of vehicles per passenger and this seems reflected in their loading levels. Interestingly, conventional wisdom gives neither of them very much space in the story of carriage evolution but the figures suggest that one might have had a more comfortable (or at least *less crowded*) ride than on some more popularly favoured systems. At the very least, it suggests that railways such as these were more influential in establishing short to medium distance *standards* than is often supposed.

A caveat should perhaps be entered at this point about the sudden climb in ranking of some railways between 1911 and 1921. The noteworthy ones are

Table 4 Passenger and Vehicle comparisons 1901-1911-1921

Note: Companies are listed in 1901 order of ranking in *each* category.

		Carriages per route mile						Passengers per route mile						Passengers per carriage				
1901 order	Company	1901	1911	1911 order	1921	1921 order	Company	1901	1911	1911 order	1921	1921 order	Company	1901	1911	1911 order	1921	1921 order
1	LYR	7.10	7.07	1	6.24	1	LB & SCR	126497	125546	1	123676	1	TVR	39818	29361	2	25386	3
2	SE & CR	5.40	4.70	3	4.33	2	SE & CR	120050	95245	3	77917	3	GER	32759	25681	3	19807	6
3	LB & SCR	5.35	5.10	2	4.09	3	GER	108756	86788	4	66245	6	CLC	30809	30101	1	21987	5
4	GER	3.32	3.38	4	3.34	4	LYR	107026	99756	2	119439	2	NSR	25345	24397	5	29472	2
5	LNWR	3.15	2.99	5	3.05	6	CLC	75422	73134	5	71035	4	CR	24956	17264	9	15658	11
6	GNR	3.10	2.93	7	2.92	7	LSWR	68967	70613	6	67351	5	LSWR	24625	23960	6	24535	4
7	LSWR	2.8	2.95	6	2.75	8	TVR	63580	67484	7	64176	7	LB & SCR	23633	24642	4	30208	1
8	CLC	2.46	2.43	8	3.23	5	CR	47734	31002	16	32188	12	SE & CR	22249	20233	7	11972	17
9	MR	2.44	2.37	9	2.50	10	GSWR	46161	35925	10	30438	14	NBR	20154	15505	13	14281	12
10	GSWR	2.34	2.12	12	2.41	11	GNR	45528	41672	8	30750	13	NER	20153	16591	12	19731	7
11	FR	2.07	1.86	14	1.70	17	LNWR	42556	37921	9	40811	10	GSWR	19698	16910	10	12642	15
12	GER	2.02	1.97	13	2.11	12	GER	38815	33046	13	26242	16	GER	19213	16801	11	12455	15
13	CR	1.91	1.80	15	2.06	13	NSR	36901	32417	15	47840	8	GWR	17836	19268	8	16108	10
14	NER	1.81	2.13	11	1.77	15	NER	36517	35285	11	34880	11	LYR	15065	14101	15	19147	8
15	GWR	1.71	1.77	16	1.88	14	MR	36260	32990	14	47290	9	MR	14841	13896	16	18901	9
16	NBR	1.61	1.72	17	1.76	16	NBR	32372	26637	17	25158	17	GNR	14678	14223	14	10545	18
17	TVR	1.60	2.30	10	2.53	9	GWR	30518	34106	12	30264	15	LNWR	13380	12679	17	13377	13
18	NSR	1.46	1.33	18	1.61	18	FR	20037	22187	18	21728	18	Cambrian	12080	12196	18	9733	19
19	GNSR	1.28	1.28	19	1.36	19	S & DJR	11643	12708	19	8255	20	FR	9693	11940	19	12762	14
20	S & DJR	1.26	1.20	20	1.24	20	GNSR	10417	10066	20	10964	19	S & DJR	9260	10606	21	6679	22
21	Cambrian	0.80	0.80	22	0.75	22	Cambrian	9635	9696	22	7266	21	GNSR	8151	7850	22	8090	20
22	HR	0.61	0.67	23	0.60	23	M & GN	8846	9773	21	6330	22	HR	7892	6586	23	5017	23
23	M & GN*	0.18	0.89	21	0.89	21	HR	4800	4388	23	3004	23	M & GN*	61923	10960	20	7098	21

*1901 figures are distorted for this system as a result of widespread use of 'foreign' stock.

Averages	Carriages per route mile			Passengers per route mile			Passengers per carriage		
Lines listed	**1901**	**1911**	**1921**	**1901**	**1911**	**1921**	**1901**	**1911**	**1921**
England + Wales	2.77	2.72	2.65	53670	49022	47239	19405	18010	17847
Scotland	1.60	1.61	1.74	32762	24664	23712	20063	15273	13619
Great Britain	2.54	2.50	2.46	49403	44159	42542	19488	17657	17270
All lines									
England + Wales	2.73	2.71	2.57	73330	73346	68721	26880	27056	26688
Scotland	1.58	1.58	1.73	35686	28125	26373	22599	17800	15241
Great Britain	2.51	2.50	2.41	66304	64727	60619	26378	25939	25118

Right *This gruesome, albeit tidy-looking collection of soul-destroying six-wheelers on the London, Tilbury & Southend Railway was typical of inner suburban working and by no means the worst which could be seen in the London area in and after 1900. However, this one, seen near Leigh on Sea, was a Southend bound* express*! The MR, when it took over the Tilbury system in 1912, decided that enough was enough as far as the native stock was concerned and rapidly consigned the worst of them to unmourned oblivion, replacing them by the type shown in the next picture* (Author's collection).

Right *This posed shot, taken in the Derbyshire area, is in fact one of the new sets of replacement bogie carriages for the Tilbury line which entered service around the time of the 1923 railway grouping. The train, in new LMS colours, still has a massive carrying capacity and there is only one lavatory-equipped carriage in the whole set, but it is a considerable improvement on its forebears.*

Table 4A Electrically-propelled stock 1921

LSWR	317
LYR	241
LNWR	185
LB & SCR	134
NER	125
MR	117
GWR	60
GCR	16
Subtotal	1195
Non-listed lines	2123
Grand total	3318

Note: The figures relate only to those eight of the 23 companies listed in Table 1 which owned electric stock in 1921. They are listed in descending order of magnitude. All were in England, but the MR, GWR and GCR figures need qualifying. The MR total was mostly made up of tramcars (Burton and Ashby line) plus its share (with the District Railway) of the London area Whitechapel and Bow stock, arising from the takeover by the MR of the LT & SR in 1912. The Lancaster, Morecambe and Heysham route — see page 255 — was the only uniquely Midland example of anything even remotely approaching conventional main-line electrification. The GWR total was entirely made up of its share (with the Metropolitan Railway) of the stock on the Hammersmith and City line, while the GCR fleet consisted entirely of 'tramcars' used between Grimsby and Immingham.

the LB & SCR, LSWR and LYR, but this reflects the fact that passenger levels were recorded in absolute terms regardless of carriage fleet whereas the carriage *totals* refer to 'hauled stock' only. By 1921, several railways, including all of these three, were carrying many of their urban passengers in electric trains, whose stock is not reckoned. Proof of this is the still low position of the SE & CR whose area was not electrified until after the formation of the Southern Railway in 1923. Other interesting 'climbers' in 1921 were the MR (probably reflecting the LT & SR again) and the NER which, by then, had a substantial (unrecorded) Tyneside electrification supplementing its locomotive-hauled fleet. For this reason, Table 4A has been added, giving the electrical multiple unit (EMU) stock as at 1921.

Particularly interesting in this matter of 'passengers per carriage' is the position of two of the English 'giants', the LNWR and MR, in 1901-1911, roughly equal at some 13-15,000 or so passengers (annually) per carriage owned. If one assumes some 300 working days per year, then the 'per day' loading is less than 50 passengers per carriage compared with some twice that total at the top of the list. However, what the raw statistics do *not* tell is how many seats per carriage were available or, even more important, how many times per day a carriage might be expected to be used. It is a fair inference that since the MR and LNWR had a considerably greater number of long-haul journeys than most, their carriages were, on average, less spartan in 'space per passenger' terms or even seats per vehicle and were used less intensively as well. If so, the apparently lowly position is less surprising.

Even so, however, a low load factor does not, in purely fiscal terms, betoken an efficient railway,

Left *The best GER expresses could rival those of most railways. This is a Liverpool Street to Clacton train on Brentwood Bank in 1910 formed of distinctly superior (and new) corridor stock for what was really quite a short-distance operation.*

Below left *There is a splendid 'time warp' quality to this GWR train between Reading and Basingstoke in July 1932; the carriages, a neat and tidy collection of William Dean's non-corridor clerestories, could well have been seen on the same task some 25-30 years earlier, as, indeed, could the engine. The carrying capacity of such a train was formidable and demonstrates the long-lasting nature of the travel styles originated in the Edwardian era.*

Above right *Many smaller railways, although building coaches for their own local services, often relied on the larger companies for most carriage provisioning for through services. One such was the Furness Railway, exemplified at Barrow* circa *1920. The train about to leave behind an imposing 4-6-4T consists of a four-coach LNWR corridor set branded 'Liverpool and Barrow', while at the rear, almost lost in the shadow of the station roof, are the two FR 'local' non-corridors which probably went no further than Carnforth. Another 'home' product stands in the bay to the right.*

Right *A variation on the 'borrowing' theme was often seen with the several 'Joint Stock' operations, particularly between Scotland and England. The Caledonian Railway held a one-third share in the West Coast Joint Stock, all the excuse it needed to use them whenever possible. A typical example is seen here,* circa *1920. If there are any CR carriages at all in this northbound nine-coach corridor express, they can only be the final pair. The rest are a typical mixture of either West Coast Joint vehicles to LNWR design or even the LNWR's own products* (R.J. Essery collection).

Right *Although the Highland Railway was the archetypal 'borrower' of other people's coaches, especially when it trundled north from Perth to Inverness with through carriages from (almost) all parts of the Kingdom, when it had to be self-sufficient in the more far-flung reaches of the system it was probably the last bastion of the pure Victorian railway. This mixed train from Kyle of Lochalsh to Dingwall in the early 1900s probably changed little for many a year afterwards — not a lavatory in sight and the best vehicle, the second one, an archaic six-wheel luggage 1st/3rd!*

Table 5 Passenger revenue 1901-1911

1901 order	Company	1901 (£1000s) Passenger	Other coaching	Total	1911 (£1000s) Passenger	Other coaching	Total	1911 order
1	LNWR	4815	1248	6063	5248	1583	6831	1
2	GWR	4329	1006	5335	5361	1440	6801	2
3	MR	2873	754	3627	3255	903	4158	3
4	SE & CR	2757	393	3150	3031	575	3606	4
5	GER	2726	345	3071	2725	431	3156	7
6	LSWR	2614	445	3059	2905	597	3502	5
7	NER	2532	482	3014	2761	625	3386	6
8	LB & SCR	2095	221	2316	2236	288	2524	9
9	LYR	2057	257	2314	2269	322	2591	8
10	GNR	1783	384	2167	1922	498	2420	10
11	CR	1512	327	1839	1530	429	1959	11
12	NBR	1450	288	1738	1498	358	1856	12
13	GCR	692	236	928	1024	394	1418	13
14	GSWR	629	129	758	674	156	830	14
15	CLC	348	60	408	373	62	435	15
16	HR	217	113	330	235	116	351	16
17	NSR	215	53	268	223	61	284	17
18	GNSR	187	59	246	192	71	263	18
19	TVR	190	22	212	193	29	222	19
20	Cambrian	137	41	178	144	46	190	20
21	FR	112	25	137	114	26	140	21
22	M & GN	79	19	98	106	30	136	22
23	S & DJR	65	18	83	78	23	101	23

Totals	1901 Passenger	Other	Total	1911 Passenger	Other	Total
Lines listed						
England + Wales	30419	6009	36428	33968	7433	41901
Scotland	3995	916	4911	4129	1130	5259
Great Britain	34414	6925	41339	38097	9063	47160
All lines						
England + Wales	33453	6156	39609	38194	8114	46308
Scotland	4084	930	5014	4215	1147	5362
Great Britain	37537	7086	44623	42409	9261	51670

however nice it might be for the passenger to find a higher proportion of vacant seats; so it suggests that yet other factors must have been present. In essence, and this is a point often overlooked, the railway was in business to make money. The slightly more modern 'social service' obligation was not really in the minds of the private companies, however laudable it may be in absolute terms. I happen to believe in the 'social factor' being applied to railways in the latter part of this century, especially if they are publicly owned, but at the time of this particular analysis it was not a prime consideration. That some of the early twentieth-century private railways managed to provide a better 'social' service in a thoroughly hard-nosed commercial environment than their own nationalized successor can do in our present day society is another matter; this is a carriage history, not a socio-political analysis! However, such ramifications cannot help but impinge throughout the century whether it be the 'fair deal' campaigns of the 1930s or the post-Beeching 'social service' obligation of the last 15-20 years. Both of them in their different ways have affected carriage design.

At the root of it all was and is *money,* so the next series of summaries (Tables 5-9) are addressed to this aspect as it affected the Edwardian period. The official statistical basis of comparison was changed between 1911 and 1921 and, in any case, was probably distorted during and after the Great War when railways were being operated in the national interest as a single system. However, the figures quoted do give a pretty well undiluted picture of the position as it was when all the private companies really were independent.

Table 5 is an unqualified raw statement of revenue in absolute terms. Five of the seven high mileage companies are up at the top again and, significantly, the same middle rank systems by mileage (LB & SCR, LSWR, LYR, SE & CR) are doing just as well as they were in the previous analysis if revenue is related solely to route mileage, while the 'big two' in Scotland (NBR and CR) are down the list again. In fact, the average performances in Scotland were nearly always less than those in England and Wales, regardless of how the comparison were drawn, which was probably a reflection of the different basic economic geography of the two statistical areas. This was, undoubtedly, one of the reasons why at the 1923 grouping it was felt inadvisable to have a separate fifth group for Scotland, however desirable this might have been on purely emotive grounds.

Table 6 is an equally raw statement of passenger train miles, and yet again the same companies dominate, save that the two large Scottish companies now come above the LB & SCR, a fact which, given the respective geographies, should occasion no surprise whatsoever. In this context, it should be mentioned that passenger train mileage figures did not differentiate between all-passenger operations, mixed formations involving some use of passenger-rated stock also conveying mail for instance, and completely non-passenger operations such as 'full' mail, milk or fish trains, for example. Perusal of both Table 5 and Table 2 will reveal what a considerable proportion of the total passenger-rated activity was involved with the handling of non-human cargoes, some 16-18% in revenue terms (on average), and no less than 25-30% in purely vehicular terms. Indeed, some railway companies would have suffered grievously had they not carried a solid non-passenger element. The GCR, for example, derived nearly 30% of its passenger-rated revenue from its non-passenger operations (probably reflecting the importance of the Grimsby fish traffic), the HR proportion was similar and the LNWR passenger-rated vehicle *fleet* was 37% non-passenger-carrying types in 1911 — probably a reflection of its importance in the mail and prize livestock business. The non-passenger element of the passenger-rated vehicle story was, in fact, of such importance that it spawned a whole range of specialized vehicles, some of which are considered later. The quoted figures, yet again, explain why.

If, however, one analyses the raw statistics on a comparative basis, a very different picture emerges. Tables 7-9 attempt to summarize the story and readers are left to form their own particular deductions. No doubt supporters of particular railways will find evidence to support whatever prejudices and preferences they may have, but overall a sort of pattern does emerge. Unsurprisingly, the revenue per route mile shows a strong dominance by the tightly knit urban/industrial companies, or those with a fair proportion of such routes. The revenue per train mile is not dissimilar, and once again the larger companies are not too high on the lists. The GWR and LNWR only reach the top five in Table 7, for example.

However, when the figures are split into passenger and non-passenger categories (Tables 8 and 9), a

Table 6 Passenger train miles 1901-1911

Note: Companies are listed in 1901 order of ranking.

1901 order	Company	Train miles (1000's) 1901	1911	1911 order
1	LNWR	26657	30705	2
2	GWR	23790	32761	1
3	MR	19899	22442	3
4	NER	15382	17419	4
5	LSWR	13029	15650	5
6	GER	12950	14030	6
7	LYR	12302	12705	9
8	GNR	12041	13054	7
9	SE & CR	11011	12867	8
10	CR	9535	10093	11
11	NBR	9246	9496	12
12	LB & SCR	8684	11088	10
13	GCR	5863	8790	13
14	GSWR	4077	4568	14
15	CLC	2516	2613	15
16	HR	1696	1750	16
17	GNSR	1421	1518	17
18	NSR	1241	1445	18
19	Cambrian	1033	1158	19
20	M & GN	907	1065	21
21	FR	702	738	23
22	TVR	675	1080	20
23	S & DJR	670	757	22
Totals				
	Lines listed	**1901**	**1911**	
	England + Wales	169352	200367	
	Scotland	25975	27425	
	Great Britain	195327	227792	
	All lines			
	England + Wales	185853	229958	
	Scotland	27380	28972	
	Great Britain	213233	258930	

Table 7 Total passenger-rated revenue rankings 1901-1911

Note: This table includes both passenger and non-passenger carrying coaching stock operated in passenger trains. Companies are listed in 1901 order of ranking per category.

	Per route mile (£)				Per vehicle owned (£)				Per train mile (£)			
1901 order	**Company**	**1901**	**1911**	**1911 order**	**Company**	**1901**	**1911**	**1911 order**	**Company**	**1901**	**1911**	**1911 order**
1	SE & CR	5172	5733	1	CLC	874	973	1	TVR	.314	.205	7
2	LB & SCR	5169	5559	2	CR	810	803	6	SE & CR	.286	.280	1
3	LYR	4162	4384	3	GWR	808	867	3	LB & SCR	.267	.228	2
4	LSWR	3407	3633	4	TVR	797	612	15	GER	.237	.225	3
5	LNWR	3130	3475	5	GCR	793	774	7	LSWR	.235	.224	4
6	CLC	2915	3063	6	HR	781	725	12	LNWR	.227	.222	5
7	GER	2767	2786	8	LSWR	767	829	4	GWR	.224	.208	6
8	GNR	2626	2827	7	NER	757	727	11	NSR	.216	.197	10
9	MR	2524	2714	9	LB & SCR	729	809	5	NER	.196	.194	12
10	GWR	2031	2262	10	SE & CR	725	890	2	FR	.195	.190	14
11	CR	1958	1827	13	MR	675	758	8	HR	.195	.201	9
12	GSWR	1899	1781	15	GNR	644	747	9	CR	.193	.194	13
13	GCR	1879	1873	12	LNWR	635	728	10	LYR	.188	.204	8
14	NER	1822	1959	11	NSR	635	651	14	NBR	.188	.195	11
15	TVR	1709	1790	14	Cambrian	627	557	18	GSWR	.186	.182	17
16	NBR	1398	1386	16	GER	607	596	17	MR	.182	.185	16
17	NSR	1389	1315	17	GSWR	595	670	13	GNR	.180	.185	15
18	FR	1023	1045	18	NBR	579	535	20	GNSR	.173	.173	18
19	S & DJR	822	953	19	LYR	512	547	19	Cambrian	.172	.164	20
20	GNSR	743	790	20	S & DJR	464	526	21	CLC	.162	.166	19
21	Cambrian	707	671	23	FR	364	402	22	GCR	.158	.161	21
22	HR	680	724	21	GNSR	337	357	23	S & DJR	.124	.133	22
23	M & GN	538	701	22	M & GN	1719*	602	16	M & GN	.108	.128	23

Averages	**Per route mile**		**Per vehicle**		**Per train mile**	
Lines listed	**1901**	**1911**	**1901**	**1911**	**1901**	**1911**
England + Wales	2655	2828	685	745	.215	.209
Scotland	1446	1423	638	619	.189	.192
Great Britain	2415	2548	681	729	.212	.207
All lines						
England + Wales	2608	2859	694	768	.213	.201
Scotland	1439	1406	646	627	.183	.185
Great Britain	2389	2582	688	751	.209	.200

* This figure is only explained by the fact that this company made much use of 'foreign' stock at this time. It is therefore listed *last* in this column.

somewhat different picture emerges. The Highland Railway, for example, suddenly climbs the table to the top of the league in revenue per passenger and also ranks high in revenue per non-passenger vehicle. In this latter category, the GCR suddenly seems a much more viable concern than its detractors might admit and the often high-ranking GER falls to bottom place in revenue per passenger. Some of the bigger English companies (for example the GWR, LNWR and MR) reveal their real strength in the revenue per passenger column, and the LNWR and MR also score well in the non-passenger revenue per route mile category. There are, of course, more than a few 'jokers', and although the much favoured GWR tends to bounce about yo-yo fashion, its position in any of the tables never falls below halfway — an underlying indication of its overall strength in all departments.

Overall, however, the various summaries tend to emphasize that there was more than a little of the 'horses for courses' element about the patterns of traffic generated. The dominance in England and Wales of the GWR, LNWR and MR in the 'size and distance' related statistics is clear, and the fact that these railways had a strong influence in the design and construction of main-line express stock is no longer surprising. The position of such lines as the LYR and SE & CR in the short/medium distance field has been commented upon, and the fact that the LB & SCR never assayed corridor stock is more than adequately explained. In Scotland, the NBR and CR never performed quite as well as English systems of similar size, for a variety of reasons, but their dominance north of the border is clearly apparent save in a few isolated instances. Which leads, fairly naturally, to a final question — was there any such thing as a 'typical' pre-1923 railway, as far as passenger carriage activities were concerned, taking all matters into account?

Perceptive readers will, perhaps, have noted that so far in this analysis no specific mention has been made of the two principal constituents of the English

Table 8 Passenger revenue rankings 1901-1911

Note: Companies are listed in 1901 order of ranking per category.

	Per route mile (£)				**Per passenger booked (£)**				**Per carriage owned**			
1901 order	**Company**	**1901**	**1911**	**1911 order**	**Company**	**1901**	**1911**	**1911 order**	**Company**	**1901**	**1911**	**1911 order**
1	LB & SCR	4676	4925	1	HR	.093	.110	1	LSWR	1039	1023	3
2	SE & CR	4527	4818	2	LNWR	.059	.070	2	CLC	1009	1081	1
3	LYR	3700	3839	3	Cambrian	.056	.052	8	GWR	963	1008	4
4	LSWR	2911	3013	4	MR	.055	.064	3	TVR	960	677	16
5	LNWR	2486	2669	5	S & DJR	.055	.058	4	LB & SCR	874	967	5
6	CLC	2486	2627	6	GWR	.054	.052	9	NER	844	751	11
7	GER	2456	2405	7	GNSR	.054	.057	5	CR	842	795	8
8	GNR	2161	2245	8	M & GN	.049	.056	6	SE & CR	839	1024	2
9	MR	1999	2125	9	GNR	.047	.054	7	MR	818	895	6
10	GWR	1648	1783	10	NER	.042	.045	12	LNWR	790	893	7
11	CR	1610	1427	14	LSWR	.042	.043	13	NSR	765	777	9
12	GSWR	1576	1446	13	FR	.042	.038	19	GER	739	712	13
13	TVR	1532	1556	12	SE & CR	.038	.051	10	HR	736	725	12
14	NER	1531	1598	11	LB & SCR	.037	.039	17	NBR	727	651	17
15	GCR	1401	1353	15	NBR	.036	.042	14	GNR	697	766	10
16	NBR	1167	1119	16	GCR	.036	.041	15	GCR	693	688	14
17	NSR	1114	1032	17	LYR	.035	.038	18	Cambrian	682	640	18
18	FR	836	851	18	CR	.034	.046	11	GSWR	673	681	15
19	S & DJR	644	736	19	GSWR	.034	.040	16	LYR	521	543	21
20	GNSR	565	577	20	CLC	.033	.036	20	S & DJR	512	614	19
21	Cambrian	544	509	22	NSR	.030	.032	21	GNSR	442	450	23
22	HR	447	485	23	TVR	.024	.023	23	FR	404	458	22
23	M & GN	434	546	21	GER	.023	.028	22	M & GN	2394*	613	20

Averages	**Per route mile**		**Per passenger**		**Per carriage**	
Lines listed	**1901**	**1911**	**1901**	**1911**	**1901**	**1911**
England + Wales	2217	2293	.041	.047	802	842
Scotland	1176	1117	.037	.045	734	692
Great Britain	2011	2058	.041	.047	793	823
All lines						
England + Wales	2203	2358	.030	.032	807	870
Scotland	1172	1105	.033	.039	742	699
Great Britain	2010	2119	.030	.033	800	849

* This figure is so exceptional that it can only reflect the fact that at this period most trains on the M & GN were composed of other companies' stock. For this reason it is listed *last* in this column.

A typical scene in the year of the grouping on the East Coast Main Line. The main train is a mixture of GNR styled elliptical roof and clerestory carriages but the leading vehicle is the NER clerestory Dynamometer car, the engine, a former NER 4-6-2, being under test.

North British Railway passenger trains changed little until several years after the grouping. This southbound express at Inverkeithing in the 1920s is typical, for, although now in LNER colours, the whole train consists of NBR stock. The main portion consists of standard robust NBR corridors with, just under the bridge, one of the newer NBR steel-panelled dining cars (see page 125). However, the principal operating interest lies in the leading carriage. It is older, of lesser quality, all third class and still gas lit, but at least it has a lavatory. The fact that it is separated from the main train by a six-wheel van suggests that it was added at the last moment as a 'strengthener' to meet some unexpectedly heavy traffic. This sort of operational opportunism was a widespread British practice.

part of the East Coast Main Line, the GNR and the NER. Both these systems were big ones; the NER was in the top three by mileage and rarely out of the top seven on any of the absolute criteria analysed, while the GNR was also always there or thereabouts. Taken overall, the GNR probably came nearer to average more often than any other railway and is as nearly typical as one is likely to get. The LSWR came quite close in this respect as also, to some extent, did the MR. In all cases, these railways operated long-distance trains as well as being heavily involved with suburban operations in the major conurbations and operating a fair proportion of non-passenger stock. This was true also of the GWR and LNWR but these two systems were in fact well ahead in terms of absolute size and would obviously dominate to some extent, however one defines the situation.

The point is that carriage design of necessity was a combination of what might be called ephemeral matters (body style, livery and decoration) combined with practical considerations (seats per passenger, type of vehicle needed and so forth). While all railways had a fairly free hand in the first of these areas, some lines needed only to consider certain aspects of the more economically based criteria. Thus, those railways which had to address *all* (or most) aspects of the passenger train field were, fairly naturally, likely to dominate those whose horizons were more restricted. This, naturally, assumed rather more importance when the railways were amalgamated in 1923, and the recorded statistics give ample evidence as to *why* certain company's design styles and approaches predominated in the post-grouping period. It was not simply a matter of *force majeure* as is sometimes supposed, but also a question of relevant experience in the context of a larger amalgamated railway. These matters will be dealt with more comprehensively in the next chapter; in the meantime, it is probably sufficient to state that the patterns of passenger traffic as revealed by the recorded statistics were there for all to see even before the 1914-18 holocaust disrupted matters in many more areas than that of the mere railway carriage.

Nevertheless, these factors, while perhaps fairly apparent in retrospect, were by no means obvious to contemporary society in the 1901-14 period. The private railways were then at the zenith of their prosperity and reputation. They were still fiercely independent and vying with each other for public patronage and approbation, even though they had no serious competition from other *forms* of transport (eg road and air) in the long and medium distance field. The railway carriage door was the point of contact with much of the public, and in consequence many railways felt obliged, for strictly business reasons, to produce something that little bit better than that of their rivals. It led to a superb flowering of elegant vehicles, superb craftsmanship, pride in the task and not a little merit. It is doubtful whether the men of Swindon, Eastleigh, Wolverton, Derby, Doncaster, York, Cowlairs et al saw it this way at the time — it was merely the norm in relation to their time. But it *was* also the end of an era (as I have entitled this very volume), and it will be the object of the rest of this part of the survey to record something of the superb contribution to transport history which these carriage builders made.

Table 9 Non-passenger-coaching revenue ranking 1901-1911

Note: Companies are listed in 1901 order of ranking per category.

1901 order	Per route mile (£) Company	1901	1911	1911 order	Per vehicle owned (£) Company	1901	1911	1911 order
1	SE & CR	645	914	1	GCR	1372	1152	1
2	LNWR	644	805	2	HR	890	725	3
3	MR	525	589	5	M & GN	792	566	8
4	LSWR	496	619	4	CR	690	833	2
5	LB & SCR	493	634	3	Cambrian	444	397	16
6	GCR	478	520	8	CLC	492	608	5
7	GNR	465	582	6	NER	491	635	4
8	LYR	462	545	7	GWR	478	571	7
9	CLC	429	437	10	GNR	478	506	10
10	GWR	383	479	9	LYR	456	578	6
11	CR	348	400	11	MR	404	488	11
12	GSWR	323	335	14	GSWR	379	488	12
13	GER	311	380	12	NSR	376	409	15
14	NER	291	362	13	SE & CR	371	528	9
15	NSR	275	282	15	LNWR	361	452	13
16	HR	233	239	17	S & DJR	346	354	19
17	NBR	232	267	16	TVR	324	372	17
18	FR	187	194	21	LSWR	302	432	14
19	GNSR	178	213	20	NBR	286	306	20
20	S & DJR	178	217	19	LB & SCR	284	357	18
21	TVR	177	234	18	FR	253	263	22
22	Cambrian	163	163	22	GER	250	294	21
23	M & GN	104	155	23	GNSR	193	230	23

Averages	Per route mile 1901	Per route mile 1911	Per vehicle 1901	Per vehicle 1911
Lines listed				
England + Wales	438	535	395	499
Scotland	270	306	406	448
Great Britain	405	490	396	492
All lines				
England + Wales	405	501	393	496
Scotland	267	301	412	454
Great Britain	379	463	396	490

The traditional British style of panelling displayed on Caledonian Railway third class corridor saloon No 46. The absence of ventilator bonnets over the door drop lights was unusual, but not uncommon on Caledonian elliptical roof stock.

The MR was probably the best known of those British companies which adopted fully square-cornered standard panelling. 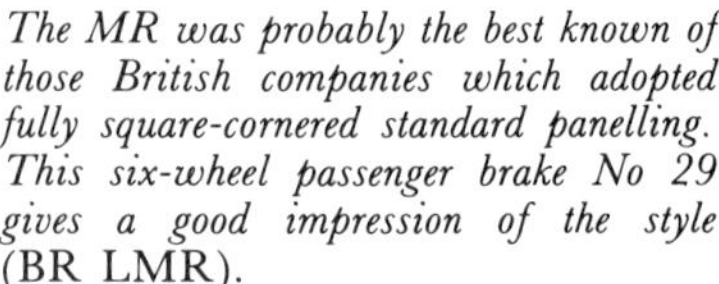 *This six-wheel passenger brake No 29 gives a good impression of the style* (BR LMR).

In 1912, the LNWR adopted a partially square-cornered variant of the traditional style. This view shows one of a series of four-wheelers built to this new style by the LNWR for its associated North London Railway. New four-wheel carriages were rather less usual after the turn of the century but by no means unknown (R.J. Essery collection).

7. The companies and their styles

The nature of the railway carriage during the 'company' period reflected a combination of what might be called stylistic preference and practical provisioning required by the traffic. In general, the visual styling (which included the livery) transcended the utilization factor so one could find a particular visual style of treatment applied 'across the board' to all types of carriage, whereas a specific type of carriage could be interpreted in a variety of different visual styles. The situation was not very dissimilar to that which influences the designer of the modern motor car or road coach. Thus, the end product tended to be a subtle combination of company stylistic preference married to an internal layout which most accurately catered for the prescribed needs of the passengers of that particular company. Small wonder that the permutations were endless and that the variety was enormous.

Attempting to bring order out of what might be regarded as incipient chaos, this analysis will first consider the various different *stylistic* approaches regardless of company) and then consider both the *types* and styles of carriage preferred by specific companies. To further simplify the analysis, the company treatment will reflect the groupings into which they were placed in 1923. The specific circumstances applicable to self-propelled (including electric) stock, Pullman and other more special-purpose vehicles will be considered separately, while the particular unique matter of those London area suburban and city lines which were amalgamated to form London Transport in 1933 will, for chronological reasons, be considered fully in Volume 2, although the origins are touched on in Chapter 15.

Vehicle styling

Basically, for the bulk of the period covered by this first volume vehicle styling was dominated by the nature of the wooden-bodied carriage. Even when the occasional use of sheet steel was adopted for the outer skin, the traditional approach died hard. Thus, many companies merely substituted steel for wood on the outside skin without real change in stylistic approach. Eventually, the different characteristics of sheet steel began to influence outward styling, but this was not a particularly significant factor during the first part of the century for most of the bigger companies.

Although the wooden-bodied carriage was put together in much the same way regardless of length, width or company, its outward styling gave considerable scope for decorative variation in such matters as panel shapes and sizes and the precise arrangement of the protective beading strips, ventilator bonnets, window frames and so forth. Virtually every individual railway adopted its own house style to a greater or lesser degree in these matters, whether it made its own carriages or had them built by contractors. Some lines maintained a recognizably similar treatment for a considerable period of time while others tended to alter the visual lines quite regularly. In the latter case, this could either take the form of a radical change or a progressive modification or refinement of existing norms. However, in spite of the many variations, most carriage styles fall into one or other of a rather smaller number of categories than one might expect. Some of these were more widespread than others, but it will help to enumerate their basic characteristics so as to avoid constant repetition later. The nomenclature adopted is that of the author and has no 'official' status in terms of historic usage.

The traditional British style

The most widespread form of body treatment took the form of a series of panels the edges of which were protected by beading strips with *rounded* corners. There would normally be a row of *eaves* panels above window level below the roof edge, a second row of panels the same depth as, and located between the windows, a third row of panels roughly matching the eaves panel along the *waist* of the carriage and a fourth row of lower body panels between the waist and the bottom edge of the body.

Within the broad definition, there was considerable scope for individual development in such matters as panel depth (top to bottom), the radius of the corner curvature of the beading, the precise location and style of the ventilator bonnets along the eaves panel and whether or not supplementary windows could (or should) be fitted above the main windows. The style went back well into the nineteenth century and did not vanish for new construction until the 1930s.

Of the more important railways, the GWR, NER, MR, LSWR and Caledonian were widespread users of the style. There were, of course, others.

The 'modified' British style

Given the traditional panel layout (eaves, window, waist and lower body), two principal variations were not uncommon, the differences usually being in the treatment of the beading. One of two common variations was adopted — all the panel corners were square or some corners only were squared off. In the latter case, it was more usual to find only the window level panels so treated, although some companies treated the eaves and waist panels in like manner.

2
2
2
2
2

THIRD
FIRST
G N R
FIRST
THIRD
314
THIRD

Some distinctly pleasant visual variations could be seen with this sort of approach as many of the pictures in this book will reveal. Railways adopting the fully squared corners with the traditional panel layout were rather few, but included some notable companies like the MR (during the 1896-1905 period) and the NER for a short while. The GER, too, came up with its own very distinctive form of treatment which was, if you like, an 'alternative modified' style!

The 'low-waisted' or 'Wolverton' style
On some railways, especially the LNWR, the traditional style of panelling was further modified to eliminate the eaves and waist panels (except on the doors) and to extend the bodyside panelling from the cornice to the waist rail between the doors. This gave a quite different visual appearance and, by virtue of reducing the quantity of beading strips, often tended to look rather more modern — or at least less fussy. The style is believed to have originated at Wolverton (LNWR) in mid-Victorian times and was copied later by several other companies, the SE & CR and its predecessor the South Eastern Railway being perhaps the most important of the others.

The twin-layer 'Howlden' or 'East Coast' style
At Doncaster on the GNR, Mr Howlden introduced a very distinctive form of bodyside treatment for the famous varnished teak coaches built there. The panelling was square cornered but was in effect in two layers, that above the waist being set back slightly from the panelling below the waist. The beading profile also varied — flat with rounded edges above the waist, half round below. Being varnished teak, opportunity was also taken to feature the grain direction as part of the treatment, horizontal in the waist and lower body panels, vertical above the waist. The style was later adopted as standard for the East Coast Joint Stock, whether built at Doncaster, York (NER) or Cowlairs (NBR).

In due course Gresley adopted it, virtually unchanged, for his own build of GNR, ECJS and LNER carriages and it remained in use until 1941, having become by then probably the longest lasting of any individual form of wooden bodyside treatment in Britain. At that time, the LNER was the only British main-line company still building traditional all-wood carriage bodies.

The twin-layer 'Scottish' style
This strictly unofficial definition seems apposite because it was particularly characteristic of several Scottish companies, especially the NBR. The 'layering' followed much the same principles as the 'Howlden' style but visually it was more like the

Top *Wolverton style LNWR panelling is displayed on this train of four gangwayed arc roof carriages in the early 1900s* (BR LMR).

Above left *This spartan four-wheeled* second *class carriage No 198 shows one of the several characteristic GER variations of traditional panelling to be seen during the early part of the twentieth century.*

Left *Typical Howlden GNR panelling on a composite brake of* circa *1897, No 314. It was a slip carriage (see page 166) and ran until 1950.*

Right *The 'Scottish' style of twin-layer panelling on yet another economical gas-lit suburban four-wheeler, NBR third class No 1072.*

traditional British panelling with rounded corners to the beading. The GNSR and the Highland also produced a few vehicles of this kind but it was less often seen in England.

Flush-sided and semi-flush-sided styles

One or two railways eschewed the use of beading strips for the most part and, even with wooden bodies, managed to produce carriages whose side surfaces were rather more akin to those of modern metal-skinned vehicles. Of course, the general shape and nature of the coaches remained similar to that of many other railways. The most noteworthy exponent was the LYR, whose carriage styling was wholly unique for many years because of this fact. In later days, one or two railways took a slightly different approach by suppressing *some* beading in favour of a more flush-clad treatment, sometimes allied to the use of *some* metal sheeting. The GWR and Caledonian were both exponents of this approach, but tended to confuse matters by continuing with a painted livery suggestive of normal traditional panelling.

Above left *These elliptical roof non-corridors, photographed soon after 1923, show the nature of orthodox LYR carriage styling with its twin-level outer sheeting. The leading coach has received new LMS colours which do not seem to have taken too well. The inward taper towards the guard's lookout was a distinctive feature of many LYR carriages, an idea also used on the LSWR 'Ironclads' — see page 128.*

Left *This 'matchboard'-panelled, cove-roofed Highland Railway corridor third was photographed in BR days at Wormit, Fife (ex-NBR), proof that not all ex-HR carriages were short-lived after 1923* (Gavin Wilson).

Below *A massive but visually well-balanced GCR 'matchboard'-sided corridor composite built in 1911 for the Manchester-London services.*

A third variant, though perhaps not really qualifying as flush-sided, was the use of a vertical tongue and groove boarding, sometimes from the waist downwards and sometime for the whole depth of the carriage side. The HR, SE & CR and GCR all, at times, built examples of 'matchboard-panelled' stock as it was known, while in pre-metal days it was always one of the characteristic features of Pullman car styling.

* * *

The above six categories probably embrace the vast majority of carriages built in Britain during the first quarter of the twentieth century and there were, additionally, styles which do not really lend themselves to analysis. These were regularly, but not exclusively, found on the newly developing electric stock (especially in London, Merseyside and Tyneside) but sometimes on particularly important special stock such as the West Coast sleeping and dining saloons. Taken with the considerable variations in roof profile and height, not to mention the infinite variety of window arrangements and carriage lengths to be seen and the multiplicity of liveries, the railway carriage scene was a decidedly colourful and cosmopolitan business before the grouping.

Against this background it may be supposed that generalization is a bit of a forlorn hope, but in fact there were many points of similarity within the apparent disparity. Most railways built broadly the same types of stock for the same sorts of services, and these will be examined in detail in the next few chapters. However, before tackling this job, it will be helpful to give a broad company-by-company review. Clearly it is not possible to mention them all or even give a proportionally correct amount of space to those which are mentioned. Rather it will be the object to examine the dominant trends which were apparent in the 1901-22 period, for these mostly set the pattern for the rationalization of post-1922 design. For this reason, the companies will be considered in the groupings into which they were put in 1923, and in descending order of magnitude of carriage fleets.

The LMS group

In 1922, the constituent companies of the LMS whose route mileage exceeded 100 were as follows, the number of passenger-carrying vehicles owned in 1921 being listed alongside:

England	Furness Railway		269
	LYR		3749
	LNWR		6239*
	MR		4331†
	NSR		341
		Subtotal	14929
Scotland	CR		2290
	GSWR		1189
	HR		303
		Subtotal	3780
		Grand total	18709

*Includes former North London Railway stock.
†Includes former LT & SR stock.

Until 1910, the NLR — see also the picture on page 100 — had built its own unique four-wheelers for almost forty years to a style which does not really fit any of the categories defined in the text. This is first class No 99, built in 1906.

Left *Britain's most numerous ever single bogie carriage type? LYR 49-foot bogie non-corridor third, LMS No 14493, seen in scruffy LMS livery sometime after 1933, unchanged from its original state. Note the air intakes to the Anderson ventilators — see page 60 — at the ends of the door-top bonnets* (BR LMR).

Right *Visual proof that the LYR could rival the rest for styling when it so chose — first class dining car No 213, built in 1907. The styling may have been influenced by the Wolverton LNWR twelve-wheelers, the two companies being close allies in many things.*

From this analysis (an abstract from Table 2 on page 87), the dominance of the three big English constituents is noticeable, representing some 75% or more of the total. All three took a quite different approach to carriage building, the LYR being probably the most consistent overall.

This railway had adopted its basic body style as early as 1876, the originator being one Mr Attock. It was in all respects a far smoother-sided treatment than that adopted by most contemporary railways, and perhaps the most noticeable individual feature was the fact that the side sheeting below the waist was set back by the thickness of the sheeting from the waist upwards. The window treatment was also particularly distinctive and neatly arranged, and the whole effect (for its time) was quite a bit more modern than most railways.

This modernity was emphasized by the fact that the LYR was one of the earlier systems to adopt the bogie in a big way; its most numerous manifestation, the 49-foot eight-compartment non-corridor third, introduced as early as 1893, was not only built for some ten years but eventually totalled 808 vehicles. This is thought to have been the most numerous single type of bogie carriage built for any railway in Britain at any time. Many other types, including some corridor stock, were built to this basic house style and even when George Hughes (the CME of the LYR prior to the grouping) moved from the characteristic arc roof to the fully-elliptical style, the body panelling hardly changed on most coaches, save for the rounding off of the lower window corners and some trivial modifications to vertical heights.

The generally smooth appearance of a typical LYR carriage was enhanced by its livery, which has been in some sources unkindly described as 'two shades of ordure'! It was in fact carmine lake on the lower panels and a brownish-orange above, eminently practical for the industrial environment in which most of them worked. The lighter colour was derived from the shade of varnished teak used in earlier days. The lining treatment was restrained compared with most contemporary systems but aesthetically very much in tune with the structural nature of the carriages. When the LYR did build a few fully-panelled vehicles in quasi-traditional style, it demonstrated that it was just as capable of delivering an elaborate fully-lined livery as anyone else when the carriage 'architecture' warranted it. The Fleetwood boat stock, for example, must have looked distinctly stylish. The LYR insignia was always very characteristic and with its white outlines set off the whole ensemble very well.

The LYR has always suffered a bad press for it carriages relative to the MR and LNWR, but this is not really fair. Its operating circumstances were very different and it was obliged to concentrate heavily on short-distance, high-capacity coaches — hardly the most suitable candidates for large-scale experimentation. Its hard horsehair third class seats became almost legendary, almost as if it was the only railway to adopt such practice, and its liking for gas lighting has sometimes been regarded as a black mark. But the MR, GWR and LNWR, to mention but three, were not exactly known for the rapidity with which they abandoned gas! Had the LYR been the sort of railway which needed, proportionally, the same number of long-distance carriages as were built by those other railways with large carriage fleets, then the available evidence suggests that it would have more than held its own. Its best corridor, and particularly first class, carriages were both luxurious and sumptuous; there simply were not many of them. Furthermore in its unwillingness to disguise its carriages with pseudo-panelling (in paint), the LYR adopted a distinctly modern approach and it was not really followed by any other railway until well after the grouping.

Although the LYR had a lot of carriages and, as Chapter 6 has endeavoured to demonstrate, generally provided a more than adequate number of seats for its patrons, it must be conceded that in terms of variety, relative to the larger amalgamated LMS, its contribution was possibly doomed to take a relatively minor place. However, its carriage works at Newton Heath remained one of only three locations which went on building new stock in LMS days (the others being Derby and Wolverton), and the operating requirements of the Central Division of the LMS (the post-1923 nomenclature of the former LYR area) were equally central to the precise provisioning of new non-corridor stock in LMS days. Furthermore, in its adoption of gangwayed centre-aisle open stock, its final experimentation with angle-trussed underframes and its eventual settling on a 56-57 foot carriage with fully-elliptical roof, it was not too far out of line with the post-1923 LMS policies which will be discussed in Volume 2.

It was, however, (and hardly surprisingly) the LNWR and MR approach to carriage building which was more in tune with the overall national picture during the first quarter of the century. Both companies operated just about every sort of passenger service from long-distance expresses to high-density suburban trains. Their carriages were, however, distinctly different.

The larger of the two, the LNWR, was possibly (along with the GWR) the most comprehensive railway system in Britain before 1923, impregnated with the sort of tradition which was well reflected in its carriages. From way back in Victorian times it had adopted a quite distinctive low-waisted form of carriage architecture which was hardly changed when the new century dawned. Allied to its equally long-lived and famous livery of carmine lake lower panels and white (actually white 'broken' with blue — see Chapter 5), it probably entered the twentieth century seeming to the outside world to have all the permanence of the Rock of Gibraltar. For the first decade or so, thus it remained. The carriage roof profile changed from arc roof to a superb low-elliptical form in early Edwardian days and became fully elliptical in 1907/8. Carriage length crept up from a sort of standard 50-foot form in 1900-1 to a 57-foot norm by 1905-10, and width increased from 8 ft 6 in to 9 ft during the same time; but the livery and decorative treatment scarcely change.

There was, however, one area where the LNWR really 'went to town', and that was in its more specialized vehicles, be they sleeping cars or Royal Saloons. They were mostly twelve-wheelers, and arguably Wolverton works, the celebrated LNWR carriage building establishment, built more elaborate twelve-wheelers than anywhere else in Britain. They will, quite properly, be given more space later in this survey, but at this point it is sufficient to state that they displayed a wholly unique visual stylistic approach, quite unlike normal LNWR practice; they rode like a dream on some of the finest permanent way in the world and can lay sound claim to having been the visual and mechanical high point of British carriage construction in the pre-grouping period. That this is a strong assertion cannot be denied, but their only serious rivals in this respect were the East Coast twelve-wheelers (see page 119) and, possibly, some of Churchward's magnificent 70-footers for the GWR (see page 135). I propose to stick my neck out and give Wolverton the accolade if only because it built rather more of them than anyone else.

As for ordinary coaches, the LNWR suddenly changed course in 1912-13 when it adopted to all intents and purposes the traditional style of panelling for almost all its general service stock. This seems to have been at the behest of Mr H.D. Earl, the carriage superintendent in succession to the famous C.A. Park, who had, *inter alia,* devised the immortal

This page top to bottom *Traditional Wolverton-style panelling on elliptical roof stock is represented by this pair of first class LNWR luxury club saloons — see also Chapter 13 — built in 1908* (BR LMR).

This unique form of LNWR panelling, though not confined to vehicles with six-wheel bogies, is often referred to as the 'twelve-wheel' style. It was introduced in 1892 and current for more than thirty years. This example, clerestory roof 2nd/3rd class dining car No 290, built in 1904, represents possibly the most stylish single variant of this distinctive treatment (BR LMR).

The post-1912 standard LNWR body architecture is exemplified by 'Toplight'-styled WCJS corridor composite No 275, built in 1913 as part of two new sets for the morning London-Glasgow service.

An early David Bain design for the MR, retaining the square-cornered Clayton-style panelling — first class dining car No 2593, built in 1903. It was also one of the first MR types to display the so-called 'clipper' profile — see page 49 (BR LMR).

Right *First class corridor carriage No 2671 was built to Bain's design in 1911 and is probably everyone's image of a typical Midland vehicle; yet it was a rare type, one of only four such carriages owned by the MR, and there were only three more in the Midland's Joint stock. This picture shows the almost unchanged livery adopted in LMS days.*

twelve-wheelers. Earl did not dare — or so it would seem — to change the twelve-wheel style (save for giving them elliptical roofs from 1907 onwards), but his later LNWR ordinary stock was, it has to be said, visually somewhat undistinguished. Being the LNWR, its new-style carriages naturally retained certain traditional features unchanged, such as door ventilators and handles, not to mention the famous livery. Earl also indulged (for a year or two) in a sort of modified style with square, lower cornered window and eaves panelling; but the last decade of LNWR coach building was a sort of uneasy visual compromise (probably unconscious) between the Churchward (GWR) and Bain/Reid (MR) style with few of the redeeming virtues of either. For example, compartment sizes in corridor stock became distinctly parsimonious compared with earlier twentieth century LNWR standards.

However, in one respect the LNWR influence was never diluted. It was of all the LMS constituents by far the most experienced in long-distance operations. In consequence, it had developed by 1922 a far more sophisticated approach to corridor coach design than almost any other British company (see Chapter 10). Its only serious rival was possibly the GWR, and this is not relevant in the LMS context. Thus, the LNWR approach to internal vehicle *layout* was of prime value in the 1920s and 1930s, and its general espousal of 57-foot (ordinary) and 68-foot twelve-wheel dining and sleeping cars became the LMS standard, probably much to the chagrin of the Midland followers. In fact, such was the dominance of the LNWR in the long-distance field that its corridor thirds *alone* outnumbered the whole of the Midland Railway fleet of gangwayed long-distance coaches.

At this point, dedicated followers of the third principal English constituent of the LMS, the Midland Railway, are perhaps muttering furiously in their armchairs! Traditional wisdom has it that the MR was the most noteworthy of the pre-1923 railways in terms of passenger comfort not just in the LMS but in Britain as a whole. It is a nice thought and I am not unknown for my espousal of many aspects of the Midland cause; but it is not quite accurate.

The MR certainly deserves total credit for its emancipation of the third class passenger from the mid-1870s (see Chapter 1), but by the start of the present century it had been somewhat overtaken in certain respects. For instance, the GWR, LNWR and even the GER had all adopted corridor trains well before the Midland. Moreover, at that time Midland carriage *design* was in a state of transition. During 1896-7, its famous carriage designer Thomas Clayton had introduced the celebrated and unique clerestory profile, and by 1900-1 this had become the standard for all new MR coaches. It was associated with the square-cornered modification of the traditional panel style and the end product was a series of highly distinctive carriages, mostly non-corridor but with a few corridor and dining car examples. The Midland was, however, in spite of its forward-looking image, somewhat conservative in terms of carriage *type* and still built a fair number of four-wheel and six-wheel carriages, some of them incorporating the pre-1896 'traditional' style of Clayton round-cornered panelling with arc roof profile. In fact, just before the turn of the century it had produced some singularly uninspiring *four*-wheelers for the Metropolitan line services to the City of London which were every bit as awful as those of the GNR or North London lines!

These facts must be put into the equation when considering MR coaching stock and it was not until David Bain (ex-North Eastern) took over from Clayton in 1903 that the MR really began to move forward again. By now, the LNWR had been building corridor coaches for itself and the West Coast Joint Stock for some years, whereas the MR had only constructed a few corridors, mainly for the Scottish Joint Stock, and even these only appeared

as late as 1898. Bain lengthened the corridor stock from 48 feet to 50-54 feet and the twelve-wheelers from 60 feet to 65 feet but retained the square-cornered panelling for a short period. He then completely revised the Midland styling to his own version of the traditional round-cornered pattern (basically brought with him from the NER) and applied it to both long-distance and suburban coaches. The main-line and some of the non-corridor lavatory stock retained the 1896-7 Clayton clerestory profile (slightly modified), but the more suburban vehicles reverted to an arc roof profile.

Ten years or so after this, the Midland, by now the last major user of the clerestory, adopted the full elliptical roof for all stock, but this was almost half a generation later than the LNWR, GWR, LYR and several others. Moreover, it was never particularly widespread and elliptical-roof corridors did not appear until after the Great War. In consequence, Midland carriages were not quite as tidy in visual style as sometimes supposed and there were still a lot of four-wheelers and six-wheelers to be seen, some going well back into the nineteenth century. However, the final MR carriage designer, R.W. Reid, had by the end of the pre-group period moved MR carriage design into something recognizably similar to that pursued by the LNWR. The standard length became 57 feet for corridor stock while 65 feet was retained for twelve-wheelers. The roof profile was consistently elliptical by now, the underframe had developed into an angle-trussed form and the panelling was basically David Bain-style with slight modification.

It is part of accepted folk myth that these features were adopted unchanged by the LMS in 1923, largely because of the dominance of many MR officers in the post-1922 management of the new company; indeed, Reid became the new LMS carriage supremo and instituted new and more cost-effective constructional methods in the 1920s which will be discussed in Volume 2. It is, therefore, not surprising that MR stylistic features were copied (they were, at the time, probably the best of all the LMS constituents), as was its magnificent all-lake livery — one of the most distinguished and practical carriage finishes of all time — but that is about as far as it went. The MR interior design concepts very soon vanished — they were basically not as well thought out or as versatile as those of the LNWR — and overall carriage dimensions and seating capacity became much nearer the LNWR/LYR standards than those of the Midland. To be fair, the Midland offered generous space in its passenger provisioning and made good-looking carriages, but after 1923 its influence was more aesthetic than practical as the very cost-conscious LMS quite speedily demonstrated during the 1920s.

These, then, were the three primary contributions to the LMS scene; but what of the remaining 20-25%? Dominant here were the Caledonian and GSWR contingents; the former was the more significant, not simply because it had twice as many carriages, but also because the GSWR was not, if we are to be honest, a profoundly significant railway in terms of its carriage stock. At the turn of the century it was producing some very neat stock of the 'modified traditional' kind, designed by James Manson (or at least attributed to him). They were neat and well finished and by no means unattractive visually, but they showed no real innovatory features compared with those of the larger companies. The GSWR lived, in carriage terms, somewhat 'under the shadow' of its English ally the Midland. It was, however, much smaller and did not get itself involved in the design of the Scottish Joint Stock — that was very much a Derby prerogative and MR designs were actually built at Kilmarnock in the late nineteenth century for Joint Stock working. Furthermore, the GSWR and MR had wished to amalgamate in the 1870s and, even though foiled in this endeavour, they remained very close associates. The GSWR adopted the MR carriage livery (to all intents and purposes) and its carriages were very Midland-like in both appearance, amenity and dimension during the Manson period. Take away the square lower corner panelling of a Manson GSWR carriage and one almost has a pre-clerestory Clayton MR coach.

Funnily enough, it was the much-maligned Peter Drummond — who made something of a 'porridge' of GSWR locomotives — who gave the company such carriage distinction as it was able to offer to the new LMS. He produced a distinctly attractive, almost fully elliptical carriage style which retained the basic Manson panelling (now rounded at all corners) but increased the overall size to something approaching modern dimensions. His use of pressed steel bogies was almost 'avant garde' and the vehicles were most certainly in the front rank for the time. But, as with the LYR considered earlier, there were not too many of them and their influence could be but minor after 1922.

It is an odd thought that the Caledonian Railway, though a fierce rival of the GSWR, suffered much the same sort of fate after 1922 as far as carriage design was concerned, even though its engines fared rather better. The 'Caley' was a much larger railway (second only in Scotland after the NBR) but, in carriage terms, it suffered from several disadvantages. Firstly, to all intents and purposes it left the design of the West Coast Joint Stock to its English partner, the LNWR. It even adopted virtually the same livery, believed to be in

Top to bottom *The Midland's elliptical roof carriages, such as lavatory non-corridor composite No 3330, retained Bain-style panelling and became the visual models on which early LMS stock was based* (BR LMR).

Characteristic Manson-styling on the GSWR is shown by arc roof non-corridor third class No 693. The apparent lack of lining suggests that it may have been a 1914-18 wartime repaint.

The visual style of Peter Drummond's new stock for the GSWR is well shown in this ex-works view of non-corridor first class No 194. The generally Midland nature of the livery is obvious, but the roof is white and there is a fine gilt line centrally on the beading, a feature not adopted by the MR (Staffordshire County Record Office).

Caledonian Railway corridor third No 982 typifies the turn-of-the-century style adopted by this famous company.

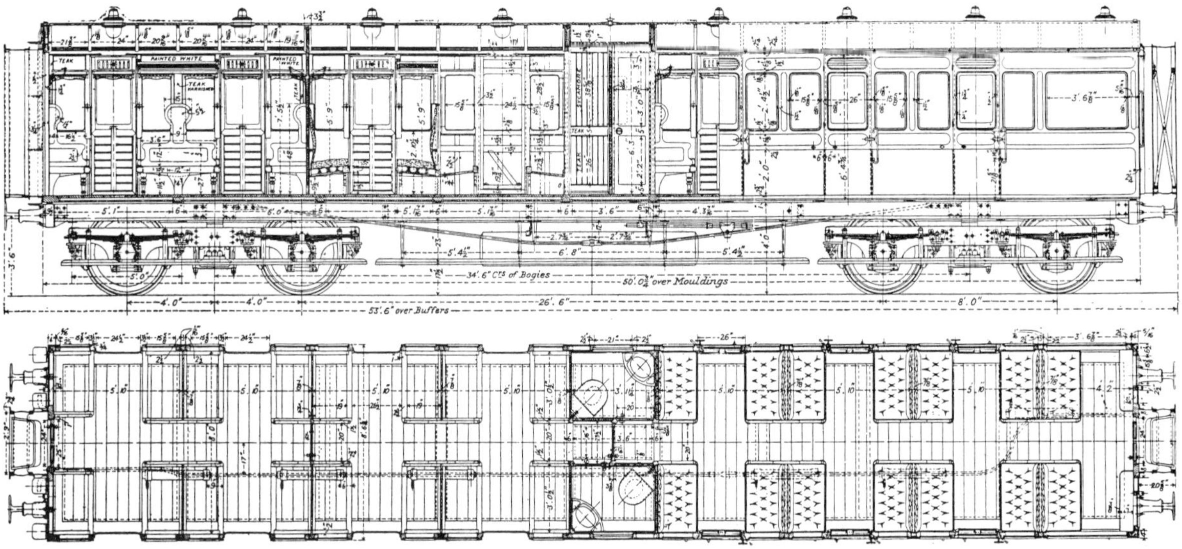

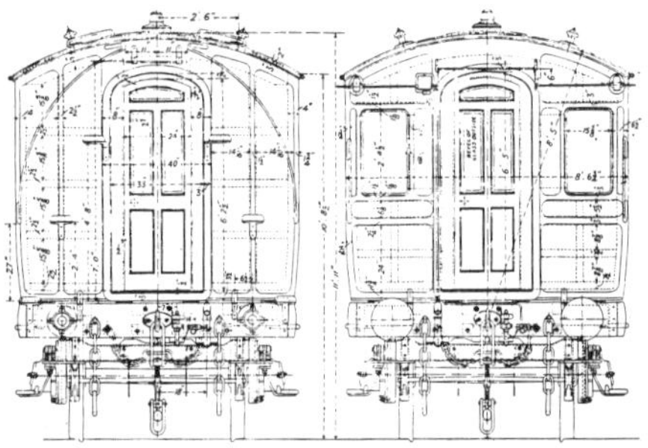

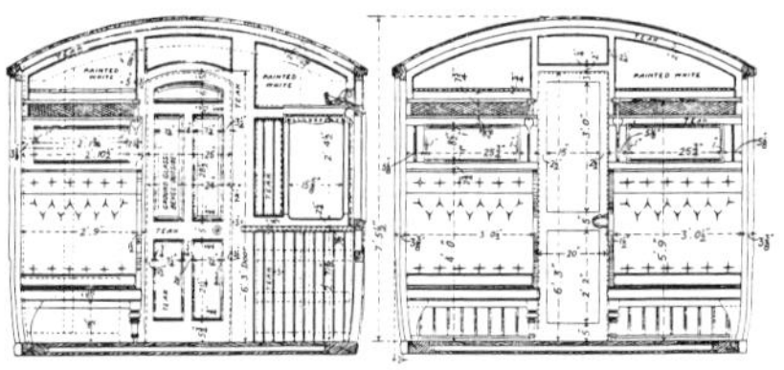

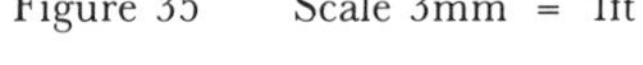

Figure 35 Scale 3mm = 1ft

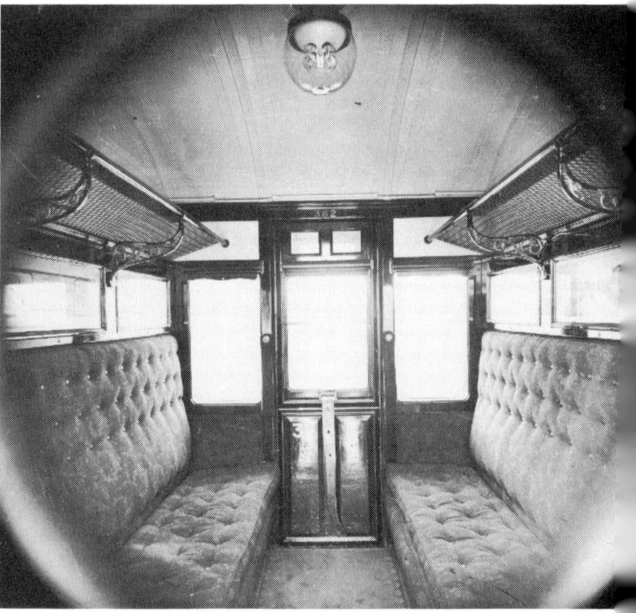

styling adopted by Drummond. The extraordinary thing is that some of the HR stock *did* survive quite well and its admittedly small quota of corridor stock was not too bad. But the fact that the LMS, soon after the grouping, saw fit to allocate quite a volume of second-line former MR, LYR and LNWR stock to the Highland area seems to tell its own story of the general backwardness of the latter's overall fleet. Only the later Drummond stock enjoyed any real longevity.

The Furness and North Staffordshire Railways both rather favoured the 'Wolverton' (LNWR) style of carriage construction, but neither of them came up with anything better than that of the larger constituents. The Maryport and Carlisle had an attractive green and cream livery allied to 'traditional' or 'modified traditional' body style but not much else, while the LT & SR and NLR systems could hardly be expected to set the Thames on fire with their carriage designs. The MR had, long before 1922-3, decided to replace the indigenous LT & SR stock with something better, and maybe the less said about the NLR contribution the better! It is one of the more amazing facts of twentieth-century carriage history that the quite appalling four-wheelers of the NLR were, for a time (after the LNWR took over), replaced by *new* four-wheelers and these archaic concepts continued to trundle up the 'Northern Heights' of the London suburbs well into the 1930s. Mark you, the CR had also built some 'modern' four-wheelers right up to the time of the grouping, so perhaps one should not be too critical.

Obviously, in a general survey such as this the subtle nuances so beloved of the railway enthusiasts have little or no place, and it may be that some readers feel that this analysis is altogether too superficial. However, if one tries to extract, from a very complex story, some continuing threads which stood the test of time — the only *real* criterion for lasting influence — then the later development of the railway carriage in the twentieth century, as far as the LMS was concerned, was strongly biased in favour of the contributions made by the LNWR, MR and LYR. These were the three main contributors to the LMS fleet which, in turn, was the major single influence in the BR continuation. It may seem to be *force majeure* but, if so, the fact should not be too unsurprising. Remember that railways were in business to make money, and their carriages reflected this fact; if the present (1980s) shape of the open second class carriage on a MkIII HST set reveals its ancestry via the LMS/LYR, so be it. History is a continuum and railway carriages are no exception.

We now turn to the next in 1923 order of magnitude, the LNER.

The LNER group

Once again abstracting from Table 2, the 100-or-more-route-mile companies which came under the LNER ownership, along with their 1921 passenger carriage totals, are listed below:

England	GCR	1694
	GER	3970
	GNR	2639
	NER	3106*
	Subtotal	11409
Scotland	GNSR	454
	NBR	2424
	Subtotal	2878
	Grand total	14287

*This total includes vehicles from the Hull & Barnsley Railway, absorbed early in 1922.

Somewhat like the LMS group, three English companies dominated the scene, this time with some 68% of the total fleet, but there was only one smaller system compared with the considerable number of such railways in the LMS group. Five out of six companies owned quite large fleets and only the GER stood out numerically. However, its numerical ascendancy was not as significant as, say, that of the LNWR in the LMS system.

The GER total of carriages included a huge number of suburban vehicles reflecting its intensive London area services into Liverpool Street. In this context it enjoyed a near territorial monopoly, save for the LT & SR, somewhat comparable with the various constituents of the Southern Railway (see below). In this respect it was different from the two other London-based parts of the LNER which had to face rather more railway competition from such rival organizations as the Metropolitan, North London and Underground systems, not to mention a degree of territorial overlap with main-line companies like the Midland or LNWR.

In consequence, GER carriage design was dominated by the needs of suburban short-distance passengers. it adopted a traditionally British form of styling but with numerous distinctive variations all its own. The eaves and waist panels were notably deeper than those adopted by most railways and the division of the lower side sheeting into a series of vertical panels on many of its carriages was wholly unique. Its livery was varnished natural wood which, when kept clean, could be quite smart, but it was by

The GER's individualistic exterior styling never quite settled down to one consistent version. Most variation occurred either below the waist or at the doors as, for example, on these typical clerestories. The nearer example, composite No 633, is more orthodox, but the full third No 522 displays recessed doors and the almost unique GER lower panelling. Above the waist they are clearly from the same stable. From the standpoint of passenger amenity, these two vehicles, with their internal semi-corridor access to lavatories, were well above average for non-gangwayed types.

The elliptical roof corridor stock of the GER, exemplified by third class No 560, showed an interesting blend of visual styles clearly derived from the clerestory period.

no means the most striking of such styles since it had nothing like the decorative embellishments carried by, say, the East Coast companies (see below). In 1919, the GER changed to a dark crimson lake colour for some of its carriages and at all times its use of large class-identifying figures on the doors was a dominant feature. In this particular, it was somewhat ahead of most companies during the early part of the period under review.

In spite of its large fleet, the GER suffered two principal drawbacks in terms of its future influence on things. Firstly, it was not a true long-distance railway in the sense of the GNR, MR or LNWR for instance, and its contribution in terms of gangwayed stock was, in consequence, relatively modest. Secondly, and in LNER terms of more than superficial importance, it was not involved with the design or operation of the East Coast Joint Stock. In both these respects, its position after 1922 was not dissimilar to that of the LYR. That it could build some very fine coaches is exemplified not just by its early use of corridor coaches and third class dining cars in late Victorian days, but also by its twentieth-century stock for the Continental boat trains and the services to the principal East Anglian cities like Ispwich and Norwich, not to mention Cambridge. But these were all 2-3 hour sort of trips (even less in the case of Cambridge and the boat trains), and the GER rarely had to address the problem of designing what amounted to an all-day or all-night travelling environment.

Thus, like the LYR, its carriage designs tended to be ignored after the grouping although, just as with the LMS in the case of the LYR, the new LNER could not ignore the traffic *requirements* of the ex-GER lines and the post-1922 design of LNER suburban stock very much reflected this fact. Another interesting influence which was at first precipitated by GER requirements was the need to design a shorter version of the LNER standard corridor coaches for use on the Great Eastern system, parts of which could not accept the longer vehicles.

Turning now to some of the other English constituents of the LNER, two of them had main lines to London, but whereas that of the GCR was a sort of appendage grafted in 1899 on to a former provincial system (the Manchester Sheffield and Lincolnshire), the whole ethos of the GNR stemmed from its role as a main trunk route from the day it opened, halfway through the nineteenth century. 'Kings Cross for the North' had been almost written into its tablets of incorporation. However, notwithstanding this fundamental difference in history, both railways had to address similar, if not identical, operating problems. In terms of vehicle design response, they did so in markedly different ways.

The Great Central entered the new century flushed with pride at its recent change of title consequent upon its achievement of the London main line to Marylebone. However, as a newcomer it had to face formidable rivalry for long-distance traffic from the three existing and well-established systems whose trains were already in fierce competition for passengers from the same or similar catchment areas, ie the LNWR, MR and GNR. In trying to face these problems, the GCR came up with some very fine carriages indeed.

At the turn of the century, the new Great Central employed traditionally panelled coaches in a nice livery of chocolate brown and French grey, later brown and cream. It built some very well-equipped corridor coaches right at the close of the Victorian era which, although by no means to the maximum length adopted by some railways, offered distinctly spacious accommodation. At times, it also favoured the clerestory roof which was a rather elegant stylistic compromise between the Midland and Great Western approaches. Its clerestory non-corridors were most definitely a cut above the average and could stand favourable comparison with anything in the land.

In 1907, the GCR went to the fully elliptical roof and a varnished natural wood livery appeared in 1910. This was accompanied by a change to a very distinctive body styling for some of its carriages combining vertical 'matchboard' treatment below the waistline and a general increase in the coach size, both in terms of length and cross-section. In the latter context, the GCR had built its London main line to a very generous structure gauge of almost continental proportions, and this permitted correspondingly generous internal provisioning for the passenger, including probably the widest internal side corridors ever offered to the British traveller.

However, the GCR loading gauge posed its own problems, just as did that of the GWR (page 134). Very large carriages could not pass freely over all 'foreign' systems, and since through coach working in Britain was a characteristic and important feature of railway working, the big GCR carriages, excellent though they were, could not offer the most effective solution after 1923. Moreover, in numerical terms they were considerably few in number compared with the GNR and/or NER fleets. Additionally, the GCR also retained a fair quantity of earlier and less worthy

This stylish GCR clerestory non-corridor third class brake with end lavatory was built in 1903. Compared with most of its third class short to medium-distance contemporaries, this must have been a more than amenable form of travel (B.C. Lane collection).

Considerable attention to detail is apparent in the finish of this attractive GCR bogie guard and parcels van, No 520, built in 1907. The carriage is unlined but the original picture clearly shows the beautifully applied grained finish of the post-1910 GCR livery. It is possible that this picture was taken to illustrate the new style.

Left *This appalling four-wheel monstrosity built by the GNR seated no fewer than 72 passengers in six compartments not much over 5 feet wide, and was one of forty such carriages when built in 1900. It was not untypical of the frugal nature of most GNR suburban stock.*

Right *In the long-distance field the GNR had to meet fierce competition, and only four years after building the four-wheelers in the previous picture it produced ten of these elegant gangwayed clerestory third class brakes with only 42 seats arranged in three open saloons and three-per-side seating, arranged 2 + 1 on either side of the central aisle.*

stock. But make no mistake about it, the Great Central carriage was by no means the inferior vehicle which its apparent eclipse after 1922 might suggest.

By contrast with the GCR, the GNR influence in carriage building throughout the first half of the twentieth century was profound — and this is somewhat surprising all things considered. In 1921 it came only third in the LNER constituent companies' carriage fleet 'pecking order', and only just above the stock of the NBR. However, numbers were not everything, as the LNWR had discovered *vis-à-vis* the Midland in the LMS group. The outcome, however, was not quite the same.

In many ways, the GNR was very like the LNWR, although considerably smaller in size. During much of the later nineteenth century they had both operated some quite dreadful carriages on their main lines considering the generally prestigious nature of both companies. However, they were both distinctly arrogant railways, full of self-satisfied complacency, and it was not until both were pushed into providing something better that improvement began to take place! In this, the competition offered by the Midland was probably pivotal to both the GNR and LNWR, while the new GCR did not exactly endear itself to any of its rivals with its rather good carriages. It is, one feels, more than significant that the GNR only began to sort matters out at the turn of the century (as indeed did the LNWR), by which time the MR had been offering superb comfort for nearly twenty years and, additionally, the new GCR was a possible threat to everyone.

The GNR responded with considerable éclat, which was to lay a firm foundation for East Coast and LNER carriage building for the best part of half a century, and its influence may, perhaps, best be summed up by the names of three people, Howlden, Gould and Gresley. Of these names, the first two are probably less well known than the last, yet they were probably more influential, at least superficially. Firstly, it was Howlden who created the distinctive 'East Coast' carriage panelling style which was worn without significant change in either style or livery (varnished teak) from the 1880s until 1941. Gould we have also met in the context of the buckeye coupling and the Pullman gangway, both being eventually adopted by the GNR as standard for long-distance stock. Gresley's influence was, in turn, both more subtle and undoubtedly more long-lasting, even though the most ardent Gresley admirers must admit that he had a good foundation on which to work which only needed a bit of refinement.

In 'surface' terms, the only thing which made the body of a Gresley carriage look significantly different from its long-distance predecessors was its full height elliptical roof and its beautifully 'domed' roof ends. In this, it was quite an achievement to improve on its forbears, for the GNR corridor clerestory was itself a thing of great beauty dating back to the late 1890s. The less said about the pure 'Howlden' body the better, with its sort of flattened elliptical roof profile which was universally adopted for non-corridor stock and its quite regular association with the most diabolically cramped compartments! In this respect, Gresley's elliptical roof suburban non-corridors were not particularly marvellous either for the most part!

It was 'below decks', so to speak, that Gresley's carriage influence was most significant. He is, of course, most famous for his fine locomotives, but he actually came to the GNR as carriage and wagon chief and had trained on the LYR. Before he left this latter railway, it had begun to experiment with an outside frame 'wide bearing' bogie of monumentally ugly aesthetic aspect but considerable virtue in terms of its ride quality. While I have never seen documentary proof of the connection, it does not seem too wild a supposition to link this LYR wide bearing bogie with the altogether more elegant

outside frame *double* bolster bogie which Gresley fairly soon designed for the GNR after he had left the LYR. The two units looked remarkably different but the resemblance in principle is there for all to see.

Be that as it may, the Gresley bogie became the GNR norm, was adopted for the East Coast Joint Stock and later the LNER, was put under many hundreds of carriages of the LNER pre-group constituents and was still considered sufficiently sophisticated to be adopted by BR in the 1950s for some of its *new* multiple unit stock. This might not be quite so glamorous an achievement as a glossy streamlined 'A4' 'Pacific', but in sheer passenger comfort terms it was certainly of benefit to far more people — and I did say at the beginning that carriages were about people!

The Gresley bogie utilized probably the finest four-wheel suspension ever adopted in Britain until quite modern days. Speaking from personal experience, its only serious rivals during the company period were the heavy LNWR and LMS twelve-wheel bogies and the LMS 9-foot four-wheeler (itself derived from the MR and LNWR types), all of which needed the stabilizing effect of screw couplings and side buffers for the best effect (see page 25). I well remember travelling to Newhaven from Leeds in 1948 when the contrast between the almost floating quality of the LNER corridor stock on its Gresley bogies was in marked contrast to the frightful antics of the Southern Railway equivalent on the boat train! At the same time, I cannot resist commenting that there were occasions when one could have wished that the East Coast had put as much effort into the carriage *interior* as it did into the wheels and suspension; however, back to the GNR.

Gresley's other principal carriage contribution was also related to wheels and suspension, namely carriage articulation wherein two adjacent carriage ends are carried on a single shared bogie. This too was a GNR innovation and will be re-addressed in later chapters; suffice to say at this point that between 1900 and 1914 the total effect of the GNR carriage revolution — for thus it was — turned out to be the dominant factor in LNER thinking from 1923 onwards. Of course, the fact that Gresley became

The first example of Gresley articulation, using the earlier GNR bogie, was East Coast Joint Stock twin corridor composite No 202/6, converted in 1905 from two 1890-built six-wheelers. In about 1914 it was transferred to GNR stock.

Top to bottom *GNR influence I — East Coast clerestory twelve-wheel corridor third class brake No 280 was one of five similar vehicles built at Cowlairs in 1901 to pure GNR style and outline.*

GNR influence II — ECJS kitchen car No 211 was built at York by the NER in 1914; again, the GNR stylistic influence is paramount. The NER-type chassis, full-length eaves panel and glass vane ventilators do, however, impart a slightly diluted GNR effect to the whole.

GNR influence III — Less well known than the ECJS was the GN/NER Joint Stock for the London-Newcastle route. GNR styling was again dominant as in this sleeping car, No 13 of 1909. The body is pure Gresley/GNR, but the NER bogies and chassis give it subtle points of difference. Identical carriages were also built on GNR chassis.

CME of the LNER may also have had something to do with it! But it was not without its technological justification.

A further contributory factor to the GNR stylistic dominance after 1922 was undoubtedly the East Coast Joint Stock. These vehicles, jointly owned by the GNR, NER and NBR, were used for the principal Anglo-Scottish services from King's Cross Although many were built at York (NER) and some at Cowlairs (NBR), the styling was normally standardized on GNR practice and coaches of basically GNR outline came out from all three locations. In fact, there is one still in existence at the NRM, a beautifully restored ECJS corridor third built by the NER at York as early as 1897 but to pure GNR style. It is true that some ECJS coaches (unlike their Midland or LNWR Scottish Joint Stock equivalent) were, during the twentieth century, built to non-GNR styling, but their influence was peripheral. This too is surprising, for the NER and NBR were by no means poor relations in the carriage field. Furthermore, whereas the LNWR and MR were absolutely dominant numerically in their respective Scottish Joint Stocks by comparison with their CR and GSWR partners, this did not really hold true for the East Coast triumvirate. Even now, therefore, it is still just a touch surprising that a railway like the GNR, which contributed less than 20% of the total LNER carriage fleet, should, in the event, have proved so dominant.

If any railway or its supporters had cause to be aggrieved by the GNR dominance in the LNER carriage field, it must surely have been the North Eastern. Second only to the GER amongst the LNER constituents in numerical terms, its carriages were, for the most part, vastly superior to most of those of the East Anglian company and, speaking from personal experience, infinitely preferable to most of those built by the GNR too. Of all the many individualistic aspects which ceased to exist at the 1923 grouping, the speedy decline of NER influence in purely carriage terms is in my opinion by a long way the most surprising of them all.

The NER was the largest of the LNER constituents, even Gresley allowed NER thinking to have more than a small place in locomotive affairs and its former officers achieved some management prominence in post-grouping days; yet its carriages seemed of little consequence after 1922 — extraordinary! This is even more inexplicable when one considers that at the turn of the century, the start of our story, NER carriage design was in the charge of that supreme carriage builder David Bain, later of Midland fame. In fact, there was more than a little collaboration between the NER and the Midland. In locomotive terms, the immortal Midland compounds were basically inspired by earlier NER experiments, and there was more than a little NER influence in latter-day Midland carriage design. Even their carriage liveries (crimson lake) were substantially similar — perhaps the 1923 grouping got it wrong!

I can offer no logical explanation for this seemingly anomalous state of affairs. It even transcended the eclipse of the LNWR styling by the MR version on the rival LMS for, as we have seen, the LNWR operating philosophy still tended to hold sway. All I can therefore do is to record the main elements of the situation as it seems from a distance of sixty or more years.

NER carriages were of the traditionally panelled kind in 1901. They were of either nineteenth century arc roof configuration or the more recent clerestory profile, a quite distinctive form which superimposed a clerestory deck on top of a basic arc roof shape without serious change of lower roof profile or bodyside styling. The latter was a particularly harmonious combination of eaves, window and waist panelling, largely attributable to David Bain. It withstood the transition to the MR in 1903, for many of Bain's carriages were not much more than NER-styled bodies married to Clayton's distinctive clerestory of 1896-7 vintage.

After Bain left, NER carriage design tended to become a bit confused — and maybe this was the problem. The roof profile became, fairly swiftly, the full semi-elliptical type, but the body styling, except for the livery, rang the changes in this manner of a debutante who could not quite make up her mind which dress she should wear for the Hunt Ball! There were experiments with straight-sided 'match-boarding' — somewhat aesthetically disastrous. There were also permutations within the 'traditional' field involving various combinations of square-cornered and round-cornered panelling; some carriages came out with top lights as an alternative to eaves panels and some did not, while corridor coaches could not quite make up their minds whether or not to suppress individual compartment doors — and so it went on. There was, in effect, no dominant and instantaneously recognisable NER approach in its latter years in the same sense as one can discern in, say, GNR, GWR, NBR or LSWR carriages, and this was a pity, for amongst all this confusion the NER built some quite splendid vehicles.

If there was a preferred single style towards the end of the pre-1922 era, it was perhaps best exemplified by the singularly well-proportioned gangwayed coaches which combined traditional panelling with something very closely approaching the Gresley pattern of elliptical roof with domed ends. The NER, possibly influenced by the GNR, adopted this profile with great enthusiasm and made some very beautiful carriages at its York works. Many of these were distinctly modern in their elimination of individual and draughty compartment doors and in their use of large picture windows. Unfortunately, the perverse British public was not always convinced (qv GWR developments — see page 136), so the poor old NER was forced to offer the older type as well; but in all essentials, the NER was probably rather more ahead of its time in terms of carriage amenity than most other companies. In terms of interior *layout* this was certainly so, and even after 1922 the Gresley-dominated LNER saw fit to continue building NER-styled corridor coaches for a year or two and to put a lot of ex-NER carriages on to Gresley pattern bogies. In this latter respect, of course, there was probably good technical reason,

GREAT NORTHERN & NORTH EASTERN JOINT STOCK . 9 .
GUARD
LUGGAGE
NORTH
EASTERN
RAILWAY
1021
LUGGAGE
THIRD
THIRD
646
N.E.R.
LUGGAGE

Left *Stylistic confusion on the NER is well represented by this group of four pictures. In order,* **top to bottom,** *they show: GN/NE Joint Stock corridor brake first No 9 in 'matchboard' style; NER elliptical roof non-corridor brake third No 1021 in traditionally panelled style: NER non-corridor third No 646 in square-panelled style with toplights instead of eaves panels; NER non-corridor brake composite No 3720 in round-panelled toplight style.*

as was also the case in the fitting of ex-NER corridor coaches with buckeye couplings and Pullman gangways after the grouping. Additionally, of course, this policy made economic sense. The NER had so many carriages that the LNER could not afford to ignore them, and their harmonization (in technical terms) with Gresley's GNR stock, combined with the relative newness of many of the carriage bodies, gave the LNER a substantial fleet, many of which lasted well into BR days.

North Eastern influence was also strong in the cross-country field (see Chapter 9), and its more specialized carriages, particularly its dining cars, could stand comparison with most. However, as with many other railways, it tended to lack the all round experience of such companies as the LNWR, GWR and MR — it was not a significant builder of sleeping cars, for example, save for its contribution to the GNR-dominated ECJS — so maybe its declining influence, post-1922, is not totally inexplicable; but it still seems surprising in retrospect.

Not too far behind the NER and GNR came the NBR, the largest of the Scottish railways before 1923, a considerable builder of railway carriages and in numerical terms above the Caledonian, its principal Scottish rival. The NBR was of course the dominant Scottish constituent of the LNER, but like the Caledonian in the LMS group, its carriage construction was insufficiently comprehensive, viewed against the needs of the post-1922 situation, to have any real long-term significance. In many ways this was unfortunate, for the North British had developed a quite distinctive stylistic approach. In terms of *type,* it was not too different from many other British systems, but its visual style, if not quite unique, was very characteristic indeed.

The NBR was, in carriage terms, the archetypal

Below *'To door or not to door?' — that seems to have been the question on the NER when in came to corridor stock. These two first class brakes Nos 1950 and 1453 are typical, and both are, in all essentials, identical. Discounting the obvious door issue, other interesting detail differences are underframe design, the presence or absence of a guard's lookout, recessed doors and so on. Both versions also appeared with each other's style of panelling! At the same time, one cannot help but remark on the extremely stylish end product, no matter what the design minutiae may have been.*

Left *The distinctive and very consistent NBR carriage styling is well seen in this period view of Tayport station* circa *1910. The scene is dominated by non-corridor four and six-wheelers, all embodying the familiar NBR cove roof profile and two-layer panelling* (Author's collection).

Below *This crisp view of third class carriage No 1730 shows an interesting NBR alternative to the corridor approach. It is a lavatory carriage with an intermediate side corridor giving access to the one toilet at the left-hand end. Almost certainly, it is this type of vehicle which forms the leading carriage of the train pictured on page 98.*

Bottom *Typical of the best NBR corridor stock was full third No 1793, built in 1906 and branded for the 'Lothian Coast Express'. It was also photographed at the same time branded 'Fife Coast Express' and was actually built as part of a set of trains for the Aberdeen services!*

Scottish railway. Its twin-layer panelling style, while not quite unique to itself (the GNSR and HR had both tried it out to some extent), was most certainly the most dominant single visual influence in carriage terms north of the border before 1923 and was not really mirrored by any English railway. Its livery, however, like that of the rival Caledonian, was by no means innovative compared with its competitors. It was one of many systems which employed an all-red colour scheme (not very different from that of the MR and NER) and, to be frank, had no prime claims to virtue. In fact, the NBR was, in twentieth-century carriage terms, something of a low-key railway compared with the occasionally ostentatious characteristics of its Scottish rival, the Caledonian, or, particularly, its East Coast partners, specifically the GNR. For instance, just as in the case of the CR (West Coast Joint Stock) or the GSWR (Midland Joint Stock), it virtually abrogated East Coast Joint design to the GNR (usually) and NER (occasionally), and with far less cause, for it was larger than either of its Scottish contemporaries. All things being equal, one might have expected NBR influence to have been proportionally more dominant (*vis-à-vis* the CR or GSWR) than, in effect, it turned out to be after 1922, especially when one considers the fact that it was the NBR which first introduced sleeping carriages to Britain, way back in Victorian times.

Towards the end of its independent existence, the NBR was one of the earlier railways to experiment with metal-clad carriage exteriors. This it did with the same sort of dull and ponderous styling as was exemplified, for example, by the LSWR with its 'Ironclad' carriages (page 128). The LNER was not wildly impressed, unlike the Southern, and this pioneering use of 'new technology' was in the event not adopted by its post-1922 successor until some 25 or more years later, and then in very different style in the form of the much maligned but rather good-looking post-Second World War LNER carriages of the 1940s designed by Edward Thompson (see Volume 2). Meantime, the NBR's best claim to fame lay probably in its corridor express stock of *circa* 1906 — a series of distinctly attractive and well thought out carriages fully competitive and compatible with most of the opposition and, in most respects, well ahead of their time.

As for the other contributors to the LNER carriage story, there are but two serious contenders, the GNSR and the hitherto unmentioned Hull and Barnsley Railway. The latter of course was in the 'under 100 route miles' category; furthermore, it was absorbed by the NER *before* the 1923 grouping. For most of its independent life, it endured something of a hand to mouth existence and could never be regarded as one of the British 'blue chip' companies. Nevertheless, it did produce some quite well thought out carriages even though its long-term influence was negligible.

The GNSR was probably even more impecunious than the Highland. Its ambitions never ventured much further afield than its own somewhat restricted territorial area, and in consequence its carriages were never much more than were seemly in the immediately local context. It had a fairly unique livery of darkish red and cream (not dissimilar, in fact, to the first post-1947 BR standard style), but this sort of claim to distinction was far too ephemeral to be of any consequence after 1922. It was, in truth, one of those many railways which, in spite of their local following, contributed nothing of profound significance to subsequent developments. A harsh judgement? Maybe — but not without foundation.

The LMS and LNER constituents between them owned something like 70% of the total passenger-carrying vehicles in existence in Great Britain at the

Three austere, almost brutal-looking steel-panelled composite dining cars were built for the NBR by Cravens of Sheffield in 1919. They were reputedly, at 47 tons, the heaviest carriages inherited by the LNER, but their influence was not profound Although later given buckeye couplings and Pullman gangways, a common LNER modification, they lasted barely twenty years, not especially good for a carriage.

Top *The almost forgotten Hull and Barnsley Railway operated some quite well-equipped carriages in its later years. This is No 25, a non-corridor brake composite, with intermediate lavatories accessed by short internal passageways* (Staffordshire County Record Office).

Above *This picture seems, somehow, symbolic of the Great North of Scotland Railway. The chronically inadequate four-wheel third is probably the more typical, but the bogie corridor composite brake is very good in both visual and accommodation terms. Its livery (red and white) was unusual, attractive and distinctively applied — somewhat in the LSWR style (see opposite).*

time of the grouping, and by far the biggest single contribution to the rest was made by the Great Western Railway. At the same time, although this great company was second in number only to the LNWR in 1921, after the grouping it had to take fourth place below the Southern Railway in the carriage numbers game and it is with this latter company that we must first deal before going on to the unique situation which applied to the carriage policy of the GWR.

The Southern Group

The Southern group was the smallest of the 'Big Four' in 1923 and by far the smallest of the three groups which were formed by amalgamation of erstwhile somewhat similarly sized pre-group companies. Yet when its carriages were totalled, it came up into an easy third place, well above the GWR. The 1921 breakdown was as follows:

LB & SCR	1871
LSWR	2649
SE & CR	2766
Total	7286

Two or three points should be made from the outset. First and most obvious is the fact that the Southern and its constituents were more passenger orientated than any other of the 'Big Four'. Allowing for the railway's absolute smallness, a carriage total greater by 1,000 or so than that of the GWR (which operated 1,000 more route miles than the SR) betokens a considerable difference in operating pattern. Not only that, but when it is further considered that there were more carriages on the newly-formed Southern Railway alone than in the whole of Scotland, which had nearly twice the railway route mileage (3,824 compared with 2,060), it will be seen how different indeed was this smallest of the amalgamated railways — and this was inevitably reflected in the carriage types it received from its constituents.

On the face of things, there was not too much disparity in totals between the SE & CR and the LSWR, and even the Brighton was not exactly an insignificant third, but there were important differences in emphasis. Two of the three systems were in essence suburban, and only one of them (the LSWR) was a 'main-line' railway in the accepted sense. This affected carriage designs and, in consequence, only the LSWR had what might be termed a comprehensive range of vehicle types comparable with those of the GWR or the other principal railways heading north and north-west from London. It might therefore be expected that, all things being equal, the LSWR would probably dominate, even though the SE & CR had marginally more carriages. To some extent this was true, but the actuality was rather more subtle and all three railways were very different.

The LSWR has embraced the traditionally panelled carriage with considerable enthusiasm and remarkable visual consistency. It entered the twentieth century with the fairly common arc roof profile which soon gave way to a sort of flattened elliptical shape very similar to that used by the GNR in the pre-clerestory, pre-Gresley days. Eaves and waist panels were quite deep and remained so while woodern bodies were made, and from the waist upwards the bodyside of an LSWR carriage was probably nearer to that of the GER than any other. There, however, most comparisons ended, for, like quite a few British lines, the LSWR had a quite unique livery which virtually defies verbal description. 'Salmon pink and brown' is quite a common nomenclature, but both tones were more than normally subtle. The upper panels were a sort of orange —pink shade, but not really the colour of a salmon, either the fresh or the canned variety. The

Below *Arc roof bogie tri-composite (1st/2nd/3rd class) No 485, typifies the LSWR approach to carriage building as it entered the twentieth century. This type of carriage contained all the seeds of that which was to become characteristic of the South Western in later years.*

Bottom *This carriage style, in effect the older form with changed roof shape and deepened eaves panelling, is probably more characteristic of the LSWR than any other in the pre-1923 period. Lavatory tri-composite No 633 is also a reminder that the LSWR retained three classes for longer than many railways and regularly used non-corridor stock with lavatories rather than the gangwayed equivalent. This example had no fewer than six lavatories, one per compartment. Its brake-ended equivalent is preserved at the National Railway Museum.*

The basic LSWR panelling style lasted almost to the railway grouping, and on the way developed some distinctly good-looking variants, including two small batches of clerestory dining cars. No 79, one of the series given large picture windows, is shown here, carried on the new outside-framed bogies also adopted for the 'Ironclads'.

nearest fishy equivalent in colour terms is probably the smoked version! As for the brown —well, what is brown? It was very dark indeed and in some light conditions took on a dark reddish hue, reminiscent of, say, an even darker version of the LNWR carmine lake. In other light circumstances it could display sort of bronze-green overtones, and at its most extreme could seem almost black —'invisible' brown might be an appropriate phase. The combined effect of the two colours (if the NRM has got it even nearly correct on the restored LSWR tri-composite) was, however, an uncommonly handsome carriage finish, especially in association with a sage green engine.

This distinctive colour scheme was applied to a wide range of carriage types from suburban non-corridors to a small fleet of corridor carriages of particularly harmonious shape. The LSWR built its corridor coaches rather wider than its non-corridor stock and this allowed the slightly flattened elliptical roof to follow a somewhat more curvaceous profile across the centre. The nearest contemporary equivalent was probably the cove roof corridor stock of the LNWR, and I consider both approaches to be amongst the aesthetic leaders at this time. The fact that both companies employed unique liveries may also have made a contribution.

Two main changes and a few minor ones took place during the pre-grouping period. Firstly was the electrification of some services from 1915 onwards, which will be considered in detail in Chapter 15. This went with a change from the two-colour livery to an all-over green shade on the electric lines. This, in the event, proved the dominant colour factor in the Southern Railway period. The second major change was the gradual introduction of steel sheeting for the outer body panels of LSWR coaches. At first this was associated with traditional woodern beading strips and, when painted, the carriages looked no different. However, when the raised beading was finally abandoned on later LSWR corridor stock, a somewhat different sort of carriage styling stood revealed.

Applied solely to corridor coaches which were quickly nicknamed 'Ironclads', this newer LSWR treatment produced a vehicle not all that different in shape from its forbears, but what might be termed their 'texture' was something new. To be honest,

No ex-works pictures seem to have survived of the LSWR 'Ironclads' when new in 1921, but this view of Southern Railway No 7714 shows one of them, little changed externally when converted for inspection use many years later. It started life as a brake first with pantry and kitchen between the three compartments and the van. The inward taper towards the guard's lookout was a characteristic feature and similar to that of the LYR (see page 104). The general style of these carriages, including the lookout arrangement, became the basis of early Southern Railway developments after 1922.

they seemed to lack something of the visual finesse of earlier LSWR corridor coaches, but like most things South Western they were very solidly built and their influence was wholly dominant in the early stages of Southern Railway long-distance thinking. It could hardly have been otherwise, in retrospect. The LSWR was the only one of the SR constituents to have any real experience in the corridor field and even then not much. The Brighton had none at all, and the SE & CR only one complete train, so by adopting the LSWR corridor coach as the basis for this new design, the Southern CME (R.E.L. Maunsell) was taking the sensible option. He could hardly be accused of prejudice since he was an ex-SE & CR man.

Thus the LSWR carriage was highly influential in setting two aspects of post-1922 Southern thinking — livery and long-distance gangwayed stock. That, however, is about as far as it went. Unlike the LMS and LNER, the non-corridor story was quite a different matter and took a somewhat unusual and remarkable turn, the origins of which were firmly rooted in the carriages of the other pre-group constituents of the Southern system. There was no such thing as a 'standard' Southern non-corridor, nor even the semblance of one.

While most of the story must, perforce, wait until Volume 2, one quite extraordinary fact must be stated at this point. The Southern Railway never built any locomotive-hauled non-corridor stock for the whole of its independent existence! It relied entirely on its pre-group inheritance. This was, of course, very much bound up with the continuous electrification of the SR which enabled pre-1923 stock to soldier on in the non-electrified areas. However, even in the electrified field, totally new stock of a purely suburban type was not found to be necessary in any great quantity until after the 1939-45 war. However, we must leave it at that for the moment and revert to the discussion of the pre-1923 situation.

Second in size, but marginally first of the SR constituents, in carriage numbers was the SE & CR. This was a working partnership established in 1899 between the South Eastern Railway and the London Chatham and Dover Railway which remained nominally independent until the grouping. To all intents and purposes, however, the SE & CR functioned as a single railway during the twentieth century and it will be thus considered in this account.

The SE & CR inherited from its partners a motley fleet of pretty appalling carriages, it being a moot point in the 1890s which of the two was the more disgraceful (probably the LCDR). Fortunately, the SER had began to improve matters, and in Harry Wainwright, the SE & CR inherited from the SER the services of one of the most forward-looking engineers of the day. His locomotive artistry is well known (*vide* his preserved 4-4-0 No 737 at the NRM, one of the visual high points of the whole collection), but what is far less often recorded is his interest in carriage matters. He had in fact begun to take a grip on things when he became Carriage and Wagon Superintendent of the SER in 1896, and in carriage terms, there was no break in SER development when the SE & CR was formed.

Wainwright's preferred visual lines were the low-waisted type — very reminiscent of that pursued by the LNWR — and this became the SE & CR norm but with a roof profile somewhat more elevated, a sort of cross between the pure cove roof and the high elliptical form. A particularly distinctive visual point was the elevated guard's 'lookout' which projected above normal roof height on brake-ended carriages. It was, perhaps inevitably, referred to as a 'birdcage' and it remained thus named to the very end, well into BR days; these carriages lasted a very long time!

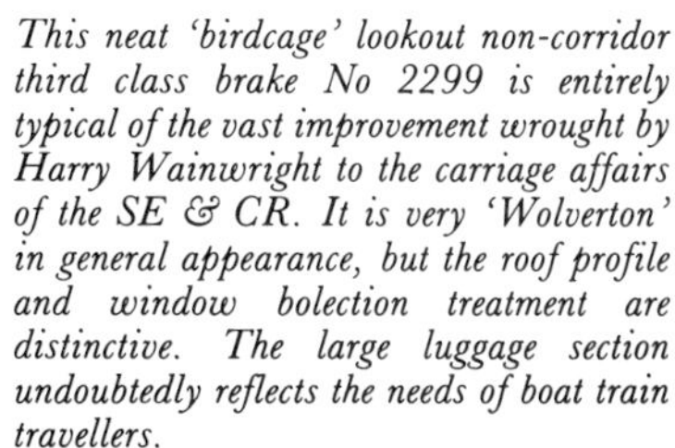
This neat 'birdcage' lookout non-corridor third class brake No 2299 is entirely typical of the vast improvement wrought by Harry Wainwright to the carriage affairs of the SE & CR. It is very 'Wolverton' in general appearance, but the roof profile and window bolection treatment are distinctive. The large luggage section undoubtedly reflects the needs of boat train travellers.

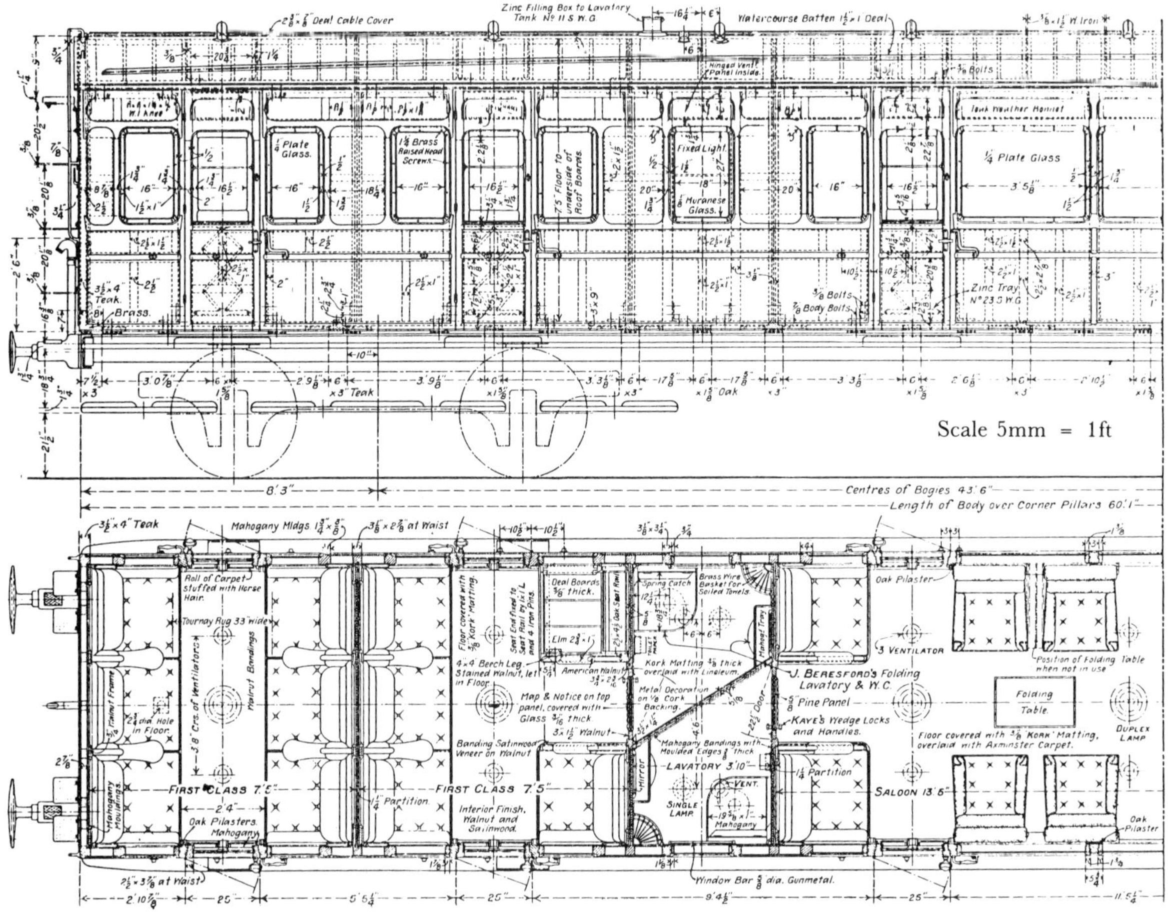

Scale 5mm = 1ft

Figure 36 *Elevation and plan of a typical, later vintage first and second class SE & CR bogie non-corridor, embodying the particularly distinctive SE & CR variation of traditional panelling. Even at first perusal, the self-evident high quality is apparent. Note, particularly, the spacious compartment dimensions.*

Below *Later SE & CR stock displayed a slightly flattened top to the raised guard's lookout such as shown by No S3321S, still looking remarkably good in early BR days. This type of lavatory non-corridor carriage was the favoured SB & CR type for most of its expresses; once again, note the long van portion. Just visible on the right is an example of the later SE & CR styling with modified traditional panelling.*

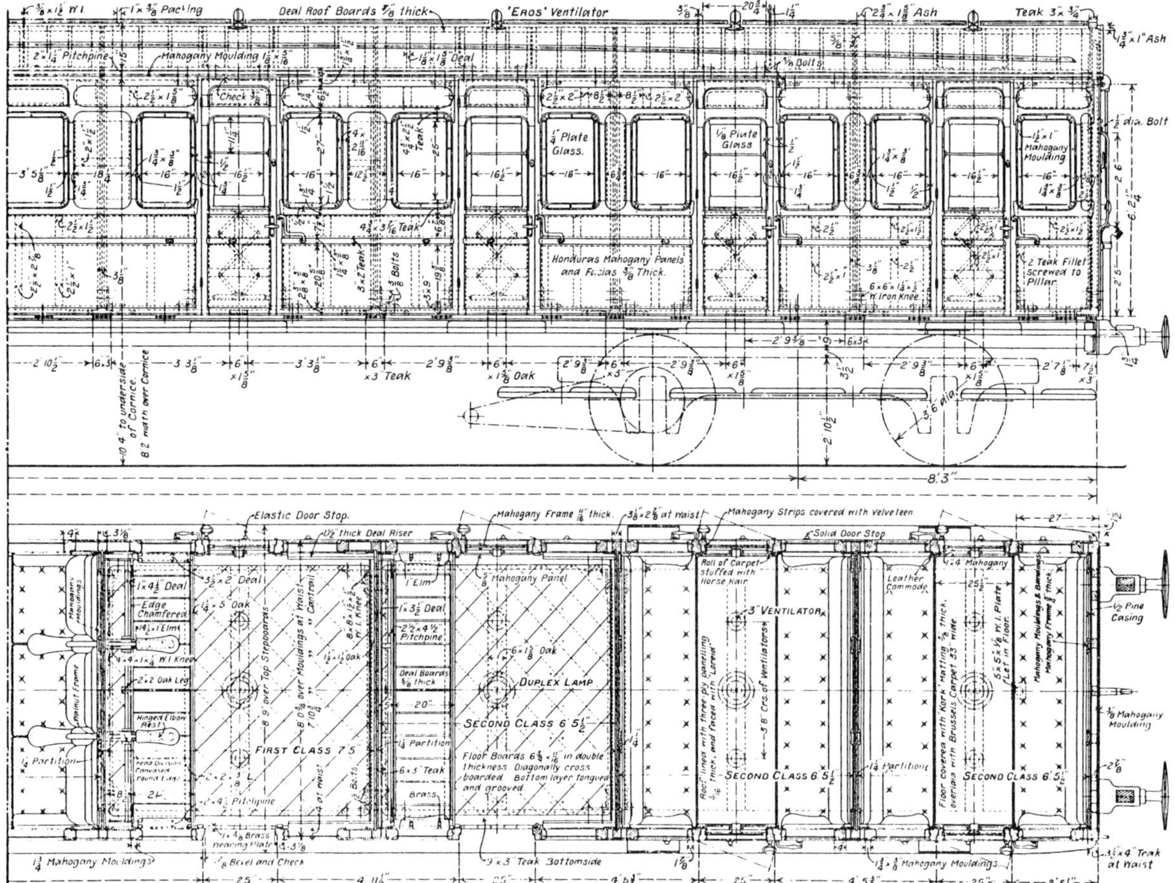

Decked out in rather austere dark lake livery of no particular distinction compared with that of, say, the MR or NER, SE & CR carriages were nevertheless distinctly well thought out in terms of passenger amenity. However, in one or two specifics the SE & CR carriages did not develop along quite such progressive lines as did those of the LSWR and this discrepancy was mainly in the long-distance field.

The SE & CR, like the LB & SCR, was a fairly tightly knit territorial company and had no really lengthy main line. London to the Channel ports of Kent was about its limit and its most prestigious services were its boat trains. Even these flagship turns (excusing the pun) were of relatively minor significance in numerical terms compared with the need of the SE & CR to provide thousands of suburban seats for the commuter services, particularly in replacement of some of the primeval relics built by its two constituents during Victorian days. In consequence, Wainwright placed very high priority in proving decent suburban stock, to the almost total exclusion of more elaborate vehicles, and did so to good effect. Hundreds of bogie coaches were built, mostly formed into neat sets with 'birdcage' brakes, and although they were undoubtedly of high seating capacity, there were plenty of them and they were a distinct cut above their predecessors in all respects. They were also a fair bit better than the suburban stock of some other London-based lines too — the GNR and NLR spring readily to mind as being two of the worst offenders. Thus, by the time of the grouping the SE & CR had virtually replaced all the pre-Edwardian horrors and possessed a fine, modern fleet of substantial and well-built non-corridor coaches which formed the basis of the subsequent post-1922 electrification. Some later examples, although keeping the 'birdcages', abandoned the low-waisted style for a very neat, part-square-cornered traditional approach to the panelling.

Meanwhile, what of the more prestigious trains? In this context the SE & CR was disadvantaged in

This turn-of-the-century bogie first/second class lavatory non-corridor in the old varnished mahogany livery is typical of the Stroudley carriage style as developed by Lawson Billinton in the 1890s for the Brighton line.

two respects — distance and catering. Dealing with the latter first, the SE & CR is only the second railway so far considered in this chapter where the role of the Pullman Car Company becomes relevant (the Caledonian was the other). The position of the Pullman Company was somewhat curious in the British context and is considered later, but as far as the SE & CR was concerned, its chief task was to provide the train catering and it was probably the principal provider of the up-market luxury as well. The preserved carriage *Topaz* in SE & CR colours at the NRM probably says all. Thus the SE & CR could not offer much experience in this field to the new Southern system. This in itself might not have mattered, but the distance factor made things more difficult, the SE & CR having no long-distance schedules of much more than 1½-2 hours maximum.

In spite of Wainwright's vast improvement in the suburban field, he seems to have seen no need to adopt corridors for the boat trains. Instead, he opted for long-distance 'lavatory' stock and very good it was too, as might be expected of him. There was plenty of seating space and much provisioning of second class accommodation (important on boat trains), but not until the very end of the period under review, in 1920 after Wainwright had gone, did the company finally adopt corridor coaches for its better trains. To be fair, the SE & CR had built its first corridor coaches in 1907 — mainly to run through to other railways — but in terms of its own domestic needs it stayed faithful to the non-corridor lavatory alternative. The 1920 corridor carriages were few in number and steel panelled, but it was only at the very end of its independent existence that the company ordered some new corridor boat trains. They came out (mostly after the grouping) with very distinctive 'matchboard' lower panelling but they were too little and too late to have much lasting effect on SR design.

The third contributor to the Southern fleet was the LB & SCR, an even more territorially compact system than the SE & CR. It held (and still holds) a popular and romantic place in the minds of many railway enthusiasts, but it has to be said that the reality often belied the romance in purely carriage terms. The Southern inherited a distinctly mixed bag of assets from the Brighton line.

Its basic carriage style was unreservedly Victorian, owing most of its visual characteristics to William Stroudley, later modified by Robert Billinton in the

In 1903, this carriage was built for the LB & SCR with the new umber and cream livery. Although similar in style to that pictured above, the more cramped nature of this third class coach is readily apparent.

The so-called 'Balloon' stock of the LB & SCR undoubtedly displayed the most conspicuous variant of the full elliptical roof ever adopted in Britain. This is non-corridor tri-composite No 629, in which only the first class compartments could gain access to the lavatories. Regrettably, for they were by no means inferior vehicles, this style did not take really firm root on the Brighton system.

1890s. It was of traditionally panelled, arc roof configuration, and at the turn of the century by no means behind the times. Indeed, when fitted with a clerestory (as some vehicles were) it was a distinctly handsome profile, nowhere better exemplified than by the magnificent 1897 Royal Train. However, things tended to get stuck in a groove at this point, with only the occasional sporadic exceptions during the Edwardian period.

The 'Brighton' changed its livery from varnished mahogany to a pleasing umber and white (more or less matching that of the normal Pullman livery) in 1903, but little else seemed to change. In part, this must be put down to Billinton's quite remarkable efforts during the 1890s to replace earlier stock. He introduced bogie carriages in 1894 to a more or less standard 48 ft x 8 ft dimension and a wide variety of designs began to appear, mostly non-corridor, non-lavatory. These continued in construction well into the present century but with little real change or improvement in the types built. Some few types had lavatories, but none had corridors, and the Brighton never built a gangwayed train for itself although it did talk about it! Compartments were often cramped and the whole ethos seemed dominated by the suburban requirement of the South London area.

This in itself would not be particularly surprising but it was exacerbated by the generally short-distance trips which LB & SCR trains ran, combined with the fact, as on the SE & CR, the Pullman Company had carved quite a nice little niche for itself in terms of higher value trade. The 'Southern Belle' was a most famous LB & SCR train, but apart from its engine there was little that was 'Brighton' about it, save for its destination.

In 1905, the LB & SCR made one of its two or three pre-1923 attempts to break the mould when it leapt abruptly from the 'basic Victorian' to the 'Edwardian monumental' style by adopting an ultra-high elliptical roof for some of its carriages. This seemed something of a shock to the system and the vehicles were quickly nicknamed 'Balloons' because of their roof profile. Length and width also increased from the Billinton standard to some 54 ft x 8 ft 6 in, but not many were built even though the variety of types was quite comprehensive. They were used for the better, longer-distance trains and boat trains, and a nine-coach special set of broadly similar, first-class-only stock was used for the 'City Limited' in 1907; but there it seemed to stick, save for a few 'Balloon' railmotor coaches (see Chapter 15).

Part of the reason for the slow forward movement on the LB & SCR was the above-mentioned Billinton re-stocking and the creaming off of the best traffic by the Pullmans, but a second contributory factor was the introduction of electrification in 1909, for which services new stock was built. This is considered in Chapter 15, but it reduced, in absolute terms, the need for many new locomotive-hauled carriages to be put into service. It merely allowed the more notorious nineteenth-century examples to be removed from the scene as electrification advanced.

Thus, even more than the SE & CR, the Brighton company came to the Southern system with a very limited range of carriages, and most of these looked distinctly old-fashioned by comparison with those of the LSWR and SE & CR. However, as we have seen, many of them were in fact quite new and, like those of the other Southern constituents, survived well after the grouping and played their part as electrification expanded in the 1920s and 1930s.

In consequence of the widely disparate inheritances acquired by the system in 1923 — and their approximately equal balance in both age and numerical terms — the Southern Railway was not faced with any clear cut options as to future carriage policy. In the event, it followed the path of expediency and economy. Thus, in spite of the mild SE & CR experiment with corridor stock, LSWR practice dominated in the long-distance sphere; in the short distance field, however, all three companies had produced a fair quantity of quite new stock, none of which had any prime claim to consideration. That of the SE & CR was probably the best and that of the LB & SCR probably the most outdated. All had sufficient life left in them for the Southern not to have to spend too much time debating the point, especially when taken together with the complications of electrification — and there we must leave it for the moment.

The Great Western group

Finally we turn in this pre-1923 review of styles to that most idiosyncratic of all British railways, the Great Western, and to those companies which were absorbed into its activities in 1923. 'Absorbed' is not too strong a word to use, for the pre-1923 GWR was dominant in its group in a way unmatched by any other British company. It vied with the LNWR for dominance in the pre-1923 scene, but in route mile terms was undoubtedly 'King', so much so that when the new boundaries were drawn, the GWR group took the name of its largest constituent company. Psychologically, if nothing else, this gave it the edge over its newly formed competitors the LMS, LNER and SR, even though it had to fall to third place in the total hierarchy and last place in the numerical count of carriages owned. It was not often that the GWR came last in anything! However, it had 'history' on its side, a trump card which it played with a monotonous and at times irritating frequency, and not always justified by events, if truth be told.

The trouble with the GWR was that its many and real virtues were marred at times by an apparent inability on its part, or that of its supporters, to see any virtue in anything which did not emanate from the 'fount of all virtue', Swindon Works! Not for nothing was it nicknamed 'God's Wonderful Railway' — there were times when it thought it was. Only the GWR could celebrate its centenary (in 1935) rather less than 100 years after it opened for business — and the whole nonsense was repeated in 1985 with 'GW 150', no less than 37 years *after* the GWR had 'Gone With Regret', as someone put it!

Tongue in cheek though these remarks may be — and, when advanced by rival railways, tinged with not a little envy — they do encapsulate a kind of reality which must be accepted (and understood) if the GWR contribution is to be properly assessed. In this respect the carriage story is no different and, like so many things GW, its twentieth-century story cannot entirely be divorced from the aftermath of the nineteenth-century epic of Brunel and the Broad Gauge, well recorded elsewhere.

Brunel's broad gauge Great Western ran its last trains in 1892 but left three vital elements which were to pervade the twentieth-century story. Firstly it made the GWR *different* from the others, a point of emphasis which still seemed to have a positive virtue to the company even after it had to run its trains on the same 4 ft 8½ in track as everyone else. Secondly, it gave the railway a more generous structure gauge which allowed it to build bigger vehicles, in terms of height and width, than most of its rivals save possibly for the 'Johnny-come-lately' GCR (page 117). Lastly, and possibly of most significance in the twentieth-century context, the genuine sadness with which the 7-foot gauge was consigned to oblivion gave the GWR in the 1890s a once and for all chance of a new beginning which was, realistically, denied to its rivals. I am inclined to believe that the sheer dominance of GWR thinking in the early twentieth-century is not unconnected with a desire on the part of the company itself to prove something, having lost the 'Battle of the Gauges'! That it did most certainly 'prove something' is a matter of historical fact, and one could even draw interesting geo-political comparisons with the economic performance of West Germany and Japan in the aftermath of the 1939-45 disaster. In fact the comparison is not so wide of the mark, for we are back to the 'people' element again, and the GWR had some very strong people.

The first name to quote in the carriage context is William Dean. He had the unenviable task of seeing the GWR through the broad/standard gauge transition, and this meant not only new engines but new coaches as well. He came up with a distinctly clever 'pendulum' type of bogie suspension and some delectably styled clerestory carriages. They owed something to the broad gauge, not least their livery, but in most important aspects they were a new concept. Dean introduced corridors, built a splendid set of new vehicles for Queen Victoria (save for her own saloon whose carcass she insisted on having re-mounted on a new frame!) and, when the GWR moved into the 1900s, Dean had set the company on a new course which it never totally deserted until much later.

The Dean clerestories may have been nineteenth century in concept but they were very much an integral part of the early twentieth-century GWR. Of all the carriages mentioned so far, they probably encapsulate more than any others the essential 'Victorian Inheritance' which was addressed in Chapter 1. Their only serious rivals were probably the LNWR, MR and GNR clerestories, all of which had nineteenth-century origins but considerable twentienth-century ramifications. Roof shape excepted, the architecture of a Dean coach, in the form of the GWR version of traditional British panelling style, became 'standard GW' until the company abandoned raised panel beading strips on its carriages. Interestingly, too, even when the GWR went to an all-metal body covering with 'painted panelling', the actual proportions of the pseudo-panelling were pure Dean!

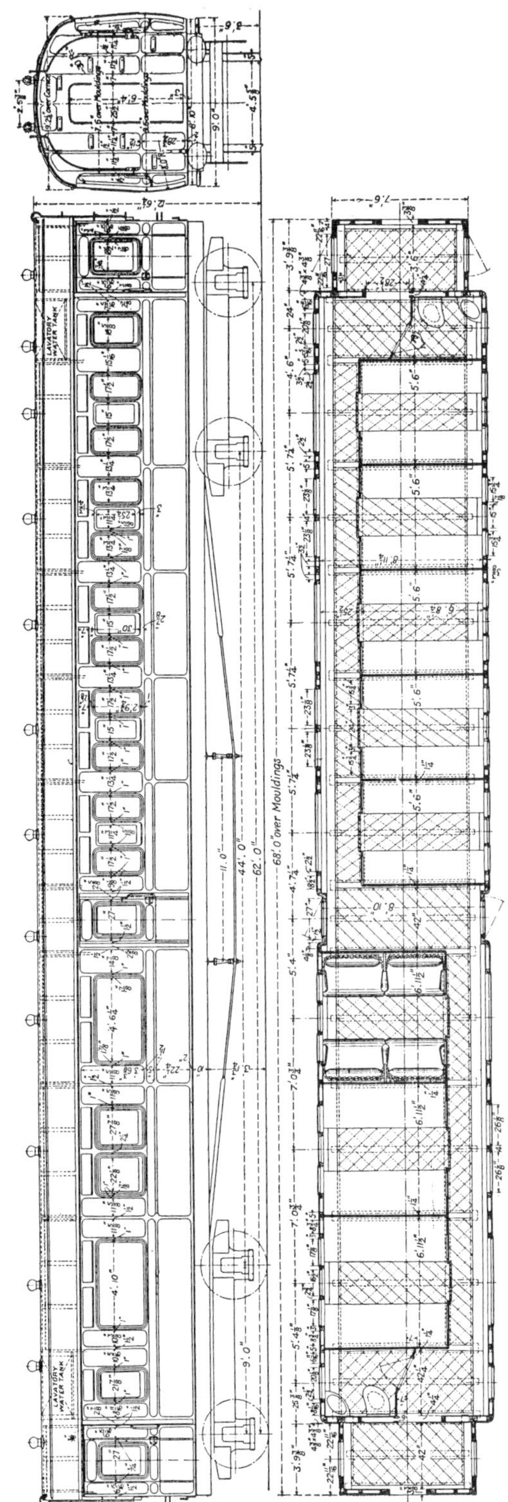

Figure 37 *Great Western 68 ft by 9 ft 6 in 'Dreadnought' corridor composite gives a clear impression of all the significant features in Churchward's huge carriages of 1905. Individual compartment doors were omitted and the carriages given recessed entrances because of the great width. For all its great size, one must note the less than generous compartment dimension between partitions. Moreover, arising from the considerable width, the first class compartments were clearly intended to seat eight rather than the more customary four or six passengers favoured by other railways, and the thirds might even be expected to take five per side at busy times.*

Had it not been for the gigantic nature of his successor, William Dean may have given more credit in the whole business than has come his way, but the man who followed him was George Jackson Churchward. Now Churchward designed locomotives of more than seminal significance but he also put the GWR well to the fore in carriage design. At this range in time, it is a moot point just how much of a particular design concept is personally attributable to the man in charge, but it does seem that Churchward did take a more direct interest than many of his contemporaries. Be as it may, however, what is certain is that shortly after he arrived on the scene, GWR carriage design underwent a quantum change — at least superficially.

Retaining the Dean panelling, Churchward in 1904 superimposed a high elliptical roof and stretched the carriage length to no less than 70 feet and its width to 9 ft 6 in. Not surprisingly, in view of their incredibly massive size by any British standard, then or subsequently, they were known as 'Dreadnoughts', an allusion to a Royal Navy battleship design of the time. In fact, length apart, their absolute dimensions have never been exceeded in British carriage history. Even the modern-day BR MkIII carriage is contained within a sort of standard 9 ft wide by 12 ft 6 in high 'envelope', even though its length is greater.

The 'Dreadnoughts', splendid though they were — and we shall meet them again — went a bit too far for contemporary thought. Their 9 ft 6 in width meant that no company except the GWR would take them, and this, along with the 70 foot length, even caused problems on the GW itself. Churchward therefore tried again, this time with the so-called 'Concertina' approach, a curious and probably rather expensive alternative, whereby a 70 foot coach was combined with entrance doors set back from the main body line. This must have caused horrendous manufacturing complications and, of course, gave rise to the nickname. It was designed to keep the projecting exterior fittings (handles, etc) within the 9 foot width, a more acceptable system-wide standard, and it had some success although it was not universally accepted.

Top *Brake third No 950, photographed ex-works, gives a clear impression of the carriage styling adopted by the GWR under Dean. The more celebrated clerestories embodied the same lower roof shape with its compound curvature. Note particularly the considerable attention to livery and lining detail even on a humble four-wheeler.*

Above *This superb view of 'Concertina' brake composite No 7672 clearly shows the distinctive characteristics of Churchward's second essay into corridor coach construction.*

This sort of 'hit and miss' approach can seem, at times, to be at odds with the normally accepted view of Churchward's sureness of approach, but it was not until he finally gave up some of the delusions of grandeur that he finally arrived at a fairly universally acceptable norm in the shape of his 'Toplight' carriages, so called because of their upper windows in the zone of what would be the eaves panels of many coaches. The LNWR and NER, to mention but two, also tried this idea. The 'Toplight' stock became very characteristic of the pre-1923 GWR, whether in the gangwayed or non-corridor field, and established standards not incompatible with those elsewhere; but they were not perfect. For one thing, Churchward had to yield to pressure and reinstate doors to all the compartments of corridor coaches — a fact which will be further examined in Chapter 10. Secondly, the finished size of a standard 'Toplight' at 56-57 ft × 9 ft or so was not dissimilar to that arrived at by many other British companies which did not have the advantages of the generous GWR structure gauge. True, the 'Toplight' story had started with the 70-foot length, but common sense had to prevail. However, a 56-60 feet long by 9 feet wide carriage was pretty commonplace long before the grouping; at the end, therefore, the GWR was not greatly different.

The GWR further compromised its position by abandoning its distinctive chocolate and cream livery in 1908 during the 'Toplight' period in favour, at first, of an all-brown livery of catastrophic dullness which was only slightly redeemed when, in 1913, it moved to an all-over dark red livery whose shade was about that of the SE & CR or North Staffordshire, but lacked the essential richness of, say, that of the MR or NER. Fortunately, it was redeemed by a fair profusion of gilt lining and embellishment and the overall effect was pleasing. At the same time, one cannot help feeling that the abandonment of the historic chocolate and cream was a foolish thing to do. The LNWR, for all its economy mindedness, would not, one feels, have so readily abandoned its own 'hallmark' livery and it is not without significance that at the time of the grouping the GWR grasped the nettle and reinstated its famous colour scheme.

Below *The first 'Toplights' retained the 70-foot length, thus allowing no fewer than ten compartments to be fitted into the full third.*

Bottom *The most familiar GWR 'Toplights' were the 57-foot corridors, here represented by one of the 1915 series of thirds, No 3923. By now, the GW had adopted angle-trussed underframes, an idea gradually taken up by most British companies. The carefully applied all-lake livery almost completely hides the fact that this is a flush-sided steel-panelled carriage* (T.J. Edgington collection).

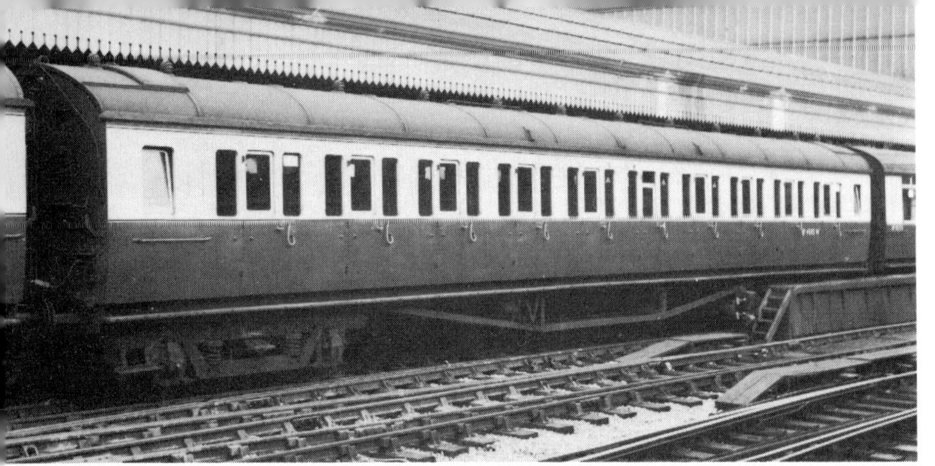

Compared with vehicles produced in the Edwardian era, GWR carriages at the end of the pre-group period became rather uninspired in visual terms. This is one of two somewhat experimental 1924 built 70 ft 8 ¼ in ten-compartment corridor thirds, No 4502 of the early bow-ended era, photographed at Birmingham Snow Hill in 1953. Vehicles of this general style superseded the 'Toplights' and will be considered in more detail in Volume 2 (T.J. Edgington collection).

This 1938 view on Aldermaston troughs shows three generations of GWR coaches. Leading is a clerestory non-corridor third, followed by a fully panelled 'Toplight' corridor brake composite with a post-grouping flush-sided non-corridor third brake bringing up the rear.

Below *The Taff Vale Railway's most noteworthy contribution to carriage development was in the field of the steam railmotor, a concept fully explored in Chapter 15. This view shows one of the 1906 batch, engine unit No 14 with coachwork by Brush of Loughborough.*

Meanwhile, carriage design itself tended to stagnate on the GWR after the 'Toplights'. There was an interesting and significant move towards steel panelling, replacing the erstwhile wood treatment, but stylistically a sort of dull complacency set in. 'Toplights' continued to be built with the new style steel-panelled treatment, but one gets the feeling, as with locomotive design, that some 20-25 years after the abolition of the broad gauge the GWR began to rest on its laurels and did not really take a subsequent firm grip on the situation until well after the grouping. What is certain is that other railways caught up and passed the GWR during the 1920s and 1930s in many respects, a point which will be taken up in more detail in the next volume.

Nevertheless, sheer size of operation decreed that the GWR influence would dominate after 1923, regardless of any inherent complacency, so it only remains to be seen what, if anything, its smaller constituent companies had to offer. The 1921 statistics for the '100-plus-route-mile' railways tend, in this context, to be all revealing in terms of passenger carrying vehicles:

GWR	5646
Cambrian	221
Taff Vale	316
Total	6183

Even if one adds even smaller concerns like the Barry Railway or the Rhymney Railway, their influence seems hardly likely to have been profound — and so it turned out to be.

We have already seen that even where one of the 'Big Four' such as the LMS or LNER absorbed several quite large fleets, the fate of the 'small fry' was pretty well guaranteed to a sort of oblivion. Only the Southern Railway showed signs of registering the nature of all its constituents, and it really had no 'small fry'. The GWR was diametrically opposite. All of its constituents could be catergorized as 'small fry', and they had no chance at all. Their eclipse was rapid and total, and in the long-term sense their influence on subsequent GWR thinking was utterly negligible They were, indeed, 'absorbed' in every sense of the word.

The Taff Vale was the largest numerically; but who, giving due respect to the sensitivities of the South Wales area, has ever seriously regarded the Taff Vale Railway as having had anything positive to contribute to the GWR, let alone the British carriage story? Even the trio of Highland TPOs is better known! This is very unfair, really, for the TVR had the longest independent history of the GWR constituents, its story going back to 1840. It did, however, in its later years, display a quite characteristic body style of by no means unpleasing aspect. Most of its carriages, though purchased from contractors, were, in fact designed by itself, and at Cathays, Cardiff, it possessed a works facility which even BR found to be of value. It adopted a similar livery to that of the GWR (chocolate and white) and in one respect was distinctive in that the upper panel beading was not always coloured black or to match the lower body panels (the normal British approach), but was simply picked out in the lining colour. It was an early user of a high elliptical roof and quite a pioneer in the steam railmotor business (see Chapter 15) but most of its carriages soon vanished. What is perhaps most surprising is that in converted form, its railmotors survived to BR days as sort of ersatz corridor thirds!

The Cambrian, alone of the small constituents of the GWR in 1923, could claim to be a genuine all-purpose railway. It showed distinct affinities with its Celtic contemporaries such as the Furness, Highland or even the GNSR — and its fate was not dissimilar. It was ignored! In stylistic terms it employed traditional panelling with an arc roof profile of somewhat Caledonian aspect. Apart from a fairly mandatory quota of conventional four-wheel and six-wheel carriages, it possessed a fair number of better vehicles such as saloons, lavatory stock and even the odd corridor coach. In fact, because of its geography, it probably possessed proportionally rather more of the better quality carriages than some of its contemporaries, but all to no avail. Its livery was quite distinctive (bronze green and 'white', later all-over green) but there is no evidence that its specific requirements loomed large after 1923. As a totally irrelevant aside, one of its more maverick acquisitions was the purchase, via the Highland Railway as agents, of the Duke of Sutherland's saloon, built in late Victorian days. The Duke had obtained in 1900 a new and opulent vehicle from Wolverton (now preserved by the NRM) and his slightly older saloon was therefore sold to the Cambrian for some reason. It became in due course GWR saloon No 9215, but in 1925 was relegated to 'fruit and parcels' status and was scrapped in 1931. This, of course, proves nothing, but is one of the many and various items of minutiae which the study of carriage history reveals.

As for the 'less than 100 route mile' constituents of the GWR, there were quite a number of them, but their influence was in all honesty peripheral to non-existent. The Barry Railway, quite a prosperous little concern, had some nice dark red carriages with electric lighting and automatic vacuum brakes but never bothered to provide carriage heating! Even so, one or two survived into BR days. A definitive history describes the Rhymney Railway as that which would

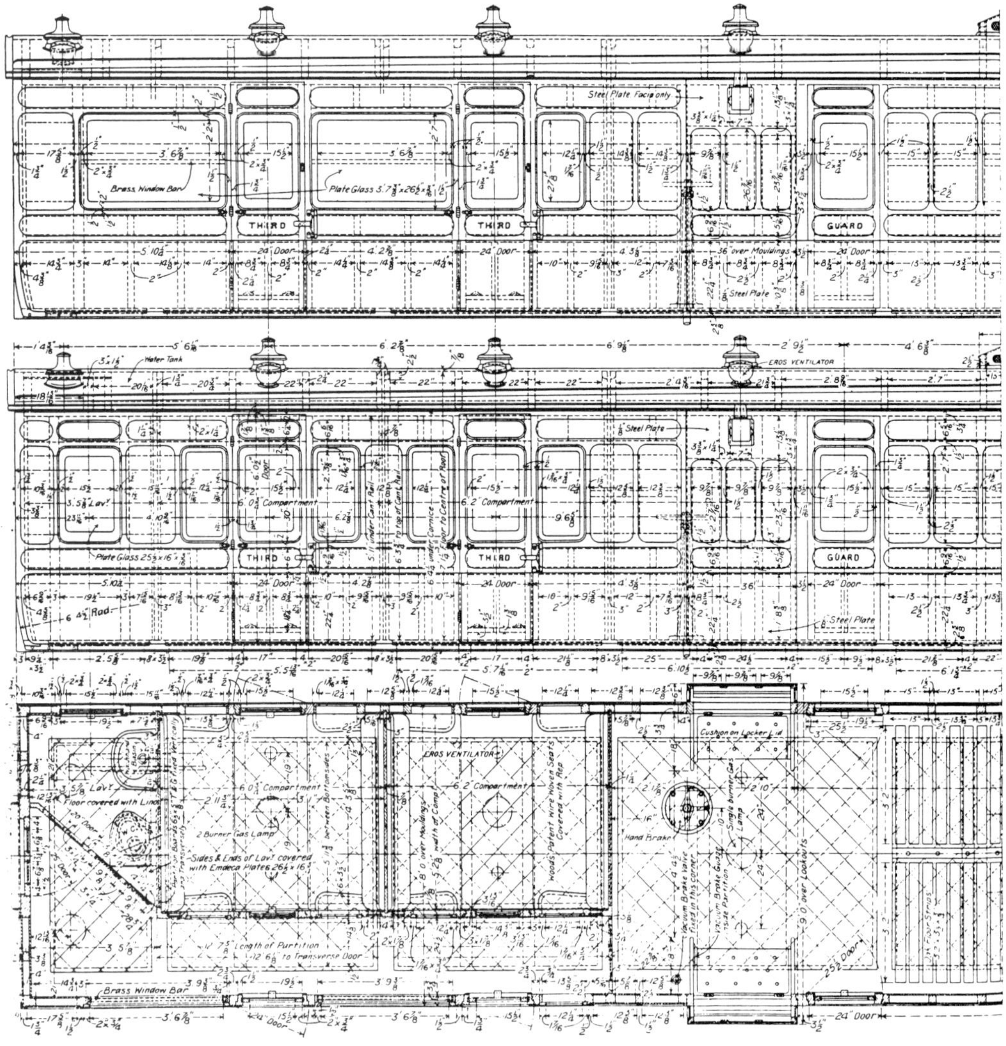

Scale 5mm = 1ft

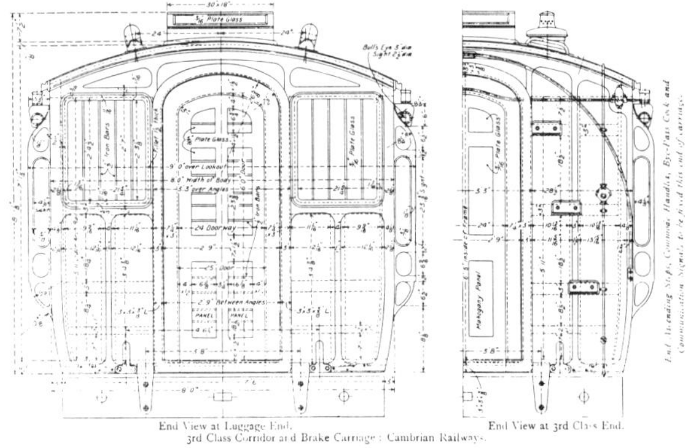

Figure 38 *The neat but hardly innovative carriage styling of the Cambrian Railway is well represented by these drawings of a corridor third brake of 1908 vintage. The central lookout is somewhat unusual and the large van suggests a form of dual purpose role. Designed as through carriages, they could clearly carry much more than the luggage of the dozen or so passengers who could be accommodated. The drain holes in the van floor suggest milk traffic (ie to cope with any accidental spillage).*

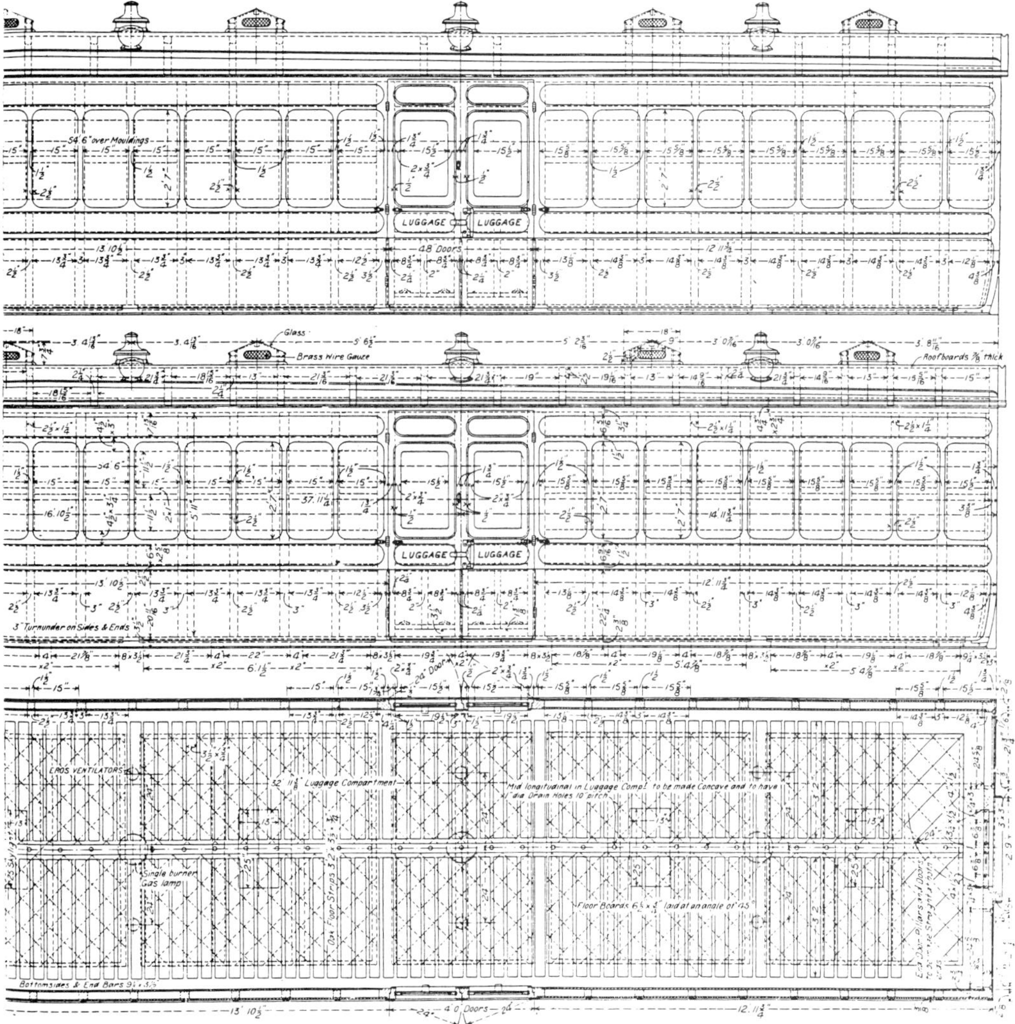

'never be described as having carriage stock that would have raised the enthusiasm of the weary traveller over its lines'! Even so, its own-design vehicles were of more than uncommonly neat outline with somewhat MR/GSWR visual overtones of the nineteenth-century kind, and a few survived to BR, generally those examples which were mounted on bogies. It was, *en passant,* the only GWR constituent to employ the Westinghouse brake and it adopted a rather attractive red and cream livery, later all red; but it signified nothing.

All told, therefore, it cannot be a source of any surprise that the 'greater' GWR, after 1923, chose to ignore any contribution made by its constituents, be it in locomotive or carriage affairs. It was in all senses rather inevitable and something of a foregone conclusion. This had curious side effects after 1922. The GWR had gained so much of its own way at the grouping that it was probably less aware than the remainder of the 'Big Four' companies of the virtues of combining the experience of its various constituents. The LMS undoubtedly gained from an amalgamation of the carriage building experiences of its various larger companies as, in a different sense, did the LNER. We have also seen how the SR had to reconcile the disparate requirements of its trunk route constituent (LSWR) with those of its tightly-knit suburban partners; but the GWR sailed serenely on — or so it seemed. That it fell on its face in carriage terms during the 1920s must await the next volume to analyse. The GWR was a magnificent railway, but in one sense the grouping did it no

Left *The later Rhymney Railway bogie vehicles lasted extremely well. This is third class No W1099W, built at Caerphilly in 1921 as RR No 58, still in service in 1954. It had an open interior with two saloons and far fewer than normal the number of outside doors for its time. The styling has a sort of GSWR look to it but the vertical sides were a distinctive, if not unique, RR feature* (T.J. Edgington).

Below right *Cheshire Lines carriages were either of GNR or GCR style. This stylish lavatory composite No 313, of typical GNR outline was built in 1911. Interior views of a similar vehicle can be seen on page 55.*

Bottom right *Like the GNR, the GCR also built spacious carriages for the CLC. This is composite No 9 of 1914 with only seven compartments in a 53-foot length. Note that CLC carriages wore the livery of the company which built them. This one is finished in post-1910 GCR style.*

favours. It was, in a phrase, too dominant by far for its own good — and therein lies the clue to the post-1922 story.

The Joint railways

It now only remains to consider the carriages of the various joint railways as they were contituted during the first quarter of the century. Effectively there were but three significant systems, the Cheshire Lines Committee, and the Midland and Great Northern and Somerset and Dorset Joint Railways.

Of the three, one of them tended towards its own design of carriages (S & DJR) while the others seemed quite content to accept the carriage designs of their owning partners. The CLC was a tri-partite concern whose owners were the GCR (formerly the MS & LR), the GNR and the MR. The M & GN was self-descriptive in ownership terms while the S & DJR was a Midland/LSWR operation. It is with the CLC, the most prosperous of the three, that we start the analysis.

The Cheshire Lines company was badly described, for much of the system was not based in Cheshire. The main artery was an alternative route between Liverpool and Manchester, and although owned by three railways the carriage stock was provided by but two of them, the GNR and GCR. The statistical summaries in the previous chapter reveal the considerable intensity of use to which the CLC was put and the carriages were dominantly of the suburban kind. In effect they mirrored contemporary company style, be it GNR or GCR, and after grouping the system continued in joint ownership, two-thirds LNER and one-third LMS. In all conscience, and notwithstanding the fact that the CLC carried a high volume of presumably remunerative traffic, its influence on carriage design was almost non-existent.

The other two joint lines were not dissimilar, and only in one case (S & DJR) were some small original contributions made to carriage design. The M & GN was marginally the bigger of the two but in carriage terms it was utterly insignificant. During much of the twentieth century and well into the LNER/LMS ownership period, it tended to make use of 'hand me down' carriages from the parent systems. Its independent history as a fully fledged joint line went back no further than 1893 when it was first incorporated, so not surprisingly its carriages were not exactly epoch-making and nothing bigger than a six-wheeler was owned before 1923, or for a few years after for that matter. Much stock was of GNR pattern but there were some residual survivors from those companies which had preceded the M & GN and, according to H.C. Casserley* it had never had any new passenger coaches built for its own use at any time. Its livery was varnished teak (GN-type stock) or Midland red (MR-type and other stock).

By contrast with the CLC and M & GN, the Somerset and Dorset Joint Railway did have its own carriages, built new for the system and liveried in

**Britain's Joint Lines,* Ian Allan, 1968.

a distinctive blue shade reserved to itself rather than simply aping the style(s) of the parent system(s). The vehicles were more closely allied to the nineteenth-century Midland styling of the pre-clerestory Clayton period than anything else but were not necessarily pure carbon copies, even in the arc roof period. However, later S & DJR carriages were fairly distinctive. They were mostly 46-foot bogie vehicles (plus a few six-wheelers) which combined Clayton's round-cornered traditional pre-1896 MR panelling style with a fairly high flattened elliptical roof profile of almost pure LSWR shape. They were all non-corridors, some with lavatories, and it was quite surprising how the mere change of roof profile could impart such a difference in overall appearance to what was, basically, a Midland type of carriage; but thus it was.

Conclusion

I am conscious that, lengthy though this review of the 1901-22 position has been, it has scarcely scratched the surface of a very complex situation, but I hope that a few basic trends have emerged, even though many small railways have been all but ignored and even the larger ones given only a brief consideration. However, unlike locomotives where one can occasionally discern truly epoch-making designs whose influence often transcended company boundaries (Churchward's on the GWR for example), there were few if any pre-1923 carriage trends which turned out to be way above the competition, even if superficial appearances seemed to suggest otherwise.

This is not to say that there were no patterns to

Top *M & GN six-compartment composite No 56 typifies the better 'native' stock of this long-gone system. The excessive end overhang of the body was a common M & GN practice with six-wheelers, presumably to keep the wheelbase within the acceptable geometry for the track curvature. Even so, the lateral displacement incurred at the carriage end —* *see also page 19* *— was considerable, and the carriage was probably uncomfortable in consequence.*

Above *'Nineteenth-century Midland panelling with twentieth-century LSWR roofs' is an apt description of the styling of most Somerset and Dorset carriages of the present century, but the guard's lookout was most un-Midland. This is 46-foot brake third No 100; the early use of colour-sensitive photographic material enables the layout of the all-blue livery with its black and gold lined mouldings to stand out clearly.*

be observed. Churchward's work on the GWR clearly laid the foundation of all post-1922 developments on that system and, as we have seen, Gresley and the GNR proved dominant on the East Coast. The LMS developed a highly consistent house style in the 1920s based essentially on Midland exterior treatment allied to LNWR interior layout, while the Southern, in so far as it standardized at all, took its main lead from the LSWR. Within these broad stylistic outlines, however, there was much variety to be witnessed within the carriage walls, so to speak, and it took quite some time for even the post-1922 companies to settle down. In part, this was more than a little the consequence of the bewildering variety of carriage layouts favoured by even the smaller companies, which topic it will be the object of the next few chapters to analyse.

8. All stations

We have seen in the first chapter how the characteristic British non-corridor compartment coach evolved from the stagecoach in the 1830s, stagnated for the best part of half a century and was eventually supplemented by the more specialized late Victorian vehicles which formed the basis of twentieth-century development. However, it is important to remember that at the start of our period by far the largest number of passenger carriages were still of the traditional compartment type. Thus, although the age of the more specialized carriage for medium and long-distance trains had dawned, they had by no means fully taken over even on the most prestigious workings, and compartment coaches were most likely to be found in the vast majority of trains, no matter what the distance travelled.

Now, it is conventional wisdom that the non-corridor coach was the characteristic vehicle for the 'stopping at all stations' suburban and local trains. Well, it did for the most part become just that, during the twentieth century, but it should not be thought for a moment that this was its only role. Many late nineteenth century 'expresses', not to mention a few twentieth-century ones, were composed of non-corridor stock. However, having entered this important caveat, it will be convenient to divide the analysis in this and the next few chapters along the lines of customary twentieth-century usage, starting with the most basic and traditional form of non-corridor carriage — ie that without even the refinement of a lavatory.

Such carriages all derived from the fundamental 'three-box' four-wheeler whose origins go back to 1830, but by the end of Victoria's reign quite a few variations had occurred in length, interior accommodation, comfort, heating, lighting and so on, so a few more definitions will not be out of place. Normally a carriage was referred to by class of accommodation offered, first, second or third. Should a carriage have two classes of compartment then it was known as a 'composite'. In this group, the 1st/3rd mix was the most common, especially as many railways had abandoned second class, or did so during the first twenty years of the century. However, 1st/2nd or 2nd/ 3rd composites could also be seen, and if all three categories appeared then it was known as a tri-composite.

Those carriages which carried a handbrake and guard's compartment were known as 'brake' carriages; normally two were found in any train and one was always mandatory if passengers were to be carried (see also Chapter 2, page 28). The brake carriage could be exclusively occupied, guard's equipment excepted, by empty space for luggage, parcels and so on, in which case it was known as a 'full brake' or 'passenger full brake'. The word 'passenger' in this context was inserted to denote *not* that the vehicle carried people but that it could operate in a passenger train. Quite regularly — in fact more commonly — a brake carriage would incorporate passenger-carrying compartments as well as that for the guard and handbrake, in which case it was referred to as a 'brake third' or whatever, depending on the class(es) of compartments provided in addition to the guard/brake space. The latter accommodation could vary in size between the minimum space necessary — often no bigger than a normal compartment — to a quite capacious loading area for luggage and the like. This space was often known as the 'van' portion because of its general resemblance to the interior of a goods van. The size of the van portion often revealed the nature of the train, in that long-distance services would, in the natural order of things, need more luggage and parcels space than a short-haul suburban train.

Sometimes one could see carriages which looked superficially like brake coaches in that they possessed a windowless luggage space as well as passenger seats. However, if this was simply a luggage compartment, 'box' or 'locker' (all these terms were used) without any guard/handbrake facility, then it was a 'luggage third', 'locker composite' or some such.

Supervening these basic descriptions related to usage were the generic terms applicable to vehicle configuration in such matters as wheels or roof profile. Thus, as an extreme example one could theoretically have such a creature as a 'bogie clerestory luggage tri-composite brake'. It would still be as much a non-corridor compartment coach as the humble four-wheel ordinary third class coach with a nearly flat roof and bare-board seats.

Of all the possible permutations of length, accommodation and so forth, the most common by far was the humble third class, closely followed by the brake third. There were, in fact, a lot of brake carriages, most of them third class, largely because of the common practice observed by many railways of assembling their vehicles in semi-permanent 'sets' of carriages, three to six being most typical. Each 'set' customarily would have at least two brakes, and since there was an amazingly large number of these fixed formations, almost as many brake carriages were being built as non-braked versions. In point of fact, the great fondness of many railways for 'set' trains could become a dominant factor in the actual planning and building of carriages.

The chief virtue of the non-corridor third class compartment coach was its 'sardine can'-like capability for absorbing lots of people and loading them quickly. Not only did each compartment have a pair of facing seats along which sitting passengers could be packed, but there was also just enough space between the seats for a third row of 'standees' at busy times. Times were often busy, trains were often well used and crowding was not at all uncommon, so the additional fact that every compartment had its own door made this really quite unpleasant form of transportation additionally favoured by the railways, solely because there were so many doors available that they could be loaded, and unloaded expeditiously.

This was not the only reason the railways liked them; they were also cheap to build and, size for size, offered more passenger seats per ton weight of carriage than any other option. This point merits further amplification. If one takes a typical five-compartment six-wheel third class carriage of the type very common at the start of our period and typically weighing around 12 tons, it could absorb 50-60 seated passengers and at least another 20-30 standing customers for a dead weight of well under 5 cwt per passenger when fully loaded. A bogie corridor coach of broadly similar carrying capacity and fitted with lavatories as well could easily at least double this figure. This meant bigger and more powerful engines, thus more capital investment and higher motive power costs, not to mention the extra vehicle costs as well.

For many purposes, until forced into doing something better, there was every incentive for the railways to pack people in and keep carriage weights down. This they did to a remarkable degree. Because four-wheelers and six-wheelers were cheap to build and showed these better 'passenger to weight' ratios than did bogie carriages, their construction continued unabated for a while. If a railway could somehow build carriages to take six per side in the third class (rather than five) without serious weight penalty then it did so. In fact, the GER even found it expedient to cut a lot of its carriages down the centre, splice in an extra foot width and put them back on the same chassis solely to get more seats without increasing train length and with very little increase in weight.

Other railways took the view that the closer you could make the distance between compartment partitions, the more of them you get per foot length of vehicle, and some very intimately sized horrors emerged in consequence. A fairly reasonable size for a third class compartment was some six feet between partitions. This allowed a 2 feet wide door between two seats, each of which occupied the space between door and partition. Five of them would just nicely complete a 30-foot vehicle, but some railways elected to put six *five-foot wide* compartments into the same space — or something equally spartan in space terms. Each compartment was still expected to carry the same number of people and on some of the more impoverished lines one could expect to have to travel quite some distance in them.

It is, of course, generally accepted that these miserably small compartments were not untypical of Victorian railways, but more than a few companies continued building them well into this century. Amongst the more notorious practitioners were the otherwise highly respected LB & SCR and GNR, neither of which donated too many favours in terms of space to the poor old third class non-corridor customer. We have seen how the GNR was dragged reluctantly into the twentieth century in terms of carriage design and eventually produced some gangwayed long-distance masterpieces — but tell that to the homeward bound traveller going to Hertford or Potters Bar! Mind you, if he was served by the North London Railway or Great Eastern he would not fare any better as many a vile four-wheeler continued to testify as it bumped and jolted its weary

GNR brake third No 571, although built in the late 1890s, was typical of the basic and spartan suburban third class carriage at the start of the century. Over 300 were built, the ten-seat compartments were only about 5 feet between partitions, yet, astonishingly, this one remained in service until 1946!

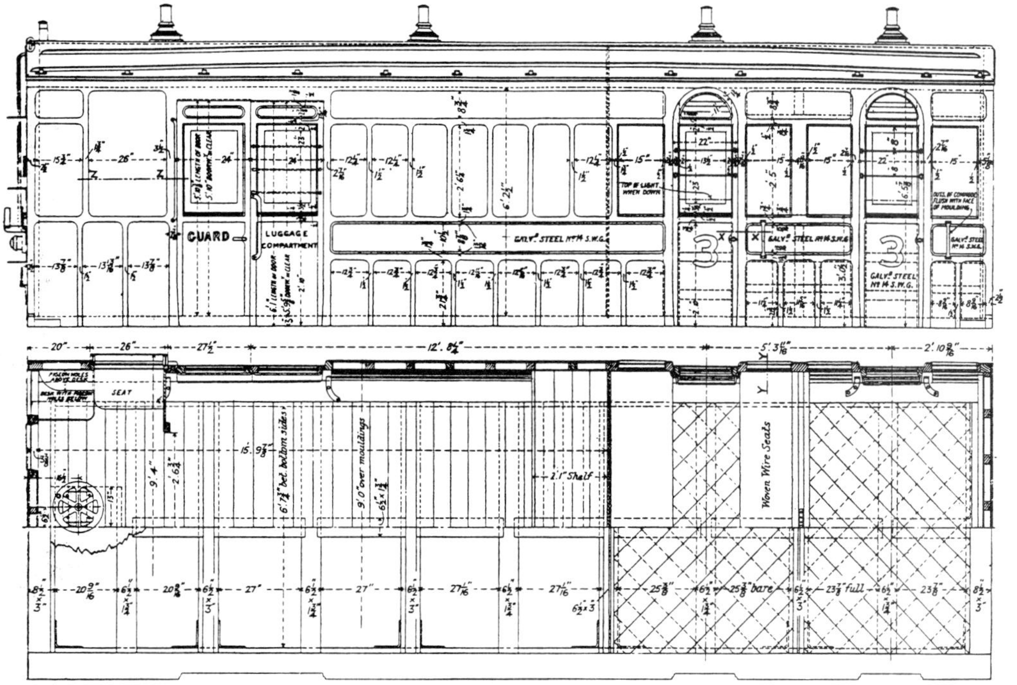

Scale 5mm = 1ft

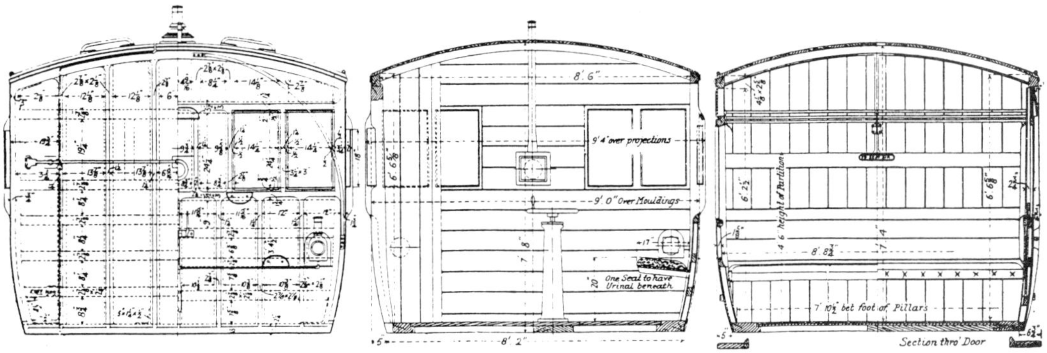

Figure 39 *Early in the twentieth century, as well as widening older vehicles the GER also built some so-called 'wide' suburban carriages. This 1902 drawing reveals the rabbit-hutch-like quality of a brake third of this miserable four-wheel series. The use of galvanized steel panelling in some areas was adventurous but there is little else save cheapness to commend it.*

This NER elliptical roof carriage seen at Scarborough, is correctly described as a 'luggage composite' with three firsts and four thirds.

Top *Later in the twentieth century the GER joined together pairs of wide arc roof suburbans to make bogie carriages. This view shows an Enfield-bound suburban train composed entirely of such re-builds.*

Above *Like the GER (and many others), the LYR also carried vast numbers of passengers but generally gave them rather more breathing space; these views show typical examples. Third class brake No 1979 had bogies and approximately 6-foot compartments even in the early 1890s, and when the company was forced into something bigger, its elliptical roof ten-compartment thirds like No 3290 were at least 60 feet long. The latter vehicle is finished in works grey (see also the picture on page 71) and is gas-lit.*

way through the London suburbs.

Nor was it only a matter of space. Seats were not exactly renowned for comfort either, and this was not just in consequence of the interlocking nature of opposing feet and knees in the cramped compartments! The seats were frequently thinly cushioned with little more than a modest concession to a neck rest and were regularly full of dirt. A slightly more hygenic option — but hardly the acme of comfort — was the slatted wood seat. This railborne equivalent of a park bench is generally supposed to have been confined to that strange and relatively unknown phenomenon the 'workmen's' train — it had something to do with not transmitting dirt from greasy overalls, as it was once said. Well, it may have been, but if so there must have been a great number of greasy-overalled workmen in the most unlikely workplaces if the carriages were any indication!

Then there was the 'toffee paper, chewing gum and tobacco trap' — that thoroughly unpleasant and almost inaccessible gap between the rear of the seat itself and the base of the seat back. It would not have been so bad had there been any real aesthetic pleasure in observing the 'decor' of the compartment itself, but it seemed that visual self-denial was to be added to physical discomfort on many of our railways. Institutional cream or off-white paint was regularly married to matchboard casing boards to produce an interior of the most depressingly Dickensian nature, by no means redeemed by the occasional picture (if you were lucky) or the generally poor quality of the lights.

Clearly, the early twentieth-century railways

Below *The NLR has received more than a few barbed comments in these pages, and these pictures may help to explain why. Composite No 18 dates from 1875 so its spartan nature, with only two lamps shared between three second class compartments, might be expected. However, it was still in use when the all-third No 245 was built in* 1906 *— five compartments, no change in style and still only three lamps! Note, too, the subtle class distinction on the outer doors — full heraldry on the firsts, elaborate monogram on the seconds, plain '3's' on the thirds. Astonishingly, they trundled on into the 1930s.*

reckoned that the third class passenger's eyesight was twice as good as that of his second or first class contemporary, so they gave him only half as many lights. It was not (usually) back to the old one light per two compartments, uncomfortably puckered into a sort of hole in the compartment partition below the ceiling, but it was not much better. If you were lucky you would perhaps get one of the newfangled electric light bulbs whose wattage was obviously the lowest which was capable of manufacture. If the dynamo was not too good and the batteries a bit flat, you were in trouble. However, it is a moot point whether the romantic-sounding gas alternative was any better. Not for the humble third class suburban passenger the glories of the chandelier. If, as was often the case, the compartment partitions did not go fully to the roof, lighting provision could often get even worse!

That there were alternatives was demonstrated by a few more enterprising railways. The newly formed GCR had some very nice suburban carriages, the LNWR, not always famed for its lavish provisioning in the Victorian period, generally gave its early twentieth-century third class passengers a more or less standard 6-foot compartment, albeit in a somewhat old-fashioned looking vehicle, while up in the North of England, the NER's carriages were better than most, but then it did have David Bain in charge at the start of the century. Even the oft-maligned LYR had probably more suburban bogie coaches, *pro rata*, than most companies and, as we have seen, did provide more than generously in terms of seats per passenger.

If, however, one can single out one particular type of carriage in this category which stood out above the rest it was probably the Midland's bogie clerestories which were being built right across the turn of the century. They were non-corridor and non-lavatory but, this apart, their internal space was every bit as good as on the main line with 6 ft 6 in as the third class compartment size and usually at least 7 ft 6 in for the firsts. The trouble was that there were not enough of them and they had to run cheek by jowl with some of the Midland's earlier stock which, in the case of the late Victorian four-wheelers for the Metropolitan line services, were every bit as dreadful as those of the GNR, GER and NLR, having 5 ft 2 in thirds and *five*-a-side firsts in an 8 ft 6 in wide body!

These non-corridor bogie clerestories were only built for a year or two but had the curious effect of helping to brand the Midland, quite incorrectly, as a clerestory railway. Basically, however, their form of construction was too expensive and their finish rather too elaborate to be really justifiable in the short-haul context. Soon after his arrival on the scene in 1903, David Bain, for all his continuance of good quality carriages in the long-distance field, pretty soon put a stop to this extravagance in the suburban category and reverted to the cheaper-to-build arc roof style with considerably smaller compartments; but

Figure 40 *The GCR demonstrated that not all London area services needed to be operated by cramped vehicles. This 1907 drawing shows a very well thought out third class brake — not quite as elegant as the GCR clerestories (see page 117) but more than adequate, nonetheless.*

Scale 3mm = 1ft

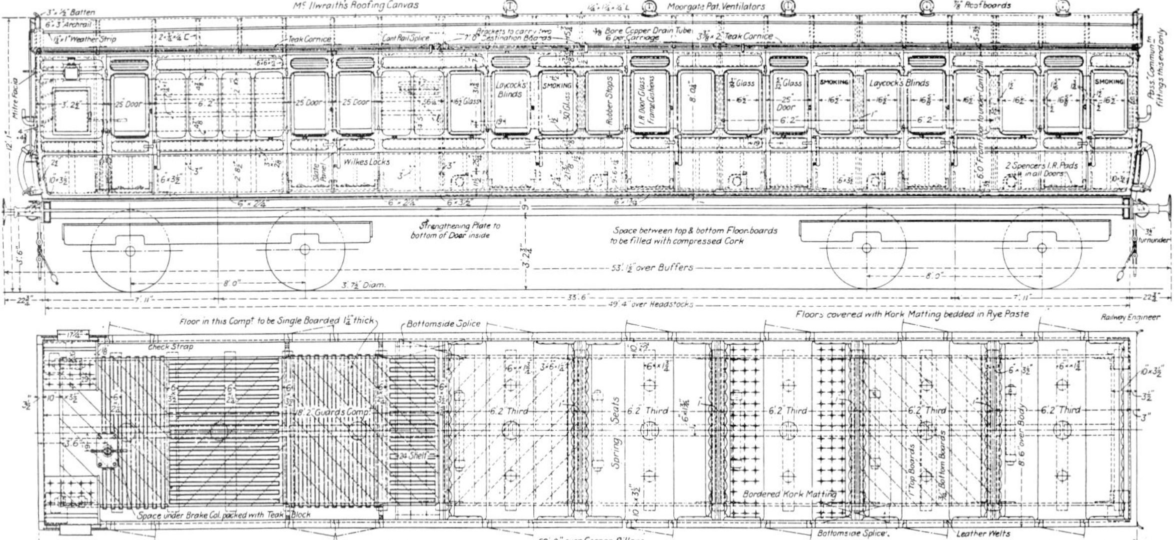

Above *Another more agreeable third class carriage in space terms was this nine-compartment NBR example of 1914, one of more than a hundred such. Interestingly, the nine-compartment third on a length of some 54-57 feet became a quite customary minimum standard for such vehicles on many railways, both before and after the railway grouping in 1923.*

Right *The best of the non-corridor breed? This is a standard 45-foot Midland clerestory suburban composite No 3205 of 1902. Its third class compartments were each 6 ft 6 in between partitions and its firsts 7 ft 9 in, both enhanced by the high clerestory roof* (Author's collection).

they were nonetheless bogie coaches rather than six-wheelers, and were at least 8 ft 6 in wide. However, the clerestories had shown what could be done, and lucky indeed were the commuters in places like the West Riding of Yorkshire where the Midland and its LMS successor chose to operate a large proportion of them for many years.

Thus far, the discussion has concentrated heavily on the conditions of travel for the third class passenger, for he indeed was the main source of railway revenue in the short-distance field as Chapter 6 has already demonstrated. However, during most of the pre-grouping era, second class passengers were carried by many of the bigger railways and, of course, all of them provided first class carriages.

There is a certain degree of ambiguity about the position of the second class carriage during this period of railway history. It was certainly of declining importance but, nevertheless, certain lines clung to it with a degree of tenacity which its basic quality may scarce have deserved. When the Midland pioneered two class only travel in the 1870s by being the first system to abandon second class, it was also its declared intention to make its own third class as good as everyone else's second class. This, for the most part, it managed to achieve, and by the start of our period there can be no doubt that except for those extreme cases of the third class 'dog boxes' already described, many railways had managed to produce quite a number of third class vehicles distinguishable from the second class only by virtue of the different designation on the doors.

At best, the second class passenger could expect little extra in the way of comfort over that provided in a decently upholstered third. There would be, perhaps, an official edict that one less passenger per side of the compartment should be conveyed (one wonders how often *that* was observed at busy times) and, in the better cases, this would be made more probable of achievement by inserting an arm rest somewhere along the length of the seat, thus reducing a five per side capacity to four, or some such. But that would be about all. If he was very lucky, the second class passenger might even get a slightly softer seat or better quality upholstery cloth, but there was not the real quantum difference between second and third class that there was between either of them and the first class carriages operated by most railways which were in most cases quite genuinely superior. In fact, when those railways which still had three classes of carriage finally abandoned second class, it was normal for them to simply downgrade the erst-

Left *In 1908, the GWR built twenty superb 60-foot 'Toplight' non-corridor firsts with no more than eight compartments, each seating eight. They were typical of the best British first class practice at the time, albeit larger than most. Such was their quality that more than forty years later they were still in first class service. This is No 8199 at Birmingham Snow Hill in 1950* (T.J. Edgington collection).

Centre left and below left *The LB & SCR 'Balloon' brake firsts of 1905 were certainly in the first rank, albeit only three in number. The exterior view shows No 27, the first of the series, containing only six seats in each of the four spacious 8 ft 6 in by 7 ft 3 in compartments; the interior view of a similar carriage shows what the passenger could expect to find when he boarded such a vehicle.*

Below right *High-capacity eight-compartment 70-foot 'Toplight' GWR brake third of 1913 marked up as 'Birmingham Division 5', its fixed set number. Note the painted panelling* (T.J. Edgington collection).

while seconds to thirds, and one doubts if many folk noticed much change. I am inclined to believe, therefore, that the perpetuation of the second class in the non-corridor field was, yet again, another example of the way in which the railway carriage related closely to the people who used it. There was a simultaneous element of both snobbery and economy about the second class carriage, and in some places it died hard.

As far as can be judged, two main groups of people used the second class. Firstly were the 'upwardly mobile' and growing middle classes. By travelling second class they asserted their better status over the hoi polloi — or maybe thought they did. Presumably one travelled with a better class of person in every sense of the word if one bought a second class season ticket! The retention of second class on the LNER in the London area until 1937 was, in fact, so as to provide a special class for season ticket holders. Secondly were those travellers who would, perhaps, travel first class on a long distance train but chose to travel second for reasons of economy. Presumably they *could* afford first class but chose to use their not inconsiderable spending power in other ways — or maybe the journey was too short for it to matter anyway. Furthermore, it was and still is characteristic of quite a few wealthy people *not* to be too liberal with their disbursements. That is how some of them became rich to start with and why so many of them managed to stay that way!

Be that as it may, the second class seems to have suffered erosion at both extremities of the social scale as the years went by and continued to decline. Interestingly, there has been a sort of contemporary replay of this phenomenon in more modern days (since the 1960s) with the gradual removal of the *first* class option altogether from many short-distance trains which are now very egalitarian one-class-only operations.

Sociologists may read what they may into the above analysis, but of one thing we can be certain, the first class carriage of the early part of the century was, almost always, exactly what it claimed to be. Very few railways failed to offer a distinctly superior conveyance for their up-market customers and there was, in truth, probably little to choose in quality between the best samples from any of them. Every passenger would normally have his own seating area defined by padded armrests and frequently by headrests as well. There would be a carpet on the floor, adequate lighting, beautiful detail treatment in the woodwork and often curtains and pictures too. There would rarely be more than three per side in an 8 feet wide carriage, or four at the most in a 9 feet vehicle, and if the compartments were much less than 7 feet between partitions, the company concerned was beginning to look distinctly parsimonious. In fact, corridors and lavatories excepted, there was little to choose between the first class compartments of ordinary non-corridor stock and that of the longer-distance equivalent.

There were, of course, a few exceptions in which the first class was not much better than the better second class offerings of those railways which retained three types, but in general, whether it be on four, six, eight or even twelve wheels, the first class non-corridor coach was no bad way to get to the office if you could afford the fare — and many could.

By the mid-Edwardian period, although vast numbers of suburban carriages were of the four-wheel or six-wheel type, there was gradually dawning a slow realization that bogie carriages were the way forward and most new building took this form. Noteworthy in this respect were, south of the Thames, the LSWR and SE & CR, both of which managed to introduce some really quite worthy carriages on their suburban services. North of the river, we have already noted the LNWR, MR and GCR, but what of the others? Well, the GWR went from almost the sublime to the ridiculous in the Birmingham area, changing rapidly from flat or clerestory roofed Dean-style four and six-wheelers (with a few bogies thrown in) to the non-corridor version of the 70 foot 'Toplights'. Their load-absorbing capacity was formidable. Even the brake thirds, for example, had no fewer than eight compartments, could seat 96 and possibly pack in 50 or more standing passengers as well.

Meanwhile, further north in Scotland, several railways leapt abruptly from spartan short carriages to quite gigantic bogie non-corridors, and the Caledonian, GSWR and NBR even put some of them on twelve wheels. Sadly, the HR and GNSR could not afford such grandiloquent gestures and neither could some of the smaller English or Welsh concerns, but, for the most part, one can at least say that the railways were trying harder than they had been. In part this was because they were facing real competition for the first time, and lest this statement should seem to be at odds with a railway network operated by apparently competing private

Another high-capacity suburban design — the Caledonian twelve-wheel non-corridors for its 'Glasgow and Edinburgh Direct' service in 1905 — seen here branded thus in the eaves panels as part of the livery treatment. The two eight-compartment third brakes and the nine-compartment full first seated 192 and 72 respectively.

companies, a few words of explanation are needful.

In the suburban field, the companies mostly enjoyed semi-territorial monopolies close in to the cities, quite unlike the longer-distance situation. Thus, while one could, for example, choose any one of four railways to take you from, say, London to Manchester (LNWR, GCR, MR, GNR), if you lived in the inner or outer suburbs, the chances were that you had only one of the competing companies within sensible walking distance of your home, whether you were a resident of the London region or any of the several industrial conurbations. In these circumstances, the only thing which could really change the situation as far as short-distance passenger comfort and convenience was concerned was a viable alternative *system* to the railway itself — and this is precisely what happened. It was called the street tramway.

The rapid growth and cheap operating costs of the electrified street tramways in the early part of the present century gave the complacent railways a considerable fright, and one can detect a very close correlation between the improved carriage stock already mentioned and the areas most affected by the new threat. Obviously, there were some kinds of service offered by the tramways (and later by the motor bus) which the railways could not match, but where the trams threatened to cream off more than just the very short-distance passengers, then the railways responded either with better carriages or better services, sometimes both.

It was not, of course, quite as simple as that, for some railways had invested quite heavily in what were fast becoming outmoded vehicles only a few years before the perceived need to improve matters. In many cases, some considerable improvement could be effected by mounting two carriage bodies of what had thus far been two separate four or six-wheelers on to one new bogie underframe. As far as can be ascertained, this method was probably pioneered by the LNWR in 1895 when it did just this for the benefit of the reigning monarch, no less! This result may still be seen at the National Railway Museum and the idea quickly spread, though mainly confined thereafter to non-corridor stock.

However, there was one noteworthy and different approach to the problem of getting a better ride quality without the expense of scrapping fairly new four and six-wheelers. This was the particular *métier* of the GNR in the person of Nigel Gresley who, rather than put two bodies on to one bogie underframe, began to employ articulation to get the same effect. Anything between two and five vehicles could thus be joined together utilizing only one more bogie than the number of carriage body units in the formation. It did nothing to improve the often spartan quality of the interior compartment accommodation offered but undoubtedly made the otherwise spine-shattering progress better! Articulation also gave the means whereby a further lease of life could be given to redundant but still quite new steam railmotor bodies (see Chapter 15) and also allowed some of the better long-distance six-wheel and rigid eight-wheel carriage bodies to carry on in

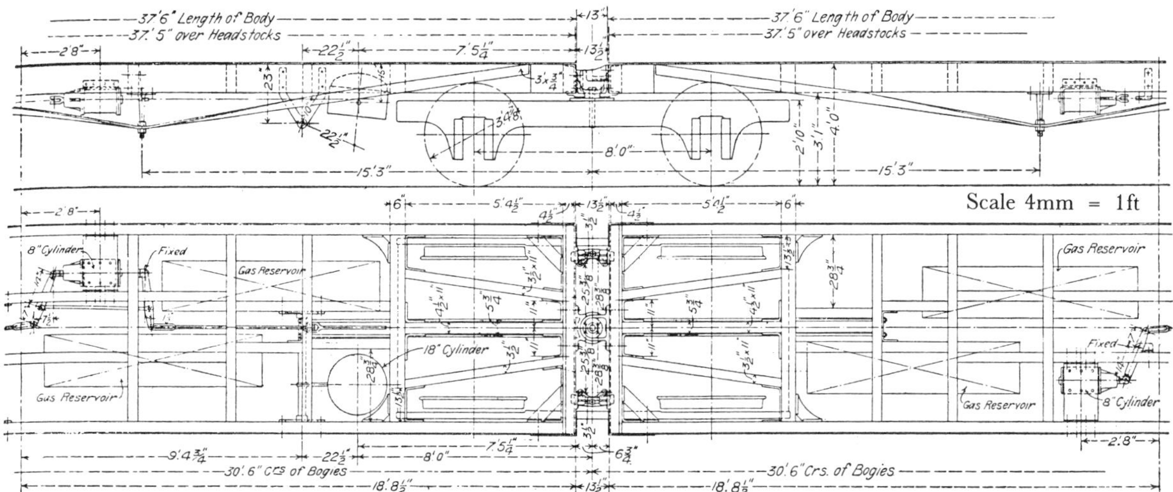

Figure 41 *Drawing of Gresley's articulated system as applied in 1908 to a pair of 37 ft 6 in carriages and utilizing the older GNR-type bogie.*

main-line service longer than might otherwise have been the case.

The problem with articulation was that if one bogie became defective, it put the whole set out of operation. If there was only a pair of vehicle bodies involved it might not be too bad, but if the ensemble was a four or five-unit formation, it could be serious and sometimes was. Nevertheless, the sheer weight-saving obviously persuaded Gresley to persevere for

Below *The picture on page 119 depicted the first quite typical form of articulation for older Howden stock. This view shows No 2116, a 'triplet composite brake' conversion in 1912 from three former six-wheelers, brake third, composite and full third, all dating from the 1890s.*

Bottom *Gresley's first purpose-built articulated carriages (as opposed to conversions) had elliptical roofs with old-style bogies. This is twin brake third No 3256 of 1912, still frightfully cramped with compartments no more than about 5 ft 3 in between partitions, each, however, now seating a dozen passengers because of the greater width. This pair were reformed in 1921 as one end of a 'Quad-Art' set, perhaps the best known form of Gresley's suburban articulated stock.*

Left *This SER 'birdcage' suburban third brake was built just prior to the formation of the SE & CR and illustrates the short 'van', very typical of inner suburban stock.*

Below *LNWR suburban stock at the turn of the century is represented by this Broad Street and Willesden set which seems to have been first and second class only when built. Note the even shorter guard/brake compartment than the previous SER example* (BR LMR).

many decades, and it was not until after he died that the LNER, as successor to the GNR, finally abandoned articulation. Of course, the high quality and general reliability of the Gresley bogie (page 119) must have had more than some influence on matters, but the GNR low-roof articulated sets were introduced well before the Gresley bogie was designed and, since they generally utilized the original type of bogie, the new Gresley version was usually confined to *new* articulated coaches, of which a fair number were also made.

Mention of the fixed nature of these GNR articulated sets, be they new or rebuilt, brings us finally in this section to the more general discussion of train formations and operations and the role of the 'set train', for it must never be supposed that the articulated combinations were the only examples of fixed formation working.

For reasons outlined in Chapter 2, the time taken for the coupling and uncoupling of individual passenger carriages tended to act against a speedy turn-round of coaches. Thus there was every reason *not* to reassemble trains on arrival at their destination; far better to have a fixed set of vehicles which would, all things being equal, meet with most demands likely to be made during a typical day. This philosophy was particularly applicable to the short-distance 'all stations' train where a rapid turn-round of a set of carriages was of considerable value in maintaining a high service frequency, especially at busy times. The GER undoubtedly holds the palm for virtuosity in this respect for its famous 'Jazz' steam suburban services out of Liverpool Street. Not only were the trains of fixed formation but the track layout at the terminus was also such as to allow the engine of the outgoing working to be attached to one end of the train at the same time as the newly arrived engine was uncoupled from the opposite end. This slick operation could, at its most efficient, send a train on its way out of the station well within five minutes of its arrival!

The GER was not, however, the only example of this sort of thing, even if it was perhaps the best known. Most railways, including even those with only a modest amount of suburban and stopping traffic, found the fixed formation train to be of considerable value, and in many cases ordered their new carriages with the express purpose of marshalling them into 'sets', as they were generally known. The make-up of these sets could simultaneously both reveal quite a bit about the nature of the envisaged traffic and also indicate something of the physical constraints of the owning company.

Firstly, the actual make-up of the train could vary considerably in terms of vehicle type, the proportions of first, second and third class seating being gauged to suit the pattern of traffic for the area in question. Secondly, the actual number of vehicles provided was

Below left *A close-coupled LSWR four-coach 'block' set No 1358, consisting of two third class brakes and two tri-composites. The latter were different, the leading example having two thirds, three seconds and three firsts, while the further carriage had four firsts, three seconds and one third.*

Bottom left *A third variety of four-coach set is represented by this late Midland example which actually entered service after the grouping. It has two third brakes, one full third and a composite (five firsts and three thirds). The MR, of course, had long abandoned three-class travel. Although the carriages are of the usual MR quality, the set is still gas lit.*

Below *The LYR had three-class travel in 1910, and its four-coach set was a little different from the LSWR version, viz two third brakes, one full third and one 1st/2nd class composite, the latter having four firsts in the centre with a pair of seconds at each end.*

rarely more than necessary in terms of passenger volume regardless of class. For one thing this reduced, in absolute terms, the capital cost of vehicles and secondly, in motive power terms, the shorter the train, the less powerful and expensive was the locomotive needed to pull it. Naturally, there were 'peaks' and 'troughs' as a typical day went by — the rush-hour is no modern phenomenon — but then, as now, if one chose to travel at busy times, one could expect crowded trains. Even in Edwardian days the railways did not like to have too much stock lying idle and not earning revenue between periods of peak demand, although things were not quite so tight as in more modern times.

One feature was, however, quite usual. This was to have trains made up of two or three identical sets at peak periods, rather than one large single formation. This then allowed one or two of the sets to be detached at quiet periods, thus reducing vehicle mileage and extending the time interval between carriage overhaul, the latter being based on miles run. It also allowed essential maintenance to be carried out on the idle sets during the slack times as well as reducing the locomotive fuel bill. For this reason, three, four and five-coach formations were particularly popular since, when multiplied by repetition, they could easily generate most of the other requirements from six to fifteen vehicles — and there were some quite lengthy caravans formed in this way.

It mattered little whether the basic unit of a set was a four, six or eight-wheeler, as the principles remained much the same. Indeed, there could also be seen some mixed formations too, not all of the same age or body style; but there was usually method in the apparent diversity, regardless of outward appearance.

In one respect, overall train length, the physical nature of a set of carriages could also be affected. As traffic increased, the capital cost of extending platforms to accept longer trains had to be considered and sometimes was, but on many occasions the railways sought to maximize capacity without increase of train or platform length. This could be done in one of several ways. We have already seen how the GER managed it simply by widening the carriages to take one extra seat per side in every compartment. Other tricks were to reduce the guard's van to rudimentary size in order to allow more passenger compartments and even to shorten the distance between carriages by using some form of fixed coupling, often of a centrally located type without side buffers. Some railways, like the Midland, introduced what was known as 'short buffer' stock to reduce the distance between individual vehicles within the set, while it was not uncommon to find cases where the standard carriage length was reduced slightly but still contained the same number of compartments. By doing this, it was sometimes possible to gain one whole vehicle without serious enlargement of train length.

If the worst came to the worse, of course, most railways were in a position to add 'strengthening' vehicles at the end of a set or sets of carriages. These could be drawn from a pool of spare vehicles and could result in some quite curious visual effects from time to time. However, one of the more characteristic features of the stopping train at this time was its generally rather tidy appearance, consequent upon the use of these matching sets. The pictures within this chapter show some of the various solutions adopted and there were many more besides these. In fact, taken all in all, the operation of the humble stopping train was an altogether more sophisticated business than its apparently lowly status might lead one to suppose.

There was one final mode of operating suburban services not so far mentioned which came gradually into more prominence as the years went by. This was the electrification of the railways, but since this regularly went hand in glove with a total reassessment of the nature of the vehicle itself, it is dealt with later and particularly in Volume 2. The country cousin, as one might call it, of this new approach, was most often manifest in the form of the self-contained 'railmotor', usually steam powered. These will be dealt with in Chapter 15.

9. Semi-fast

One of the dangers in trying to establish some broad generalized patterns in a basically complex field is the definition of categories and the blurring of edges where one category merges into another. The so-called 'semi-fast' train was and still is a prime case in point. There was, however, a certain type of operation which developed in Britain during Victorian days which, while not being exactly an all-stations local was most certainly not a long-distance express either. In its most classical form, it would normally cover longer overall distances, typically in the 25-100-mile category and would omit stops at some or all of the smaller intermediate stations. It was fairly characteristic on the mid-distance cross-country routes and not at all uncommon in what might be called the 'outer suburban' commuting environment. In the latter case, a train would, typically, pick up its load at the outer stations of its route and then run non-stop through the inner suburbs. It is a practice still widespread in the modern era.

When this type of train first came to be recognized as a separate sort of creature is conjectural — probably quite early in Victorian times — but what is certain is that the carriages provided were, in the early days, no different from those used on any other services, and this remained the case for most of the last century. However, in the present century this intermediate range operation became increasingly the area wherein one could find that euphoniously sounding vehicle the 'lavatory non-corridor' carriage, and it is with these vehicles that this chapter is concerned. As usual, however, it is necessary to start with a few comments about the origins of the type.

The non-corridor lavatory-equipped carriage first appeared in the later nineteenth century when it was introduced as a first tentative step towards improving amenities on the long-distance trains. Indeed, the Midland Railway, which built some of the finest examples of the genre in the late 1890s, described many of them as 'Express Lavatory Stock' and put them on its main trunk services. Other railways did likewise and it was only with the establishment of the gangwayed corridor coach that the lavatory non-corridors began to be moved across to the intermediate distance services. This process of 'cascading', as it is now called, was only in its infancy during the first part of the twentieth century and, in fact, many railways deployed lavatory stock rather than corridor vehicles on their expresses well into the 1920s and 1930s. For the most part, these superficially less venturesome systems were those whose main lines did not offer really long-distance travel. Thus, for example, the SE & CR remained very much wedded to the lavatory non-corridor style, even for its most prestigious boat trains, until almost the end of its independent existence — and they were often things of great luxury and splendour. However, even such giants as the Midland were by no means extravagant in corridor coach provisioning at this time and it was only a few systems, notably the GWR and LNWR, which had whole-heartedly embraced the corridor during the Edwardian period.

Thus it is probably most accurate to say that the more modern-day association of lavatory non-corridors with an intermediate sort of operational role was never more than a gradually evolving concept during the pre-grouping period. Many of the vehicles to concern us had actually been built, by and large, for express services and probably only a minority of lavatory non-corridors were actually designed and built purely for the intermediate tasks until after the railway grouping.

So much by way of background, but what of the vehicles themselves? Structurally, of course, they were little different from orthodox non-corridors save for the insertion of the lavatories in place of some of the passenger seating areas. They were built to the usual ad hoc mixture of lengths, roof profiles and wheel arrangements but there was never any one dominant approach as to what, precisely, constituted the ideal arrangement. In this respect, there was a fundamental difference between lavatory and non-lavatory stock. In the latter case, regardless of external stylistic difference there was a broad measure of consistency between railways as to the basic arrangement of the carriage. In truth, there could be little variation save the overall vehicle length and compartment size, but the lavatory non-corridor was a different creature altogether.

For one thing, there never seemed to be any measure of agreement either between railways or even within one railway as to whether all or merely some compartments should have access to lavatories and/or whether such provisioning should be exclusive to the upper passenger echelons or provided on a more egalitarian basis. Furthermore, even if one could detect a sort of underlying principle at work — by no means easy — there was still no dominant solution. Things had reached their most confusing right at the turn of the century and a few examples must serve to suffice for the whole; although late nineteenth century in origin, they more than typify the early twentieth century state of affairs.

Take the LNWR, for example, a railway which, like its GNR rival, seemed often to display a chronic indifference to the plight of its customers until late

Left *This Webb radial chassis West Coast Joint Stock tri-composite, No 25 dating from the late 1880s, is typical of the first use of lavatories, ie for express use in pre-corridor days. Only the first class has lavatories and there are two coupés (see page 165), one of which, at the far end, is the solitary second class provisioning. Converted to bogie form, this and many carriages like it enjoyed a considerable twentieth-century life in the intermediate role before eventual scrapping.*

Below left *Characteristic use of non-corridor lavatory stock in the early twentieth century — a Highland Railway express at Druimuachdar Summit,* circa *1905. All but one of the carriages visible in the picture have some lavatory provisioning, many of them being quite generously served.*

Below and bottom *The LSWR clearly exemplified the indecision regarding the quantity of lavatory provisioning to be provided. Much early lavatory stock favoured the first class, as in arc roof tri-composite brake No 447, and this philosophy was repeated in the early cove roof stock. Later, carriages like full third No 390 gave four out of seven compartments the choice, one for ladies only. The final solution was lavatories for all — see the picture on page 127.*

in Victorian days. It had obviously embraced the non-corridor lavatory carriage by the 1890s and had more or less settled on a standardized 42 foot or 45 foot length, but the variations of layout within that length defied all logical analysis; it was almost as if every single batch of carriages was built to fulfil slightly different criteria. Thus, totally new layouts were introduced for very minor changes in overall accommodation offered — all very confusing.

On the other hand, that much praised system, the Midland, seemed at times to get itself into a total confusion of principle. In 1896 and 1897 it had introduced some of the finest express trains seen in Britain between Bradford and Bristol and from London to Manchester. They were non-corridor but otherwise beyond comparison in their use of a dramatic new clerestory style and spacious compartment sizes. They were nominally two class only (first and third), but on more detailed analysis they actually turned out to be *six* class trains, viz first class dining and lavatory, first class lavatory only and first class non-lavatory, this whole threefold subdivision then being repeated in the third class end of the train! One needed to be something of a Sherlock Holmes to be able to find the right place in a train under these circumstances; yet this sort of nonsense went on right through the early decades of the present century. The obvious solution was the continuous corridor, already fully developed, but this did not always happen, so one must try to answer the question 'Why?'. It probably resulted from a complex interplay of public demand, economic factors and train weight considerations.

The provision of lavatories was an obvious first step in the improvement of travelling conditions for the long-distance traveller, but regardless of the precise layout adopted, the lavatories took up floor space at the expense of seats. They also involved extra fittings and internal doors, not to mention the essential plumbing, so foot for foot, a lavatory carriage was more expensive to build for less actual seats than its non-lavatory equivalent. This commercial disadvantage was set directly opposite the growing passenger demand for better facilities and it was probably a matter of fine judgement on the part of the railways when it came to assessing the balance between higher capital cost and the likely effect on passenger revenue if such cost was not incurred.

It was probably this specific aspect which caused many railways to come up with the already mentioned halfway solution, where some compartments did have lavatories and others did not. It showed willing if nothing else, one supposes, but at its more parsimonious could produce the sort of train where one carriage had a token lavatory or two, the rest being the mixture as before. The LYR was rather fond of this solution and was by no means alone. We have already noted a Midland example and most railways could offer similar instances.

Another factor was overall train weight per passenger carried. Even if the economics of lavatory provisioning *vis-à-vis* passenger revenue could be accepted, the mere fact of reducing the number of seats within an otherwise unchanged carriage configuration to make room for the lavatories meant either that more carriages were needed for the same loading levels or that new and bigger carriages must be built. Either way, one had a heavier and probably larger train and this, in turn, posed questions of the locomotive fleet which, frankly, some railways were incapable of answering. It is not at all without significance that the move towards larger and more powerful locomotives took place at the start of the twentieth century when passengers were making more and more sophisticated demands on the companies in terms of carriage amenity.

In consequence, many lines, especially those with relatively shorter principal routes, tended to favour the lavatory non-corridor over the corridor alternative since it still offered an appreciable seat for seat weight advantage compared with the gangwayed carriage. However, in those instances where railways chose the lavatory alternative for express working, there was often a determined effort to provide every compartment with toilet facilities and this led to some very ingenious interior layouts showing probably more variety of approach than in any other generic type of carriage. Thus there gradually developed two quite separate strands of lavatory non-corridor design. Firstly, there were those where lavatory access was only provided for some of the compartments. These were often, but not always, of late nineteenth-century origin, but were used well into this century increasingly in the 'intermediate' role. Secondly were those carriages which offered lavatories for all. These were normally intended for express working and many remained thus employed well into the 1920s, albeit 'cascaded' later.

There were many ways by which lavatories could be incorporated in a carriage design and most possibilities seem to have been tried somewhere along the way. Most of them, however, fell into one of three principal categories:

1 *The 'between compartments' approach.* This traditional method, the simplest solution to the problem, undoubtedly derived from late Victorian practice wherein erstwhile non-lavatory coaches were converted to the lavatory style by the simple expedient of removing the seats from one compartment and converting it into a toilet or toilets. The LNWR and MR were masters of this particular technique and,

Left *This SER six-wheeler, No 21, is the classic example of the conversion of an original compartment into a pair of lavatories, probably in connection with its rostering as part of 'No 2 Boat Train'. The bar with handles across the carriage end was for turning on the gas lamps — see Chapter 4.*

Below left *LB & SCR brake tri-composite No 5189, built in 1905, bears all the stamp of the typical non-corridor lavatory fitted through carriage. It contained five first, five second and 26 third class seats, probably a fairly accurate breakdown of the likely customers. The one third class lavatory served all three compartments by means of intermediate connecting doors at the far side.*

Figure 42 *This floor plan and some typical interior elevations show the very thoughtful provisioning in Wainwright's 1st/2nd class 'semi-corridor' lavatory composites for the SE & CR boat trains at the start of the century. It is no way inferior to contemporary corridor stock and, for once, gives specific details of upholstery: 'electric blue' velvet (2nd class) and figured claret velvet (1st class).*

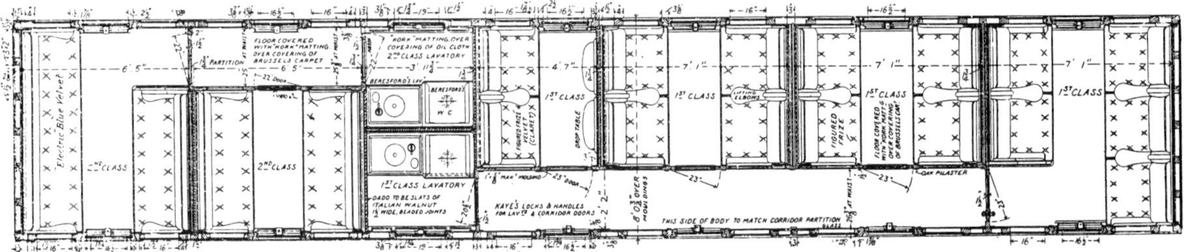

Scale 3.5mm = 1ft

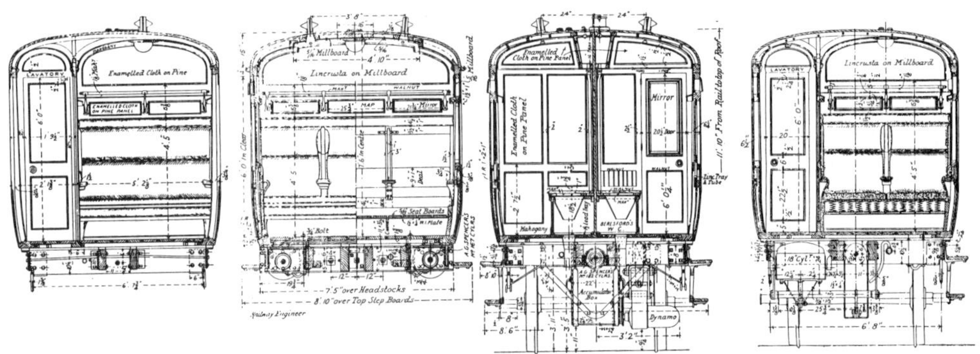

quite apart from its modest conversion cost, it also resulted in a quite spacious lavatory area. New carriages built to this principle generally saw a reduction in the size of the lavatory compartment (between partitions), often either to allow for some recovery of passenger seating space or to permit more lavatories to be incorporated.

2 *The 'short passageway' approach.* A disadvantage of the first solution was the fact that each lavatory could only really serve one compartment, therefore a common minimum provisioning had to offer at least two sets of toilet apparatus. This could be circumvented by two adjacent compartments sharing a single intervening lavatory, provided some sort of 'walk through' passageway could be offered. In effect it was a sort of mini-corridor, but saved a considerable number of lavatories.

3 *The 'semi-corridor' approach.* In this solution, much favoured by the NER and later the LNER, the short passageway was extended probably halfway along the carriage to allow all compartments to be served by fewer lavatories. Apart from the lack of connecting gangways, this type of carriage was close to being a true corridor vehicle but, properly planned, it could offer more seats than an orthodox corridor coach with fewer lavatories than the 'between compartment' type. For a given vehicle length, its seating capacity approximately equated to the 'full-lavatory-provisioned' version of alternative 1 above. This variation could in some cases lend itself to subsequent conversion to the full corridor form.

Apart from the semi-corridor type of solution either of the other two approaches could be used either in the partial or full provisioning of lavatories, and there were no really dominant styles. However, if full provisioning was wanted in the traditional mode, then anything up to six lavatories could be provided and considerable numbers of vehicles with just this sort of lavish facility were built for either all or some of the various classes of passenger. In this context, as might be supposed, the first class passenger was the best treated, but the days when this type of customer was the only one deemed to have such bodily needs had long gone. The second class (where it still remained) was usually well served and the third class by no means ill provided.

At their best, lavatory non-corridor coaches could provide a very civilized form of travel, provided there was no prima face need for mobility within the train (to a dining car, for example), and nowhere was this better exemplified than in the already-mentioned boat trains of the SE & CR. Study of the floor plans of a typical set of vehicles reveals considerable ingenuity, and it was normally achieved within a neat external style and considerable visual harmony. The SE & CR was by no means alone in this respect as some of the pictures in this book reveal, but it can stand as very typical of the best contemporary practice. In fact, this is one area in carriage design where

The lack of some outside doors at the left hand end of 'matchboard'-panelled NER lavatory third No 959 reveals it to be a typical 'semi-corridor' carriage wherein all compartments could gain access to a pair of centrally located lavatories. The passageway for the right-hand four compartments was on the far side of the vehicle, the general floor layout being much the same as shown in Figure 42.

3083
G.N.R.
GUARD

THIRD
N.E.R.
3712

MIDLAND
THIRD
2951
FIRST

Top to bottom *GNR lavatory third brake No 3083, built in 1908 for the King's Cross to Cambridge and Grimsby services, shows an alternative style 'semi-corridor'. A pair of open saloons gained gained access to the lavatories by means of central aisles between the seats. It seated only 42.*

NER lavatory third class No 3712 shows the full side-corridor layout whereby all compartments were served by a single lavatory without the expense of end gangways. For some reason, these carriages are annotated on the record as being for 'emigrant traffic'!

This Midland composite solution dates from 1906. Clerestory brake composite No 2951 permits only one each of the two classes of compartment to gain access to the lavatories. This approach lingered until the end of the MR period and beyond, for example the picture on page 111. (BR LMR).

This 'non-corridor five compartment, five lavatory "slip" composite brake' of the LNWR, No 6078, represents possibly one of the most extreme solutions to the through carriage business. It has two guard/brake compartments and a pair of 'birdcage' lookouts to assist the guard in the 'slipping' process. Only three were built to the new 1912 LNWR carriage panelling style, obviously intended for one specific service (two working, one spare — a common situation); it has not been possible to ascertain the service on which they ran.

the differences between the best and the worst companies were far less pronounced than in other fields. On the whole, they were all pretty reasonable.

An important use of the lavatory non-corridor coach was in providing through services, without change of vehicle, to a multiplicity of smaller destinations not served by a full train. In twentieth century terms, it no longer had the monopoly in this role, having first to share it with and then be supplanted by the corridor vehicle, but it led to a flowering of many ingenious composite carriage designs. The problem with a through coach was that it had to provide seats and lavatories for at least two and possibly three classes of passenger plus space for the luggage and, regularly, a guard's compartment as well. In this latter form it was known as a 'brake composite' or 'brake tri-composite', and the railways had real fun trying to get the balance right. This was equally true of the corridor equivalent, but the non-corridor was possibly the more catholic in terms of sheer variety.

For one thing, a through carriage probably mirrored in terms of its passenger load the economic breakdown of the two or three classes of traveller conveyed. However, the proportions of each were often difficult to achieve. Suppose that the numbers of first, second and third class travellers were likely to be in the ratio 2:1:8, for instance, a quite plausible division, then how do you get a single carriage to satisfy this demand? The fact is that most railways tended to take an inspired guess. Some companies contending three classes often provided equal numbers of compartments for all three, typically two of each. The LSWR was one such, and a real manifestation of this can still be seen at the NRM in the form of the preserved tri-composite brake No 3598 wherein are contained six compartments (two of each class), six lavatories, a luggage van and a guard's compartment. It is a real *tour de force* but by no means untypical. One does, however, suspect that until the second class compartments were downgraded to third class, the latter passengers probably had a bit of a raw deal in terms of the seats-per-passenger ratio.

Individual companies tended to favour different approaches in this matter of composite coach design. The Midland, for instance, having but two classes to cope with, tended to favour the first class customer both in terms of the proportion of compartments offered and in the provision of lavatories. In spite of its high reputation, it was distinctly parsimonious in the latter context, and the high seating quality of its third class could often be negated by some shortfall in lavatory provisioning in the long-distance trains — and it made very few carriages with lavatories for all compartments save in the corridor field.

Notwithstanding the above remarks, companies could go to some lengths to get the class balance more nearly correct and this led to that wonderful institution, the 'coupé' or 'half' compartment. This made tacit recognition of the fact that straight multiples of a whole compartment did not always get things right in terms of seat numbers, but that a half-compartment (ie one row of seats facing a plain partition wall) might just do the trick. It was, in fact, a bit wasteful of space, since two half-compartments (say first and third class) would each need a separate door and floor area and thus occupy more length than a single complete example of either type, but this did not seem to put the railways off. The idea originated in the nineteenth century and was probably inspired in the first place by the need to fill up the odd few residual feet of length in a carriage which could not, for some reason or other, be extended or reduced in length to accept a whole number of reasonably standard compartments. The oldest extant example is to be found at the NRM in the shape of Queen Adelaide's carriage (London and Birmingham Railway No 2) built as early as 1842, but the custom died hard.

At its most extreme — and some railways seemed to thrive on it — it could lead to a situation where in, say, a tri-composite there would be but two or three second class seats in a solitary second class half compartment, sometimes with an exclusive lavatory

Right *This early version of a so-called 'LBL' lavatory set dated from the three-class period on the LYR and was very sparing of lavatories, two first class compartments only being served. The seconds (in the middle carriage) and the thirds were denied, as were half the firsts!*

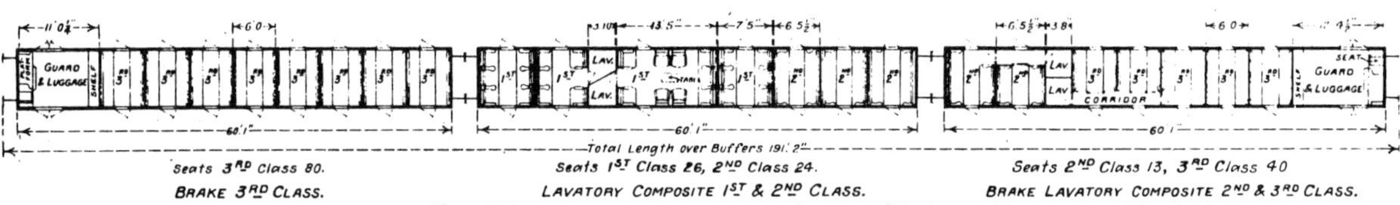

Below Figure 43 *In 1913, at about the same time as the LYR example, the SE & CR also introduced partial lavatory provisioning on some of its outer suburban and semi-fast services, but to slightly better effect. This floor plan shows a typical version made up from three 60-foot carriages of the style shown in Figure 36 (page 130).*

for those same few seats. Needless to say, under certain circumstances this could make the coupé very popular indeed; not for nothing were they often called 'honeymoon' compartments! The LNWR was particularly fond of them at the turn of the century.

Just as the lavatory non-corridor displayed many more subtle design variations than did the more suburban type of vehicle, so too did its operation defy simple analysis. Many of them were formed up into sets for the more important services, but a huge number were regarded as 'loose' vehicles to be added to or removed from trains at will. We have already seen their role as through carriages, conveyed perhaps at the end of a principal train and detached intermediately for working to a different destination. Sometimes this was achieved without stopping the main train by the ingenious process of 'slipping' the carriage from the rear. The GWR, LNWR and to a lesser extent the Midland were all rather fond of this technique. It later became commonplace with corridor carriages too, but certainly began with the lavatory non-corridor.

A 'slip carriage' had to be a self-contained 'train in one vehicle' and was, for the most part, a brake composite or brake tri-composite. It carried its own guard who, at the appropriate moment in the journey, could activate an ingenious mechanism whereby the slip carriage could be uncoupled from the main train while in motion without fracturing the train brake pipe (see page 30), thus allowing the slipped carriage (or carriages — there could be more than one) to freewheel into the station as the main train receded into the distance. It saved much transit time for the main train but, of course, was impossible to repeat in the reverse mode when it came to attaching the carriage to an inbound service, but it was popular.

Another common use for the lavatory carriage — again with perhaps a slight emphasis on the composite type of vehicle — was in order to enhance the quality of a particular service without going to the expense of providing all lavatory stock. It was particularly common, for example, to find a lavatory composite sandwiched between two non-lavatory third class brakes for the sort of 25-50-mile trips quite common throughout Britain. In fact, the LYR actually built new sets of coaches to this philosophy for its not inconsiderable traffic across the Pennines between Leeds, Bradford and Liverpool (the 'LBL sets'). These could hardle be classed as short-haul suburban, but there they were, nonetheless, with but one or two first class lavatories puckered in amongst non-lavatory compartments!

Excursion trains were another likely spot for the odd lavatory coach. Here the objective was to maximize seating capacity but, perhaps, make a slight concession or two possibly for PR purposes. Thus a lavatory coach would find itself at the end of a string of suburbans on its way to Southend or the Clyde Coast for example. It was all rather random and there was little pattern to any of it. They could even be found quite regularly as 'strengtheners' on the end of corridor expresses.

This particular part of the narrative has dwelt at

some length on the operational variety and particularly the variable internal arrangements within the non-corridor lavatory coach, for it is perhaps its most interesting single feature and much more could be said did space permit. However, it should be sufficiently clear by now that there was more than a degree of 'ad hoccery' about the whole business and it seems to me that this is symptomatic of some degree of uncertainty on the part of the railways themselves, individually and collectively, as to what should be the proper solution. However, such a statement presupposes that the nature of the problem was capable of precise identification, and there is little firm evidence that this was the case. A very wise, now, deceased, railway engineer once told me that he had found decision making to be easy; it was the identification of the *problem* that caused him all the headaches! This seems to be the key to understanding this very fascinating group of carriages.

There is no doubt that the railways moved quite sharply from a period of considerable complacency in the late nineteenth century to one of greater awareness in the early twentieth. Competition from the road was just beginning both in the field of public transport and in the slow but, as it was to prove, inexorable move towards private mobility in the shape of the motor car. One doubts if it was quantified with any great precision, but one can sense that the railways were beginning to feel that something ought to be done in terms of both meeting new competition and trying to satisfy greater customer expectation.

The difficulty was that any improvement to the carriage itself, or the services provided, would invoke greater capital expenditure, be it on vehicles, locomotives or infrastructure, and the railways were commercial companies trying to make profits. There was thus every incentive to keep expenditure within bounds, and against this background the lavatory non-corridor carriage must have seemed an attractive and less expensive option than the full corridor alternative. To this must also be added the fact that social habits and travel patterns were changing quite markedly in the Edwardian era. After sixty or more years of staid Victorian rectitude, the Edwardian period undoubtedly saw a considerable change in public attitudes from the Monarch downwards, and it would be ridiculous to think that this did not have its effect in the field of passenger travel. 'Emancipation' is not, perhaps, too strong a word.

In effect, therefore, the railways were faced with a period of great adjustment and change at all levels and had to try and respond, simultaneously, to all manner of different stimuli. That they managed to do so pretty effectively, all things considered, is one reason why the Edwardian era, short though it was, is often regarded as the high point of private railway development, particularly in the passenger vehicle field. In a sense it was inevitable since the pace of change was forcing the railways to pursue more experimentation than at any time in their previous history. This took on both a technological and sociological form in carriage terms and the lavatory non-corridor was a particularly good example of the interplay in the socio-economic field. The fact that it could appear in so many different forms was no more than a reasonable response to rapidly changing demands and expectations.

With the benefit of hindsight, one can realize that for all their valiant attempts the railways never got it quite right, and that the non-gangwayed lavatory vehicle, however well designed, could never really match the gangwayed alternative. This did not stop the railways trying until well beyond our immediate period, and many of the products of this particular school of carriage thinking continued in use until almost the end of the steam railway itself. But the real future lay with the gangwayed carriage and to this we must now turn attention.

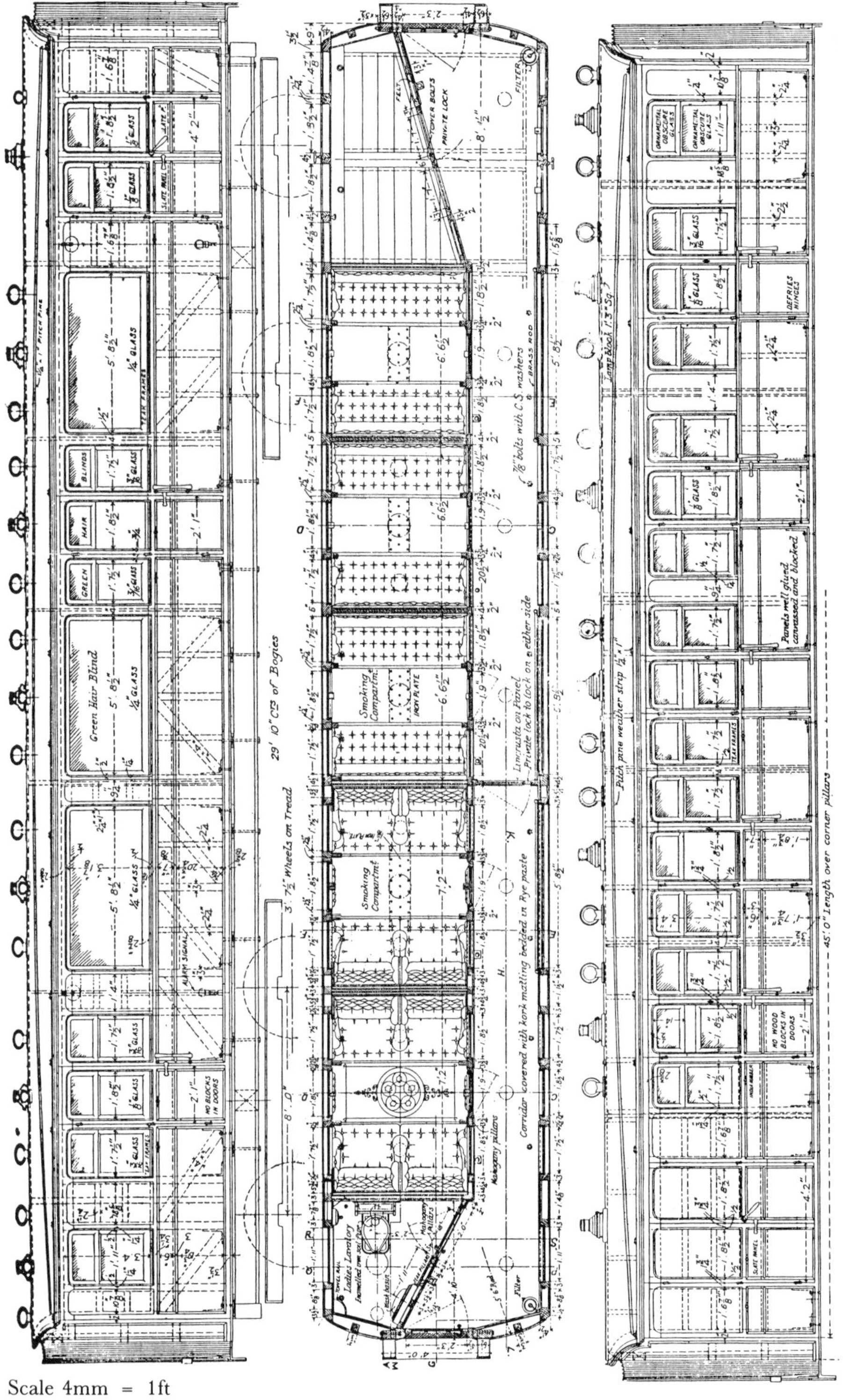

Scale 4mm = 1ft

Figure 44 *These elevations and floor plans, albeit of a relatively small carriage (45 ft by 8 ft 6 in), show the essential layout of most British side-corridor stock of the twentieth century. It is, in fact, a GCR example from 1900, internal sections of which are featured in Figure 33 (page 67).*

Right *The essential difference between 'corridor' and 'open' stock is shown by this pair of GER interiors, dating from* circa *1910.*

10. The general service long-distance carriage

There can be little doubt that the gangwayed bogie carriage has proved the most versatile single vehicle type which the railways, whether of Britain or elsewhere, have ever produced. Its adaptability seems virtually without limit and it is the essential common factor linking this and the next few chapters. It was the adoption of the gangway which made possible most of the amenities which we now take for granted on the train, and although in Britain such vehicles were by no means in the numerical ascendency over the already considered non-corridor types, their infinite variety was such that it is necessary to devote several chapters to them. Indeed, this particular section concerns itself only with what is usually called 'general service ordinary stock'.

The origin of the gangwayed carriage is firmly American, and we have already seen that the first British example was in 1869 with Queen Victoria's LNWR-built Royal Saloons in their original 'twin' form, now preserved united on a single 'modern' (1895) twelve-wheel chassis at the NRM. Somewhat more general use of the gangway did not occur in Britain until a generation or so later in the 1890s, but its well-nigh universality was very much a twentieth-century phenomenon, established as such beyond doubt in the period covered by this particular volume.

The technicalities of the gangway itself have been covered in Chapter 3, but a paragraph ot two must needs be added at this point by way of further definition. In the existing literature of railway carriages, words like 'corridor', 'gangway' and 'vestibule' are often hurled around with a careless disregard of their precise meaning. In fact, the same word can often be ascribed to entirely different features, or two different words used for the same feature!

As far as this book is concerned, the 'gangway' is the apparatus fixed to the carriage end by which the passenger moves from one vehicle to another — in other words, it is a technical term. The word 'corridor' refers to an internal passageway generally located *at one side* of a carriage from which access can be gained to compartments, kitchens, lavatories or whatever. The word 'vestibule', frequently used as a synonym for gangway (reflecting its American form of usage), is more correctly used (in the British context) in reference to an internal lobby, usually with outside doors, from which access can be gained to the internal corridor or the gangway between vehicles (or both simultaneously). So far so good, but there is the special case where the passageway for passengers runs along the longitudinal centre of the vehicle between seats on either side, such as are found in dining carriages and the like. This is the common

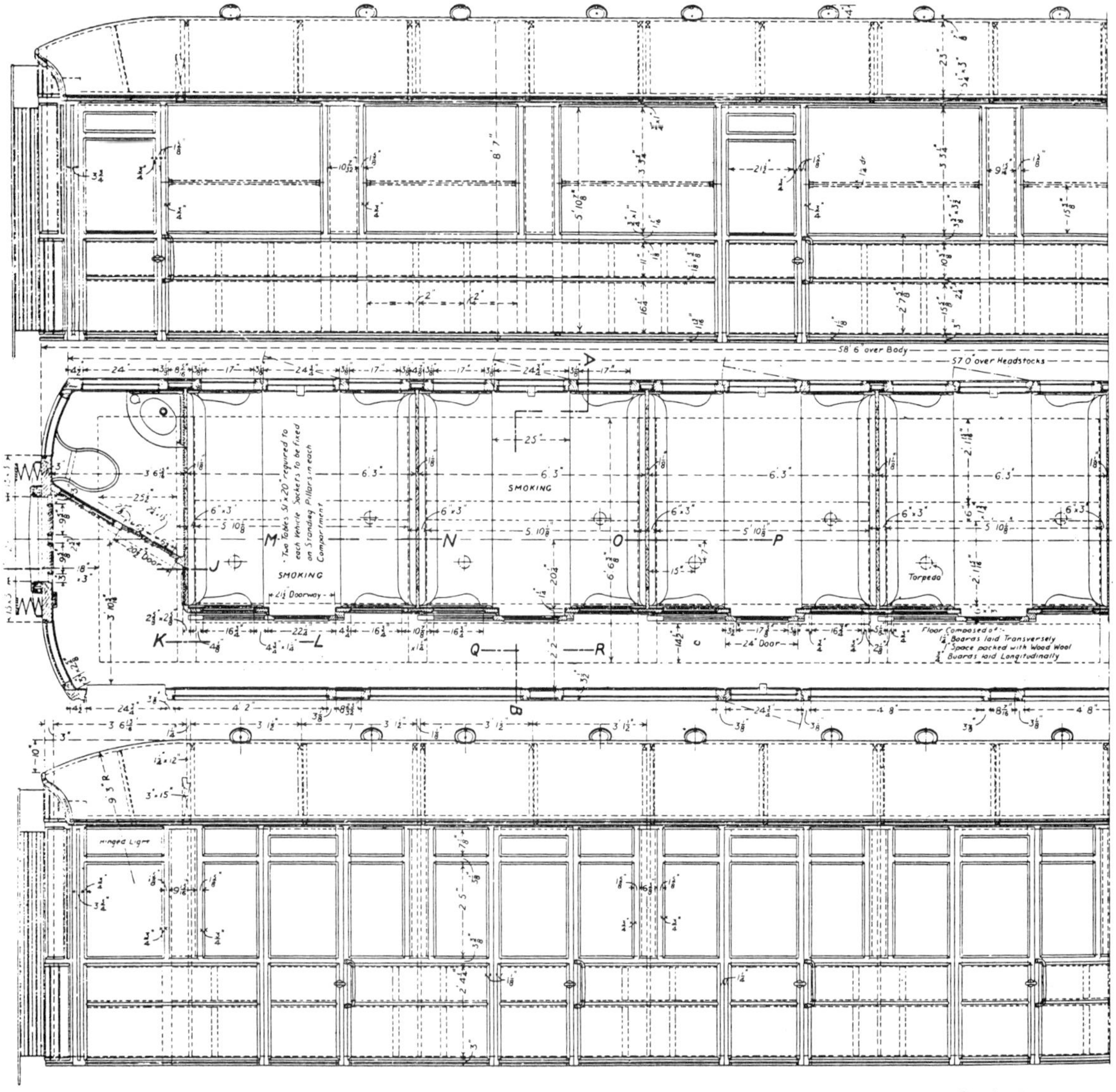

Scale 5mm = 1ft

Figure 45 *Half elevations and plan of a typical Gresley styled 58 ft 6 in ECJS corridor third of 1907. The carriage was exactly symmetrical about its centre-line, and the basic design hardly changed for the next forty years.*

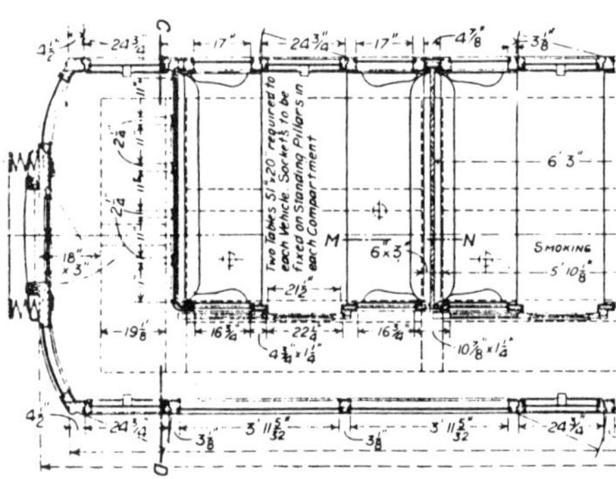

Scale 4mm = 1ft

Figure 46 *Third class carriages to an approximately 50-54-foot length usually had one less compartment than the 57-60-foot type. This plan shows a York-built ECJS example, contemporary with Fig 45 but only 53 ft 6 in long.*

Above *The toilet layout shown in Figure 46 seems to have been something of an East Coast speciality. This is an earlier clerestory example, ECJS No 94, built in 1903 to the same 53 ft 6 in length, this time with only one intermediate lavatory and two end vestibules.*

modern approach but historically its nomenclature is confusing. Some railways, for instance the LYR, called it a 'centre corridor', but since it had no walls this seems a bit of a linguistic inaccuracy; others adopted the terms 'passageway' or 'gangway', while after 1922 the LMS use the word 'vestibule' to denote this *type* of carriage! Since its most obvious differentiated characteristic was the open nature of its interior (ie not cluttered with intermediate walls and partitions), it seems logical to use the word 'open' to define the type, whether or not it possessed vestibules or gangways! This, indeed, is current BR form, so let us use it throughout.

So much for the semantics; what of the vehicles themselves? Essentially they can be classified into two families, 'corridor' and 'open', and this will be the basis of our analysis of ordinary stock.

In the 1900-1925 period — and later, for that matter — by far the most typical gangwayed carriage was of side corridor configuration. Early pioneers were the GWR, LNWR and, surprisingly, the GER, but by the end of the nineteenth century most long-distance systems which had tried it out at all had copied the basic arrangement. For one thing, it was extremely logical. Take one ordinary non-corridor carriage composed of conventional compartments, add a lavatory at one or both ends, place a passageway along one side, encapsulate the whole within the confines of an acceptable overall carriage size, add gangways at both ends and there you have it — the basic gangwayed corridor coach. All else was mere adaptation, and still is to all intents and purposes. It is in the adaptation that the real interest lies, for the railways demonstrated a remarkable versatility in playing 'variations on a single theme'.

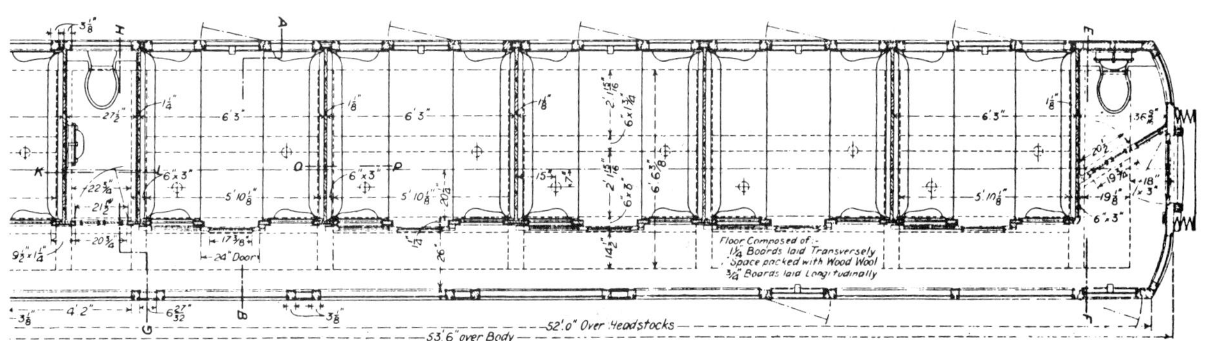

Firstly, it must be understood that in Britain the individual compartment was for the most part *de rigueur* in those days and woe betide the railway company which decided to break with tradition too dramatically. Thus, yet again, we come face to face with the interaction between people and vehicles as far as the railway carriage is concerned. Now, whether or not the reactions of individual companies were conscious or not is pretty well irrelevant at this distance in time, but they did reflect a genuine social reality in their almost universal adoption of the side corridor vehicle — and it was not solely a matter of practicality. The British liked their compartments. They always had and, I guess, given a free choice, they probably still do today. Nor am I free of prejudice myself, for nothing delights me more than to find my train formed up from the increasingly rare side corridor vehicles still to be seen on BR. The British are not wildly sociable people, and the compartment offered a sort of privacy which was jealously guarded in railway carriage terms for more than half of the present century!

Why this should be so is beyond my competence to analyse, but it seems real enough — or else why would the railways have gone to the trouble of making vehicles by the thousand over the years which

Left *The classic GWR 'Toplight' corridors evolved from the 'Dreadnoughts' via the 'Concertinas', and these views show the start and finish of the process 'Dreadnought' full third No 3277 and 70-foot (actually 69 ft 11¼ in) 'Toplight' full first No 8337, brand new in lake livery in 1914. Note that as well as a full set of compartment doors on the far side, each of the eight compartments had a door on the* corridor *side as well, a somewhat outmoded practice at this time* (Below T.J. Edgington collection).

Below left *MR composite No 3421 — see the drawings on this page.*

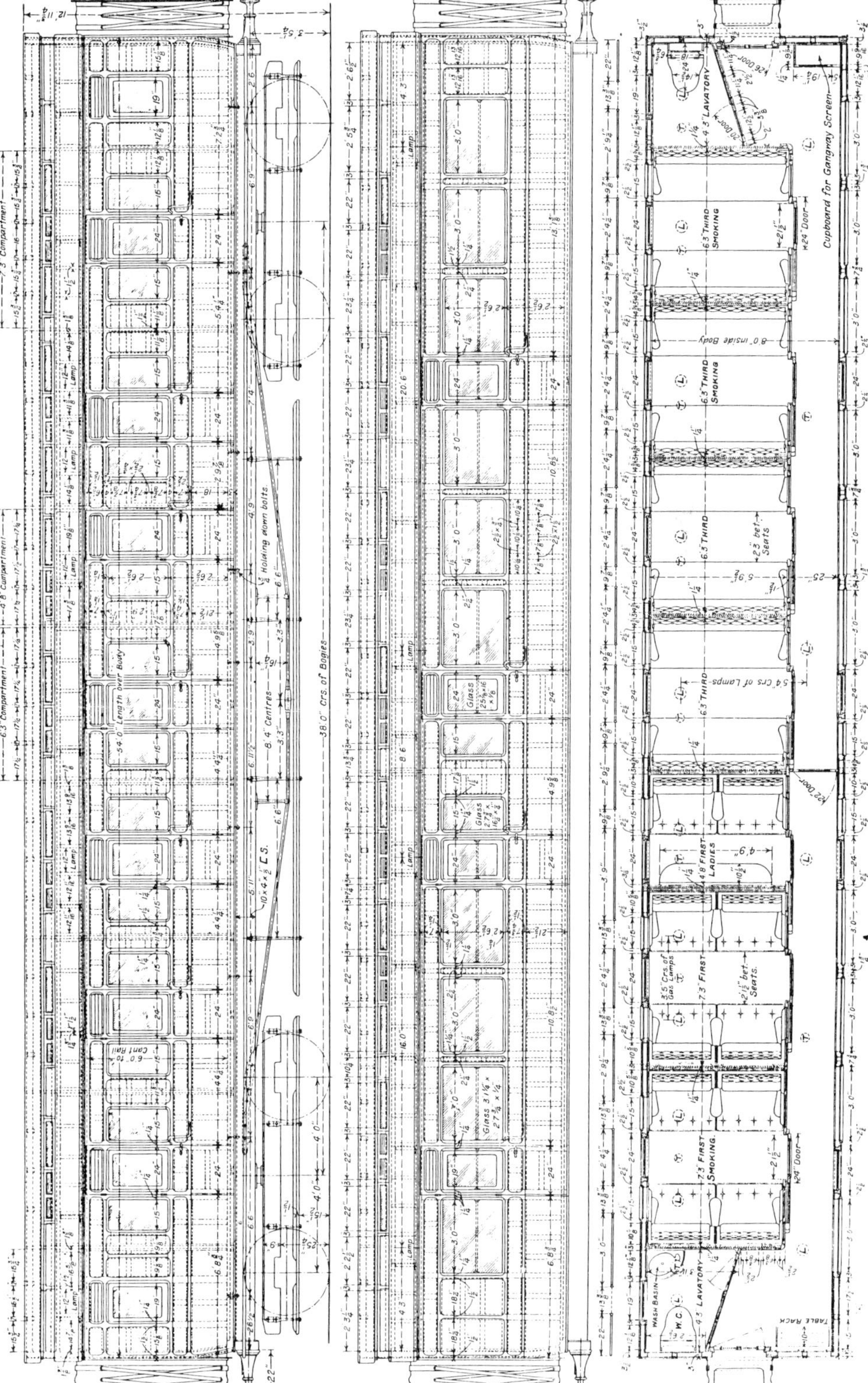

Figure 47 *Elevations and plan of a 54-foot Bain corridor composite built for the Midland Railway in 1909. Note the first class half-compartment* (BR LMR).

Scale 3.5mm = 1ft

were intrinsically more expensive than their open equivalents? They needed more partitions, doors, fittings and so on, and regularly provided a smaller number of seats per vehicle; but that was what was wanted, so the railways tried their best to provide, and right royally they succeeded. This attitude extended, in fact, well beyond the period under immediate discussion, but it was firmly grounded in the Edwardian age.

Setting aside the superficialities of style, roof profile, livery and so on, the basic corridor carriage was designed so that within the defined company length and width the best use could be made of available space. Typically, two particularly characteristic forms emerged which were to stand the test of time, the full third and the composite. The style of the full third was normally some 7-8 compartments plus two lavatories within a 50-60 foot length and an 8 ft-8 ft 6 in width. A typical desired compartment dimension was about 6 feet long, and the lavatories were about 4 feet, so a seven-compartment third plus two lavatories nicely fitted into a 50ft length; this was a very common choice, give or take a foot or so, perhaps best exemplified by hundreds of LNWR vehicles. Add an extra compartment and the very common 56-57 foot dimension emerged in consequence and variations within this arrangement were based on similar principles.

Thus, for example, the Midland, which favoured a somewhat more spacious 6 ft 3 in to 6 ft 6 in third class compartment, tended to go for a six compartment 48-footer at the turn of the century, extended to about 54 feet for the seven compartment version of the 1903-10 period. At the other end of the scale, the GWR 'Dreadnoughts' could get ten third class compartments plus lavatories into their 70-foot length. These carriages also managed to incorporate a corridor which changed sides halfway down the vehicle.

The composite was rather more of a problem. For one thing, there was always present the need to assess the relative proportions allocated to the various classes in terms of compartment numbers. Even had this basic decision been made with any degree of consistency, which was rarely the case, it could then be further confused by the need for *three* classes to be accommodated by those railways which still retained the second class option. Now, logic would suggest that the solution *should* have been to offer full first and second class carriages was well as full thirds, and this was a quite common solution in the four and six-wheel era. However, virtually all corridor carriages were of bogie type, and to allocate a complete vehicle of this larger type to either of the upper echelons would, in most cases, provide too many first and second class seats relative to the third class. The statistics analysed in Chapter 6 make this point only too clearly. Most railways did, in fact, build a few full firsts, but only used them on their heavier trains. For most purposes, three or four first class compartments within a composite would suffice to meet the need.

The main structural problem with a composite was to resolve the conflict between the increased length needed for the first class compartments and the understandable wish to use the same length of carriage in the interests of chassis standardization. The 'full' option was, of course, quite simple, in that six first class compartments, for example, would occupy much the same length as seven second or third class compartments, and this was the commonly adopted solution in these cases. The composite, however, was different, many indeed were the variations thereof and a few examples must needs serve to illustrate the whole.

For general use, a sort of half-and-half layout was adopted, typically 3 + 3 or 3 + 4 (either way round). Should this result in one fewer compartment overall than for a full third, the extra space gained, possibly 3 feet or so, could either be given to the lavatory compartments or provide, perhaps, extra internal luggage storing capacity. Thus, for instance, some of the six-compartment LNWR 50-foot composites had more or larger lavatories than the seven-compartment thirds. If, on the other hand, a company did not wish to reduce compartment numbers, it was

Left *This LSWR corridor composite No 999 has a fairly normal corridor side arrangement for the period, but displays a common stylistic variation, that of having drop lights opposite those compartments* not *served by outer doors — compare the picture on page 176.*

Below *The familiar corridor brake third could come in a variety of forms and compartment numbers. These three are typical, the references to 'handing' referring to the location of the brake end when viewed from the* corridor *side. They are: 50-foot three-compartment RH GER No 31 (above); 57-foot four-compartment RH CR No 1365 (below); 57-foot five-compartment LH LNWR No 6742 (bottom). Note that all of them have individual doors to each compartment* (Top BR LMR).

sometimes possible to reduce (slightly) the dimensions of both compartments and lavatories to fit them all in. A parallel alternative to either of these solutions was to incorporate a coupé, rather than lose a whole compartment. The Midland was quite fond of this trick and its 54-foot composites often had two-and-a-half first plus four thirds.

The exact number of compartments could be misleading in terms of perceived class proportions in the vehicle. In a corridor carriage, a third class compartment would always be assumed to have six or even eight seats available (the latter being typical for stock 9 feet wide) whereas the first class would mostly have but four seats per compartment (up to 8 ft 6 in wide carriages) and either four or six for a 9 feet wide example. In fact, many a 9 feet wide carriage was given but four seats per first class compartment, and no better provisioning has ever been made for the first class traveller since then, save at times on 'supplementary fare' services. Thus, a three first plus four third composite (a very typical form) would have a seating capacity of some 12-18 plus 24-32.

These figures, of course, did not reflect the true balance of cutomers within the train itself, but then it would not be very likely that a composite would run on its own. It would typically be operated with several thirds, and many railways chose to operate mostly composites rather than full firsts on even their longer trains. Two composites, placed 'first class to first class', would give the same number of seats as a full first but offer greater flexibility of operation. The MR was paricularly wedded to this approach.

The brake-ended corridor coach came in all three principal varieties (first, third and composite), but dominant again were the thirds and composites. On most railways, a fairly standard brake third layout was adopted with a lavatory at the non-brake end, followed by as many or as few compartments as were thought desirable before the van portion was reached. In general, the size of the latter tended to reflect the probable amount of luggage anticipated for the whole train, so on longer-distance services there were as few as two or three compartments with a large van, while at the opposite extreme, five or six compartments

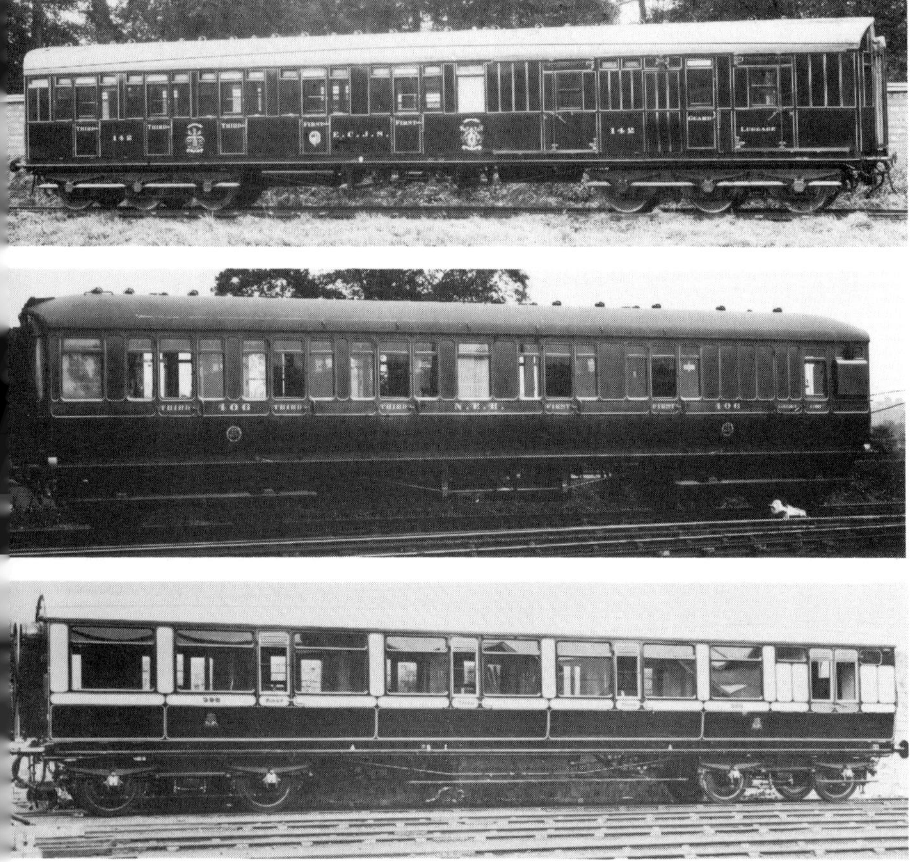

The five-compartment layout (two firsts and three thirds) was probably the most common form of corridor brake composite. Two of these three examples are of this kind, the third, the WCJS coach, having six compartments. In order, the types are: 65 ft 6 in twelve-wheel 'matchboard'-style LH ECJS No 142; 53 ft 6 in LH NER No 406; 57 ft RH WCJS No 398 (two firsts and four thirds). The layout of ECJS No 142 is given in Figure 48 and is reasonably typical for all, save for the precise location of toilets and first class compartments.

The much rarer corridor brake first is represented by these spacious examples, built within a year of each other in 1905-6. Both had but four seats per compartment. GNR No 217 is a five-compartment LH brake while MR No 2656 is a four-compartment RH example — this is the corridor side. Note the distinctive early MR practice of repeating quarter and drop lights opposite all compartments but without *a full set of corridor doors; larger windows appeared later (see page 109)* (Lower BR LMR).

with a shorter van would be preferred. Most long-distance companies could offer examples of all types, three to five compartments being probably the most customary.

The brake first was something of a rare bird, and still is for that matter. Unlike the full first, the relative sparseness of the brake first had little or nothing to do with the problem of compartment numbers as such. In fact, one might argue that a three or four compartment brake first would be just about right for many services in terms of accommodation *vis-à-vis* the rest of the train, but this would put the first class customers at one end of the formation. Many railways, however, preferred to put their first class seats in the middle of the train, flanked by the seconds (if present) and thirds. This had the effect of giving the first class customers the shortest walk to the dining car, if provided, and, except at terminal stations, was likely to put the first class section nearest to the entrances and exits from the platforms — all most laudable, but not always as practical as it may seem.

The alternative solution of firsts at one end, thirds at the other and dining facilities between them is much more common these days in Britain (reading 'second' for 'third'), and is the standard method of forming up a gangwayed train. However, until BR days this was by no means always the case, so the brake first tended to have some rarity value. Insofar as one dare generalize in these matters, it was probably the LNWR and particularly the MR which partially favoured the end location for the first class passenger, although neither did it exclusively. On their Anglo-Scottish trains, for example, it was quite common to see them formed up with the first class at the London end (avoiding a long walk from the platform barrier) then the diner(s) and then as many thirds as might be needed. In the case of the MR, since these trains often reversed their direction of travel at Leeds, the first class end was also at the platform end on arrival in Glasgow too — very clever! However, before taking this discussion of the complex business of marshalling a gangwayed train any further, we must first look into the role of that astonishingly versatile carriage, the corridor *composite* brake. Many railways had, or seemed to have, almost as many of these as they had brake thirds and the reason is not hard to find.

Like their non-corridor predecessors, corridor composite brakes were the logical choice for through workings. In fact they were even better, for the gangway allowed the passengers full use of the train's facilities right up to the point where the vehicle was detached to follow its own individual route to journey's end. Thus it was by no means uncommon to find trains carrying quite a number of such vehicles, each of which was bound for a different 'ultima

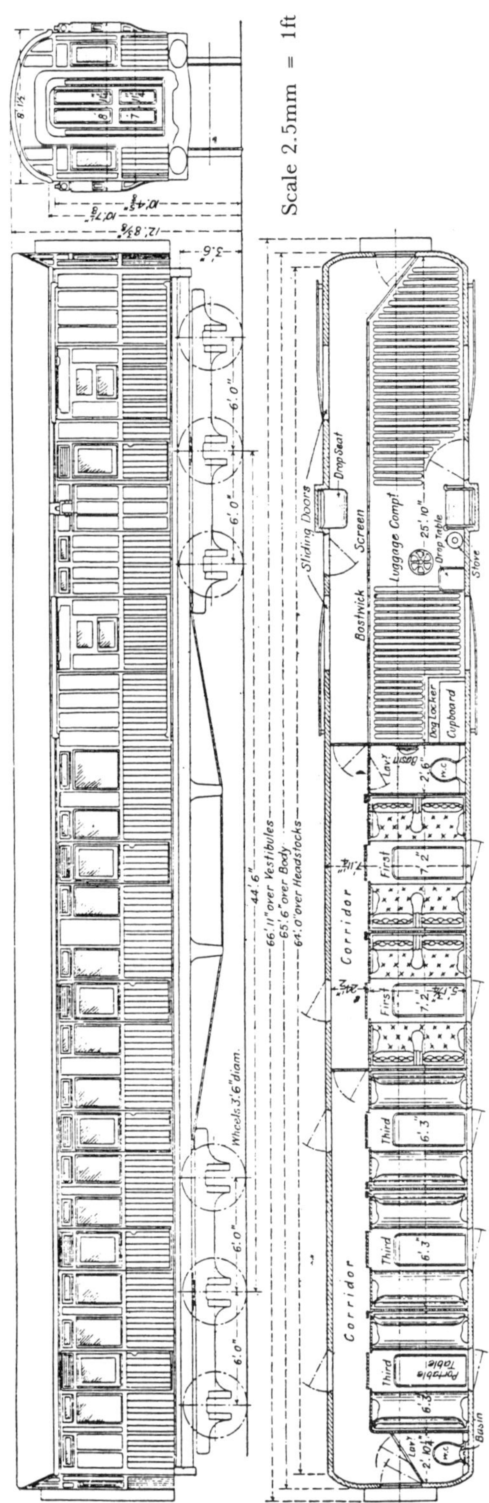

Figure 48 *Elevation and plan of the ECJS corridor composite brake illustrated on page 176. In this case, the toilets were 'outside' the compartments and the first class at the 'van' end of the carriage.*

Thule'. Furthermore, on some services the first class accommodation within a typical single brake composite might even suffice for the whole train, in much the same manner as did the first class compartments within a non-brake composite under different circumstances.

In terms of interior layout, the brake composite followed that of the brake first or third, but normally the van was shorter and it was rare to have fewer than four compartments (1 + 3 or 2 + 2) and far more likely to be five or six (2 + 3 or 2 + 4). There would often be a second lavatory between the last compartment and the van and, hardly surprisingly, many railways made extensive use of coupés in their brake composites. At times it went to ridiculous extremes, but no one could argue that the railways were not trying their best. In fact, the sheer variety of corridor carriage layouts within the same set parameters is only explicable in terms of the railways making a conscious effort to match their carriage provisioning as precisely as possible to the nature of specific services. It reached its ultimate form in the 'dedicated' set formations for specific services (see Chapter 13) but, within the 'general service' category, most railways managed to provide themselves with a sufficient measure of choice in order to achieve, or try to achieve, a precisely correct mix for most purposes.

Take, for example, the matter of the 'handing' of brake carriages. Perusal of any corridor coach plan will reveal that the van can either be at the left-hand or right-hand end of the vehicle, relative to the corridor and passenger spaces. There is no hard and fast rule about it, but, to avoid ambiguity, references to 'left-handed' and 'right-handed' brakes in this survey will relate to the position of the van when viewed from the *corridor* side. There is no prima facie case for 'handing' a brake-ended carriage. The normal ramifications in service will pretty soon guarantee that the vehicle at some time in its life gets itself 'inside out', so to speak, as a result of negotiating loops, triangles, reversals of direction and all the other track complexities which the railways in their heyday could provide. So why was it done?

As far as I can determine, there were only two reasons for this phenomenon, both concerned with train marshalling. In a perfect world, a set of gangwayed carriages would normally have a brake vehicle at each end, van portions outwards. Now, some railways, particularly such influential concerns as the LNWR, liked to maintain the corridor down the

The corridor brake composite was ideally suited for slip working — see page 166 — and the GWR was probably the prime exponent. This is 'Toplight' 'slip brake composite' No 7101 (BR/OPC).

same side of the train throughout. This was said to be because the LNWR wished to have the corridor on the 'west' side of its mainly north-south trains. Apparently it was to avoid passengers getting too hot on long sunny days! The LNWR certainly put most corridors on the west side on many occasions, but this inevitably meant opposite-handed brakes at the ends of the formation, however many intervening carriages might be present. This particular obsession even went as far as 'handed' composites from time to time in order to allow the first class portions of two adjoining coaches to be connected together with the corridor on the same side or to put them next to the diner(s). This was all most commendable, but rather presupposed that nothing would ever happen to alter the formation of the train — a vain hope in most cases.

Paradoxically, the second reason for 'handed' brakes arose from precisely opposite criteria, the wish to alternate the corridor from side to side between each vehicle. There was a sort of feeling, arising from the fact of the corridor coach having its passengers distributed towards one side of the vehicle, that it would, in some way, be loaded more heavily on the compartment side. The GWR 'Dreadnoughts' displayed a corridor which was switched across the vehicle at the mid point for this very reason. The effect was at best marginal, but took on somewhat absurd characteristics when some railways decided to balance the perceived asymmetric loading by alternating the corridor side between adjacent vehicles, as if it could in some magical way cancel out the lop-sidedness! I have never seen any good argument advanced for this quaint custom, but when allied with fixed sets of corridor coaches it inevitable meant that those sets containing an *odd* number of vehicles threw up opposite-handed brakes at their extremities.

The most noteworthy practitioner of this approach was probably the LSWR which set much store on five-coach sets (usually two brake thirds, two thirds and one full first). In this it was often followed slavishly by the Southern in more recent times, but mercifully the more corridor-orientated railways fairly rapidly abandoned the nonsense and settled on a single configuration, dominantly right-handed. By BR days, all new side-corridor brake coaches of any type were exclusively right-handed. Mark you, there was still (save in BR days) much scope for variety in terms of compartment numbers and whether or not (in the case of a brake composite) the first class should be at the end of the vehicle or adjacent to the van. By means of such inconsequential ephemera,

First class two-seat coupé (for ladies only) in a Midland corridor composite brake of 1903 (BR LMR).

Top *This elegantly styled five-coach set of LNWR cove roof corridors clearly demonstrates the 'corridor down one side' principle. From the near end, the types are: brake first (two compartments), first (six compartments), two thirds (seven compartments), brake third (four compartments). All were 57-foot carriages and the small number of compartments was probably generous to a fault; but what a nice train for 1905! The formation also demonstrates the 'first class at one end' philosophy, and if a dining car was included it would have been inserted between the first and third class portions* (BR LMR).

Above *Another elegant set, this time LSWR, illustrates the 'alternating side' corridor principle and a different class distribution. From the near end the types are: brake third, third, two composites (first class portions adjoining), brake third. In this case the firsts are in the middle of the train, and note also that the brake end has no gangway (it was later modified), symptomatic of the 'set' principle followed by the LSWR. Other LSWR sets had one full first and two thirds rather than as shown here. In my view, this and the preceding LNWR train represent some of the stylistic high points of the pre-group era.*

the delights of the carriage student were much enhanced!

It was, of course, the principal long-distance companies which led the way in terms of corridor coach design — and there seems to have been more than a bit of 'over the shoulder' looking at the offerings of the rival concerns. Thus, within broadly similar parameters, the companies came up with quite a few variations. The dominant concerns were, not unnaturally, the LNWR (including the West Coast Joint Stock partnership with the CR), GWR, Midland, GNR and NER (including their various joint activities) and, in Scotland, the CR and NBR, though the latter pair tended to be of lesser significance than their respective English partners.

This led to more than a few very splendid carriages being put into service on the longer-distance routes which, fashion apart, would not disgrace the modern railway. Take those arch rivals the MR and LNWR for example. They were in fierce competition for much of the traffic between London, the Midlands, the North and Scotland, and their carriages could not have been more different during the Edwardian period. Both companies entered the century with a sort of 48-50 ft x 8 ft 6 in standard dimension, the LNWR with an arc roof profile, the Midland with its classic clerestory. In terms of compartment size and general elegance the MR probably held the edge, but in its espousal of the corridor principle the LNWR was second to none. In the early 1900s, both companies made changes. The MR extended its carriage length to 54 feet, retaining broadly the same stylistic features, but in 1905 the LNWR made a great leap forward with some of the finest corridor vehicles ever seen in Britain up to that time. They were 57 feet long by 9 feet inside with a handsome cove roof profile (see page 37) and extraordinarily spacious compartments. The full third had but seven of them and the full first only six, the latter, moreover, with but four seats per compartment. They also came in at over 30 tons per vehicle, an awful lot of weight for only 24 first class passengers; but they were sumptuous. In due course, they were built with full elliptical roofs but, interestingly, they

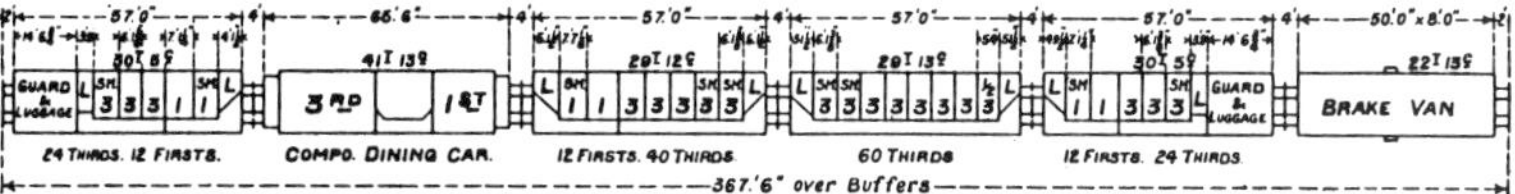

New Train, Day North Express, L. and N.W.R. 57ft. 0in. x 9ft. 0in. Stock. Side doors.
36 First Class. 148 Third Class. Total passengers 184.

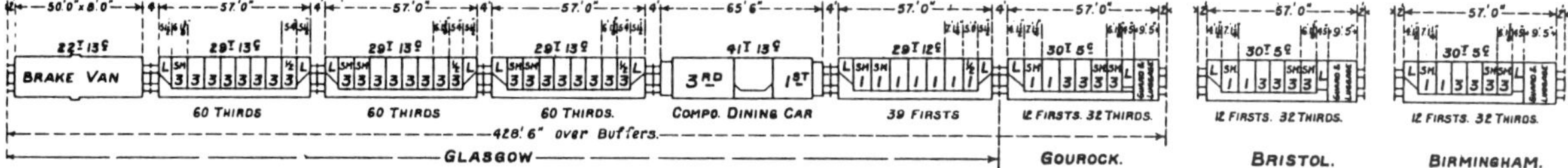

New Train for 10 a.m. ex-Euston, Scotch Express, L. and N.W.R. 57ft. 0in. x 9ft. 0in. Stock. Side doors.
75 First Class. 276 Third Class. Total passengers 351.

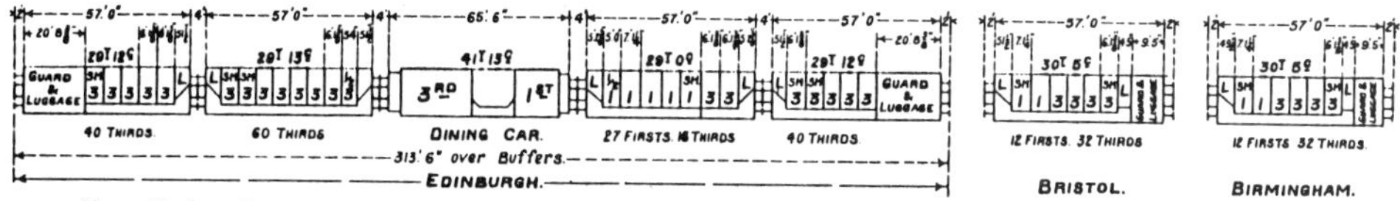

New Train, Scotch Express, Edinburgh Portion, L. and N.W.R. 57ft. 0in. x 9ft. 0in. Stock. Side doors.
51 First Class. 220 Third Class. Total passengers 271.

Figure 49 *This contemporary drawing shows typical LNWR/WCJS formations used in 1913. The trains were mostly new-styled carriages such as shown on page 108, save for the twelve-wheel diners and the full brakes.*

were usually confined to the English routes where the LNWR met with competition from several rivals. The West Coast services, however, continued until about 1912-13 with the old arc roof style, save for one spectacular exception (see Chapter 13).

The MR and the GWR (also in rivalry with the LNWR) seemed unwilling to match this LNWR grandeur and continued to provide the mixture much as before, and even the LNWR seemed to think twice about these excessively generous compartment sizes before many years had lapsed. Interestingly, all three companies settled down to very similar provisioning, based on a 57 feet by 9 feet dimension, during the Great War period. Exterior styling apart, there was little to choose between them by, say, 1918 in terms of their then current building programmes. As has already been mentioned, the GWR after the Dean period came to this situation by means of a short-lived experiment with 70 foot coaches ('Dreadnoughts' and 'Concertinas') before it finally settled down during the 'Toplight' era to something very close to the LNWR/MR approach.

Down the East Coast, as has been seen, the GNR

This 1908 53 ft 6 in NER corridor third No 1920, without compartment doors, was distinctly ahead of its time, and it was a generation later before its LNER successor standardized the same principle. Even the NER was forced into retaining an all-door configuration on many of its carriages (see the picture on page 123).

design influence gradually became dominant and this really started with some magnificent twelve-wheel corridors built at the turn of the century. There were not many of them, but in terms of the competition from the other Northern routes they were every bit as good and offered particularly welcome improvements in the third class — probably to meet the Midland's aggressive aompetition. These pioneer clerestories were, however, soon to be rendered obsolescent, if not obsolete, by Gresley's introduction of his new corridors with their very 'modern'-looking domed end roof shape, thereafter to become dominant both in ECJS and later LNER days. Their length tended to settle down at a foot or two longer than those of most companies at the time, eventually standardizing at around 58-61 feet, give or take a few inches.

In one respect, the companies so far considered had one particular design point in common, the retention of outside doors to all compartments. It is true that the GWR 'Dreadnoughts' abandoned this feature, but it turned out to be too advanced a concept for the time, so back came the doors with the 'Concertinas' and 'Toplights'. There was, however, one railway which made more than one valiant attempt to move forward. This was the NER which, for its own domestic use, produced a whole range of carriages especially attractive both outside and within. Those without compartment doors were a definite cut above most of the competition but clearly met with some resistance since the NER also felt obliged to produce some all but identical repeats with a full array of doors. In their liking for individual doors, one can only conclude that the British travelling public showed similar resistance to change as they did with the move to open carriages (see below).

The NER, for all its size, tended to live somewhat under the shadow of the GNR as far as long-distance carriages were concerned, especially in its jointly-owned operations. The ECJS examples are, of course, relatively well known, but the situation was further diluted from the NER standpoint by the GNR/NER joint stock which operated the London-Newcastle services. These too, although much less well known than the ECJS fleet, tended to follow the latter pattern, so the purely NER designs tended to be concentrated in the provinces where, perhaps inevitably, they received rather less attention than might have been the case had they been regularly seen in London. In this respect, the regional nature of the NER seemed to put it at a disadvantage, size of system notwithstanding. At the same time, it should be recorded that many GN-styled Joint Stock coaches were built by the NER to its own somewhat shorter length and on NER design chassis.

Right Figure 50 *Part elevations, plans and selected cross-sections of the celebrated Caledonian 'Grampian' corridor stock of 1905. Details of the bogie can be found in Figure 7 (page 23).*

A somewhat similar fate befell the two principal Scottish companies which operated corridors, the NBR and CR. Their services to England were largely in the hands of the ECJS and WCJS respectively, so their own individualistic contribution was generally confined to their purely domestic routes. In this context, they both proved capable of producing some quite splendid offerings of which perhaps the most celebrated were the Caledonian's 'Grampian' twelve-wheelers. These highly praiseworthy vehicles came out as early as 1905 and exhibited a near GWR size in terms of length and profile, being 65 feet by 9 feet with an almost fully elliptical roof. Internally they were conventional enough in layout, but their considerable length allowed a considerable enhancement in seating capacity. Unfortunately, as with many other rather good carriages, there were too few of them to count for much in subsequent years, and the CR soon went over to the 57 foot type, very similar to its English contemporaries.

The NBR's equivalents to the 'Grampians' were some rather stylish vehicles built for the Fife and Lothian Coast Expresses (and other purely Scottish services) in 1907. Like most railways at this time, the NBR had also decided to espouse the full height roof but came up with its own subtly distinctive form which, when allied to its equally characteristic panelling treatment, produced a rather different-looking vehicle — albeit with little in the way of interior innovation. Another disadvantage as far as the NBR was concerned in terms of long-term influence was the fact that not only did it participate in the ECJS, but also that its services via the Waverley route to England were in the hands of the so far unmentioned Midland-Scottish Joint Stock (MSJS), later renamed M & NB or M & GSW as appropriate. Just as with the other two Anglo-Scottish joint fleets, so too in the case of the MSJS, the English influence was dominant, this time pure Derby. This led, in time, to the somewhat amusing situation of Midland-designed vehicles being operated in LNER colours after the post-grouping division of the M & NB stock between its LMS and LNER partners.

Meanwhile, what of the smaller concerns, sparing the sensitivities of their followers? Here again there were quite perceptible differences both between Scotland and England and, south of the border, between the London-based and the provincial systems. Moreover, even the nature of the various London-based systems caused differences to appear.

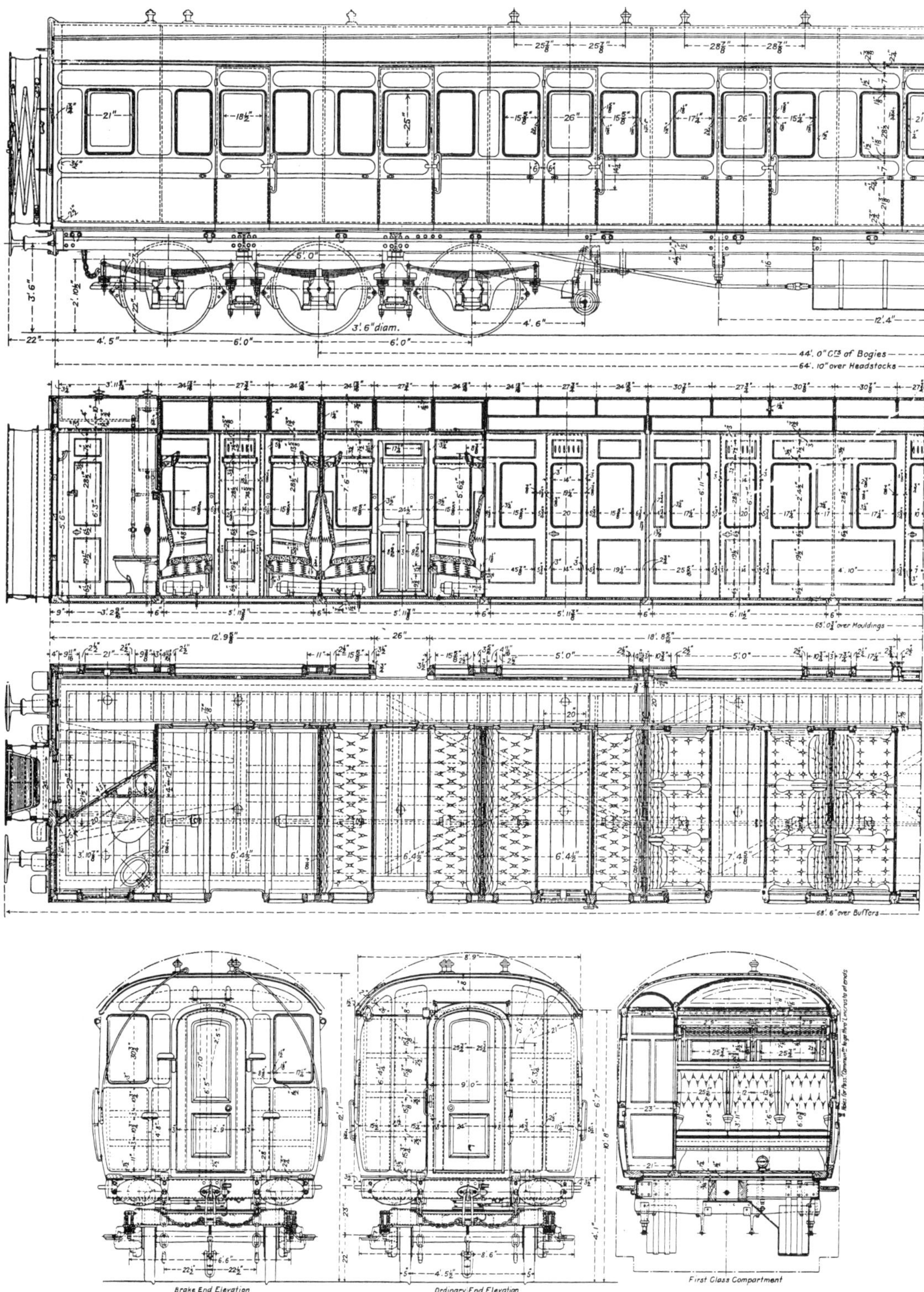

Scale 4mm = 1ft

However, before considering these rather subtle influences, it will be convenient to conclude the Scottish survey.

Apart from the NBR and CR, the main Scottish user of corridor coaches was the GSWR and in Peter Drummond's time some very attractive vehicles emerged, somewhat in contradiction to his less than universally approved locomotive designs. However, like the other two big Scottish companies, any possible GSWR influence on a larger scale was heavily eroded by the dominance of the English element (Midland) in the M & GSW fleet of corridor coaches. These were always pure Derby and frequently identical to the domestic MR product. In fact, even before the grouping, the GSWR found itself operating Derby-designed vehicles under its own banner as a result of its share of 'cascaded' former M & GSW coaches. In this, of course, it was no different from the NBR or CR. Nevertheless, the Drummond coaches were good, and in their extensive use of pressed steel bogie frames distinctly ahead of much of the opposition.

Drummond, of course, had come to the GSWR from the Highland Railway, and one can detect some degree of design linkage between his latter-day HR coaches and those he built for his new company. However, the HR was a somewhat impecunious system and did not build many corridors on its own account. To be honest, it hardly needed to, being fed, so to speak, at Perth with the products of Derby, Wolverton, Doncaster et al as they converged from their various points of origin on to the Southern end of the famous Highland main line to Inverness and the far North. What a spectacle that must have been in its heyday! Thus, apart from a few carriages built for services between Inverness and Glasgow or Edinburgh, the HR did not bother too much with corridors and the GNSR was much the same, although it had produced some excellent examples of the type as far back as the 1890s.

Back in England, one can clearly differentiate between the provincial and the London-based systems. Thus, for example, although the GCR might not have been as important in absolute terms as, say, the LYR, the fact of its main line to Marylebone caused it to tackle the corridor coach problem with some vigour. In a sense it had no choice because it was entering an already competitive field against some real giants. In a fairly modest start at the turn of the century it displayed some imaginative internal touches, not least being the admirably wide corridors compared with the competition. This was a much appreciated improvement, albeit at the expense of compartment width. This, however, can be seen in retrospect to have been little more than a final flowering of the Manchester, Sheffield and Lincolnshire Railway approach (the pre-1899 name of the GCR). Once the GCR began to build to the limits of its structure gauge for the London Extension, its new 'matchboard'-sided corridor coaches commanded immediate attention. They were better than the more famous 'Barnums' (see below), not least in their styling — large, dignified and on the whole harmonious. They kept the wide corridors, and some of them even had a patent form of anti-telescoping device fitted to their headstocks which caused a great deal of contemporary technical interest. They certainly gave plenty of space inside for all their passengers.

The other two so far unconsidered London-based concerns with any pretensions to corridor coach status, the LSWR and the GER, could not have been more different. Alone of the constituents of what was to become the Southern Railway, the LSWR had trunk route status and, in consequence, started to tackle the corridor coach implications of its competition with the GWR for the West of England traffic. It did so in a distinctive way, not so much in terms of vehicle quantities, types or styling, but by a quite positive attempt to translate the undoubted advantages of set train formations (see Chapters 8 and 9) to the altogether more complicated business of long-distance operating. This has already been touched upon earlier in the chapter but this seems, perhaps, the best point at which to amplify the topic; the LSWR, while not alone in producing sets of corridor coaches, was undoubtedly the leader, as indeed was its Southern successor.

The practical advantages of set formation trains of time-saving on coupling, marshalling and so on, have already been discussed, particularly in the non-corridor field, but they are equally applicable to corridor vehicles if some sort of standardized pattern could be evolved. Interestingly, most of the 'corridor' lines tended, at best, to go for only a few regular sets of vehicles, each being 'dedicated' to one or two specific services, the LNWR, for example, being one such system. The balance of services on these lines would be operated more often than not by a suitable assemblage of vehicles formed up to meet specific operating requirements. The LSWR was different. It took the view, quite deliberately, that if one could arrive at a suitable fixed formation for most of the time, then at periods of pressure one could augment the principle either by having a few spare or 'loose' vehicles (dominantly thirds) or even use two identical sets rather than one only. On the whole, it seems to have worked and the Southern continued the general idea right into the post-Second World War era. In fact, after the grouping the idea translated quite well across to such large systems as the LMS which became quite adept at using what it called 'Inter-Corridor sets' (an abbreviation for standardized Inter-District corridor formations of three or four coaches) for many services.

Back to the LSWR, however, and what can be said is that even the building of its corridor coaches was carried out with the deliberate intention of forming the vehicles into sets. The individual carriage running numbers, the 'handing' of the brakes (if relevant) and the fact that the sets were regarded for decades as having almost permanent status (they were branded by number on the the outer brake ends) were all reflected in the end product — and the vehicles themselves were not bad either. The earlier examples were typically LSW in styling (low elliptical roof, traditional panelling and so on) but were 9 feet wide and quite lengthy (57 feet) by company standards. However, before the grouping, the LSWR entered somewhat pioneering territory by being one of the first companies to experiment with the more widespread use of steel, particularly in the exterior panelling, in its so-called 'Ironclads'. They were hardly things of great aesthetic distinction — some would even call them dull and boring — but, like many things LSW, they were built like the proverbial battleship and stood the test of time. Southern Railway practice came much under their influence for many years and they too tended to the 57-foot length already considered above.

Top left *The NBR introduced this seven-compartment corridor first in 1907, but built a few more in 1921 so they must have been more than adequate. They certainly provided a very clear view on the corridor side as exemplified by No 460 of the 1921 series.*

Above left *Peter Drummond's GSWR corridor stock, though not particularly well known, was more than uncommonly handsome and spacious as well as being typically British, points well shown in this brake third No 64. The full thirds had only seven compartments in a 57-foot length. Most railways at this time would have used eight.*

Right *The spacious 2 ft 6 in wide corridors of the new GCR trains are shown clearly in this view of first class No 1299 of the 'armoured' series.*

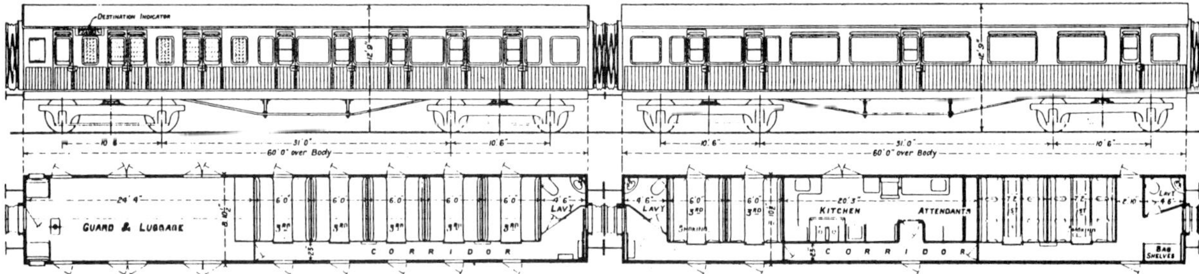

Corridor Third Brake Carriage. To carry 40 Passengers. Corridor Composite Kitchen Car. To carry 12 First and 16 Third Class Passengers.
Diagram of London, Manchester and Bradford

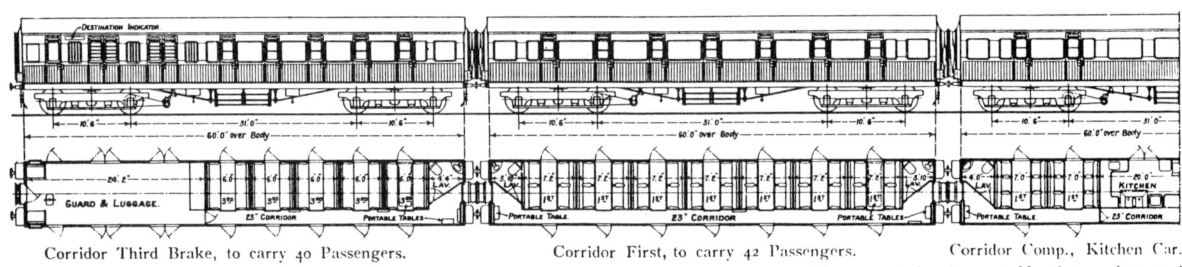

Corridor Third Brake, to carry 40 Passengers. Corridor First, to carry 42 Passengers. Corridor Comp., Kitchen Car.
Diagram of London and Manchester Armoured

Figure 51 *Floor plans and simplified side elevations of the trend-setting GCR 60-foot corridor trains of 1915, one of which was fitted with the so-called 'armoured' anti-telescoping device at the carriage ends, details of which are also shown (below).*

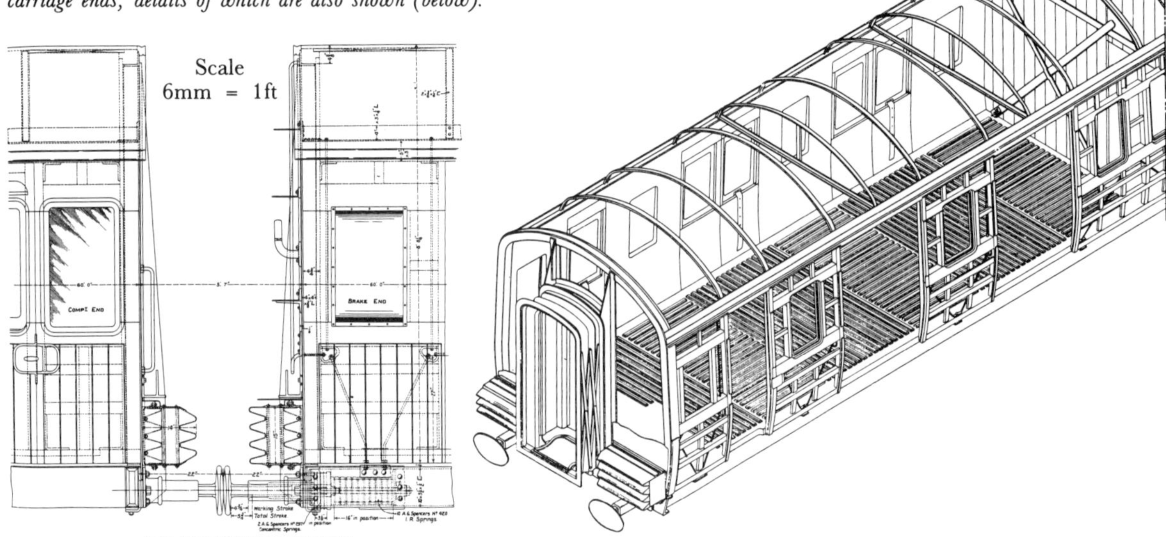

The GER, on the other hand, although having been an early pioneer of corridor stock, tended to remain somewhat on the periphery of things. Its vehicles, be they clerestory or elliptical, were always neat and unfussy, and some of the boat train formations were distinctly superior; but somehow they never seemed to catch on either in popular acclaim or in subsequent LNER days. Perhaps it was because few could believe that a railway capable of such diabolical atrocities as were provided for its suburban services could ever be capable of producing anything decent in the longer-distance field. It was manifestly unfair, as a study of some of the pictures in this book will reveal, but it seems to have been real enough. Nevertheless, after the grouping the impoverished LNER must more than once have had

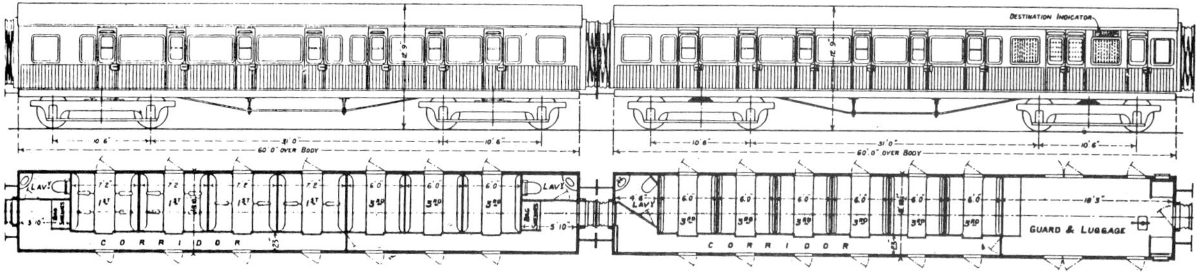

Corridor Composite Carriage. To carry 20 First and 24 Third Class Passengers. Corridor Third Brake Carriage. To carry 48 Passengers.
Express Train; Great Central Railway.

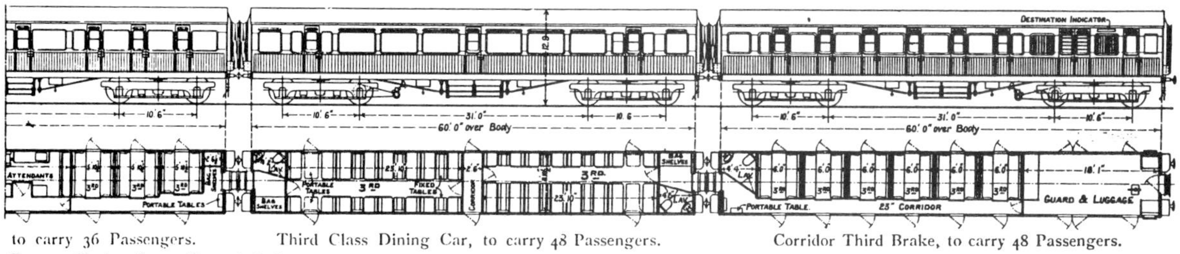

to carry 36 Passengers. Third Class Dining Car, to carry 48 Passengers. Corridor Third Brake, to carry 48 Passengers.
Express Train, Great Central Railway.

cause to be grateful for the quality of the better GER corridors; they certainly lasted for a long time and were by no means the worst of their kind, although they tended to be shorter in length than most contemporary corridor coaches.

A rather different story is to be told of the SE & CR, a railway not renowned for its corridor stock. In fact, to all intents and purposes, it had none to speak of save for one or two rather curious exceptions, including an altogether rather splendid clutch of brake composites. Interestingly, these were not built for local consumption but more in accordance with a 'keep up with the Joneses' philosophy. We have seen how the SE & CR produced some distinctly superior non-corridors, but where through services were concerned it obviously felt it needed to be on a par with the companies with whom it exchanged traffic. It thereupon proved that it could come up with the goods if necessary. Its introduction of corridors for its own services was caught up inextricably with the grouping but, for the record at this point, it should be stated that the final SE & CR corridor designs were of distinctive 'matchboard' style which formed the pattern for the Eastern section of the SR after 1922, even if not in quite such a seminal way as did the 'Ironclads' of the LSWR.

As for the Brighton influence on corridor coach evolution, it may safely be ignored!

Corridor coaches on both the larger and smaller provincial companies, if built at all, tended in layout terms to copy the patterns of the larger concerns but some interesting vehicles emerged. Even the Cambrian and Furness Railways had a few, but perhaps the most significant contribution, as far as future influence in Britain was concerned, was that of the LYR, an unlikely contender for honours one might feel. Over the years, the Lancashire and Yorkshire has been given less than due credit for its often innovative approach to the business of operating a railway. We have already noted its quite generous provision of bogie coaches in the non-corridor field and equally one could instance the work of George Hughes in the sphere of locomotive development. There will also be cause to come back to the LYR in the story of steam railmotors and electrification (in Chapter 15) but what is perhaps less well known is its influence in the field of gangwayed carriage design.

As fas as side corridors were concerned, the LYR examples were from the outset built to quite full dimensions — 56 feet by 9 feet. Originally with arc roofs, they went straight to the full elliptical style early in the century and thereafter mirrored contemporary fashion in terms of layout and operation. Thus far they would merit no more and no less attention than those of many another company, but in one important respect the LYR turned out to be a significant trendsetter on a nationwide basis, and this was its espousal of the open saloon interior as a common alternative to the conventional side corridor — which nicely sets the scene for a discussion of the second principal type of gangwayed ordinary mentioned early in this chapter.

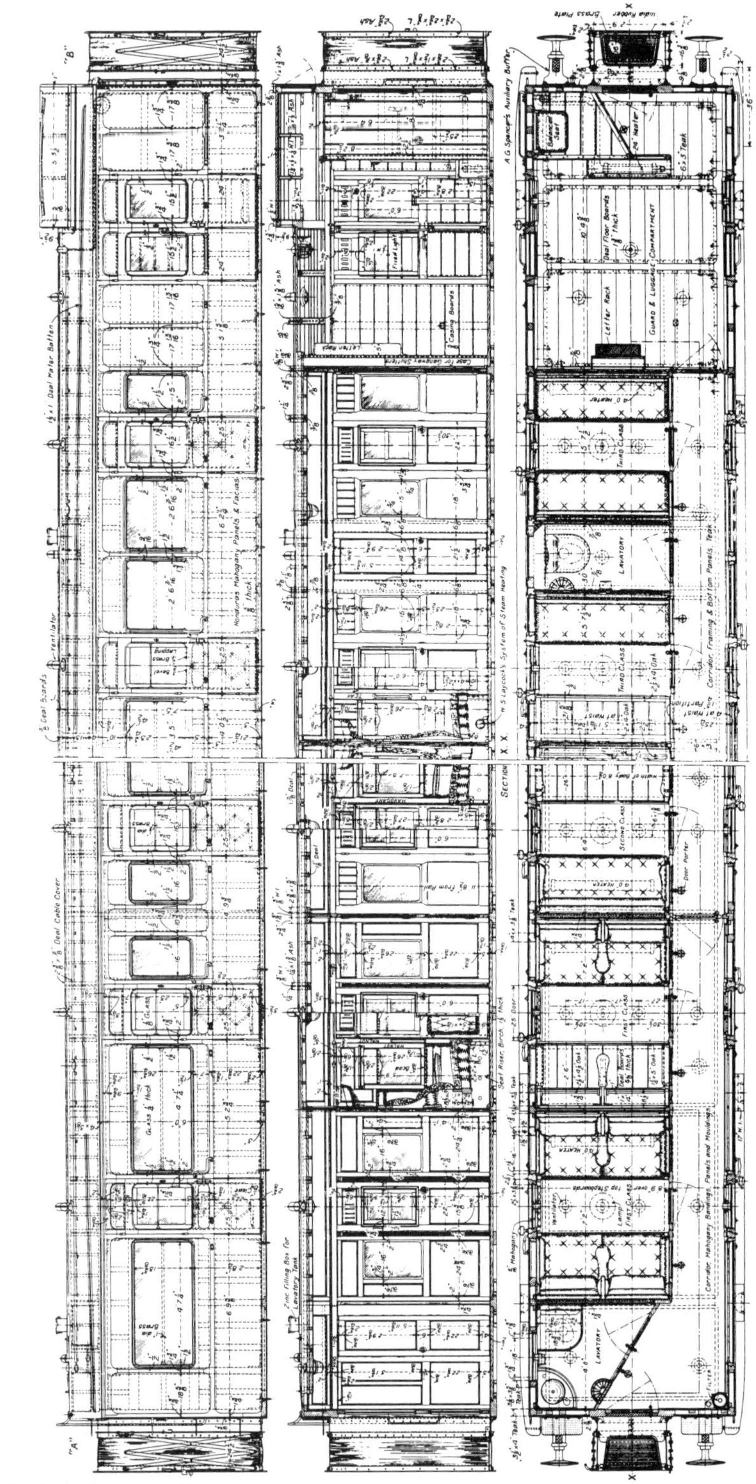

Figure 52 *A rare but by no means inferior essay into the side-corridor field — elevations and plan of the exceedingly well-appointed bogie tri-composite corridor carriages built by the SE & CR for through operation to the North and West via the LNWR, MR and GWR.*

Scale 3.5mm = 1ft

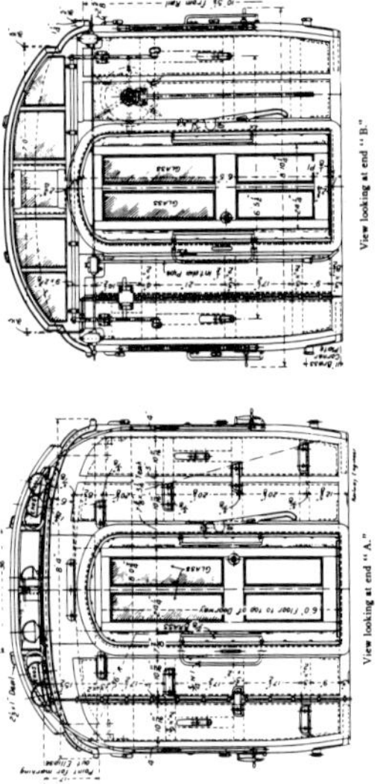

Above right *Probably the first serious attempt at open stock was represented by six so-called 'Picnic' saloons by the LYR in 1900-01. They were true harbingers of the later and ubiquitous open third. No 2509 was the first and only one to be built without gangways (added later). The use of traditional panelling, a treatment always confined by the LYR to its carriages with open interiors rather than the orthodox LYR styling gave distinctive visual characteristics to the carriage.*

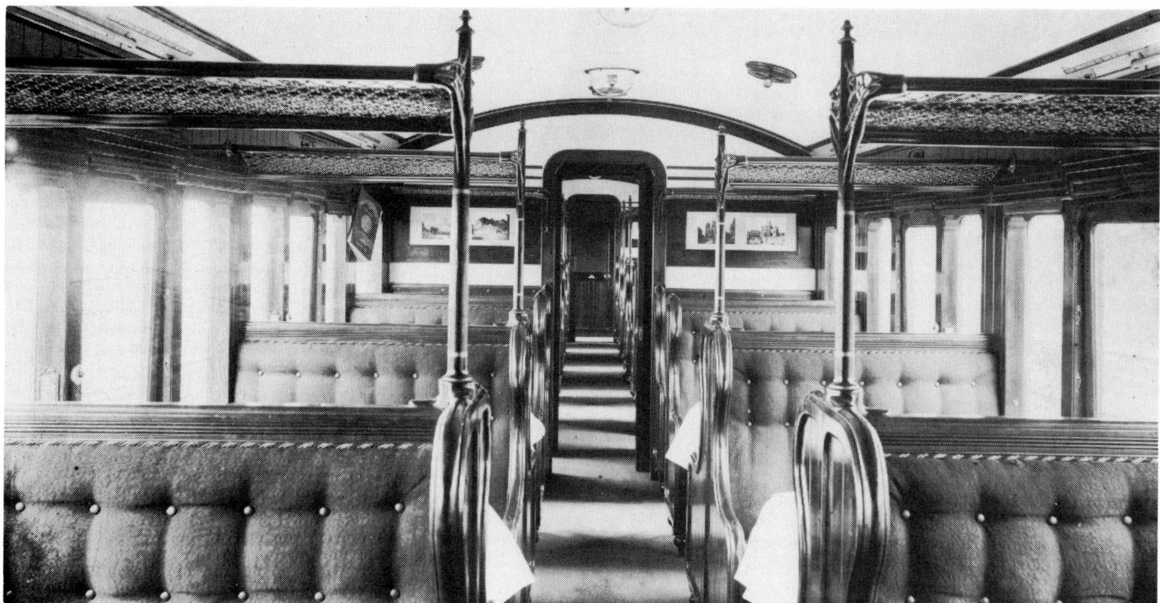

The open configuration began in the dining car field, having obvious practical advantages in the context of meal service, but for many years this was the only type of carriage which displayed this form of interior layout. Even those relatively few open carriages without a kitchen/pantry area were always regarded as dining carriages, and several railways built the odd example from an early date, back in the 1890s in some cases. However, as far as can be ascertained it was probably the LYR which first began to consider them as an alternative to side corridors for ordinary, as opposed to dining, use. The reasons cannot be determined exactly, but alone of the pre-grouping companies the LYR regarded them on virtually equal terms with the side corridor type, and thus began a trend which in BR days was virtually to eliminate the good old side corridor style for new construction. Of course, it was never quite as simplistic as this in real terms and for many decades open stock was regarded more as a supplement to rather than a replacement of the side corridor approach, particularly in the third (now second) class field.

Like them or loathe them — and both views have their adherents — the open carriage configuration possesses certain advantages from the railway company's point of view. For one thing it is cheaper to make, having less internal partitions and, save for a few exceptions which can realistically be ignored, considerably fewer outside doors. Secondly, and this time from the passenger standpoint, if four per side seating is required in a gangwayed third class coach, then the 2 + 2 seating of an open carriage is marginally more comfortable than the four per side corridor style. If three per side in the third class compartment is favoured (common in later LMS, LNER and BR days), then an open 2 + 2 arrangement actually offers 33% more seats per vehicle without too much loss of comfort. These latter considerations have obviously proved decisive in modern BR planning, but it may well be that the LYR was the first company to see it that way.

In terms of styling, the LYR open stock generally differed from the side corridor equivalent in a number of ways, some significant, others not. For some reason, whether arc or elliptical roof, most of them abandoned the characteristic and somewhat spartan Attock styling (page 106) in favour of a more traditional style which embodied distinctly pleasing proportions and a somewhat more elaborate lining

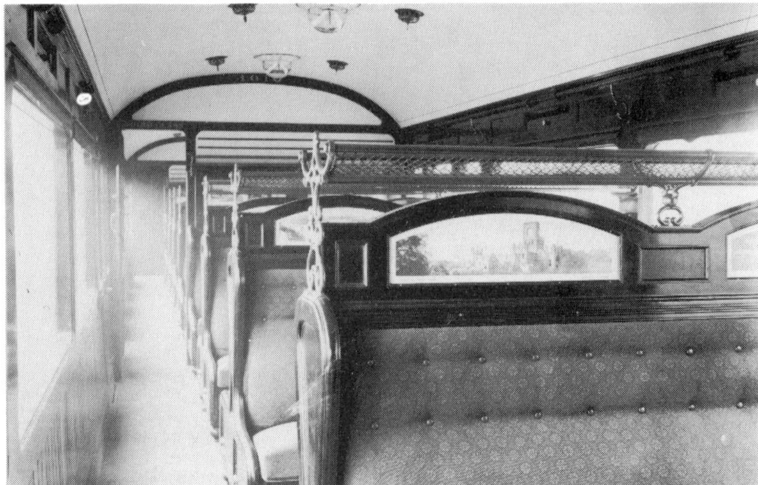

Above *Open composite No 865 typifies the later and more familiar elliptical roof 'fireproof' stock of the LYR. The large picture windows are prominent and, again, it was given traditional panelling.*

Left *Another LYR experiment in 1908-09 produced some fascinating carriages described as 'open side corridor', again with large windows. They displayed conventional LYR exterior styling, and the interior of the first example, No 1010, is illustrated. Although the general idea did not catch on, the LMS found use for them for many years.*

treatment. This may have been a shrewd publicity move, for when allied as it was in the elliptical roof variants with large 'picture' windows in each seating bay, it really did make the carriages look very modern by comparison with those of many other lines.

It was some of these open coaches which formed the basis of the celebrated LYR 'Fireproof' trains. In Chapter 4 the reluctance of some railways to abandon gas lighting was mentioned, and the LYR was one such. In 1913, it produced a series of metal-clad carriages with much supplementary fire-resistant material in an endeavour to stave off the need to move, exclusively, to electric lighting. They were distinctly attractive and gracious formations and, being placed on the prestigious residential expresses, sometimes known as 'Club' trains, operated by the LYR to Southport and Blackpool, they were given all the publicity which the company could muster. With an Aspinall 'Atlantic' or Hughes 4-6-0 in charge, they were no mean advertisement for a so-called 'provincial' railway. However, their influence in the 'fire-proof' sense was far less significant than the implications of their layout. Indeed, it is not too far fetched to presume that the LYR experience of ordinary open stock was by no means the least of the reasons why the LMS adopted the idea with great vigour after the grouping (see Volume 2).

Now, lest it should be thought that the LYR was the only major company to experiment with gangwayed open coaches for non-dining services, this impression must be corrected. Several of the pre-1923 companies tried the idea with a greater or lesser degree of success, including a few unlikely contenders such as the Caledonian. However, of those which did persevere, one can perhaps single out the Midland and the Great Central as being the most noteworthy.'

During 1909, the Midland Railway had put into service a handful of 'Vestibuled Excursion Coaches' as it called them. As mentioned on page 171, the use of the word 'vestibule' was somewhat misleading and the LMS took up the term after 1922 to denote the open configuration, but in essence they were gangwayed clerestories with open saloon interiors. Although relatively few were built, they must have struck something of a receptive chord because after the Great War, almost on the eve of the grouping, the MR repeated the exercise, this time using a 57 feet by 9 feet elliptical roof body as the basis. Their exterior treatment was entirely traditional and they employed a very characteristic twin window arrangement per seating bay (one fixed and one drop light) but their influence was profound. None had actually been built when the MR was succeeded by the LMS, but the new company promoted the designs with vigour, adopting them as the first of the new standard carriage types. There is a fair amount of evidence that they were intended primarily as excursion stock, but, no doubt bolstered by the LYR experience, the LMS quickly came to regard them as one-for-one equivalents of side corridor coaches and used them accordingly, thus establishing the beginnings of the modern day 'open second' as it is now called.

It is, in fact, rather doubtful if these MR/early LMS open carriages were ever seen as particularly significant trendsetters at the time for, superficially, they did not look too different from most other coaches and there were not, until the 1920s, very many of them; but the same could not be said of the Great Central 'Barnums'. These huge vehicles, of quite distinctive, almost slab-sided construction with 'matchboard' panelling, emerged on the scene in

Right *The GWR did not really espouse open stock until after the grouping, but some of its turn-of-the-century so-called 'corridors' displayed semi-open interiors. This is an unidentified Dean clerestory third.*

Below *The true trend-setter? LMS 57 ft 56-seat open third No 4649 built to Midland design, was not put into service until after the grouping. Hundreds were built over the years, undoubtedly representing the most significant move away from side corridors thus far seen* (BR LMR).

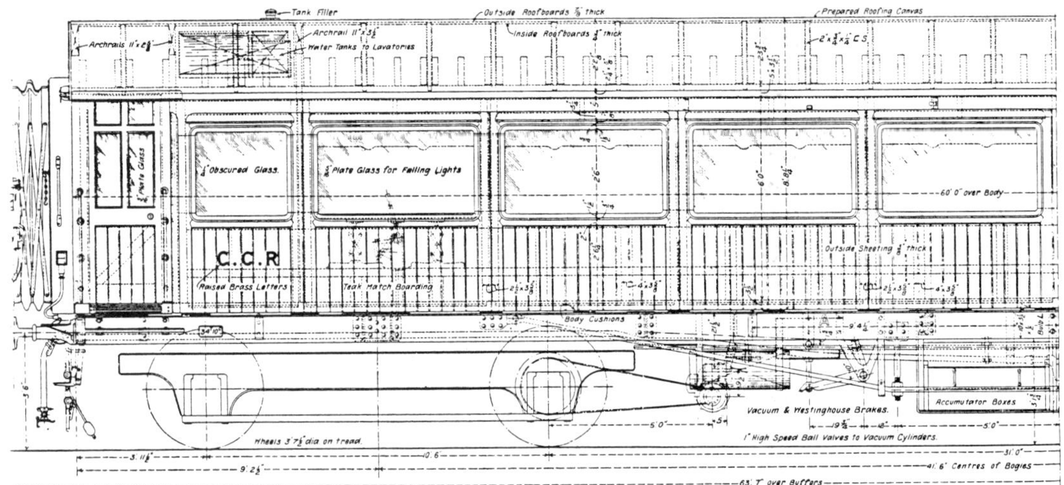

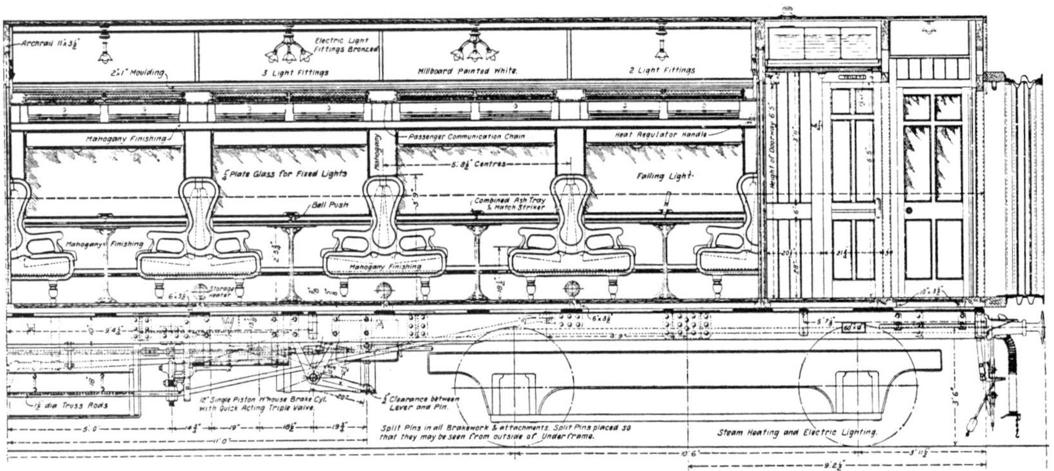

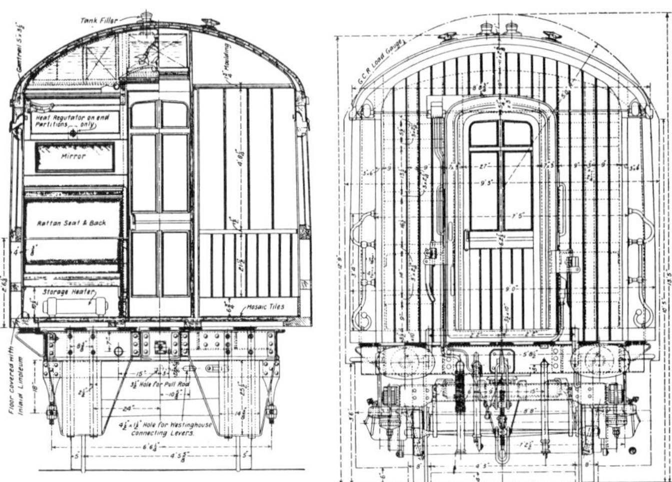

Scale 4.5mm = 1ft

Figure 53 *Selected drawings of the well-known GCR 'Barnums'. Never built in great quantity, many of their features, not least their large windows and overall size, anticipated several aspects of more modern practice.*

Right *The open version of a coupé is well shown in this NER elliptical roof first class example of* circa *1908. In open carriage parlance, this would be known as a 'half-bay'.*

1910. Built to the full dimensions of the GCR London Extension structure gauge, they offered open accommodation in a very spacious envelope. In all conscience they cannot be regarded as the most visually pleasing of coach design, or the most significant, but they were certainly noticed at the time and one or two still survive in preservation. Their nickname is believed to derive from the contemporary fame of the Barnum and Bailey circus elephants — an allusion to their great size. Such is the odd nature of popular perception that their historical relevance has regularly been over-emphasized. Interesting though they were, nothing quite like them was ever seen on British metals either before or since, but their fame seems assured.

Turning, finally, to the types and interior layouts of open general service coaches in the pre-grouping period, once again the early examples turned out to be prophetic. By far the most common was the full third, the ancestor of the modern open second. Typically it would have seven or eight bays of seats, two per side, in facing pairs and quite regularly with a table. Intermediately there would be one or possibly two transverse partitions defining smoking and non-smoking areas, and the lavatories would usually be at one or both ends of the carriage. Full firsts and composites would be much the same, the full first normally deploying one less seating bay for a given coach length just as in the side corridor equivalent, and with the composite there was again the problem of organizing a mixture of first and third (second) class bays so as exactly to fit the carriage length. The open equivalent of a coupé was sometimes to be seen, ie two seats in a sort of half-bay, either side of the central aisle. First class bays almost always had an asymmetric aisle with single seats on one side, twins on the other — the 2 + 1 arrangement so familiar today. If, by any chance, one encountered a 2 + 1 *third* or even *second* class open coach one could be fairly sure it was either a non-kitchen dining vehicle or had started life as such.

Brake-ended open coaches were much fewer in number relative to their non-brake equivalents than in the side corridor field and were almost always third class. Open brake firsts were exceedingly rare as were open brake composites, and the latter were rarely if ever used in the same mode as the side corridor brake composite. This curious distinction remained right through the company period and into BR days. In later days one might have no choice but to occupy an open coach in the third (later second) class part of the main train, but if you were travelling in the through coach, detached *en route*, the compartments reigned supreme.

There for the moment we must leave it, although the story was by no means over as the next volume will, hopefully, reveal.

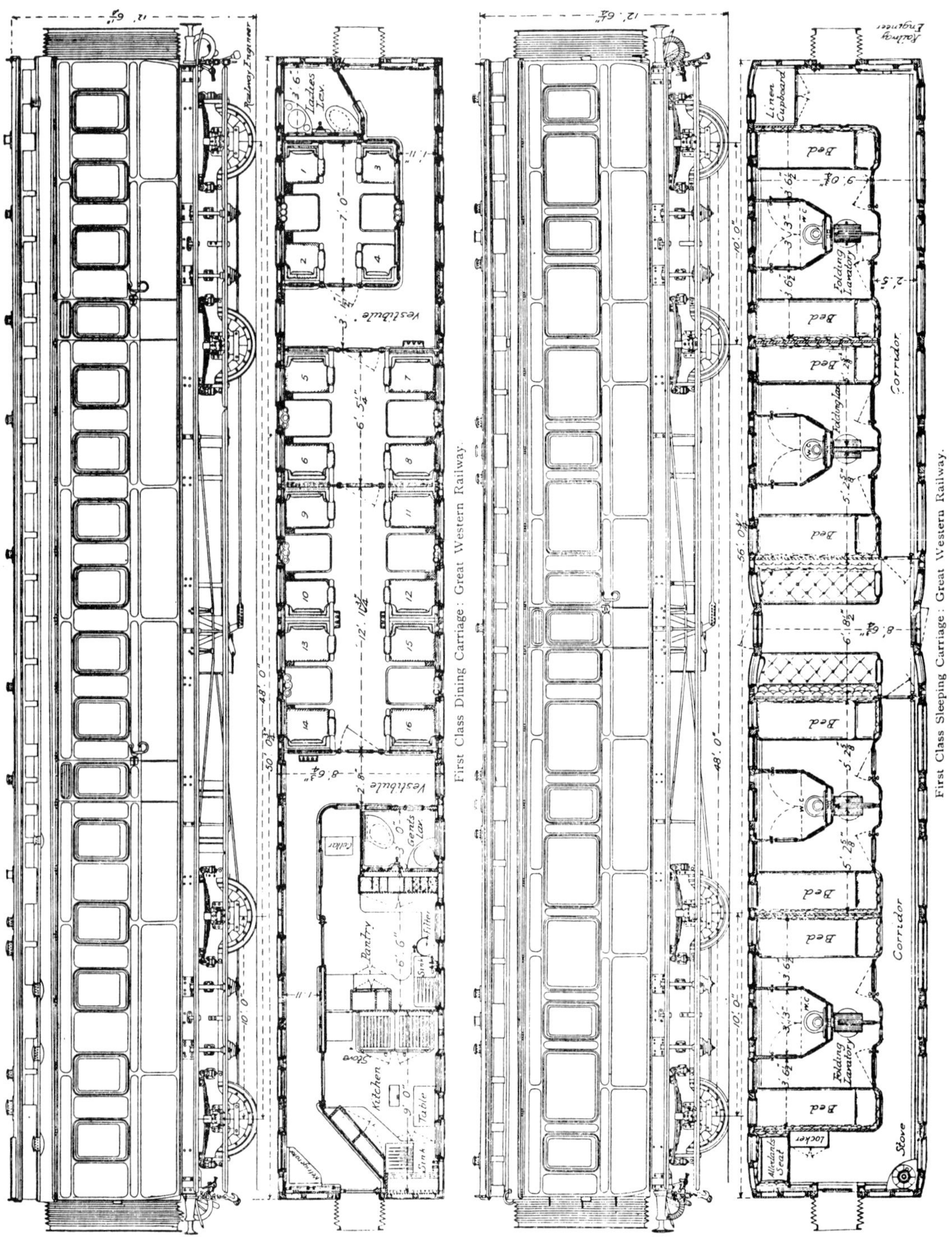

First Class Dining Carriage: Great Western Railway.

First Class Sleeping Carriage: Great Western Railway.

Scale 3mm = 1ft

11. Mobile hotels

With the possible exception of the ocean liner, there can have been few more gracious ways to travel than were provided by the Great Trains during the heyday of the mechanized railway. To be strictly truthful, one should perhaps say 'are' rather than 'can have been' since the modern railway is still quite capable of offering stylish travel when it so chooses. The trouble these days is that there are so many alternatives from which potential travellers may choose that, in proportionate terms, the railway's share of the market has declined and this has inevitably caused a reduction in the total number of prestigious trains. Moreover, life styles have changed and too many people nowadays seem to be in too much of a hurry to be able to enjoy the more leisured progress of a well-endowed train. 'Travelling hopefully', it would seem, has been thoroughly superseded by the wish to arrive, and this has just as inevitably caused changes to the nature of the railway carriage as it has in other walks of life. However, it was not always thus, and in terms of vehicles Britain made its own highly distinctive contribution.

Central to the whole business of civilized long-distance travel were two principal types of vehicle, supplemented occasionally by carriages of a third group. The two main categories were sleeping and dining cars, while the third and smaller group were the various forms of 'private' saloons, covered in Chapter 13, which could be hired by those who so wished. Together, these three types of operation inspired the building of vehicles which for the most part were both refined and beautiful and which have rarely, if ever, been surpassed in terms of sheer quality, be it inside or out.

The most sophisticated requirements of the long-distance traveller were first addressed beyond the shores of Britain, notably in America, and it has to be conceded that many of the early British dining and sleeping cars drew heavily on American experience, particularly influenced by the activities of the Pullman Car Company. In fact, so important was the influence of the latter that it has been felt desirable to include a separate chapter on this very theme. However, in the strictly British context things had settled down quite nicely to a recognizably 'modern' approach by the start of our period, most of the experimentation having been carried out, as in most other areas, during the last decade of Victoria's reign. This relatively late start can, for the most part, be attributed to the geographically small nature of Great Britain compared with many parts of the world. There were few journeys which lasted appreciably more than twelve hours, and none at all which spanned the twenty-four-hour spectrum, so the carriage needs in Britain were from the outset different in scope. Nowhere was this more true than in the field of sleeping cars, the first of the categories to be considered.

Figure 54 *Elevations and floor plans of William Dean's splendid dining and sleeping cars for the GWR in 1896. Their internal arrangement set most of the basic standards for the next century, regardless of subsequent changes.*

The British sleeping car began, so history tells us, with the North British Railway in 1873, closely followed by the LNWR and, two or three years later, the Midland, the latter in the form of its imported American Pullmans. For the rest of the nineteenth century, various different approaches were tackled, mostly concentrating on internal layout about which there seemed to be no single agreed solution. From the outset, however, it was a facility for first class passengers only and this did not change until as late as 1928. Part of the reason was cost, the other part being mostly related to the nature of the service and the social mores of the time.

It is an inescapable fact that a bed takes up more floor space than a chair, so, for a given size of carriage, fewer sleeping passengers can be accommodated at floor level than if they were sitting on conventional seats. There must, therefore, be a premium charge for the use of a sleeping carriage — but then one is saving the cost of a hotel room. There can be no doubt that the early railways concluded that only their first class clients would want to or be able to afford these extras and also that they would expect for their money a considerable degree of comfort, privacy and amenity. In consequence, the British sleeping car was always exceedingly well equipped, whatever its layout.

There was, in fact, a somewhat more economical alternative, the 'Pullman' section. This idea, imported from America, consisted of facing pairs of seats (on either side of a central aisle) which at night could be drawn towards each other to form a bed, and a second 'bunk' lowered from a folded position in the ceiling. This ensured that when converted for night use, a Pullman sleeper could carry as many recumbent passengers as it could seated customers by day — a very practical solution in the context of multi-day travel in North America. However, privacy at night was achieved by little more than curtains drawn down the aisle and shutters or screens between individual section. Moreover, there was no room to change into night attire and, frankly, the

L M S
SLEEPING
CAR

Left *Interior view of Pullman 'sections' made up for night use on the Midland Railway in the 1890s* (Author's collection).

staid Victorians *did not like it!*

Although the MR persevered with this approach to some extent until the start of the present century, the typical British sleeping car was designed to provide a series of private bedrooms, each self-contained as far as possible. For one thing, there was scarcely any need for it to have a daytime function (journeys were too short) and the customers liked their privacy so from the start of the present century the sleeping car was almost always a purpose-built vehicle rather than one with a conversion option. It still is, for that matter, and during most of the last 100 years its interior layout has hardly changed, having settled down to one basic and overriding form in the 1890s with very few noteworthy exceptions.

The characteristic British sleeping car was and still is a side corridor compartment vehicle, each compartment functioning as an individual bedroom, with either single or double occupancy. There are the usual lavatories at the corridor ends and, regularly, an additional compartment for the travelling attendant. Frequently in Edwardian days there would be one non-sleeping compartment provided with a few comfortable seats for use as a smoking saloon, but this idea was quickly abandoned — it was a bit extravagant and the all-sleeping configuration (save for the attendant) became standardized.

Within each compartment, the railways spared no expense to make the facilities as self contained as possible — washbasins, coathangers, shelves, even hooks on which to hang the pocket watch being all provided. About the only thing which was not present on an individual compartment basis was a lavatory and given that the compartment was rarely more than about 6 ft 6 in by 4 ft 6 in (some doubles were about 6 ft 6 in square) this was hardly to be wondered at. Even so, there was usually what might best be called 'emergency provisioning' — at least for the men folk!'

All in all, the sleeping car was a masterpiece of compact planning and, in most cases, of considerable merit too. Of course, not all railways needed to (or did) provide such vehicles, so the design influence was dominated by the long-distance concerns, particularly the Great Northern (including its NER partner in the ECJS), the Great Western, the London and North Western (including as it did all the designs for the WCJS) and the Midland (including all the MSJS designs). As we have seen, most of them had settled on a fairly universal layout by the start of the present century, but there were still some variations on the theme to be observed. Comparisons are always odious, but risking a personal view, it seems to me that the dominant influence, both in contemporary terms and in relation to their future influence, was provided in the fleets owned, maintained and operated by the East and West Coast rivals; they did, after all, operate the most numerous and the longest distance overnight operations.

Centre and left *Classic twelve-wheel clerestory sleeping cars, LNWR No 151, built in 1904, and MR No 2767, seen in post-grouping LMS markings, built in 1911. Both could sleep eleven first class passengers, mostly in single berth compartments* (Top BR LMR).

Both organizations favoured the twelve-wheeler for a variety of reasons and, additionally, both of them also tended to be dominated by one only of the respective owning companies, the GNR (ECJS) and the LNWR (WCJS). The twelve-wheel preference is easy enough to explain, being mostly connected with matters of weight. If to a normal corridor coach one added the extra weight of washbasins, beds, sundry internal fittings and a whole host of additional ancillary features below the floor (eg heavier-duty batteries to cope with the greater demand), the weight limit for an eight-wheeler was soon exceeded, and if one was going to have to contemplate twelve wheels, one might just as well go for the largest and most versatile vehicle which *could* be carried on twelve wheels — typically about 65 feet long and 40 tons tare. In consequence, there were spawned some truly memorable carriages on both sides of the country, and it would be a brave man who attempted to adjudicate between them. If forced to a decision, I would favour those of the West Coast, not because I have specialized in their study but mainly because there were rather more of them, there was slightly more consistency in design and, on the whole, they did tend to be more influential in the design of subsequent LMS and BR vehicles than any of the others; but in truth there was little to choose.

Both favoured the clerestory at the start of our period, and beautifully elegant they were, an attribute which was not changed when, during the Edwardian period, the full elliptical roof was adopted. They literally (and most appropriately) rode like dreams, and in the case of the West Coast examples at least three of them were considered good enough to be transferred, without significant structural or mechanical modificaion, to the LNWR (later LMS and BR) Royal Train. This role they continued to fulfil until 1968, over sixty years after the first of them had been built. There can be little doubt that had the East Coast Royal Train (see Chapter 13) been used appreciably for overnight travel, some of the ECJS sleepers would have been similarly distinguished. Of all the lost causes in the field of

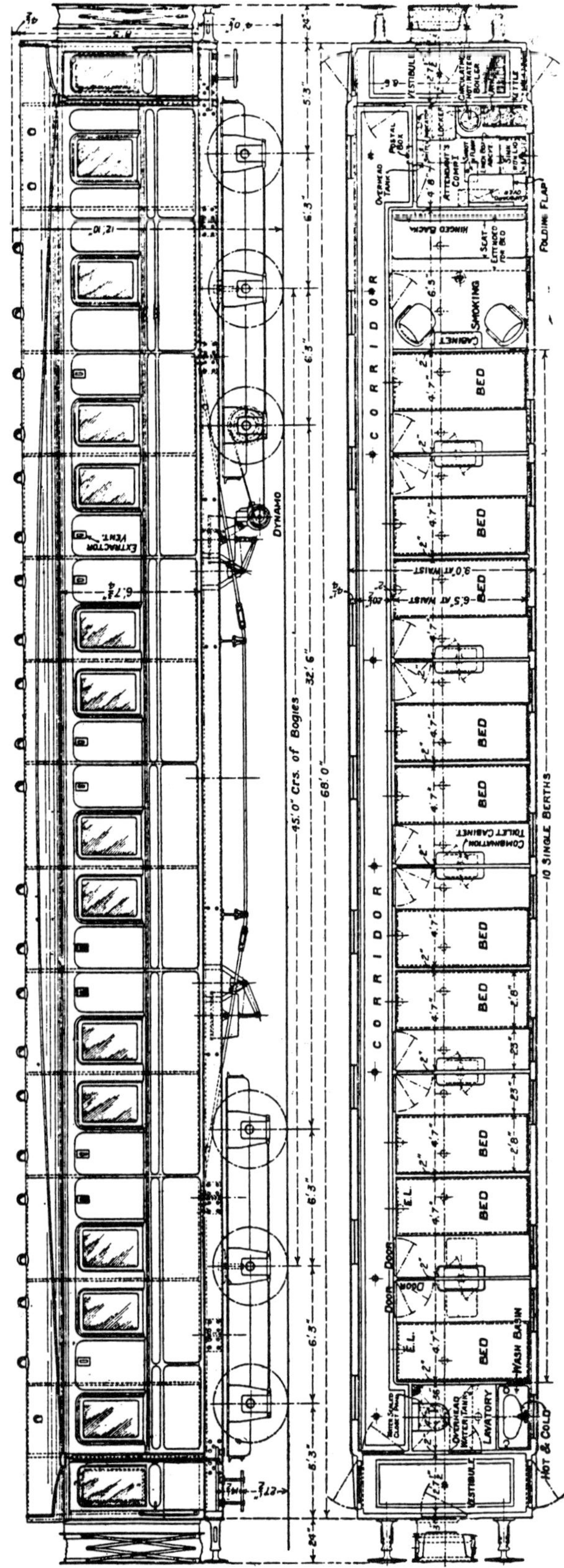

Scale 3mm = 1ft

Figure 55 *The finest of the pre-group sleeping cars were probably the 68-foot twelve-wheelers introduced by the LNWR in 1914. This drawing shows the arrangement as built — little different from a modern-day plan. One survived in Royal Train use until 1968.*

railway carriage preservation — and there have been more than a few — the absence of a genuinely original Edwardian sleeping car is by far and away the most significant omission in my view — they were magnificent.

However, the East and West Coast routes did not have a total monopoly of the elegant overnight trade, a fairly respectable 'second eleven' being provided by the Great Western and the Midland. Each, in its own way, was distinctively different. The Great Western was in fact the first company to standardize the side corridor style, and during the Dean period its side corridor sleeping cars could stand comparison with any whether in terms of practicability or visual harmony. However, the GWR did not have the sheer distance of those routes which headed north from London, so its fleet was never anything like so big. Moreover, its few Edwardian sleepers did not stand the test of time as well as those of the East and West Coasts. There were four massive twelve-wheel 'Dreadnoughts' built in 1907 which lasted less than thirty years, and a pair of eight-wheel 'Toplights' of no great distinction which were later rebuilt into twelve-wheel composites of the most monumental dullness — and that was about all in the pre-group period.

The Midland was rather better, but if truth be told, not much. Its sleeping cars had initially mostly been in the Pullman mode with its centre aisle and 'pull-together' sections. Right at the start of the century, its latest offerings were still partly of this kind — a clutch of four Pullman-type twelve-wheelers containing a mixture of sections and individual compartments served by a side corridor. Visually they were most striking with a high clerestory roof, but were soon rebuilt to an all side corridor arrangement. Even so, they did not survive beyond the early 1930s, a similar fate to that which befell the more orthodox 'British' Midland sleeping cars of the Bain era. They too were often twelve-wheelers, typically elegant clerestories but finding little subsequent favour.

In one respect, however, the Midland was a bit more adventurous in its building of a composite sleeping car type, a handful of which were constructed during the Bain period. They were not true composites in the sleeping car sense because only the first class compartments had beds, third class being accommodated in conventional seated

The curious 'half and half' pattern of composite sleeping car, No 124 of the WCJS (Author's collection).

compartments. However, they were quite spacious, had fewer than the normal number of outside doors and ample luggage space. In this respect they were distinctly better than some of the so-called composites of the West Coast, a series of distinctly peculiar vehicles, well recorded, which grafted a 9 feet wide first class portion containing sleeping compartments on to an 8 ft 6 in wide portion containing the orthodox third class seating accommodation. They were grotesque, and the true composite sleeping carriage had to await the post-grouping period for its appearance. Needless to say, the LMS, which inherited both the West Coast and Midland exemplars, had little time for either of them after the early 1930s.

Thus it was that the two principle Anglo-Scottish routes dominated the sleeping car scene in Britain, and continued to do so. What, however, of the rest? Well, in point of fact there were not many of them and since it is not the purpose of this book to chronicle every single vehicle built by every individual company, two final examples of the genre must needs suffice. They could not have been more different or, in a sense, more surprising, coming as they did from the LSWR and HR respectively.

The LSWR examples were conventional enough but rather larger than most of the matching corridor fleet. In truth there can have been little use for them, and one suspects that it was more of a gesture to keep pace with the rival GWR than anything else. They were, however, rather handsome in a typically South Western way and their relatively few patrons to the deepest West Country must have been pleased enough at the time. They were, in fact, sold off later to the GWR itself.

It has already been remarked that the Highland

Most but not all sleeping cars were twelve-wheel types. Here are two eight-wheelers from companies not particularly famed for their sleeping car provisioning: the compartment side of LSWR No 42, one of four built in 1908, and the corridor side of Highland Railway No 8, one of this company's only excursions into the sleeping car field (Gavin Wilson Collection).

was served by through carriages from many parts of the kingdom, so its building of two sleeping carriages in 1907 was something of a surprise. They seem to have been dedicated to the overnight Inverness-Glasgow service (one each way each night) and were composites, first class sleeping, third class ordinary. Built in Drummond's rather distinctive 'matchboard' style, all but unique to the Highland, they did not last long in their original form and by LMS days they were operating as corridor third brakes with a very long van portion in place of the erstwhile first class sleeping accommodation.

If sleeping cars were most noteworthy for their limited nature (in terms of operating company), the same was not true of the second major category of mobile 'hotel' vehicle, the dining car. By the turn of the century, 'meals on wheels' had become an accepted part of longer-distance travelling, even for those railways which could not offer the sort of distances which would justify sleeping cars, and by the 1923 grouping there were relatively few of the major railways which could not offer at least one or two quite sumptuous catering vehicles. As with sleeping cars, there was a strong Pullman influence, deferred to the next chapter, and in the case of on-train catering, it was actually a Pullman service in 1879 between Leeds and London which began the whole business in Britain. From these tentative beginnings there had developed by the turn of the century a fairly characteristic dining car form which was to stand the test of time well into the modern era.

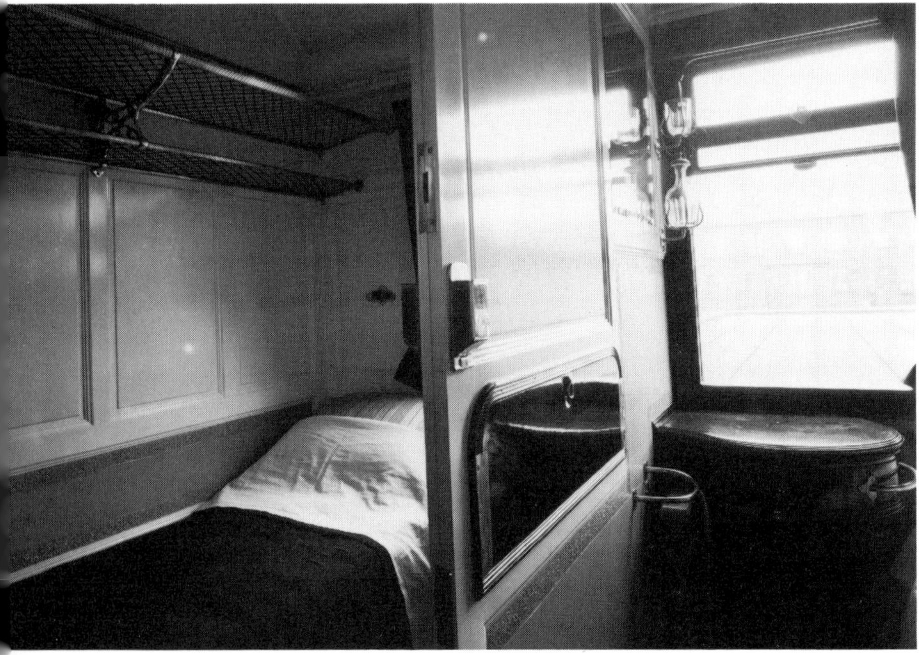

Above left and left *Contrasting compartment interiors of the LSWR carriage shown on page 199 and GN/NE joint car No 12 of 1909, the LSWR example having the wood panelling and brass bedstead. The GN/NE interior has interconnecting berths with the sliding door open between them; an exterior view of a similar type is shown on page 120.*

Right Figure 56 *This group of elevations and plans shows typical dining car arrangements, both centre and end-kitchen. It is noticeable that the greater size of the GWR 'Dreadnought' of 1904 permits more people to be seated, albeit at rather closer seating pitch than the 1912 GNR and NER examples. The NER car is illustrated on page 14.*

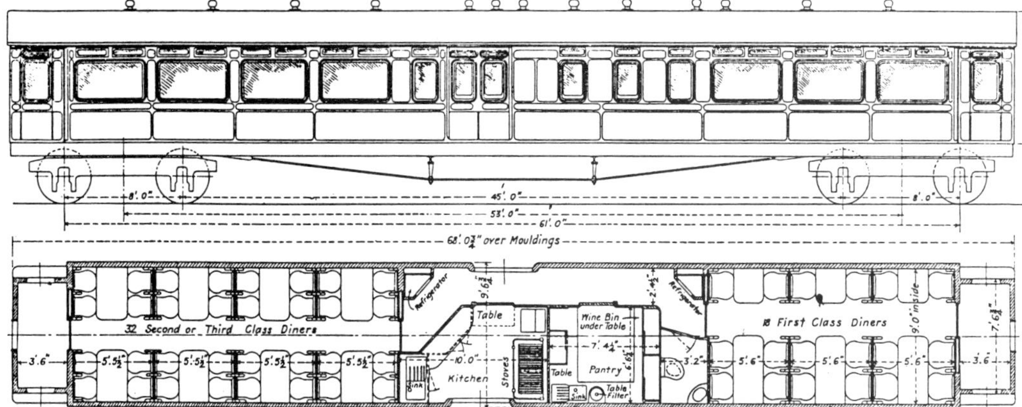

'Dreadnought' Dining Car, Great Western Railway, 1904

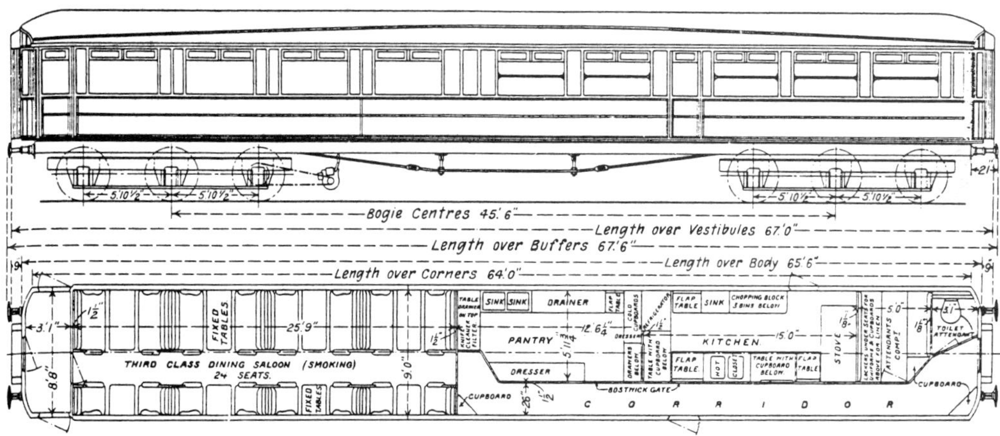

Third Class Dining and Kitchen Car, Great Northern and North Eastern Joint, 1912

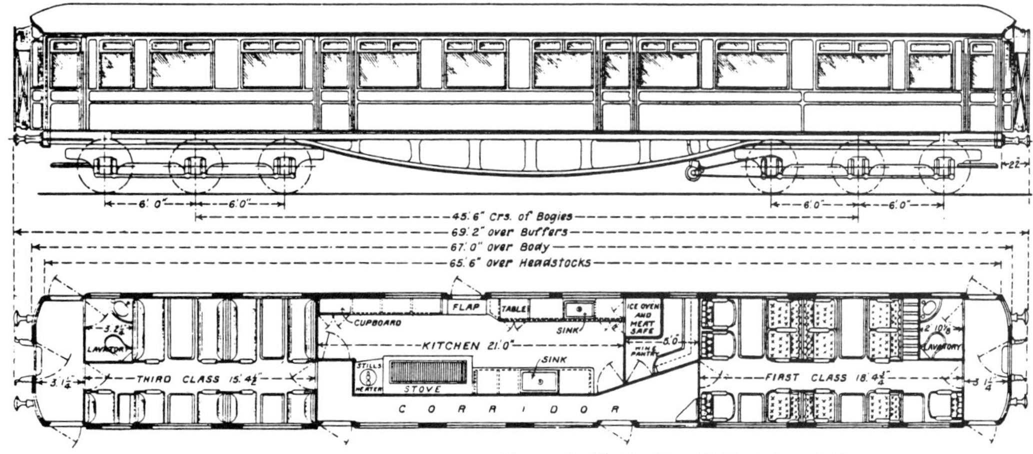

Composite Dining Car, North Eastern Railway, 1912

Scale 2mm = 1ft

These dining cars, built for the M & GSW Joint services in 1920, formed a typical operating pair: kitchen first and open third. The vehicles are M & GSW Nos 216 and 394 respectively (BR LMR).

The typical British dining car consisted of a combination of food preparation and food serving areas, the kitchen and pantry commonly occupying anything from 25-50% of the length of the vehicle with the seating normally arranged in 2 + 1 form separated by an aisle. Four-seat to six-seat bays were the common standard, although there were exceptions at both ends of the scale and the seats could be arranged in one of two principal layouts. That with the kitchen/pantry portion at one end and the seats at the other was known as an 'end kitchen' vehicle, that with the service section in the middle, flanked by seating bays at both ends, was the 'centre kitchen' variant. The latter was almost invariably a composite with the kitchen and pantry separating firsts from thirds while the end kitchen type could be either one class only, divided by a partition into two classes, or even used for all classes, in which case it was known as a 'common' diner. From this it will be appreciated that dining facilities in Britain were not confined to the first class passenger during this period, unlike the case with sleeping cars. Interestingly, this universal provisioning has been somewhat eroded by latter-day BR policy, and it is now quite regularly impossible to obtain a full meal service on a modern InterCity train without first taking a first class ticket — so much for late twentieth century egalitarianism!

Like sleeping cars, dining cars generally carried much more equipment than ordinary day carriages so, like their overnight contemporaries, they regularly displayed the twelve-wheel form. There was also much in common in terms of length and exterior styling but, of course, there the resemblance ended. However, before coming on to this aspect of the story, a few more general points need to be made.

Firstly, although all classes were catered for, the second class option was very much in decline even on those railways which still retained all three, so the dominant trend was first, third or 'common'. Secondly, it was found from experience that the typical kitchen of a dining car was well capable of serving more meals than there were seats in the diner itself. This gave rise to a second type of dining vehicle which had no kitchen but whose seating areas were arranged in the characteristic dining car form, ie open interior with central aisle. These were and are regularly referred to as 'open' diners as opposed to 'kitchen' diners. A fairly typical pairing might be a kitchen first with an open third, but there were many variations. In certain circumstances, it was possible to find a kitchen-only vehicle flanked by open coaches, but this practice did not become particularly widespread until after the grouping. An alternative solution, regularly practised on the LNWR for example, was to have two quite separate kitchen diners in different parts of the train and, if need arose, provide removable tables which could be fitted into some of the side corridor compartments for the overflow trade.

As for the vehicles themselves, it seems fair to state that with the exception of Royal and some special saloons the interior furnishing of a British dining car was the most splendidly opulent of any of the vehicles built by the railways. They moved slowly from ponderous late Victorian to a slightly less oppressive form during the period under review, but at all times

Style on the GCR. This splendid vehicle, open third class dining car No 1602, was built for the London Extension of the GCR right at the end of the last century. The interior was truly first class standard, while the exterior seems to have been inspired by Wolverton (LNWR).

GER kitchen interior of 1912. The ingenious storage arrangements for crockery etc are quite typical, and various utensils are seen hanging below the outer casing of an auxiliary water tank — see page 58.

The GWR 'Concertina' period 70-foot first class dining cars of 1906 established a general end-kitchen layout on the GWR until the grouping. They were less spacious than the 'Dreadnoughts' but still rather larger than found anywhere else.

the use of decorative finishes was high on the priority list. Whether it be inlaid veneer, marquetry panels, flamboyant Lincrusta panelling or superb quality upholstery, the diners usually had some or all of them. Polished and carved wood detail was common, associated with delicate mouldings and decorative light fittings. Built-in bottle holders, courtesy lights and push-buttons to call the attendant were all commonly to be found and, particularly significant, there was much less difference between first and third class than in most carriages. Most third class diners were literally first class in their provisioning, and it was often difficult, if not impossible, to tell the difference. In fact, unless the first class diner was one of those relatively rare birds (inspired by Pullman) with single seats on both sides of the aisle, there often was no difference save, perhaps, for a slight reduction in the length of each seating bay in the third class section. They really were splendid and many railways vied with each other in terms of elegance and style.

As for kitchens and pantries, these were veritable masterpieces of ingenuity. They normally used compressed oil gas for fuel and literally every nook and cranny was pressed, cleverly, into service. This did, of course, lead to some particularly odd-shaped cupboards and storage areas, but space was at a premium and none was wasted. Thus, for example, in a kitchen not much more than 10 feet by 6 feet, one might regularly expect to find anything between six and twelve burner rings and at least two ovens, each capable of holding a 30 lb turkey.

It would be impossible to identify the best company in the dining car sense but, of course, matters of scale decreed that some railways needed to build more than others. In the purely numerical sense, the LNWR probably held first place and, at its peak building period, it was sending new twelve-wheel diners into service at the rate of one per month. Splendid though they were, who is to say that they were better, in absolute terms, than the four cars which were all that were ever built by the LYR or the spectacular one or two individual vehicles of such railways as the GSWR.

The other big companies in the dining sense were the East Coast triumvirate (particularly the GNR and NER), the Midland and the Great Western, but the GER, the nineteenth-century pioneer of third class dining cars in 1891, had some quite incredibly good diners, particularly associated with its boat trains, while the LSWR slotted some distinctly stylish clerestories into the middle of several of its five-coach corridor sets. The 'upstart' GCR added its quota and, short of letting this chapter degenerate into a catalogue of vehicles built, it seems best, for once to let the pictures tell the story. Happily, dining cars were well-photographed vehicles (possibly because they had a sort of 'flagship' status) and it seems a pity not to give many of them an airing! If, however, I was forced to give an opinion, I would award the absolute decor prize to a quite splendid Adam-style one-off built by the GNR for its Harrogate service. From the outside it was rather ordinary, but inside it was a tour de force (see the picture on page 207) No doubt the Harrogate destination was not the least of the reasons for its styling!

At this point, and as a link to the Pullman chapter, it should perhaps be mentioned that several railways were quite content to leave the bulk, if not all, of their catering to the Pullman company, and amongst the more important lines in this respect were the LB & SCR, SE & CR and Caledonian, although there were others.

During the pre-group period, the full meal dining car was the archetypal catering vehicle, those passengers with less gastronomic propensities having to make do with either their own pre-packed picnics or the now long-gone railway picnic hamper, a thing of great splendour which, happily, I am just able to recall from the days of my childhood when my father would obtain one at London prior to a journey north. They were amazingly good value and it was always a moment of great excitement to see what might be contained therein. There were some surprises! These hampers were in a sense precursors of the modern buffet car, a vehicle which did not really achieve any great significance until the 1930s and which did not really come into its own until the modern day. However, this survey of the pre-group catering vehicle would be incomplete without mention of a few of the early attempts which were being made, even at the start of the period, to provide an alternative to the full meal. They were not very numerous, nor very well known, but were of interest, if only because they were ahead of their time.

Allowing a year or two of latitude in respect of its building date (1898), pride of place in the innovation stakes early in the century goes to the GCR which, coincidentally with the opening of its London Extension, not only built some exceedingly well-appointed conventional dining cars but added a buffet car design by way of bonus. This was regarded with considerable contemporary interest and was a very well thought out design, but it did not at the time start anything in the way of a trend, possibly because at that period even those third class passengers who partook of meals were solidly middle class and could readily afford the full meal option. In any case, the fad for 'fast food' is very much a modern innovation.

One of the nice things about the well-run dining car until, in fact, quite recently was the regular service of afternoon tea, and this seems to have inspired such railways as the LNWR to experiment with a minimum facility catering vehicle, usually called a 'tea car'. These were corridor thirds with two central compartments converted into a miniature kitchen/pantry/service area. They seemed to be used on cross-country journeys to provide a form of corridor refreshment service; one could not actually consume the food at its point of preparation since there were no dining seats as such. It was not a true buffet car but must have had some success, the

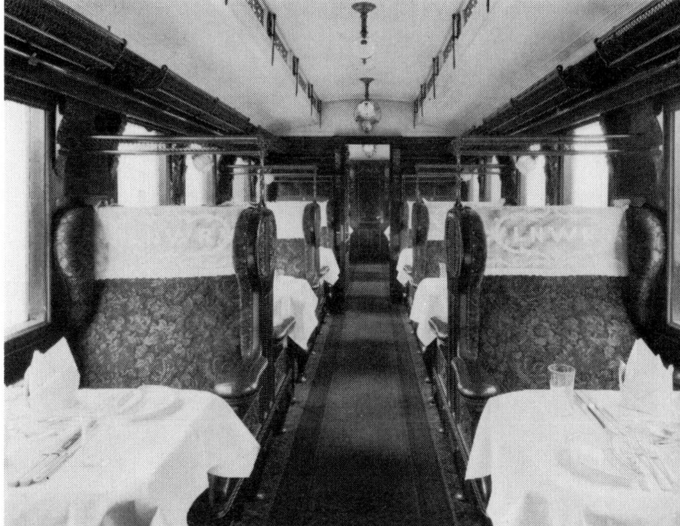

Right, top to bottom *Contrasting first class interiors of typical GNR and LNWR clerestory twelve-wheel dining cars* circa *1905, together with a comparative view of a GWR elliptical roof 'Toplight' period example, No 9561 built in 1922* (Centre BR LMR).

Top *Ten years or so after they were built, Gresley modified some of his GNR predecessor's twelve-wheelers to accept the new larger window style introduced* circa *1906. It gave an even more elegant look to what were already stylish vehicles. This is the centre kitchen composite No 2993, modified in 1913.*

Above and left *The GER built relatively few dining cars but this clerestory example for the Continental boat trains was very good. The company favoured leather upholstery in the first class, shown to good effect in the interior view of the same car, No 24. The later GER elliptical roof cars of 1912 were finished in almost identical manner.*

Right *This must surely have been Britain's most elegant dining car interior ever — GNR No 3250, the famous 'Harrogate' car built in 1912.*

Below right *The first LSWR dining car venture consisted of adding a clerestory to its basic corridor coach style. The centre kitchen composite was preferred and the result was pleasing (see the picture on page 128). This view shows the third class section of No 67, one of an earlier series with three windows per seating bay.*

LNWR eventually placing a dozen or so in service. They were not, however, repeated after the Great War.

The sleeping car and the dining car have stood the test of time, albeit with some minor changes, but the third category of travelling 'hotel' vehicle, the special saloon, was very much a child of its time. In the days when everyone from the highest to the most humble travelled by train, there was a small but identifiable demand by specific types of clientele for semi-private travel facilities, and the railways sought to meet this demand by offering as an alternative to the normal form of carriage the exclusive use of a special saloon in exchange for a specified number of fares. These vehicles are somewhat inextricably mixed up with the Royal saloons and are considered in Chapter 13.

Below *The GCR's pioneering Buffet Carriage of 1898. From the left-hand end, it consisted of a buffet counter, a central kitchen with gas range, an attendant's compartment and three third class compartments plus lavatory. Strangely, this fundamentally sound idea did not catch on until more than a generation later in the 1930s.*

12. The Pullman contribution

There can be few more evocative yet misunderstood words in the field of travel than 'Pullman'. It can define a railway carriage, refer to a style of travel, be applied to other forms of transport than rail or even be used to designate an up-market waiting room, yet all in all it is no more than the surname of a famous American entrepreneur who had a vision back in the last century, one George Mortimer Pullman. No doubt Mr Hoover met with much the same problems in the field of domestic appliances as years went by.

Pullmans have been with us, in one form or another, for most of the twentieth century and long before, and it is vital that their place in railway history is properly understood. It is quite complex, but fortunately there is some considerable specialized literature on the subject (see the Bibliography) so we need only consider the essential outlines here, concentrating mainly on those relating to the vehicles themselves. Even in this context, however, there are two main strands of development to the story, the use to which the vehicles were going to be put and the nature of the vehicles built to fulfil this requirement. Logically, one should start with the nature of the services themselves; this time, however, we must spend a little more time than usual in the pre-twentieth century period.

Pullman carriages were developed by George Pullman himself in North America and were designed from the outset to offer extra comfort and amenity for those passengers who could and would pay for it; the 'would' is important in the British context! From the beginning, there was always an expectation of greater style and comfort in a Pullman vehicle, thereby explaining the subsequent adjectival use of the word. The first Pullman cars (always 'cars', by the way, *never* carriages) were imported into Britain by the Midland Railway in 1874 and put to work on its lines. They were owned by Pullman himself, in the shape of his American Pullman Car Company and 'plied for hire' on the lines of whichever railway system was prepared to accept them. Although the Midland ordered some almost identical carriages for itself, the name 'Pullman' could only be applied, strictly speaking, to those vehicles owned and operated by the Pullman Company. Thus, in effect, some Pullmans were not 'Pullmans' even though they looked as if they were! The subsequent confusion can readily be appreciated.

How, then, did the Pullman Company make its living, since it did not actually collect the fares for the journey itself, these being kept by the parent railway? The method was to charge a supplementary fee for the use of the Pullman Car and keep all the catering and other incidental revenue thus generated. Since people tend to part with their money rather more readily if treated in a civilized fashion, the emphasis in a Pullman was always firmly on the aspect of 'service'. The attendants were always attentive and always smart; they pandered to every wish of the passenger; they took pride in remembering the names, seating preferences and even the favourite drinks of their regular clientele — and so forth. There was, in truth, more than a bit of the snob element to it all, but interestingly it was eventually made available to third class passengers

Left *Parlor Car 'Prince' was built in the USA in 1888 as part of the first British Pullman car set with 'closed' entrance vestibules. It is seen here as re-modelled in 1915, carrying the familiar umber and cream livery in its first variant, ie with a cream-coloured 'headboard' above the windows.*

Right *The stylish twelve-wheel 'Arundel', here seen at Brighton in the older Pullman colours, was a sumptuous parlor car imported from the USA in 1899. It did not remain long in this form, being rebuilt with a kitchen and renamed 'Majestic' in 1905. This and the previous view give a good comparison between the eight and twelve-wheel American style bogies regularly used for Pullmans at this time.*

too. Pullman cars, by tradition, concentrated on the dining and sleeping car side of things — this was, after all, a reflection of their American origin — and it stayed thus throughout, although in Britain it tended during the present century to be mostly a catering operation.

The independence of the Pullman Company from the various British railways remained intact throughout the company period and into early BR days, at which point it tended to become rather anachronistic and caused not a few problems until the company was taken over, absorbed, bought out, or call it what you will, by BR in 1954. Today the word is used solely to denote a style of travel and has no corporate meaning in Britain.

Because the Pullman Company relied heavily on the willingness of independent private railways to accept its cars, there was always a degree of *frisson* in its relationships with the companies. Some liked Pullman, others did not and the rest were indifferent, so the operations were never to be evenly spread throughout Britain. Wales, for example, was a Pullman 'desert' until a much later period and for rather different reasons. In fact, during the 1901-23 period, Pullman operations were mostly confined to the South of England, but more of these details anon.

The first Pullman cars to run in Britain were actually built in America but with dimensions to suit the smaller British structure gauge. They were shipped in component parts across the Atlantic where they were reassembled, initially at a special sub-section of the Midland Railway's main works at Derby. The cars were, therefore, thoroughly American in concept and design and they remained thus for some three-quarters of a century, long after all construction had moved to England.

The American influence was both conceptual and structural, the latter being somewhat a consequence of the former. Their layout almost always followed the open style with centre aisle and seats on each side. This was true whether the vehicle was a day carriage or a 'Parlor Car' as it was called — the spelling of 'parlor' was long kept in its original 'old English', later American form — or whether it was for sleeping purposes, in which form the Pullman 'section' was typical — see page 195. The Midland tried out both types, and just to proclaim its own independence called its own day carriages 'Midland Drawing Room Cars' rather than Pullman Parlors. They were, in fact, much the same sort of animal.

To be honest, The Midland did not find its espousal of Pullman-style travel to be a total success. The open plan and supplementary charges were both in the nature of mild disincentives in those days and seemed to supervene the improved facilities and vastly improved riding qualities of the vehicles themselves. The Midland was quite good at this sort of thing itself anyway, so maybe the comparisons were not quite as dramatic as they would have been on other lines. Be that as it may, during the rest of the nineteenth century, the various imported Pullmans tended to be shifted around from system to system, and although the MR remained half-heartedly faithful to at least a few Pullman sleeping cars, most of Pullman's fleet (if not sold to the Midland and others) tended to find a more welcome home in the south, particularly on the LB & SCR.

Below *The almost 'Gothick' interior of 'Arundel' typified most turn-of-the-century Pullman parlor cars. Two almost identical armchairs and a section of a similar interior survive at the National Railway Museum.*

Thus matters remained, more or less, until George M. Pullman's death in 1897.

Meanwhile, the vehicles themselves were heavier and larger than anything else in Britain at the time of their introduction and for many years afterwards. They were also immensely stronger than British-built coaches. In part this was a consequence of both their layout and their ancestry. Their American origins decreed a much stronger basic construction because of the generally less well engineered lines on which they ran in the USA. Their open layout, devoid of too many intermediate partitions and with doors at the extremities only, meant in fact that their strength could be built into the sides, floor and roof uninfluenced by compartments and outside doors. In fact, the wooden-bodied Pullman carriage was built on the integral box-girder principle and had no separate underframe or chassis. The whole carcass was immensely rigid and most of the ancillary features were, literally, fixed to the outside. This structural form withstood the transition from open to closed vestibule entrance lobbies in 1888 and from the favoured clerestory from of the nineteenth century to the elliptical roof of the twentieth. Roof apart, the structure of the preserved 'Topaz' at the NRM (built in Britain in 1913) is all but identical to that of the first to be imported almost forty years earlier.

This integral box structure also withstood the transition from wood to steel at a later date, and it was not until well beyond the period of the first two volumes of this survey that Pullman actually made use of a standard British body form when the last vehicles were ordered in 1959 by the 'independent' Pullman concern, now wholly BR owned. Until then, Pullman was, to all intents and purposes, alone.

It was alone, too, in the realm of carriage styling. For some 75 years from the 1870s to the 1950s, Pullman cars were flat sided. One is tempted to call them 'slab sided', but this would be an insult to the decorative efforts of their makers. The styling was, in fact, a straight copy of contemporary American practice, miniaturized by about 10-15 per cent to suit the more restricted British loading gauge. In the wooden-bodied era, which lasted well into the present century, there was, typically, a lower body treatment of vertical 'matchboarding', above which was a definite waist rail followed by the window-level features. The windows and their intermediate panels were always decorated, at times flamboyantly, and until the 1950s the lavatories *always* displayed a lovely oval stained glass window. Above the window was the headboard on which, most commonly, would be emblazoned the word 'PULLMAN' in an ostentatiously sized but stylishly executed elongated serif style of lettering. They often ran on American-pattern bogies, they almost always sported a highly finished and distinctive livery and they nearly always carried names, not numbers. It was not until Pullman cars entered the third class arena that 'Car No XXX' was seen on the sides of the vehicles; even then the first class cars continued to bear names.

The famous 'umber and cream' livery of the British Pullman car was not, as is often supposed, written into the tablets. In fact it did not become the normal scheme until the 1900s when the association with the LB & SCR was strong. As we have seen (page 133), the latter company introduced the livery early in Edwardian days and at this range in time it is a moot point whether Pullman copied Brighton or vice versa. The Pullman livery change is variously quoted as 1902 or 1906, the Brighton being 1903-4. What can be said is that prior to this time Pullman often used its own dark olive brown and green colour scheme (as in North America) with a profusion of gilded scrolls and curlicues, the bane of the life of any modeller! In the 1901-23 period, those on the SE & CR and Metropolitan Railway carried a distinctive dark red scheme, in the former case matching that of the SE & CR and faithfully reproduced on the preserved 'Topaz' at York. It was not until the 1920s that all Pullmans became two-tone brown and cream.

So much for the (mostly) pre-twentieth century background to the twentieth century Pullman story. It is by no means simple and the continuation was less so. Allowing a bit of licence as to dates, the story of the present century began, for practical purposes, in the late 1890s, first with the death of Pullman himself and then with the introduction of a second complete train of Pullmans on the LB & SCR in 1898 supplementing the earlier 1888 set, the latter, incidentally, being Britain's first electrically-lit train.

Even so, by the turn of the century, Pullman's toe-hold on the British mainland was at best precarious, however defined. When the founder himself died, the pioneering Midland had already decided it could build its own diners and sleepers every bit as well as could Pullman, and either did so or bought the erstwhile Pullman vehicles rather than run them under Pullman's own banner after the original contract had expired. Since the Midland was the major long-distance user of Pullman cars, this was rather a blow, scarce mollified by a small purchase of four Pullman-bodied sleeping cars in 1900 which were actually put on Midland-pattern running gear and flew Midland insignia from the outset. By 1907, only the LB & SCR, LSWR and the Highland were operating Pullmans.

In fact, while drawing heavily on the Pullman influence in terms of vehicle types and, to some extent, styling, all the British long-distance companies tended to take the view that they preferred

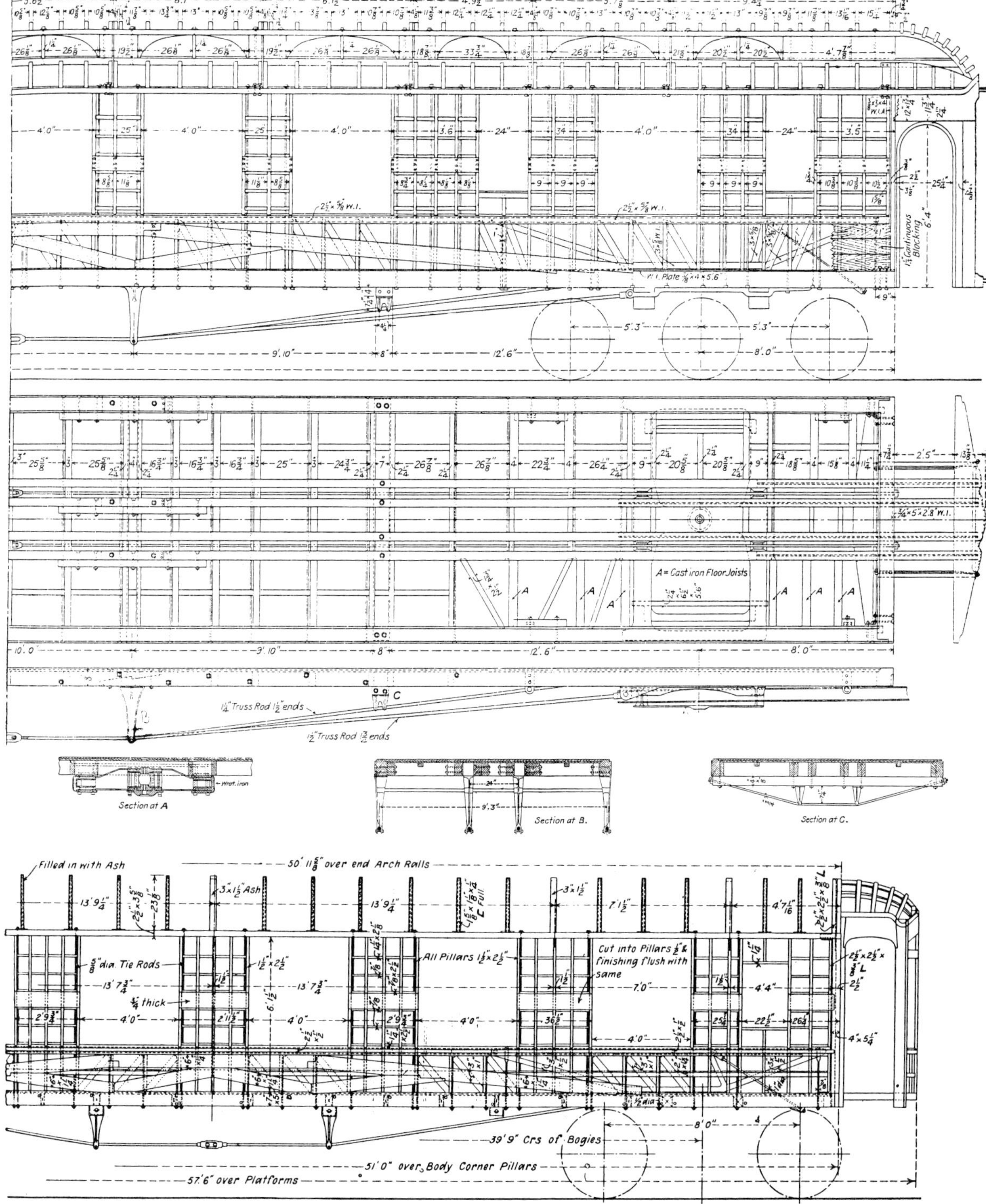

Figure 57 *The basic structure of wooden-bodied Pullman cars is shown in these drawings of a 1905-built clerestory American car and the similar but smaller British-built SE & CR example of 1913 with elliptical roof.*

Scale 4mm = 1ft

Left *The last Midland association with Pullman — sleeping car No 36, one of a batch of four introduced in 1900. Note that although still very American — the bodies were built there — the carriage is running on Midland pattern bogies* (BR LMR).

Left *The famous pioneer 'Southern Belle' Pullman set of 1908, brake-ended 'Alberta' at the near end. This was a completely twelve-wheel formation embodying the new elliptical roof profile but still bearing all the traditional Pullman hallmarks. Note the lack of end gangway.*

Opposite page *Interior view of the bar counter in Pullman buffet car 'Mayflower', one of two built in 1910 by the Birmingham C & W Co and used on the Metropolitan Railway* (Staffordshire County Record Office).

to build and operate their own sleeping and dining vehicles, so Pullman was forced to look elsewhere. Its saviours turned out to be the mid-range companies, especially those in the London area. As has already been pointed out, few of the Southern companies themselves built either dining, sleeping or even gangwayed vehicles, and this gave Pullman the opening it needed. A fairly thorough and successful assault was made on these lines and the company which benefitted most was the Brighton concern, closely followed by the SE & CR. The LSWR began to build its own diners, but on the other two lines, increasingly after 1910, it was Pullman cars which provided most if not all of the catering right through into Southern Railway days, and it is no coincidence that its offices eventually settled down at London Victoria (jointly operated by the LB & SCR and SE & CR) and its repair works became located first at Longhedge (SE & CR) and later at Preston Park, Brighton (LB & SCR).

Thus began an association which lasted half a century or more and was bolstered by a fairly rapid seried of changes in the structure of the company following the death of the founder himself. The story is complex and well recorded elsewhere, but the salient facts are that in 1907 ownership of the company was transferred across the Atlantic to a new organization headed by Mr Davison Dalziel, who was also Chairman of the famous Wagons-Lits Company based in Belgium and founded by the celebrated George Nagelmackers. In fact, and brushing aside all the tortuous ramifications of company finances and organization, the so-called independent British Pullman Company was, as near as makes no odds, a wholly-owned subsidiary of Wagons-Lits until 1954, as anyone could guess who had travelled with either of them. Staff uniforms, crockery, cutlery, and even the basic *modus operandi*, although independently branded and marketed, were too close for it to be coincidence. It was, if you like, the railway equivalent of the familiar 'badge engineering' in the motor car business of the late twentieth century!

Pullman in Britain ceased to import American-built cars in 1906, thereafter relying on British works to satisfy the demand. Even this was not as simple as it may sound. Brand new vehicles were usually built by outside contractors such as, for example, Cravens of Sheffield and the Birmingham C & W Company, but they were still very American in concept and construction, and Pullman issued the specification; there was no 'off the peg' purchasing of standard designs. Pullman itself also built 'new' cars, but these were most difficult to define. Many of them were, in fact, comprehensive rebuilds of older cars while others were in the form of old underframes fitted with completely new bodies. For example, a particularly astute purchase by Pullman of some ex-Great War ambulance coaches provided some splendid underframes on to which were grafted new bodies to launch Pullman into the 1920s era. Obviously, by this time, the 'integral wood box girder' form of construction had been supplemented by this later subterfuge, but outwardly there was little apparent change in appearance.

Nor did it stop there. For all the outward opulence, Pullman was a very shrewd practitioner of 'make do and mend'. While it might be necessary, for technical reasons, to upgrade the running gear (possibly even the kitchen equipment), if the armchairs and other such fitments were still sound, reupholstery and reinstatement into a so-called 'new' car was quite customary. This went on right to the end and beyond, and is one of the reasons why the preserved 1913 'Topaz' was displayed for many years *sans* seats; when the 1960 Metro-Cammell cars were put into service by BR, their original loose armchairs were purloined from the vehicles they replaced! 'Topaz' lost most of its armchairs as a result and it was not until 1984-5 that the NRM was able to make restitution of this fine car by commissioning exact replicas of the original tables, table lamps and armchairs. However, back to the pre-group era.

The first manifestation of the new order was a splendid set of British-built cars for the LB & SCR 'Southern Belle', as it was called in 1908. It was the Brighton's third full Pullman set and became justly famous for both its quality and its clientele between London and Brighton. Its successor, the electrified 'Brighton Belle' of 1933 et seq, became equally celebrated, although this latter train must await Volume 2.

To be honest, London to Brighton was hardly the most suitable route to act as the standard-bearer for the Dalziel Pullman philosophy. For one thing, the distance was really too short to provide scope for all that Pullman could and would, given the chance, try to do. A fifty-mile run through the North and South Downs, lasting little more than an hour, was not really adequate time in which to deploy the particular style which was 'Pullman'. However, it does seem to have been the first twentieth century manifestation of that most distinctive feature of British Pullman operating — the provision of meals at all seats. This may, in the event, have turned out to be the most significant factor. In North America, 'Pullman' was synonymous with high-quality *overnight* travel; Dalziel made the British equivalent synonymous with day travel in association with 'refreshing the inner man'. The one feature which made British Pullman travel in the twentieth century so agreeable was the tacit assumption by Pullman that one would prefer to take a meal without having to go to a separate dining car. Even in North America this was a rare possibility. Thus, whether first or third class (practically speaking, second class may safely be ignored in this context), this was what one expected of Pullman (and usually got) for one's supplementary payment.

Interestingly, the one main-line company which seemed to have grasped this point in relation to its own dining cars was the pioneering Midland. Almost alone in the pre-grouping period, the Midland encouraged 'all the way' travel in its dining cars and transmitted this idea to some extent to its LMS successor. One can perhaps conclude that the Midland's long association with Pullman in the last century may have had something to do with it.

The long-term effect, as far as Pullman was concerned, was that the provision of kitchens was a vital part of its operations. If a train was 'all Pullman', then every second or third vehicle (first *or* third class) would be a kitchen-equipped car, and if running singly there would almost always be some minimum catering facility as well as the passenger seats. Thus, for example, when Pullman managed to get a couple of cars on to the outer suburban services of the Metropolitan Railway, they were catering vehicles, albeit in modern parlance more correctly referred to as buffet cars. The same idea was translated with considerable success to the catering services of many trains on the post-1922 Southern Railway, of which more in Volume 2.

Meanwhile, the other two principal Pullman activities in the pre-grouping era of the this century could not have been more dissimilar or more widely geographically spread. Staying, for the moment, in the South of England, we must now address that most

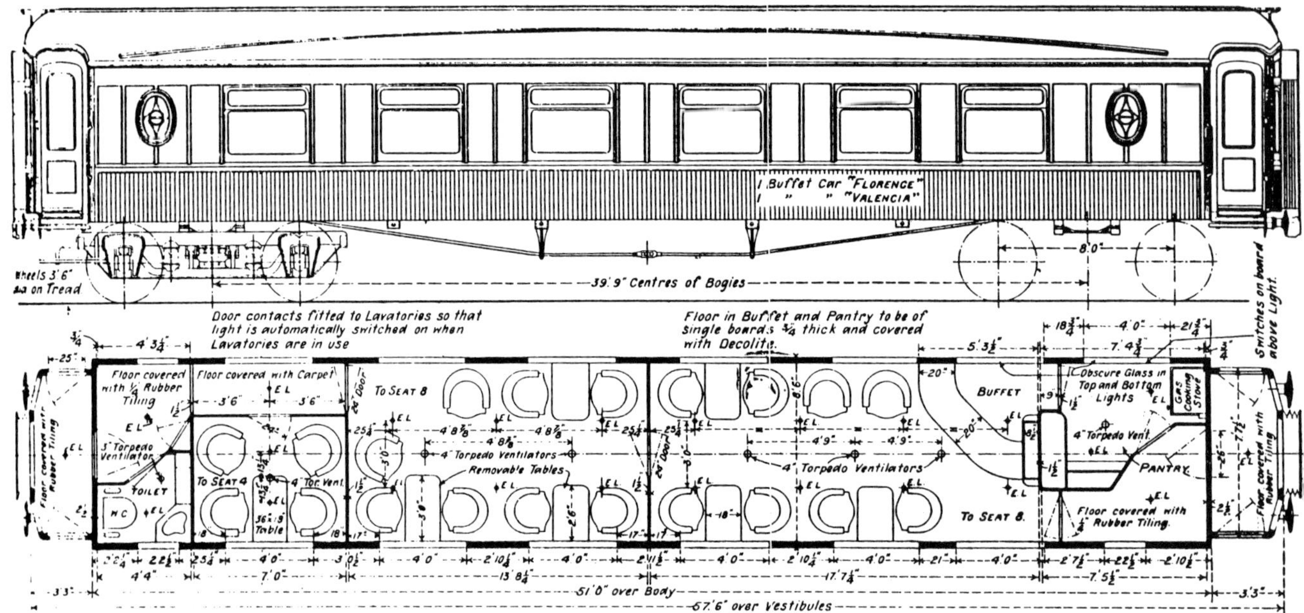

Scale 3mm = 1ft

Figure 58 *Elevations and plan of typical 57 ft 6 in buffet/parlor cars 'Florence' and 'Valencia', built in 1910 for the SE & CR. The preserved 'Topaz' of 1913, at the NRM, is an almost identical full parlor equivalent.*

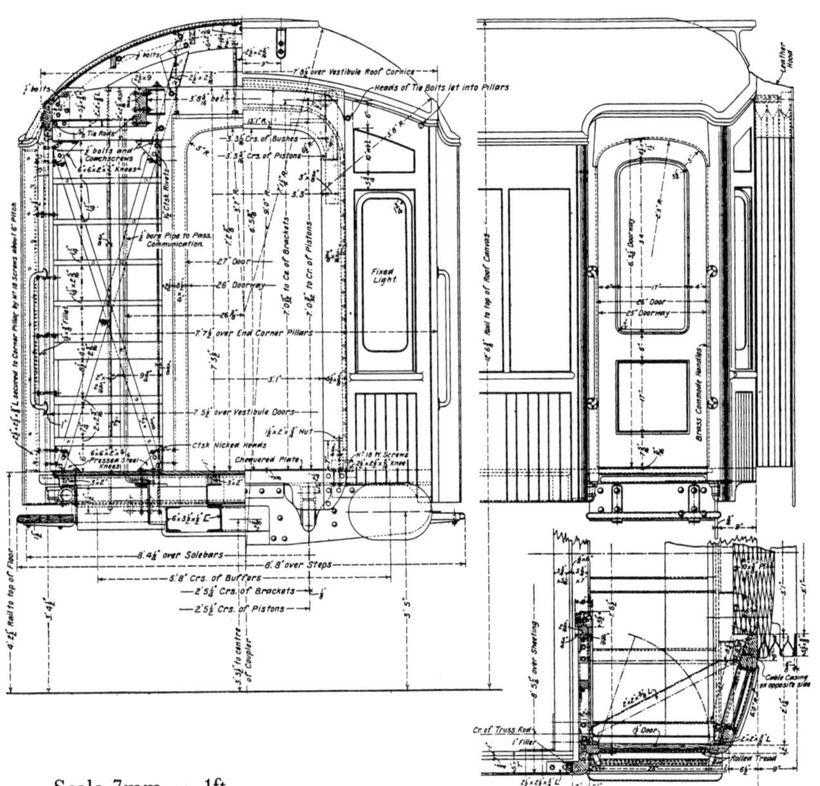

Scale 7mm = 1ft

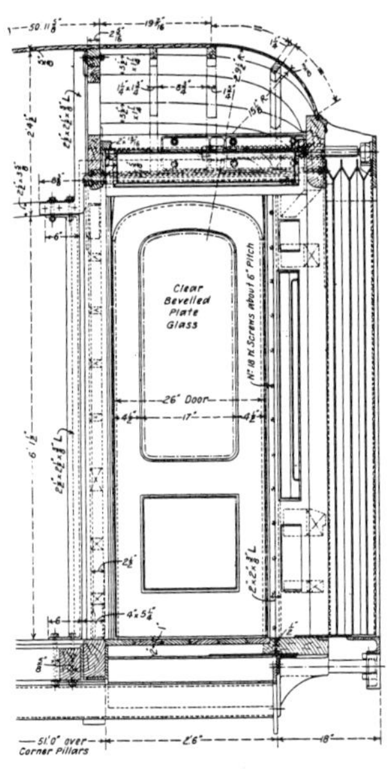

Figure 59 *Vestibule end and framing detail of the 1910 Pullmans for the SE & CR.*

Above *Parlor Car 'Emerald', built by the Birmingham C & W Co in 1910, was turned out in SE & CR dark red livery, carrying the somewhat rare circular Pullman badges used on a few vehicles at this time. It was replaced in 1960 by the modern 'Emerald', now preserved at the NRM.*

Below *The years between 1920 and 1924 saw a great upsurge in Pullman car building and refurbishments, most of the consequences being felt in the post-grouping era. It also saw the last flowering of the classic twelve-wheel wooden-bodied cars, two of which are featured here: 'Arcadia', built in 1920 by Clayton as a kitchen and parlor car and remodelled by Pullman in 1924, as shown, to a brake parlor first; 'Malaga', a kitchen/parlor car built by Pullman itself in 1921 and seen here on 'Golden Arrow' service in the post-1928 umber and cream colours with dark headboard. It survives in preservation, thanks to the Ian Allan organization.*

interesting railway, the SE & CR. This company, even when operating as two separate systems (SER and LC & DR) during the nineteenth century, had always witnessed the SER part in some rivalry with the LB & SCR for cross-channel patronage, but in the 1890s the SER had gone to the rival American Gilbert Car Company to obtain some suitable vehicles by which to counter the Brighton Pullmans. These vehicles (see page 11) were very much like Pullmans, but it was not until 1910 that the SE & CR decided to throw in its lot with Pullman. There thus began a separate and profitable association (of which the preserved 'Topaz' is the prime exemplar) of Pullman with a second major part of the south-of-the-Thames railway scene. By 1922, all the best SE & CR boat trains were, like the best Brighton services, Pullman-operated and, with the limited continued espousal of Pullman by the LSWR for some services, the stage was set for the continued linkage between Pullman and the SR after the grouping.

While all this was happening in the south, the main trunk lines (LNWR, GWR, MR etc) were all busily developing their own 'in house' services without the help of Pullman, though doubtless influenced by some aspects of the Pullman style. It therefore must have seemed that the future of the Pullman Company lay within its southern redoubt; but this was to underestimate the tenacity of Dalziel's company. Pullman never stopped trying to persuade the various railways to accept its cars, and eventually an unlikely breakthrough was made in Scotland in the shape of the Caledonian Railway which entered into a twenty-year agreement with Pullman in 1914, embracing all its non-WCJS catering services. This led to the building of an opulent fleet of Pullman dining cars, all with suitably Scottish-sounding names of considerable resonance. Thus there entered the scene 'Flora McDonald', 'Lass o' Gowrie', 'Fair Maid of Perth' and many others, not the least of which was the unique Pullman observation car 'Maid of Morven' which plied its trade on the Oban line, displaying a quasi art nouveau observation verandah to all and sundry and causing much comment both in the contemporary and subsequent railway press. It was the only British Pullman observation car until after the Second World War.

Now, apart from the 'Maid', the Scottish cars were quite different from what later became to be understood as normal Pullmans (ie parlour cars or parlour/kitchen cars).They were pure 'all-comers' dining cars in the best Wagons-Lits tradition (first and third class) and were simply slotted into normal Caledonian trains as required. Their umber and cream livery did not fight too strenuously with the Caledonian colour scheme, but in 1923, with ten years of the contract still to run, they began to look somewhat visually incongruous amongst the ever-increasing flood of LMS-liveried crimson lake coaches. In any case, the LMS did not favour Pullman, so when the contract came up for renewal, the LMS, like the nineteenth-century Midland a generation earlier, bought up the cars rather than renewing the contract, painted them red and proceeded to add them to its own not inconsiderable fleet of dining carriages. As such, some of them survived until well after nationalization.

Not for the first time, this part of the narrative has exeeded the strict bounds of the period covered by this first volume; thus was the nature of Pullman, however. It never quite followed the normal ground rules.

By the end of the pre-grouping period, Pullman had rather recovered from the low point of the early century. It was well established south of the Thames, had a firm foot-hold in Scotland, was one of the few civilizing influences on the Metropolitan Railway and was even beginning to make successful overtures into East Coast, later to become LNER, territory. This led to a considerable flowering of activity during the

Left *This Pullman in BR red and cream livery,* circa *1950, was one of the many pure dining cars built to a Caledonian Railway order. It entered service as 'Meg Dods' in 1923, was sold to the LMS in 1933, becoming LMS No 217 in the composite dining car series and was scrapped in the form seen here as Sc217M — quite a history!* (F.W. Shuttleworth).

Above right *Interior view of what is thought to be No Sc217M,* circa *1950, scarcely changed from its original state and still in amazingly sound condition* (F.W. Shuttleworth).

1920s to 1950s period, but will have to await the next volume to resolve. The common factor in all these operations was catering, and by way of concluding this first encounter with the Pullman company, a few further words on the vehicles themselves will not be out of place.

One could always recognize a Pullman from the outside, partly from its livery but also from its shape, and this was just as true of the interior. We have seen how things began as a mixed day and night activity, but by the twentieth century Pullman was a dining operation. Its foundation was the full parlour car, with the kitchen/parlour as a close second, be it first or third class. Within the carriage, the layout was of the open configuration, dominantly individual armchairs in the first and 2 + 1 fixed seating in the thirds (introduced in 1915). A full parlour would almost always include two small compartments (or coupés) at the extremities between the main saloon and the end-located lavatory. These havens of privacy (almost always four-seaters) had a side corridor alongside and were much sought after. The name 'coupé' was very much a Pullman interpretation, for they were, in every respect, of full compartment size, unlike the honeymoon half compartments (page 165) normally called coupés. Kitchen/parlours had one such feature, the kitchen itself occupying the other end of the car, and this internal configuration remained very consistent throughout.

Other arrangements mostly followed either the individual dining car layout or the buffet car style, and for some 'all Pullman' sets a brake-ended version was also provided. These seem to have appeared originally as first class cars with 'Alberta' and 'Verona' on the 1908 'Southern Belle', but increasingly the brake-ended Pullmans were of the third class type. In fact, one of the first of the 'lower order' Pullmans was a brake third.

Within the carriage, first or third, the decor was unmistakable with its coved ceilings, considerable use of inlaid or carved woodwork (often both) and the ever-present table lamps, an indispensable accompaniment to Pullman travel and, in the pre-BR era, regularly stamped with the name of the car itself. A clock would normally be present (until more recent years), and floors would be carpeted. So good, in fact, were Pullmans that even the third class option was usually equatable with most *first* class diners in the non-Pullman field. That it could all be provided — and make money — at a cost of only a few shillings (10-30p) plus a meal price no more than that to be found on a normal railway-owned vehicle was one of the more astonishing facts of this highly idiosyncratic organization.

Pullmans were rarely built in vast batches, usually coming into service only when specific needs arose. In consequence there were rarely more than a handful of identical specimens, and during the present century lengths varied between about 57 feet and some 68 feet, as did the choice between eight or twelve wheels; but they were all in the family. In consequence, when, as often happened, Pullman switched its cars from one service to another, it was not always possible that the more casual traveller would notice the change. Nor was it common for a complete set of new cars to be provided for a fresh service. It would, more typically, be a mix of new, refurbished and old. This too remained characteristic, but those readers who would know more will need to refer to the more detailed specialist works; it is a fascinating tale.

Pullman's influence was simultaneously both more and less significant than might be supposed. In the positive sense it showed what could be done, but some of Pullman's thunder was stolen, in the British context, when such systems as the GWR, Midland, East and West Coast Joint services and others demonstrated a quick ability to learn, copy and eventually replace Pullman with vehicles every bit as good. Thus Pullman never gained the same stranglehold on British train catering services as did its Wagons-Lits partner in many European countries. Even after the grouping, although Pullman maintained a high profile in certain areas, the traditional twentieth-century non-Pullman lines (essentially the LMS and GWR constituents of the post-1922 scene) were not involved until after nationalization, and for rather different reasons.

However, in spite of many disincentives, by the end of this first period of study, Pullman in Britain had well and truly arrived and still had its finest hours to come.

13. Special carriages for special purposes

We turn now and finally in this review of orthodox locomotive-hauled passenger carriages to those special vehicles which most railways could offer, even if only on a unitary basis, to those travellers who merited VIP or other special forms of treatment. By their very nature, they have always been at the forefront of such limited literature as the railway carriage has inspired, so I have tried hard to resist the temptation to wax too eulogistic and at too great a length about them. Much has been written already, and sheer repetition would border on plagiarism, but they cannot be ignored. For one thing, the various special and other carriages, however defined, were almost always at the apex of design, fashion and construction, and collectively they displayed in a far more tangible form than any other group of vehicles the sheer skills, ability and pride in the job which characterized the railway carriage builders. Limited they may have been in terms of those who were privileged enough to ride in them, but in all their glory they represented all that was best in British carriage building, and it would be unfair to those who built them not to comment on their place in the scheme of things. They were magnificent and, happily, one can still stand open-mouthed in admiration at the sheer quality of their workmanship, for many survive in preservation to the immense benefit of all.

At the top of the heap stood those vehicles built for or associated with the demands of the Monarchy, and there can be no doubt that during the Edwardian period of the pre-group age the ultimate high point of carriage design was reached in those vehicles provided for that most characterful of sovereigns, King Edward VII. The King liked trains and indeed had some splendid ones built for him — but they did not happen by accident, and yet again we must back off into the Victorian era to set the scene.

Queen Victoria embraced rail travel in the 1840s and was undoubtedly instrumental in helping to make railways respectable; she was, however, more than a bit conservative in her wishes and by the end of the nineteenth century had more than once frustrated those railways, notably the LNWR and GWR, which wanted to deploy their latest technology in the service of their Queen. She was more than happy to go on using her old vehicles, and the best that either the GWR or LNWR could do was to obtain her agreement to remount old carcasses on new running gear. The Queen was quite content with this compromise solution, the only genuine exemplar of which, the LNWR saloon, remains preserved for all time at the National Railway Museum. The GWR equivalent is long gone, in spite of the valiant attempts by Tussaud's Waxworks to persuade us otherwise in their imaginative but artificial recreation of the 1897 GWR Jubilee train at Windsor station.

King Edward VII had none of his mother's inhibitions. His nineteenth-century carriages (provided for him as Prince of Wales) were generally rather more modern than the Queen's, and when he became King the approaches of the principal railway companies regarding new Royal Saloons were very well received. Indeed, it is said that he hated Queen Victoria's saloons and the NRM knows of only one recorded instance where her preserved saloon was used by the new King after her death.

First in the strictly twentieth-century field was the London and North Western Railway, the owner of Queen Victoria's principal saloon and the traditional provider of vehicles for the Windsor-Balmoral pilgrimage via Ballater (GNSR) station. However, before going on to the realization of this wish by both railway and sovereign, a brief last mention of the nineteenth century is necessary in the shape of two railways, the GWR and the LB & SCR. Both had built almost brand new Royal Trains of considerable distinction in 1897 and, the GWR Queen's Saloon excepted, these were all but twentieth century in concept and much to King Edward's liking. Not surprisingly they survived well, and, in fact, it would not be bending regal history too much to postulate that the elegant Brighton clerestory set was, to all intents and purposes, designed more to meet Edward's requirements than that of the elderly Queen. She was not best known for her pilgrimages to Brighton, or to the races for that matter!

However, the long-distance journeys north were not well provided for in terms of the new King, so the LNWR moved in swiftly, obtained approval in mid-1902 for a brand new Royal Train and managed to deliver the principal saloons by Christmas of the same year! These two fabulous twelve-wheelers were supplemented by no fewer than *six* matching a semi-royal carriages a year or so later, and the whole ensemble was a visual and technological *tour de force*, never surpassed and scarcely approached since. The LMS kept it intact until 1941, and some bits of it survived until the late 1960s in regular royal service. It was eventually augmented by the addition of matching sleeping and dining cars of the conventional Wolverton type together with a couple of brake vans for the train crew, the latter being superseded in 1923-4 by a pair of corridor first brakes. Amazingly, seven of these carriages survive, five in the NRM

Right *This view of the LB & SCR Royal Train of 1897 shows that the Brighton line was just as capable as anyone else of producing elegantly styled carriages if it so chose. However, only the Monarchy benefited!*

Right and below right *The 1897 GWR Royal Train embodied the so-called 'Royal' clerestory, a roof profile of great beauty with its distinctive overhanging domed-end shape. No new principal saloon was built, so the style was only used on new vehicles such as the Lords and Ladies in Waiting saloon No 9003, seen here in the new single-colour livery, sometime after 1909. The interior was every bit as elegant as the outside.*

collection (two Royal Saloons, both brake firsts and the royal dining car) and two (the staff diner and semi-royal) in private ownership.

The special vehicles themselves, although a mixture of eight and twelve-wheelers, were of the classic Wolverton 'twelve-wheel' exterior styling and entirely in tune with the style and fashion of the day. Their visual lines, both inside and out, broke away from the stuffy Victorian, and since they have been described many times in some detail I have let the pictures tell the story. What is, perhaps, most important about them is that they established the 'travelling palace' concept for the first time in a truly comprehensive way, by marrying the quite well established family saloon idea (see below) with all that was best in modern technology. Moreover, although their own clientele was very restricted, many of the ideas which they pioneered eventually became characteristic of much general service stock — much more quickly, in fact, than is often supposed. Indeed, the dining and sleeping cars allocated to the LNWR Royal Train from *circa* 1904 onwards were unmodified examples from the LNWR/WCJS fleet and little changed thereafter.

If, however, a single vehicle can be identified as being the most significant contribution to this essentially twentieth-century approach to the VVIP train, then there is only one serious contender — the magnificent carriage built across the turn of the century by the LNWR for the 4th Duke of

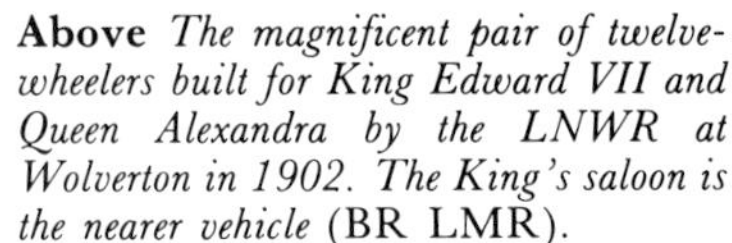

Above *The magnificent pair of twelve-wheelers built for King Edward VII and Queen Alexandra by the LNWR at Wolverton in 1902. The King's saloon is the nearer vehicle* (BR LMR).

Left *Interior view of the 1902 LNWR Royal saloons taken from the Queen's parlour and looking through the vestibules to the King's lounge. As preserved at the NRM, these carriages display the later interior decor introduced by Queen Mary* (BR LMR).

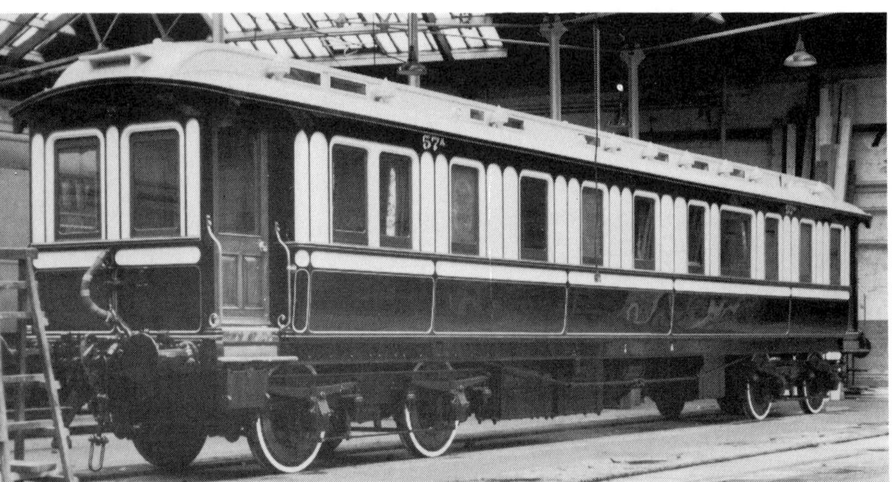

Below left *Saloon No 57A, the fine carriage built by the LNWR at Wolverton for the 4th Duke of Sutherland in 1899-1900, which established virtually all of the features subsequently to be found in most British Royal carriages. The picture was taken at Wolverton in 1958 when the saloon was first restored. It now resides at the NRM, York, having been further renovated during 1979-80* (F.W. Shuttleworth).

Above right *East Coast Royal Saloon No 396, built at York by the NER in 1909 for Queen Alexandra. In LNER days it was converted to a dual purpose saloon for the King and Queen, and in 1962 it was again refurbished for Queen Elizabeth II and the Duke of Edinburgh. In this final form it, too, now resides in the NRM collection.*

Sutherland, again, happily, preserved in the NRM Collection. This was a family saloon writ very large indeed. It was, in truth, the final flowering of the Victorian era but spent the whole of its operational life (1900-48) in the twentieth century, and King Edward VII travelled in it from the very outset whenever he visited his aristocratic friend at Dunrobin Castle where it was housed. Small wonder that the LNWR Royal Train of 1902-4 drew heavily on the ideas first put into tangible form for this influential Scottish nobleman; the King was most impressed with its vastly better amenities than that of his mother's ancient conveyances and said so. Why, the Duke's saloon even had its own private kitchen! Furthermore, the Duke's unique facility to use his carriage on demand in the Highlands as a mobile home must further have appealed to the new King.

Thus it was that King Edward VII was the first beneficiary of the better technology and up market provisioning which the railways could now provide; but it did not stop there, this was merely the beginning.

It was not to be expected that the East Coast companies would stand idly in the wings allowing the LNWR to gain all the kudos from its new, very visible Royal Train, so in 1908-9 they replied in kind with another sumptuous pair of saloons for Edward VII and his Queen, accompanied by a handful of equally grand semi-royals. These carriages were, naturally, in the Gresley East Coast style, although one of the principal saloons was actually built at York (NER). These two saloons were regarded as East Coast Joint Stock, unlike those of Wolverton which were jealously protected by the LNWR and distinctly *not* joint stock! In exterior design terms, the East Coast pair (also preserved by the NRM) lacked a little of the delicacy and visual harmony of normal Gresley-styled vehicles, being somewhat overblown in their overall proportions and mounted on heavy NER-type chassis, but inside they were probably unmatched for quality in the 'quasi-Adam' style. The wood veneers in the principal day compartment of the King's saloon, No 395, are probably without peer in any British-built carriage.

The East Coast set was in much demand for trips to Sandringham (King Edward VII's favourite abode), not to mention race meetings and the like, but it was never used quite so often in the overnight or long duration role. In consequence, it never acquired sleeping or dining cars on a permanent basis and was never quite as flexible in the operational sense as was the LNWR set. It was probably for this reason that it lasted even longer, making its final run in full formation as late as 1961 (for the Duke of Kent's wedding in York), the principal saloons themselves being used intermittently for yet another decade or more until the mid-1970s. Long before then, the original King's saloon had been converted for the fairly exclusive use of Queen Mary, and was later to be similarly employed by Queen Elizabeth the Queen Mother after the deaths of King George VI and Queen Mary in the early 1950s. However, the further adventures of these two splendid Edwardian Royal Trains will have to await the next volume.

By 1910, counting the late-nineteenth-century LB & SCR and GWR trains, the reigning monarch now had four complete sets of carriages to choose from, but still there was more. Early in the century the SE & CR had produced its own saloon for the King, and in 1910 the Midland Railway got into the act with a splendid Royal Saloon, No 1910. Surprisingly, given its reputation, the MR never built a full Royal Train, but could provide a more than passable substitute by combining this new carriage with its better family saloons, dining cars and corridor stock and occasionally did so. Likewise, too, sometimes the railways south of the Thames utilized their better saloon carriages in the service of the Monarch, rather than venture into exclusively royal provisioning. In this, they were often assisted by Pullman in the form

Above *Surprisingly, the MR Royal Train, apart from the principal saloon, No 1910, was formed from better quality general service stock. The main saloon, numbered for its year of manufacture, is seen formed up as the second vehicle. The rest of the train, save for the third carriage, a nineteenth-century Clayton clerestory dining car, is pure David Bain. No 1910 survives in preservation; sadly it no longer has its original interior fitments.*

Left *The King's ECJS Saloon No 395 of 1908 was later converted for HM Queen Mary's use and, later still, refurbished for HM Queen Elizabeth the Queen Mother. The furniture has changed but the fantastic sycamore wall panelling and 'Edwardian Adam' decor may still be admired at the NRM.*

Left *In 1914, the GNR built two almost identical first class saloons, Nos 3099/100. In practice, they turned out to be almost exclusively VIP saloons for use with the East Coast Train. This view shows the interior of No 3099.*

Right Figure 60 *Elevations, plans and sections of LNWR six-wheel Invalid/Family saloon of 1902. Six wheelers were still quite common in the normal compartment coach field, but their continued use for a somewhat specialized vehicle was, by this time, somewhat rare.*

of its best parlour cars; the use of Pullman cars for royal journeys on the Southern lines continued well into the BR period.

As will be appreciated, Royal Saloons tended to be somewhat one-off vehicles and generalization is not readily possible. It therefore seems more sensible to cover some of their more noteworthy ramifications by using a rather higher proportion of illustrations to depict their considerable variety and the quality of their detail and finish. Much the same sort of approach also seems valid for the next group down the hierarchy, the many and various forms of private and family saloons. We have already encountered some of the grander examples of those built for use in support of the Royal Trains, and a point not often appreciated is the fact that most of these vehicles could be hired, if not required by the Royal Family, by any person willing to pay the cost — probably something in the order of 12-24 first class fares. After all, the Royal household paid and still does pay the railway for the provision of the Royal Train, so why should not this privilege be extended to anyone whose pocket was deep enough? The railways saw no reason why not.

The idea of a special saloon for private hire was a concept dating well back into Victorian days, and the majority of such vehicles were actually built during the nineteenth century. They did, however, reach their peak of luxury during Edwardian times before their inevitable and early decline in favour of the motor vehicle. After all, it was the more wealthy folk who would, all things being equal, be amongst the first to espouse the motor car. But the so-called family saloon, or whatever other name it was given, was often the carriage builders' *tour de force,* short, that is, of the even more elaborate Royal Saloons.

In this context, the word 'saloon' can be misleading. In railway terms it regularly described a complete vehicle (dining saloon, sleeping saloon and so on), but could also be used to indicate one specific area within the carriage, ie the 'day' saloon as opposed to the 'night' equivalent. In this work, the word will hopefully be confined to references to the whole vehicle.

The family saloon, with its close ally the so-called 'invalid saloon', can trace its origins back to the pioneer sleeping cars of the 1870s, and probably even earlier. Typically, the vehicle would have accommodation for the family itself, the servants (in a second or third class type of compartment of course) and all the luggage and paraphernalia of the late Victorian travelling entourage. There would be much luxury in the family compartment(s), characteristically armchairs and/or settees together with tables, carpets and

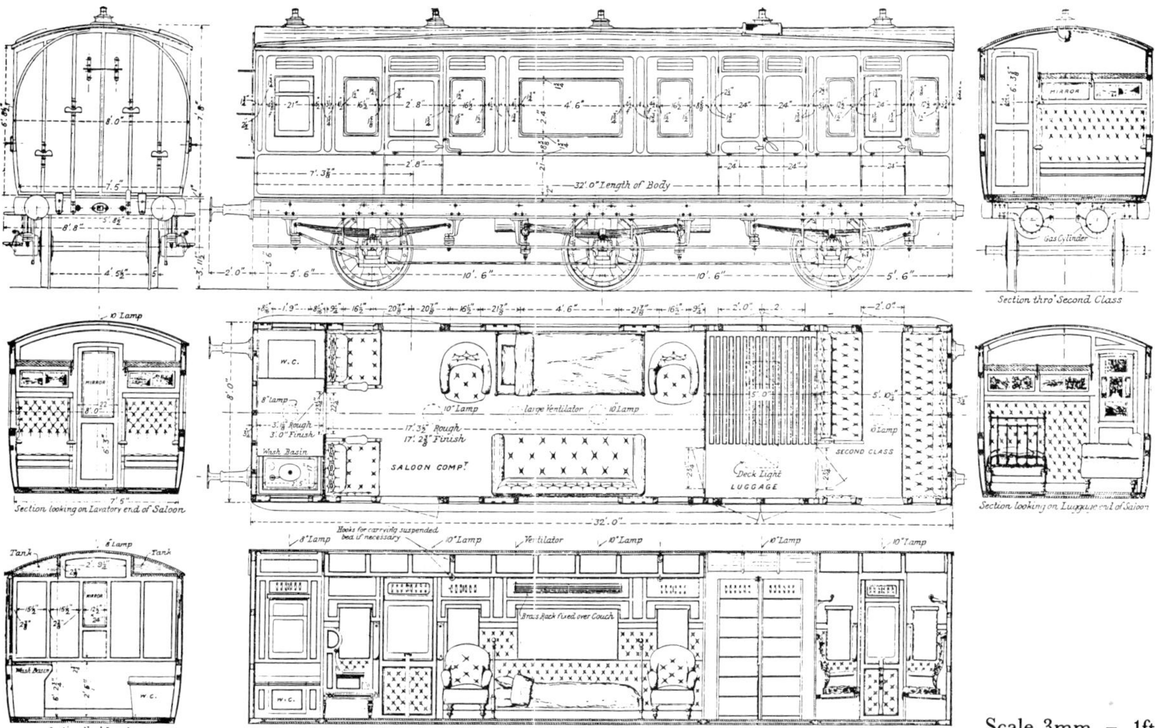

Scale 3mm = 1ft

Left *Interior view of a Dean GWR family saloon with suspended couch for the use of invalids.*

the many florid excesses of the time. The vehicle would have lavatories and usually be well lit and heated. Typically, the servants' compartment would be separated from the family apartment(s) by the luggage space, but at least the staff would usually have a lavatory. Most of these saloons contained the sort of furniture which could be turned into beds at night — hence the design linkage with sleeping cars — and the only significant difference between the pure 'family' and the specialized 'invalid' variant was the ability of the latter to admit a stretcher or wheelchair to the main compartment by means of wider doors. They would also, as a rule, have a proper bedstead for the invalid passenger. Some saloons, indeed, were convertibles.

The Victorian family saloon was normally a six-wheeler and, quite regularly, two or three would be seen on the longer-distance trains, but by the start of the present century a somewhat paradoxical situation was beginning to develop. On the one hand demand was reducing, probably because of the generally improved nature of general service sleeping and dining cars, while on the other those few vehicles which *were* built embodied even more luxury and were normally carried on bogies. However, Royal Trains excepted, it was a last desperate fling, and although such renowned companies as the Midland, LNWR, East Coast lines and GWR made valiant attempts to cater for this trade, it soon disappeared and the only really long-lasting special saloons were those considered for royal or VIP use. The remainder

were either scrapped, turned into railway officers' saloons or downgraded into third class vehicles with redesigned interiors (see Volume 2).

Lest it should be thought that the specialized saloon was the exclusive prerogative of the first class passenger, this might be an appropriate point at which to mention that other early twentieth-century oddity, the 'picnic saloon'. These were dominantly third class and were for hire by private parties for excursions, or even attached to service trains. Their layout was usually spartan but friendly, with seats round the periphery of the open interior and long tables down the centre. They were the precursors, one supposes, of the modern road coach which in turn has superseded the early-twentieth-century open-topped charabanc. Either way, just as with the more opulent saloons, the picnic versions did not long survive the onslaught of road motor transport, although at least they did last a bit longer, quite a number surviving even the Second World War. Some, indeed, were actually conversions of erstwhile first class family saloons.

There is a distinct 'grey area' dividing the generally available special saloons and those which were dedicated for the exclusive use of specific groups of people. Clearly, of course, these included those for the Royal Family, but there were other kinds too and these must now be considered, though they are, in truth, difficult to categorize. In the strictly pre-grouping context, there seem to me to be three areas of prime interest, two of which were available for public use, the third category most definitely not.

Dealing with the latter group first, this was the domain of the travelling boardroom, usually known as Officers' or Inspection Saloon. There were not many of them but when very senior railway management decided to inspect the line, they regularly travelled as well as Royalty, sometimes even as part of the Royal Train. The vehicles usually contained one or two lounges, one at each end, with panoramic views both from the sides and ends of the coach to aid the business of 'inspection'. Between these two areas there would usually be some sort of service facility, almost always including kitchen and toilet, sometimes even a sleeping berth or two or a bathroom. Within the confines of a normally-sized vehicle, little in the way of creature comfort was spared to create the most agreeable self-contained travelling environment for those privileged to use them — and they rarely had gangways to connect them to adjoining vehicles in the train. Most of the time this was not necessary because an 'Officers' Special' usually consisted of the saloon itself together with a well-turned-out locomotive and little else save for the chef and the rest of the train crew, in that order of priority for the most part, one suspects!

Most railways owned at least one of these rather self-indulgent vehicles and several still survive both in museum collections and private ownership. Naturally enough, the larger and more self-important railways produced the more grandiose and long-lasting specimens, but some of the really quite minor systems also went in for either delusions of grandeur beyond their status or the most extraordinary one-offs imaginable. Two must suffice as exemplars, one from each of the opposite extremities of the scale.

The so far scarce-mentioned Taff Vale Railway had a most comical set up — a rather grand, if somewhat ancient, clerestory officers' saloon permanently coupled to a separate 'dining room'. The latter was

Far left *'Spartan but friendly' — a typical picnic saloon interior, in this case a turn-of-the-century LYR six-wheeler* (Author's collection).

Left *In 1912, the Cheshire Lines Committee obtained what it chose to call a first class family saloon, No 201, of typical GNR external style. In fact, it rather seems that this opulent vehicle was mainly used by railway officers. This interior gives an idea of the comfort in which they patrolled their domain. There was also, needless to say, a kitchen!*

Right *Lancashire and Yorkshire No 1 was, as its name implied, very much an 'Inspection Saloon' with its almost glasshouse-like array of windows. The folding steps allowed for between station stops and the central service area was small.*

a converted six-wheel full brake with no windows, but which was wallpapered inside — one of only a very few British carriages ever to be so finished and almost certainly the only 'full' brake! Its curiosity value is such as to merit even the rather poor quality picture reproduced alongside. Equally bizarre in its own way was the principal saloon of the London, Tilbury and Southend Railway, a sort of mock 'Gothick' creation with elliptical roof, domed ends and a pair of extraordinary fireplaces, one in the centre of each end where the gangway would normally have been located. Again, visual confirmation is appropriate, since the Tilbury was hardly renowned for most of its carriages.

The more celebrated railways tended to build their officers' saloons in the general style of their main-line carriages, and the illustrations show something of the variety. Of those which survive for posterity, we might perhaps single out one or two. There is, for instance, a rather nice vehicle, No GE1 in private ownership, which, for all its latter-day alterations both by the LNER and BR, is still recognizably Great Eastern, even though its open verandah at one end gives it a vaguely American feel. Splendid too are a pair of ex-LNWR saloons — a massive twelve-wheeler now in private ownership and, most amazing of all, the former LNWR Chairman's saloon, built in 1920, which at the time of writing is still in service with the Royal Train, being used for its traditional purpose of carrying railway officers travelling with the Royal Train and cleared for 100 mph running, no less!

This astonishing vehicle has been used by all manner of people as well as railway officers — King Edward VIII, General Eisenhower and Winston Churchill to name but three. It is expected that by the time this book appears, it will have gone or be about to go into honourable retirement, having been earmarked by the NRM for permanent preservation in the National Collection.

In some respects, even more exclusive than the Officers' Saloons were those extremely rare creatures, the 'Club' saloons, if only because there were so few of them. Their origin is a bit obscure but casts a fascinating glimpse into the travelling mores of the day. In essence, they were used on public trains by fare-paying passengers on a regular daily basis, but there all resemblance to normal commuting ends. They were firmly, if not exclusively, a Northern phenomenon, closely connected with the prosperity of the Yorkshire and Lancashire textile industries. Within these areas, many of the more wealthy businessmen chose to live away from their 'dark satanic mills' in more salubrious places such as Blackpool, Southport, Morecambe, Llandudno, Windermere and so on. If sufficient patrons were agreed as

Left *The curious Taff Vale Railway inspection ensemble referred to in the text. The 'dining car' is at the far end* (Author's collection).

Below left *Exterior and interior views of the amazing LT & SR Directors' saloon, complete with its internal fireplaces. The outside shows it in the 1920s as LMS No 2799, and the interior view shows the far end of the vehicle* (Top R.J. Essery collection).

This page *This trio of Club saloons from the NER, MR and LYR respectively were used on the Hull to Bridlington, Morecambe to Leeds and Manchester to Blackpool services. Apart from the MR example, an ex-family saloon, the other two were purpose-built* (Centre BR LMR).

Left *Club chairs in a club carriage — a view of the inner sanctum of another NER vehicle.*

Below right *LB & SCR continental boat express at Newhaven Harbour, 1908. Note the Pullman car midway down the formation.*

Bottom right *This view of WCJS No 386, the 'Aberdeen' brake composite from the '2 pm' train, shows the basic carriage styling used on the famous Wolverton trains of 1907-08. The large-size windows were usually found only on the corridor side of the side-corridor vehicles.*

to their times of travel, it was not particularly difficult to persuade the railways to provide a special saloon for this distinguished and usually first class clientele. It was known as a 'Travelling Club' and was attached to a regular morning and evening working to and from centres like Leeds, Bradford, Manchester, Liverpool and the like. Club saloons were either purpose-built or converted from other conventional stock, and were dominantly of open configuration, a sort of cross-breed between the more common family and officers' saloons. The LYR, LNWR, MR and NER were quite good at this sort of thing and there were others.

The third category of carriages in the pre-grouping period were those provided for particular services only. In a sense, this is an appropriate group with which to conclude this chapter for these carriages bring us back to a somewhat more democratic patronage than the exclusive vehicles so far considered. The only thing which governed their use was whether or not one's travelling needs coincided with the services to which the carriages were allocated. If so, then there was no need to be a club member, a railway officer, a member of a well-heeled family or even the sovereign. All you needed to have was the price of the ticket — and this could even be third class.

This concept of specific sets of carriages for particular workings reached its apogee after the grouping and began in Victorian times, so the period under discussion had certain evolutionary qualities, some of them of quite prime significance. The obvious contender for this type of service was, of course, the already considered Pullman, but the railway companies themselves seemed quite willing, on occasion, to join in the party. During Victorian times, the GWR, MR, WCJS and GER, to mention but a few, had all in their own way produced some splendid 'dedicated' sets of vehicles. The first true corridor train was GWR, the first long-distance corridor was WCJS, the first all-class dining service was GER and the Midland's special sets of the 1890s have been mentioned already, so the idea was not new. But the Edwardian period saw it reach new heights of splendour — and it was not simply in the long-distance field. Even the short-distance railways like the LB & SCR made their mark.

So far, this narrative has not been noteworthy for its praise of the Brighton line, save for its use of Pullmans and a commendatory mention of its late Victorian Royal Train, but there was one rather shining exception to the fairly unmemorable quality of most domestic LB & SCR stock for anyone other than first class passengers. When Billinton introduced his somewhat avant-garde 'Balloon' stock (see page 133), there was included among them a really quite splendid boat train set for the Newhaven services; it was non-corridor but it did have an adequate provision of lavatories for a not too lengthy run, and the opulence went down below the first class level. For the Brighton it was amazing, but sadly was not repeated. The real contribution was to be that of the more long-distance lines, and these were mostly north of the Thames or even north of the Anglo-Scottish border; moreover, the GWR was not exactly to the forefront either!

We have already noted, *en passant* such vehicles as were provided for the Caledonian 'Grampian' corridor trains, the NBR Fife and Lothian coast expresses, the LYR 'Fireproof' stock for its business trains and the GNR and/or East Coast twelve-wheelers, all superb in their own way, but if asked to provide a couple of prime examples, then I would argue that the LNWR/WCJS contribution stood supreme at this time. However, such a categorical statement needs qualification.

Wolverton (LNWR) was by no means the only carriage building establishment of merit. It has already been described how it was that many railways moved rapidly from late Victorian complacency to early-twentieth-century achievement; but it does seem, as already averred in the twelve-wheel field, that Wolverton managed somehow to get the overall mix more consistent than anywhere else. Its only serious rivals were Swindon (GWR), Doncaster (GNR), York (NER) and, conceivably, Derby (MR), but none of these places managed to deliver with quite such panache as did this venerable Buckinghamshire establishment during 1907-8, when it put into service probably the finest sets of carriages ever built in Britain for the *non-supplementary fare-paying passenger*. The emphasized qualification is important.

I refer, of course, to the celebrated '2 pm' and 'American Boat Train' stock. In a sense, they could well have come into Chapter 10, but somehow they seem more appropriate here. As vehicles, they were probably no better, technologically, than those of maybe half a dozen other lines, but conceptually they were real pioneers, setting standards which were never approached, let alone exceeded, for decades. They were so good, in fact, that the LMS (in succession to the LNWR) did not feel the need to replace them on their original designated service until more than twenty years after they were introduced.

Left and right *These interior views sum up the luxurious character of the 'American Special' and '2 pm' trains. They depict, in order: 'small' first class compartment, American stock; second class compartment, American stock (the American and '2 pm' thirds were all but identical to this); first class compartment, '2 pm' stock; second class dining car, American stock. The dining areas of all three classes on both trains were virtually indistinguishable from the version shown.* (BR LMR).

To get this into perspective, one only needs remark that the famous Deltics and their 100 mph trains of the more modern BR era lasted only some 16 years (1962-78) with at least three changes of coach style and at the time of writing the 1978 HSTs are likely to be replaced in 1991 after only 12-13 years of operation on the East Coast Main Line, and even so they have needed an intermediate face-lift (1985-7) on the way!

The sets of coaches provided in 1907-8 by the LNWR for its services — the '2 pm' was, in fact, WCJS but the design was pure LNW — embodied the classic twelve-wheel design philosphy which had gradually evolved over a fifteen-year period (1893-1907). Apart from the full kitchens and full brakes of the Boat Trains which were eight-wheelers, all were mounted on the well-proven LNWR twelve-wheel chassis and it does seem likely that no compromises were ever made in such mundane matters as weight per seat. They were opulent trains; even if one was travelling second or third class, one had no draughty compartment doors, the diners were superb and nowhere else in Britain was there anything quite like them. To be candid, they were ahead of their time, drawing much of their quality from the immediately preceding LNWR royal coaches of 1902-3, not to mention the 1904-6 sleeping and dining cars, themselves a considerable cut above average.

The 'American Boat Trains' — designated for the Liverpool (Riverside) to Euston services — were undoubtedly designed to impress the transatlantic clientele, and probably copied, if only subconsciously, some American ideas. Even so, an 11 ft 9 in by 6 ft first class compartment with but three arm-chairs and a settee was going some, even by USA criteria, especially when the journey time was no more than about four hours maximum! Nevertheless, since these splendid carriages were still somewhat restricted in their patronage being boat trains, it was the '2 pm' which turned out to be the real show-stopper.

In superficial terms, the '2 pm' West Coast stock was not perhaps quite as lavish as that of the American specials, although externally it looked much the same. The diners were, in fact, a few years older and still deployed the clerestory roof, but they were extremely elegant and, moreover, first and third class only. The side corridor stock was orthodox insofar as a five-compartment brake third, some 65 ft 6 in long without compartment doors and weighing some 40 tons could be considered orthodox. Even at maximum capacity (40 passengers) it was one ton per *third* class traveller, and the said traveller did not have to pay a penny extra for the privilege. Suggest that to a harassed second class commuter into London in the 1980s, crammed six-a-side in non-corridor side-door compartment stock of much more recent build!

The pictures appended herewith probably tell it all. The LMS and LNER could not improve on matters until the 1930s, while the Southern and GWR never did so as far as the third class passenger was concerned, so it does not seem unreasonable to conclude our review of pre-group conventional carriages on this mid-Edwardian high point. Nothing better was ever offered to the ordinary traveller, even though objectivity forces me to admit that the same LNWR, only five or six years later, produced some distinctly mean 57-foot eight-wheel coaches for the 10.00 am WCJS train, almost as though it knew it had gone too far. Although it made quite a splash about them at the time, one feels it was a sort of hollow claim — and there we will leave it for the moment.

14. 'They also served'

Before leaving the realm of conventional locomotive-hauled carriages, we must not forget the many thousands of vehicles which found their way into passenger trains but which did not carry passengers as such. Their importance has already been touched on in Chapter 6, but we must now take a closer look at this very important aspect of railway travel. First, however, a brief word about the subject in general.

From almost the very beginning of railways, the speed of transit afforded by the passenger train relative to most other contemporary forms of surface transport, has always been a key factor in terms of patronage, and from the earliest days there have always been certain types of cargo whose nature was such as to make time in transit an important consideration. Probably the earliest manifestation of this type of demand was the carriage of mail, and as early as 1830 the railways began to carry mail on their best trains. This concept was gradually expanded to embrace all manner of traffic until a whole generic group of vehicles had been evolved whose running characteristics in terms of their vehicular quality was fully compatible with passenger carriages but whose body structure was adapted to a whole range of different uses. Collectively, this group of vehicles is usually referred to as 'non-passenger-carrying coaching stock' — a cumbersome phrase but pretty well self-descriptive. These are the vehicles with which this chapter is concerned.

Obviously, there is a degree of blurring at the edges, for we are dealing with vehicles whose cargo could, in some cases, equally well have found itself forming part of the more humble goods or freight train, but from the earliest days there have always been certain types of commodity whose nature was such as to encourage their owners to pay a little more for the speedier transit which a passenger train would guarantee. This in turn stimulated the railways to make rather superior vehicles with better brakes, running gear and so on, the higher capital cost of the construction of which would, all things being equal, pay for itself by virtue of the higher charges which could be commanded for their use. These vehicles tended to fall into quite distinct categories, and this will be the basis of the analysis which follows.

The brake, luggage and parcels van group

The 'passenger full brake', to use its proper title, is the most obvious extension of the passenger carriage into the non-passenger sphere and, in purely vehicular terms, is no more than the logical consequence of expanding the van portion of many a brake-ended carriage to the point where one can do without any passenger-carrying compartments. The logic behind this course of action was no more than the natural outcome of the sheer volume of luggage which, increasingly during late Victorian and Edwardian days, the ever-growing number of passengers wished to take with them on their journeys. This led quite regularly to situations where, especially on the longer-distance trains, the luggage capacity of a normal brake-ended coach was insufficient, and the railways found it expedient to make carriages purely for luggage. It was equally logical to let the guard ride in them and, if the service so demanded, fit them with gangways as well. They were cheaper to build than a passenger-carrying vehicle and offered useful extra capacity for conveying other things than passengers' luggage should space and demand permit.

Of the various 'extras' which could be conveyed in this fashion, there soon turned out to be a profitable trade in such things as parcels and newspapers. In both cases, there was a degree of urgency in terms of transit time and the railways soon discovered that by putting a full brake into the train instead of a brake-ended passenger carriage, there was often sufficient space available to convey this extra trade without disadvantage to the original primary luggage function. Of course, many of them were pure luggage vans but increasingly the sheer versatility of a 'carry-all' vehicle unencumbered by the demands of the passengers themselves led to a situation where special-purpose vehicles purely for parcels or newspapers were built *without* guard's accommodation and also added to the main trains. This was an even cheaper option than the full brake with guard's space, and became extremely popular with those railways which had a fair volume of this traffic. All that really mattered in these cases was that the carriage itself should be capable of operating at passenger train speed. In fact, so lucrative did this trade become in some cases that special workings consisting of nothing but parcels and newspaper vans became quite common, the only condition then being that one of them, at least, should have somewhere for the guard to ride and also be fitted with the mandatory handbrake.

In the earlier days, it was more customary for such vehicles to copy standard passenger carriage styling, since more often than not they would be formed up as part of a passenger train, but it was not absolutely necessary and more than one railway could see no point in spending too much money on the vehicle itself. Thus, provided the couplings and brake gear were compatible with passenger train operation, it

A typical passenger-rated bogie full brake van from the turn of the century — LB & SCR No 438, built in 1900. Note the huge 'chimneys' for the oil pot lamps.

East Coast gangwayed bogie full brake No 6 was typical of many hundreds used on long-distance services by most major companies. The 'Luggage' branding, though wholly appropriate, was by no means universal on such vehicles.

A 70-foot twelve-wheel luggage van was a distinct rarity, but GWR No 876 was one of a pair built in 1910 as high-capacity baggage vans for the Fishguard boat trains. They could carry 20 tons of passenger luggage and after the Great War were re-classified as newspaper vans (T.J. Edgington collection).

The SE & CR adopted very much a 'goods vehicle' outline for its passenger luggage vans with no concession to 'coach' styling. This design became the basis for the ubiquitous Southern Railway general utility vans in the post-group period. In spite of appearances, their running gear had all the necessary refinement for high-speed operation and the design was long-lived. Many later examples survived well into the 1980s.

This non-gangwayed newspaper van No 208 of the NER was also a full brake — note the guard's lookout. There was always a degree of blurring at the edges in the description of this group of vehicles, and after 1923 the LNER simply classed them as full brakes.

was not unusual to find some of these vehicles being built to quite a utilitarian, almost freight-vehicle outline. This in turn led to a further sub-classification of 'general utility van' (GUV) to cover almost any kind of vehicle which might be expected to find itself either attached to a passenger train or forming part of a parcels or newspaper train merely by virtue of the load it carried. This type of operation continues to the present day and in the 1980 it is rather more common to find such vehicles displaying semi-freight wagon characteristics than purely passenger vehicle styling.

The dedicated mail vehicle group

The carrying of mail by train has always been an important part of railway operation, and right from the very beginning the Post Office has always insisted on speedy transit. In fact, during the seminal period of railway development, the mail trains were always the fastest in the business and in some cases passengers were prepared to pay extra to be conveyed on the postal trains. Indeed, famous named trains such as the 'Irish Mail' can trace their origins right back to this evolutionary time.

In most cases, mail vehicles ran as part of a mixed passenger and mail train and only rarely were all-mail formations operated. However, whether in mixed formation or exclusively mail, at heart of the postal operation was that unique vehicle, the 'Travelling Post Office' (TPO). This type of carriage could trace its origins back to the start of Victoria's reign, and by the turn of the century had developed very sophisticated characteristics. Its name was self-descriptive and many of them actually carried a late fee posting box into which one could post one's letters direct.

In structural terms, the TPO almost always mirrored that which was most up-to-date in contemporary coachbuilding practice. Typically, it would contain a multiplicity of sorting racks and shelves along one side of the carriage at which employees of the Post Office could sort the mail traffic as the train proceeded. Until very recently (1971), these facilities were regularly supplemented by the unique apparatus devised originally in 1838 whereby mail bags could be despatched from or collected by the train without the need to stop or even slow down. There were few more spectacular sights than to see a postal train exchanging its mail bags at high speed during the time when this practice was customary.

Because the mail pick-up apparatus was always at the near side of the line, TPO vehicles were usually built one-sided with the pick-up nets on the near side and the sorting racks on the off side of the carriage. Furthermore, in order to give an uninterrupted run of sorting shelves, it was equally customary to offset the gangways to the near or pick-up side of the carriages. These structural constraints meant that the vehicles not only had to be turned before their return journeys, but also could not be gangwayed to the normal centre-gangway passenger-carrying vehicles in the train. This, of course, ensured the security of the mail vehicles but also meant that all mail vehicles had to be marshalled together rather than mixed up with the passenger vehicles, the ultimate form being a full mail train. The most celebrated of these was the 'Night Mail' or 'West Coast Postal', whose departure from Euston (LNWR) at 8.30 pm, was not only more than normally ritualistic but whose operation itself was given the sort of special attention which might normally have been expected only if it was carrying a full load of the most influential people in the land.

Of course, not all mail vehicles were dedicated TPOs, and even the main users of these specialized vehicles also needed many carriages purely for the storage of mail bags and parcels *en route*. These coaches were little different from the normal luggage/parcels/brake vans already considered, and some railways owned only these types. In fact, there was more than a little chopping and changing of usage, and once again the categories could become blurred. Indeed, at peak times all manner of non-passenger coaching stock could be pressed into service for the carriage of mail, and it was always common for a few mail bags to be carried in the guard's van of many ordinary passenger trains, especially those operating in the more sparsely populated areas.

Top to bottom *Although not strictly twentieth-century (it was built in 1895), this GWR Dean clerestory No 596 merits inclusion if only for its most unusual configuration. It was a third class and Post Office van, fully equipped with mail pick-up apparatus and gangwayed only at the mail van end. It was not unusual for passenger accommodation to be provided on mail trains, but not normally in the Travelling Post Office itself!*

This is the classic form of TPO from the route which made most use of the type, the West Coast main line. WCJS No 437 was a 57-foot sorting van, built in 1910 with pick-up apparatus, and is shown here posed with its nets extended. Note the offset gangway to allow more space on the far (sorting) side of the carriage (BR LMR).

This rather noble-looking clerestory mail van, No 351 of the LB & SCR, was built in 1897 but is seen here with King Edward VII's monogram. It was converted to a full brake in 1921.

Left and below left *LNWR No 329 and NER No 181 are entirely typical of the better horse box designs of the pre-group period. They look very different but both embody similar features: (from left to right) fodder and 'tack' compartment, livestock area and the groom's compartment in the form of a coupé* (Top BR LMR).

Left *The demands of circus traffic gave rise to the need to carry elephants. The size and weight of these animals precluded the use of normal livestock vehicles so the more robust covered carriage truck was commonly adapted for the purpose, the animals entering the vehicle through the end doors. This is NER No 167 in LNER days.*

The livestock group

The bulk of animals carried by the railways were conveyed in normal freight trains utilizing cattle wagons, vehicles of little sophistication and scarcely better than open wagons with added roofs. They were partially open-sided above the waist as a rule and there was no provision at all for any accompanying stock handler or herdsman. Most of them had but rudimentary brakes and suspension and only a few had any capability for high speed. For the most part, these vehicles sufficed for large-scale stock movements but there was one group of livestock whose movement demanded (and received) better treatment. These were the high-value animals normally conveyed in considerably smaller numbers than the large herds of cattle and flocks of sheep which formed the bulk of livestock traffic.

The dominant species was the horse, and the most characteristic passenger-train-rated livestock vehicle was a horsebox. These were normally four-wheelers with accommodation for no more than two or three animals in well-padded stalls, along with storage space for tack, fodder and bedding straw and almost always with a half compartment for the groom. These distinctly superior vehicles arose from the fact that, as a general rule, horse traffic was very much up-market, being confined in the main to racehorses in transit to meetings and private carriage horses accompanying their usually wealthy owners on holiday or elsewhere. The so-called 'horse and carriage' trade was a very lucrative source of revenue for the railways and even quite modestly sized stations were expected to keep at least one horsebox and carriage truck (see below) in readiness for whatever business might arise. For this reason, even the smallest railways could muster quite a few horseboxes, while the larger organizations could number them by the hundred. Because of the high-value nature of the animals themselves and their rather more important status, the railways charged more for their conveyance and, in consequence, were able to provide vehicles which could safely be attached to passenger trains, or even be operated in special trains should occasion demand. They were usually finished in passenger carriage styling.

There were two main offshoots from this principal category. First was the carriage of prize cattle, almost always pedigree breeding bulls. These animals were less common than horses, but their conveyance, when called for, was just as important and the resultant vehicles were rather similar, if somewhat less elaborate. The second category was the travelling circus animal. In the days before motorized heavy road transport, the railways were sometimes called upon to convey complete circuses and deploy all manner of specialized vehicles, but again speedy transit was of the essence — frequently overnight — so passenger-rated vehicles were called for, not just for the animals but also for the human artistes and their accompanying scenery, tents and other paraphernalia. The livestock could often be accommodated in conventional horseboxes or prize cattle vans, but some species, for example elephants, needed somewhat stronger provisioning. This regularly took the form of specially strengthened carriage trucks or similar vehicles. In this context, there was much in common between the circus train and the requirements of the travelling theatrical companies; their transport problems also embraced personnel, costumes and scenery.

These needs, and many others too numerous to mention, gave rise to the considerable growth in demand for provision of one or more items from the next group of vehicles to be considered.

The carriage truck group

The carriage truck, as its name implies, was developed originally for the conveyance of horse-drawn carriages by rail, usually in company with the horses themselves (see above). The origins of the type go back to the dawn of the steam railway when, as an alternative to the conventional railway carriage, it was not unheard of for the more wealthy folk to travel in their own horse carriages firmly strapped down on to the top of a flat truck. Even when conventional coaches improved and the railways stopped allowing owners to travel in this way, the gentry still liked to take their equippage with them and the carriage truck continued to develop. By the time of this survey, the basic vehicle had developed into two specific variants, the 'Covered Carriage Truck' (CCT) and the 'Open Carriage Truck' (OCT). The names are self descriptive, the open version being, of course, the lineal descendant of the pioneer type. Whether open or covered, they were built to a variety of sizes and lengths, most common being four-wheel and six-wheel examples.

As a general rule, covered carriage trucks were usually fewer in number and confined to what were reckoned to be more valuable loads. In Edwardian terms, this often meant the newfangled motor car, and this new usage is worthy of more than a passing mention. In a curious anticipation of the modern 'Motorail', and before the real threat of the car had become apparent, the railways seemed to go out of their way to encourage the conveyance of motor cars, and produced some very stylish CCTs branded for motor car traffic. Of course, the modern trunk roads did not exist in the form we now know them; many indeed had not been built. With the benefit of

Left *Caledonian Railway CCT No 138 was a typical six-wheeler with visual points in common with both passenger and freight stock. It had spoked wheels, a very goods-truck-like handbrake and the end doors are simply tongue and groove boarding, but the bodyside styling is pure coachbuilding.*

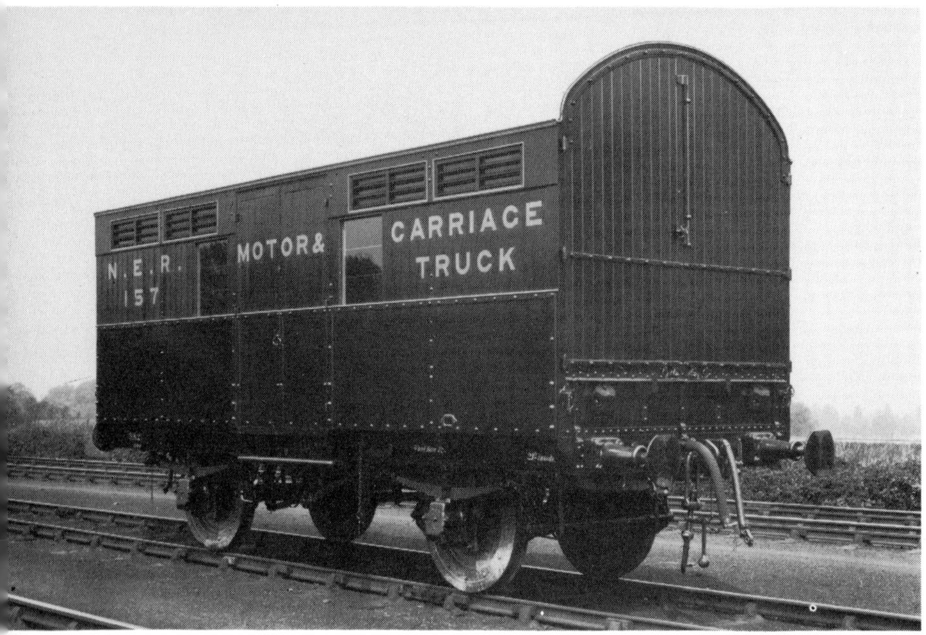

Left and below left *These two views show contrasting examples of CCTs adapted for motor car traffic in the early days. NER No 157 has distinctly 'freight vehicle' characteristics, but LNWR No 603 was clearly designed and painted to draw attention to itself* (Below BR LMR).

Opposite page *The open carriage truck came in a variety of forms and these three examples are typical. LYR No 147 is a very long wheelbase four-wheeler with no side planking; LNWR No 280 probably represents the most numerous single type, a fairly conventional four-wheeler with side members of modest height; and LNWR No 12015 is an example of the somewhat less common bogie type. It started life as a scenery truck but is seen here modified to carry containers of joint LNWR/LYR ownership.*

To Carry 6 Tons
147
L.Y.R
Tare 8.10.1

L & N W R 280 To Carry 5 Tons
S A

hindsight, it does rather seem that the railways never realized that the car would be a serious long-distance threat to their basic passenger trade, but rather tended to regard it as a substitute for the older 'horse and carriage' traffic. It was, of course, confined in those days mostly to the more wealthy who, presumably, would want to take their cars with them on their travels just as they had hitherto conveyed their horse-drawn rigs. This development saw a more or less continuous growth throughout the first half of the century and it is only in the more modern era that the whole business has had to be re-marketed in a somewhat different way.

The OCT could be used for a whole range of vehicles from horse-drawn furniture vans to farm machinery, but as with the covered version the principal distinguishing factor was the ability to be loaded 'over the end' rather than from the side. This was done by means of 'end loading' docks at the larger stations, where there would be some form of flat plate above the buffers connecting the vehicle floor with the loading bay itself. This had obvious advantages when the cargo needed to be wheeled on to the vehicle, but did not prevent side loading in some cases or even a quite different form of use for theatrical scenery, containers or any other high-speed cargo whose nature made the provision of an easily loaded passenger-rated vehicle with a large floor desirable. There was thus a degree of overlap between the carriage truck and general utility categories, and different railways had different names for them. However, the pure carriage truck was always recognizable by its ability to be loaded from the end. Thus, if an otherwise similar vehicle did not have this end-loading facility, including end doors if of the covered variety, it could not properly be called a carriage truck. The accompanying pictures indicate just some of the variety to be seen in this very large group of vehicles. There were many more and they earned much revenue.

The perishable cargo group

The final group of non-passenger-carrying coaching stock to be considered is that which most closely approximated to conventional goods vehicles. Some of them were, in fact, no more than goods trucks which had been given brakes and running gear to allow them to be worked safely in passenger trains. Their origin is obscure and almost certainly bound up with the total inability of the typical nineteenth century British goods train to be operated at anything like the transit speed required for perishable goods, and although this book is essentially about passenger carriages it is necessary at this point to refer briefly to the other side of railway operation, freight traffic.

It is one of the more severe indictments of the development of railways in Britain that their sheer success in capturing just about all the available land transport market in the nineteenth century bred a degree of monumental complacency in the board rooms of most railway companies when it came to vehicle provisioning for cargo handling. This typical four-wheeled British goods wagon was a poor thing indeed, usually devoid of both automatic brakes or any degree of sophistication, but for almost a century it had a virtual monopoly of the traffic so there was no real incentive to change its nature, particularly in terms of the speed at which it could run. In fact, it was not really until the 1950s and later that any real improvement began to take place on a widespread basis, by which time it was often too late to avoid losing the traffic to the road competitor with results which are now obvious to all.

Nevertheless, there were a few readily definable high-value traffics which demanded a higher transit speed even in the early days, and the railways were never slow in addressing the problem if they thought there was revenue to be gained, so in some areas they genuinely 'tried harder'. One way was to add the odd perishable goods vehicle to a passenger train, thus guaranteeing better speed provided the vehicle could operate in this mode. In effect, this was one of the first tentative moves on the part of the railway towards the much higher-speed freight service which is now commonplace. However, during the steam period it never went much further than an occasional fully braked freight train and, in consequence, there was always a place for those somewhat rare vehicles which could be hitched on to a passenger train.

The types of commodity carried should occasion no surprise: milk, fish, meat, vegetables and so forth. Many areas of the country could usually generate a wagon load or two of such items on almost a daily basis, so what more natural than to load them into a passenger-rated vehicle which would not have to endure the interminable delay of the loose-coupled and unbraked freight train? There can have been few places in rural Britain which did not respond to the undoubted advantages of being able to despatch the odd load of surplus fresh meat or liquid milk to the ever-growing towns with the guaranteed assurance that the railway would get the produce to market still fresh, usually the same day or, at worst, the next morning. In consequence, there grew up a considerable wagon-load traffic of perishables which would regularly find themselves attached to the first passenger train of the day — the 'early morning milk train' in very truth. Of course, the vehicles provided were more sophisticated and the rates for their use more expensive, but on the whole it was a valuable service in the pre-motorized era and the fact that

Right *The LNWR was the biggest single British operator of non-passenger coaching stock, so no apologies are necessary for yet another example from its diverse fleet. This is open fish truck No 439, one of many specifically built for carrying loaded boxes of fresh fish. It may not have looked like a conventional carriage but its mechanical specification allowed it to be treated as such in terms of the speed at which it was allowed to operate* (BR LMR).

Above right and right *The covered van with slatted sides was a very common solution to the problem of handling several different kinds of perishable traffic. These two very similar vehicles, MR No 95 and LYR No 25 are for fish and milk traffic respectively* (Top R.J. Essery collection).

These stylish six-wheelers are very much in the carriage building tradition. LSWR No 163 was for milk traffic, and LMS No 4296 was built at Wolverton in pre-group days for West Coast fish traffic. After the grouping, it was re-designated as a meat van. Such change of usage in the 'perishable cargo' category was by no means uncommon (Below BR LMR).

there may have been no more than one vehicle load from any one location posed no real problem while ever there was a passenger service to which it could be attached.

To some extent, the coming together of these individual loads at more central locations enabled the railways to operate high-speed 'perishable' trains under full passenger-rated regulations, much in the manner of mail and parcels trains, but it was not necessary *per se* and it was just as common to see such vehicles working to London, Birmingham and other big cities as part of the passenger service. Of course, in exceptional cases it paid the railways to operate all-fish, all-meat and all-milk trains, especially from those locations where one might reasonably expect to be able to load a full train from the outset. The Aberdeen and Grimsby fish trains spring immediately to mind in this context. In some cases, the railways even transported *live* fish in mobile 'fish tank' vehicles so as to ensure even greater freshness on arrival.

In purely vehicular terms, the demands of this sort of traffic could be met by wagons and/or vans which could span the range from vacuum-braked open goods trucks to purpose-built and elaborate vans, scarcely distinguishable in appearance from most other coaching stock. At the margin there was always a degree of uncertainty as to whether a particular vehicle constituted a fully-braked goods vehicle or was genuinely non-passenger coaching stock. Some railways hedged their bets and classified in both ways, so it is difficult to be more specific; it was all part of the passenger business in the broadest sense.

15. Alternatives to convention

As has already been related in the context of many different types of vehicles, the first two decades of the present century were a time of great change in railway travelling habits culminating in the move to ever more grandiose conveyances for the more prestigious trains. All of the vehicles so far considered, however, be they humble suburban coaches or palatial special saloons, have one point in common; they were marshalled into trains and hauled along by locomotives. The same period, however, was also noteworthy for the first significant moves to some form of self-propelled passenger-carrying vehicle. This quite distinctive alternative form of passenger conveyance in the form of the ubiquitous diesel or electric multiple unit is very much the norm on many parts of the current railway scene and is likely to become more so during the next century, but it was the first twenty years or so of the present century which saw the real beginnings after a few late nineteenth century experiments.

The spur to change was the growing road competition, first in the form of the street tramway (see Chapter 8), supplemented increasingly by the motor omnibus and road coach; while the 1920s were probably the first decade during which the private motor car was first seen as a threat. To be honest, the railways did not seem to give this last competitor much serious thought until after the Second World War but it did have an effect, particularly in the country areas before then. However, in the context of this volume the real threat was the rapid rise of alternative forms of mechanized *public* transport and it was this aspect which lay at the heart of the new ideas.

The railway, for all its many virtues (not least its solidarity, reliability and safety), is by nature a somewhat inflexible form of transport with a multiplicity of fixed structures to maintain, not to mention its vehicles, even the meanest of which are normally heavier, stronger and more expensive to built than the road equivalent. To combat road competition, the railways therefore had to seek more economical ways of doing a task which hitherto had enjoyed something of a methodological monopoly even though the railways themselves competed with each other for custom. They were now all under threat.

The self-propelled option offers quite a few theoretical and practical advantages for short-to-medium-distance operations. It avoids the extra expense of a separate locomotive, it offers some greater degree of design freedom, its power output can, be more exactly matched to the load to be carried and it affords at least a possibility of trying to avoid the railway equivalent of using a sledgehammer to crack a walnut by providing vehicles just sufficiently large, but not too large, for the task. This latter point, however, can also be its undoing.

Electrification

Perhaps surprisingly to some people, the oldest alternative *form* of propulsion to steam was electricity, which first emerged on the scene in 1879 and was destined to become the principal motive force for much of the world's railways. In Britain, electrification was a slow process and its development, while beginning to achieve some dominance in certain specific areas during the Edwardian period, was much more spectacular during the periods covered by the second and third volumes of this series. However, its origins were Edwardian and can conveniently be considered here.

Without doubt, the various activities of the Metropolitan and District Railways and the London Underground group, all later to become part of the unified London Passenger Transport Board (LPTB), were the most striking single manifestation of railway electric traction during the first part of the twentieth century, but their story merits more detailed treatment than can be given at this first general encounter with alternatives. In any case, their own version of the grouping did not take place until 1933, well into the period covered by Volume 2. Since the formation of the LPTB was so pivotal in the whole development of London's transport needs, along with the Southern Railway electrification of the 1920s and 1930s. I have chosen to consider the fuller story in that context; but one cannot dismiss the entire subject quite so baldly, even at this stage.

The establishment at the turn of the century of both the pioneer deep-level 'tube' lines in London (always electrically powered) and the electrification of the so-called 'surface' routes of the Metropolitan and the Metropolitan District Railways can be seen, in retrospect, to have had an influence well beyond the confines of the routes concerned. On the technical side they began to establish standards of traction and current collection which became widely influential; in operational terms they began to develop a pattern of frequent trains at such short intervals as to make a knowledge of the timetable unnecessary (at least in the principal built-up area) and, perhaps above all, they were amongst the first railways to undertake a major 're-think' in terms of vehicle design. It is with this particular aspect of the story that this part of the

account will be concerned, for therein lay a strong link with those few of the main-line railways which assayed electrification.

Given that there have been and will always be exceptions to any generalization, it does seem to me that the most dominant design feature of early electrical multiple unit (EMU) stock, as it is called, compared with its locomotive-hauled predecessors is the more widespread use of an open-plan interior layout, relatively uninfluenced by any previous kind of railway vehicle. When this was married to a form of exterior styling which drew much of its inspiration from North American inter-urban and 'streetcar' design, the end product was a distinctly new look.

That many of the new electric trains should draw some inspiration from contemporary road practice is not entirely surprising, given the early history of railway carriages (see Chapter 1). Moreover, several of them arose out of competition with the new electric street tramways which were proving very popular. Thus the end door with the transverse *and* longitudinal seating, so characteristic of the typical British tramcar, was also a commonly seen 'new' arrangement on the electric trains. It had considerable merits in terms of fairly speedy loading and unloading, it gave plenty of room for standees and, supplemented by intermediate central doors, is still a very characteristic form on the London Underground network of the present day.

Of course, the highly characteristic double-deck tramcar body style could not readily be translated into railway form — it was too tall — but the railway lent itself to longer, wider and more massively built vehicles, so it is hardly surprising that many systems looked across the Atlantic to America where the street-car had taken on a much longer bogie form, of more orthodox railway carriage shape. Neither must one discount the influence of developments in mainland Europe where railway electrification was pursued with rather more vigour than in Britain in the early days.

Whatever the precise reasons, many new electric carriages in the London area and elsewhere took this new form and, particularly in the case of systems which had no pre-history of compartment stock such as the deep-level tube lines, it became a standard type. The forefather of them all was probably the celebrated 'padded cell'-type carriage design of the City and South London Railway of which an example is happily preserved at the London Transport Museum, but this quickly gave way to altogether more elegantly styled vehicles on such pioneer cross-London routes as the 'Central London', 'Great Northern, Piccadilly and Brompton' and so forth. The circular geometry of the tube tunnels forced, of course, a characteristic profile for these new carriages which must, at first, have seemed strange, but which is now so familiar as to cause scarcely a second glance.

The so-called 'surface' routes of what was to become London Transport, the Metropolitan and the Metropolitan District (later, more simply, the 'District') lines, had much older origins and began life as steam systems with conventional compartment stock. In consequence, when they were electrified a mixture of purpose built open EMU stock and conventional compartment stock hauled by electric locomotives was to be seen, and this division of style

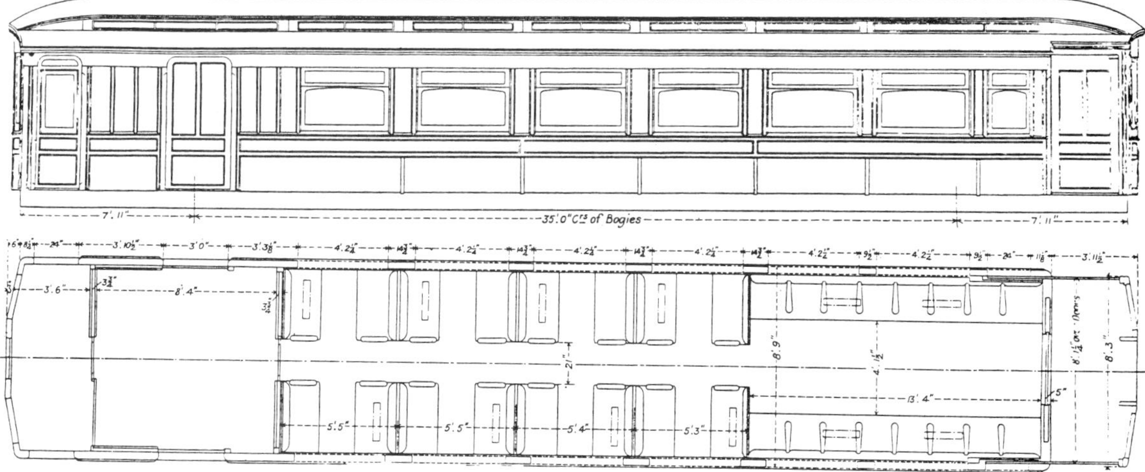

Electrically Operated Carriages, Metropolitan Railway.—Motor Car.

Above left *The now familiar mixture of transverse and longitudinal seating in deep-level tube stock is well illustrated by this view of a Charing Cross, Euston and Hampstead carriage of 1920. This route is now part of the much longer Northern Line of London Transport.*

Left *Two 1905 Metropolitan open motor cars flank four carriages of bogie compartment stock originally built for steam services in a typical mixed formation operation* en route *to Baker St,* circa *1910.*

This page Figure 61 *Elevations and plans of the stylish clerestory open stock introduced by the Metropolitan Railway in 1905.*

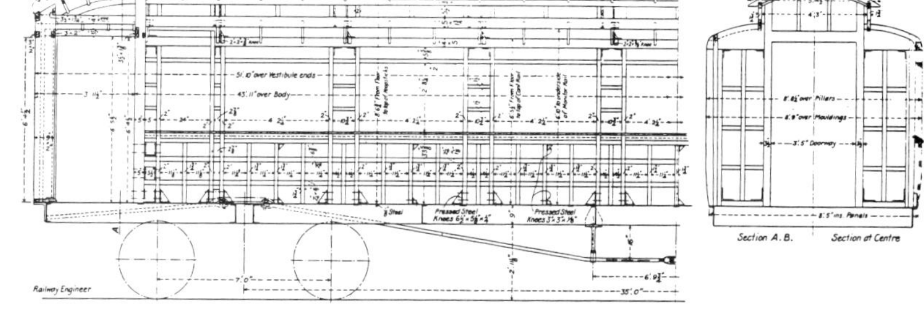

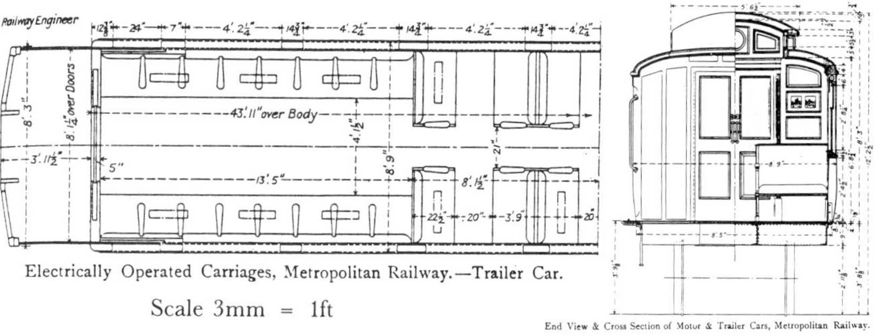

Electrically Operated Carriages, Metropolitan Railway.—Trailer Car.

Scale 3mm = 1ft

End View & Cross Section of Motor & Trailer Cars, Metropolitan Railway.

was exceedingly long-lived, surviving on the Metropolitan until well after the Second World War. However, when the Metropolitan and the District built EMU carriages, they too chose the new open-plan layout for the most part and even adopted the clerestory roof form which made the carriages look even more transatlantic.

Compared with the purely 'London' railways, and with two notable northern exceptions, the main-line railway companies were somewhat slow to adopt electrification for suburban purposes, and even by the time of the railway grouping by far the bulk of the short-haul commuter traffic was still firmly in the hands of the old faithful steam train with its individual carriages. Competition forced improvements to the actual vehicles (see Chapter 8) but the capital investment in locomotives was, presumably, such as to oblige most railways to look long and hard at the economics of electrification before making changes. It is a matter of history that many of them never did, but where the change was justified it tended to be more than usually interesting.

Remaining for the moment in the London area, the effect of the new underground electric lines, was

This third class motor driving car from the LNWR shows off the neat lines of the celebrated 'Oerlikon' stock of 1914. This stock was the only major instance of the LNWR panelled livery being applied to a non-beaded exterior.

beginning to have some effect, both in operating and in terms of attitude. Thus, for example, the GWR got into the act via the Hammersmith and City route by collaborating with the Metropolitan, while the London, Tilbury and Southend Railway went into joint ownership with the District Railway in some stock for through working.

North of the Thames, the only other railway seriously to entertain electrification was the LNWR which put conductor rails on to its Watford local lines and built for them some very stylish new carriages, again mostly end door and open plan. Memory recalls them as being of more than normally fine riding quality. Like the GWR and LT & SR, the LNWR also had a link with one of the London-based systems, but this time, rather unusually, it was a deep-level tube system, the forerunner of the present Bakerloo Line. This meant that the normally dimensioned LNWR stock could not penetrate the tube system, so the tube trains went out to Watford instead, wearing LNWR colours and joint insignia for a while and looking distinctly diminutive out in the open alongside the LNWR main-line trains. Even today, Queens Park station on the Bakerloo still bears witness to this historical curiosity.

It was, however, south of the River Thames where the main-line companies seriously considered and eventually embarked upon electrification during the 1910-23 period. In all cases the catalyst of change was the electrified tramway, and the reasons for it being more prevalent south of the river was a consequence of the somewhat peculiar geography of the railways in and around London. If one looks at the familiar system map on any London Underground station, one cannot fail to notice that the bulk of the routes lie to the north of the Thames. The Metropolitan and District lines and all the deep-level tubes are predominantly found in this area, and this goes right back to the time when these various lines were in private ownership. Consequently, it was mostly the underground lines which met tramway competition in North London.

In part, this fundamental difference was accentuated by the fact that many of the main lines north of the Thames were not only genuine long-distance concerns (GWR, GER, LNWR, MR, GNR and so on) but also since the earliest days their termini had been forbidden to penetrate central London any further south than the line of the modern Marylebone and Euston Roads. Moreover, the traffic patterns of these longer-distance routes was subtly different from those in south and south-west London, even that of the LSWR. In effect, therefore, what is now London Transport filled the gap between the two sets of London-based railways and established a pattern which, for all its subsequent augmentation and change, persists to this very day.

Thus, the SE & CR, LB & SCR and LSWR could all bring their lines right up to Thames-side, and had done so. This was through the very heart of tramway territory in the 1900-20 period, and the first line to meet the new challenge was the Brighton. Adopting what was, for Britain, a very unusual single phase, high-voltage AC systems with overhead pick-up wires, the LB & SCR installed very successful pioneer electric trains on the South London line from London Bridge to Victoria via Denmark Hill in 1909, the whole service going electric by 1912. Meantime, a second overhead service on the Crystal Palace lines had started in 1911. These 'elevated' electric routes, as they were called (by virtue of the overhead current collection), were the pioneers of what was to become the whole Southern Railway electric network, but they did not survive long after the grouping in their original form — and this seems an appropriate point at which to raise the more technical business of current collection as far as trains are concerned.

In essence, an electric train, be it a multiple unit (ie traction motors mounted on some or all of the passenger carriages) or a locomotive pulling carriages, must both pick up and return the current. Pick-up can be either from a trackside conductor rail or an overhead conductor wire, return being either via the running rails or a fourth conductor rail. This in itself can be complicated enough, but when taken with the fact that the supply voltage can be anything from 5-600 volts DC to 25,000 volts AC, the potential for lack of standardization is enormous — and so it turned out to be as far as the Southern Railway was concerned in 1923. By the way, the London Underground systems and their associated links with the main lines were to a still different system, the now familiar fourth conductor rail method seen all over London Transport.

Although the Brighton pioneered South London suburban electrification, close on its heels was the LSWR which brought in a 600-volt DC conductor rail method in 1915 and by 1923 had well over twice as many actual vehicles in service than on the earlier Brighton system (300 out of an SR total of 434 to be exact) and rather more routes electrified. By now, the SE & CR had also got as far as the planning stage and was proposing a 1500-volt system with two conductor rails. The new Southern Railway, quite logically, should see no sense in all this; *force majeure* prevailed and the LSWR 600-volt DC method was adopted as standard although the Brighton overhead lines were developed for a short period before conversion to 600 volts. Naturally, the former SE & CR routes, after grouping, were electrified on the LSWR system from the outset, and basically, apart from subsequent slight voltage upgrading, the Southern electric, to this day, betrays its pre-group history in terms of current collection. Ironically, the Brighton had chosen an overhead collection AC method which, modified to 25kv, is now regarded as the BR standard!

Although this narrative may seem at times to have strayed somewhat from the specifics of vehicle design, the peculiar and unique nature of the London area electrification cannot really be ignored for fuller understanding of a rather complex subject. Moreover, it will need to be readdressed frequently in the context of both post-grouping and post-nationalization developments. In its own way it turned out to be just as powerful a manifestation of the complex relationship between people and railway vehicles as any of the other issues so far considered.

The Brighton actually built new stock for its 'elevated' electrics but did not copy the new open-plan style of the underground railways. Instead, it adopted a modified compartment style with an internal passageway (not a true corridor) and partition heights less than full height of the roof, save for the divisions between the 1st and 3rd and smoking and non-smoking areas. Stylistically, the South London stock exhibited square-cornered panelling and a somewhat more rounded arc roof, but the Crystal Palace sets reverted to customary LB & SCR styling and both versions were very much in the traditional mode.

This was even more so with the LSWR services where all the 'new' electric three-car trains were, in fact, rebuilds from the older (1904 vintage) four-vehicle 'bogie block' sets and thus very much in the customary LSW stylistic idiom. However, their new driving cabs, with a pronounced 'V' shape (often nicknamed 'torpedo' ends), along with the new all-green livery, gave them a superficial air of newness. They were, however, just as traditionally non-corridor as in their steam-hauled days.

This non-corridor compartment type of EMU, adopted by both the LB & SCR and the LSWR in their different ways, not unnaturally became the SR norm after 1923, and when the ex-SE & CR lines were added to the electric system in the 1920s, they too made much use of rebuilt ex-SE & CR steam stock. In fact, all three constituents of the SR contributed steam-hauled coaches to the new company

The diminutive appearance of the tube stock on the 'open road' is seen in this view of a five-car set of London Electric Railway/LNWR joint stock on the LNWR 'new' lines near Kenton. Two styles of vehicle are featured on this northward extension of the Bakerloo line.

This page top to bottom *A three-car train of LB & SCR South London stock on the overhead electrified system at Wandsworth Road. The distinctive square-cornered panelling is readily apparent.*

This Southern Railway view shows a very characteristic form of operation — an eight-car train made up entirely of converted steam stock from the LSWR and LB & SCR.

The substantial American-built stock for the original LSWR Waterloo and City services was astonishingly well finished for such a short distance operation. The attention to detail, especially in the woodwork, would not have disgraced a main-line express.

Above right *The LYR electrics were built in several batches over a period of years, starting with clerestories in 1904 and followed by elliptical roof stock from 1910. This view shows a mixed four-car set with two of each type. The driving ends when originally built had a pronounced inwards taper to the front windows, later altered to the full width arrangement shown here. Note the elaborate lining.*

Right *The distinctive lines of the later LYR elliptical roof stock are well shown in this 'works grey' view of third class motor car No 3065.*

which were subsequently converted to EMU form, so even after 'Southern Electric' had become something of a household phrase, the pre-group origins of many of the new electric trains remained obvious for decades.

Before finally leaving the London area, brief mention should also be made of that mildy curious operation, the 'Waterloo and City Line'. Built, as its name implies, to link Waterloo (LSWR) with the City of London, it was the only pure deep-level tube line never to be integrated with London Transport. Its first cars were both American in style and origin, and to this day it is the only pure tube line which is operated by British Railways.

Outside the London area, and disregarding such odd freaks as the Swansea and Mumbles (incidentally, the oldest passenger-carrying line in the world opened in 1807), the Grimsby and Immingham and the Burton and Ashby Light Railway routes (all of them essentially no more than glorified tramways somewhat in the American 'inter-urban' mode), the only two main-line railway companies which made any sort of progress with electrification in the pre-group era were the LYR and NER. It is interesting that, yet again, these two companies whose carriage building has often tended to be ignored (because they did not go to London?) were both pioneers in the new technology — and neither of them did it by converting elderly hand-me-down steam stock either. Moreover, the LYR was actually the first railway in Britain to electrify what amounted to a main line (1904).

Both companies adopted the new open interior, end door approach and did it in some style with, if anything, the palm going to the LYR for its efforts north and north-east of Liverpool. In truth, there was probably little in it either way, for the Tyneside electrics of the NER were distinctly attractive and well found vehicles; but the LYR efforts were on a

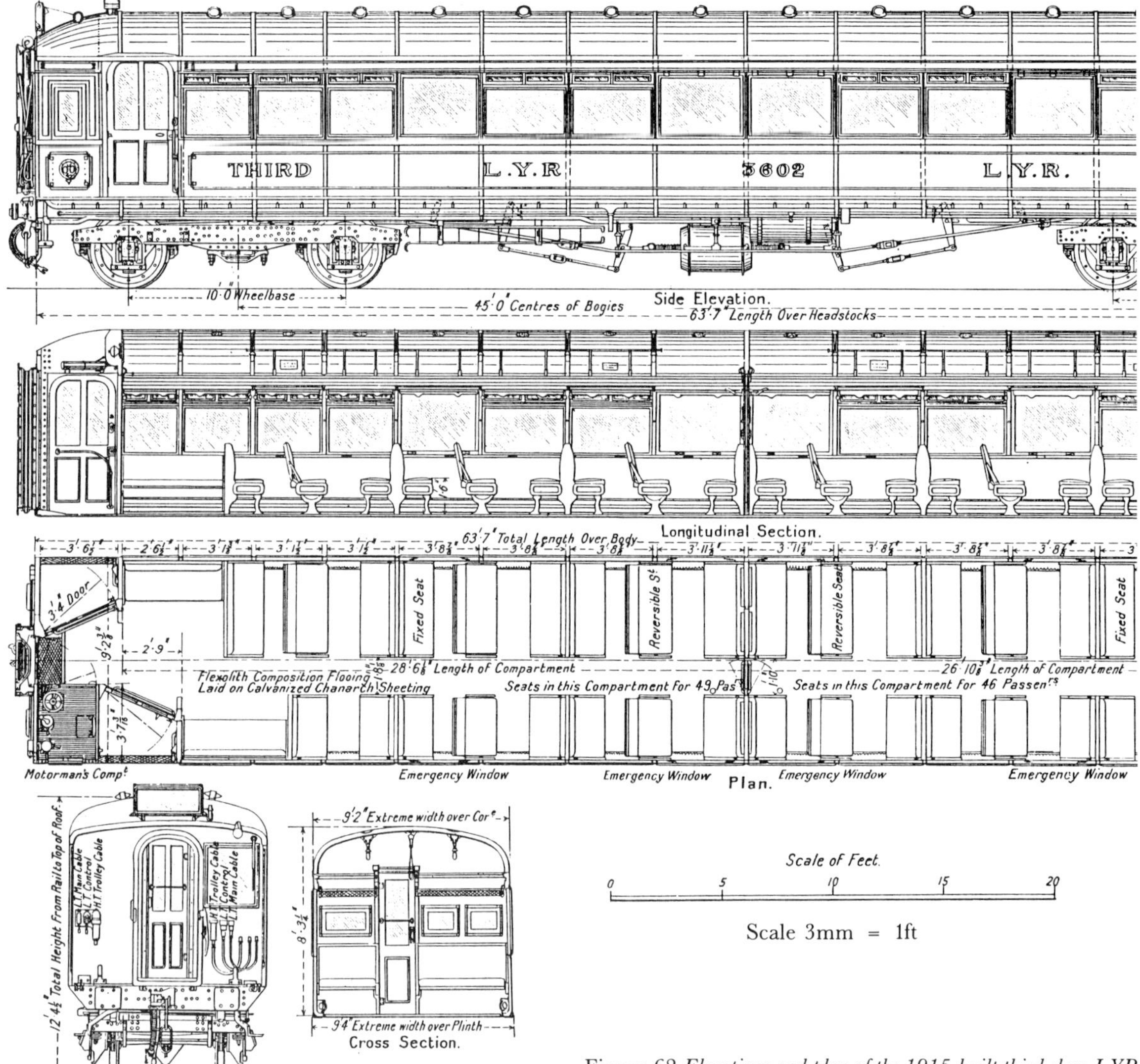

Figure 62 *Elevations and plan of the 1915-built third class LYR trailer cars.*

truly spectacular scale in terms of both vehicle shape, construction and size. They were of all-steel construction, of almost GWR 'Dreadnought' proportions and even wider (10 feet) in the case of those carriages reserved exclusively for the Liverpool-Southport and Liverpool-Ormskirk services which had a generous loading gauge. They were in fact the widest railway vehicles ever built in Britain and decorated most flamboyantly with, for the LYR, a massive amount of lining and florid insignia which must have looked good set against the rather sombre basic colours. Their interiors, too, were different. Drawing from both contemporary American inter-urban and British tramway styling, they managed to provide what to me seems to be an attractive and acceptable improvement on conventional contemporary suburban coaches, for they were, after all, only commuter trains. Perhaps the somewhat fashionable nature of the residential districts between Liverpool and Southport had something to do with it.

Scarcely less attractive were the somewhat smaller vehicles of the so-called 'lightweight' stock, built for through running on to the Liverpool Overhead system. If anything, these were even more flamboyantly decorated than those on the Southport services. Clearly this was the dawn of a new era, and the LYR could see no reason why it should be, or need be, too coy about its achievements.

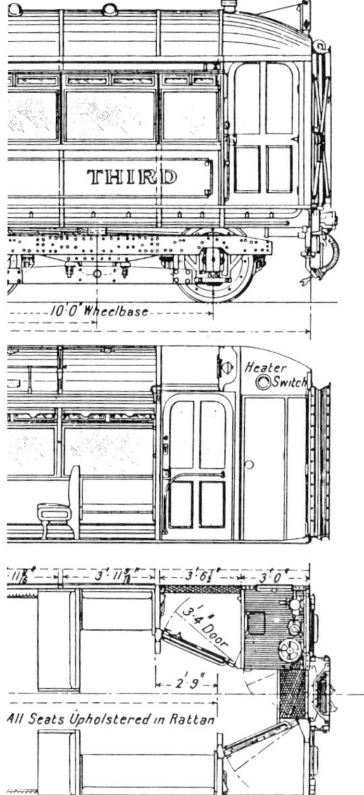

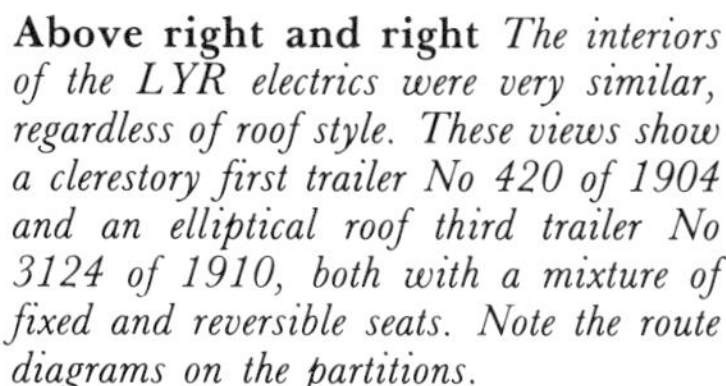

Above right and right *The interiors of the LYR electrics were very similar, regardless of roof style. These views show a clerestory first trailer No 420 of 1904 and an elliptical roof third trailer No 3124 of 1910, both with a mixture of fixed and reversible seats. Note the route diagrams on the partitions.*

Below *Composite No 1005, one of the flamboyantly decorated 'lightweight' LYR cars for working on to the Liverpool Overhead system.*

This page top to bottom *Interior of prototype LYR 'lightweight' car No 1000. The first class areas were much the same as on normal LYR electrics, but these slatted benches with their 'carpeted' seats were much inferior to normal third class LYR practice.*

The markedly American nature of the Mersey Railway electric stock is well exemplified by this mixed set of later elliptical roof motors and original clerestory trailers at Birkenhead Park.

Three typical NER Tyneside electric cars — a motor luggage first is nearest the camera and behind is a pair of full thirds.

Right *A single-unit Tyneside electric train — NER Motor luggage composite No 3770 with a cab at both ends.*

Below right *The Midland's rather half-hearted attempt at electrification in the Morecambe area took the form of central motor cars flanked by two trailers. The carriages, though not very good in either style or comfort, were, however, different from all other MR stock* (BR LMR).

Furthermore, it augmented its electrified system by tackling the Manchester-Bury route some eleven years later with some equally fine vehicles. The carriages built for all these services lasted well into the LMS era and the first replacements did not appear until 1940-41.

Mention of the Liverpool Overhead in the context of the LYR serves as a reminder that London was not unique in having its own 'dedicated' electric railways. Liverpool could sport two such. The 'Overhead' was a quite distinctive operation in the dockland area which, by virtue of its route set on gantries above the streets and docks, was the nearest thing Britain ever came to having an 'elevated' urban railway in the American sense of the word. 'American' too were its carriages, as indeed were those of that other Liverpool system, the Mersey Railway, which operated what amounted to not much more than a shuttle service from the Wirral peninsula, under the Mersey itself and into the heart of Liverpool. The 'Overhead', sadly, is no more, but the old Mersey lines along with those of the Wirral Railway and the LYR Southport lines still form the nucleus of the modern 'MerseyRail'.

Just as the LYR had adopted electrification in advance of the London-based companies, so too did that other large English regional company, the North Eastern, when in 1907 it began to operate electric trains in the Tyneside area. They were somewhat similar, if slightly smaller in overall dimensions, to the LYR carriages, but whereas the LYR broke entirely new stylistic grounds, the NER vehicles did perhaps carry a slight hint of contemporary company fashion, save for their livery, a striking new red and

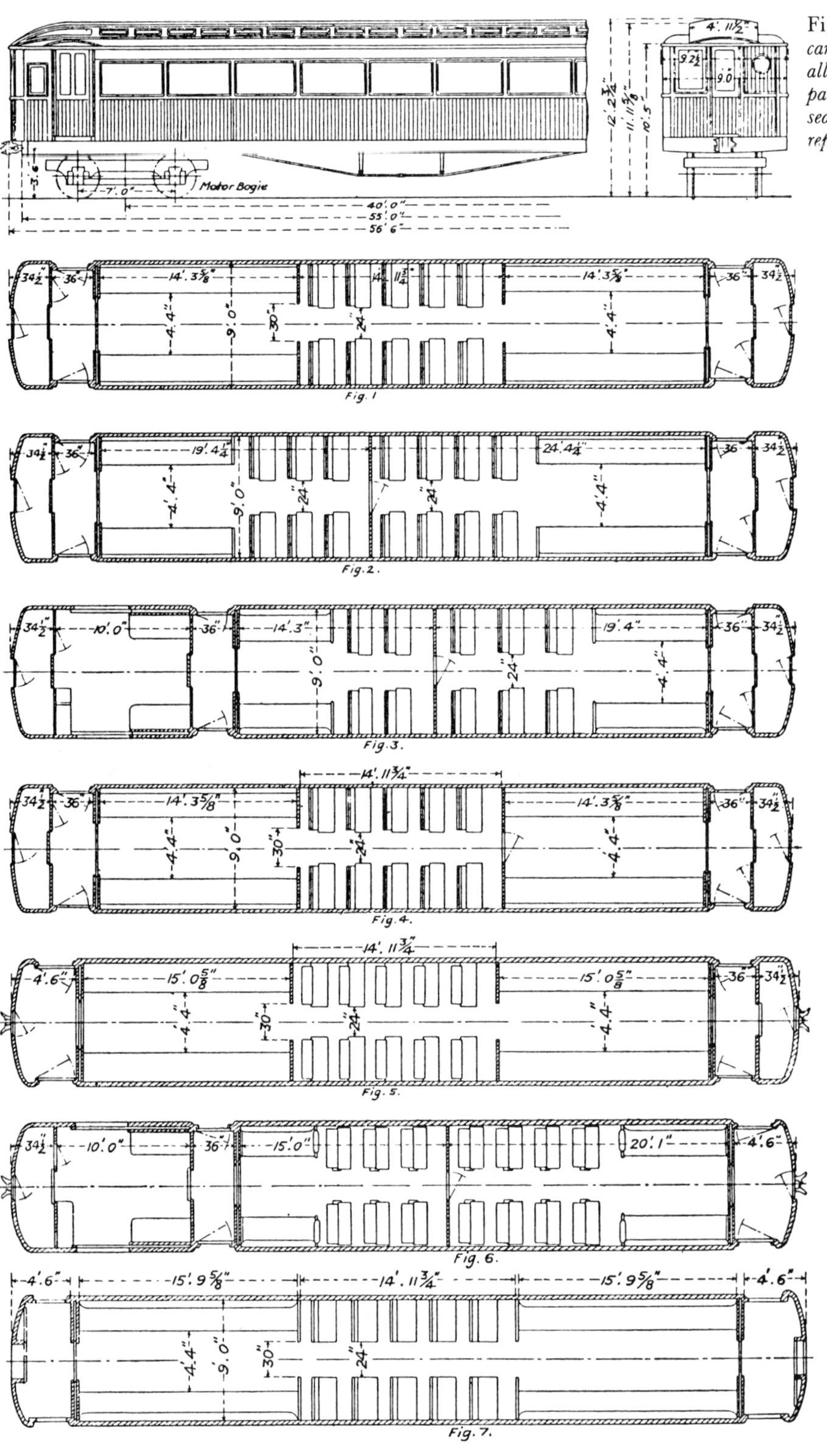

Figure 63 *The original Tyneside electrics came in quite a variety of internal layouts, all displaying the characteristic mixed pattern of transverse and longitudinal seating. No fewer than nine variations are represented by these contemporary plans.*

1. Third Class Carriage (Motor).
Third class compts. 64 seats. Two driver's compts. Two vestibules. Weight, 29 tons 1 cwt.

2. Third Class Carriage (Motor).
Two third class compts. 60 seats. Two driver's compts. Two vestibules. Weight, 29 tons 1 cwt.

3. Third Class Carriage (Motor).
Two third class compts. 42 seats. One luggage compt. Two driver's compts. Two vestibules. Weight 29 tons 1 cwt.

4. Third Class Carriage (Trailer).
Third class compts. 64 seats. Two driver's compts. Two vestibules. Weight, 23 tons 1 cwt.

5. Third Class Carriage (Motor).
Three third class compts. 64 seats. One driver's compt. Two vestibules. Weight, 28 tons 19 cwts.

6. First Class Carriage (Motor).
Two first class compts. 44 seats. One luggage compt. One driver's compt. Weight, 28 tons 17 cwt.

7. Third Class Carriage (Trailer).
Three third class compts. 68 seats. Two vestibules. Weight, 21 tons 5 cwt.

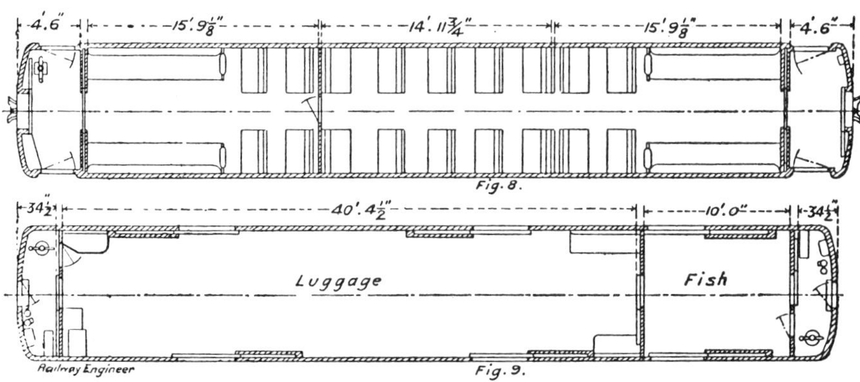

8. Third Class Carriage (Trailer).
Three third class compts. 64 seats. Two vestibules. Weight, 21 tons 15 cwt.

9. Luggage Van (Motor). One luggage compt. One fish compt. Two driver's compts. Weight, 34 tons 10 cwt.

Scale 2mm = 1ft

cream colour scheme. Like those of the LYR, they survived well into the BR period, but the story of their eventual replacement is rather more complex and very much a part of the latter-day BR development to be considered in the final volume.

Of the other main-line companies, wherever located in Britain, none can really be said to have achieved anything of great significance in terms of pioneering electrification. Several had thought about it and, as we have seen, the SE & CR had got as far as the planning stage by the time of the grouping, but of the others only the Midland possessed any purpose-built hardware, aside that is from its interest in the District Line via its ownership from 1912 onwards of the London, Tilbury and Southend Railway. The Midland's own home-produced product was a small clutch of not particularly exciting vehicles for an experimental overhead electrification project carried out in the Lancaster, Morecombe and Heysham area, of all places. It survived well into LMS and BR days but was never of more than marginal significance, save in a quasi-experimental category.

The best, therefore, that can be said about the moves towards electrification during the pre-group era is that they showed an increasing awareness of a growing problem. However, while some were distinctly well thought out, there was no real appreciation of the virtue of some sort of standardization in terms of technology. The legacy of this inconsistency is still with us, albeit perhaps less visibly obvious than in those pioneer days if only by virtue of the somewhat greater vehicle body design harmonization of the BR period.

Perhaps the most surprising feature of the whole business is the lack of interest in electrification shown in the other three great industrial conurbations of Birmingham, the West Riding and Glasgow. True, Glasgow did have its own underground, but this was not much more than a glorified electric train set, devoid of any pointwork and operating on a self-contained city centre circular route in tube-type tunnels. Even the vehicles had to be placed on the track with a crane! It was never considered to be a railway in the fullest sense and was usually referred to as the 'subway'. It was, however, full of character and, re-equipped in the early 1980s, still survives to this day.

Glasgow, as the centre of a large industrial complex, had to wait until BR days for a proper electrified suburban system — and a very good one too — but the West Midlands and the West Riding are at the time of writing still waiting for the sort of electrified suburban network which would be normal in almost any other comparably sized industrial regions of the world. Perhaps this is because, unlike London, Lancashire and the North East, neither the West Midlands nor the West Riding during the company period were served by but one big company which regarded these areas as its home territory. In Birmingham, the GWR, LNWR and MR eyed each other suspiciously while at the same time having bigger fish to fry, while in the West Riding, although almost everybody got into the act (GNR, NER, LYR, LNWR, MR, GCR et al), nobody seemed to be able to capture the leading role. The modern-day legacy of these competitive nonsenses is still there for everyone to see.

If electrification was less than universally successful in the pre-group period, the other alternatives were no better. It was, one supposes, inevitable that the newfangled internal combustion engine would be tried out somewhere, and this led to a minor outbreak of some pretty comically styled petrol-driven railcars, some of them being 'petrol-electric', ie petrol engines generating electrical energy for traction motors. This was an idea pursued with rather more vigour in North America, but the British contribution was, in global terms, of monumental insignificance. The NER was again to the fore, and, to be fair, probably tried harder than anyone, but the only others worthy of even passing mention are perhaps the GNR and

Left and below *'Dignity and Impudence' seems an apt description of these NER petrol-driven vehicles. No 3711 is a diminutive petrol-engined railcar, employing a form of direct drive, whereas No 3170Y, seen in early LNER days, was described as a 'Petrol-electric-autocar'. The petrol-driven generator was located in the body superstructure at the left-hand end, and the whole ensemble was styled rather in the manner of the contemporary 'enclosed'-type steam railmotors.*

Bottom *LB & SCR petrol-electric railcar No 3 was one of two supplied by Dick Kerr and Co in 1905, broadly identical in size and configuration but with somewhat differently styled bodywork, the tramcar inheritance of which was clear. They did not last for more than five of six years in passenger use, being transferred for inspection use on the overhead electrified lines in 1911.*

the LB & SCR, both of whom tried out some near-identical four-wheel petrol cars of Kerr-Stuart origin. They were quite neat in a sort of 'modified tramcar' style but, like the NER contribution, they came to nought.

In the context of Britain's railways, it did seem that tradition died hard. Perhaps the most astonishing manifestation of this was the building of a brand new *horse-drawn* carriage by the NBR for its Port Carlisle branch as late as 1908! However, this was distinctly maverick.

Steam railcars and derivatives

The real bastion of the traditional approach to the problems of competition was that uniquely Edwardian phenomenon, the steam railcar, or steam railmotor as it was sometimes called, and it is with this vehicle and its derivatives that the rest of this chapter is concerned.

It was entirely predictable that when the pre-group companies began to feel the competitive winds blowing from road and tramway competition, they should try to modify the traditional steam train to a more economical form. What they were striving to do was produce a smaller powered, cheaper to build and cheaper to operate unit which would not be as much of a drain on financial resources as the larger, more conventional locomotive and carriages approach. This was achieved by making use of what was normally a self-propelled single unit vehicle embodying a combination of a small locomotive portion with a passenger-carrying area. Many were built by a considerable number of railways (see Table 10).

In terms of structural form, two alternatives were to be seen: the 'rigid' railcar, wherein the locomotive part was mounted on the same frames as the carriage portion, and the 'articulated' version whereby the powered end, although semi-permanently attached to the carriage, could pivot independently. On the rigid railcar, the purely engine portion was, in effect, a sort of steam-powered traction bogie, whereas with the articulated type the configuration was somewhat more that of a conventional locomotive whose boiler pivoted along with the driving wheels.

Either variety could be found in either of two styles

Table 10 Purpose-built steam railcars 1902-11

Note: The totals refer to the number of passenger-carrying units — several railways (eg GWR/LYR/Taff Vale) had 'spare' engine units. The list refers to Great Britain, excluding Ireland.

Years built	Company name	Rigid pattern			Articulated pattern			Grand total
		'Open' loco	Enclosed loco	Sub total	'Open' loco	Enclosed loco	Sub total	
1904	Alexandra Docks		2	2				2
1903	Barry		2	2				2
1911	Cardiff*		2	2				2
1905	Furness		2	2				2
1904-5	GCR		3	3				3
1905	GNR				6		6	6
1905	GNSR				2		2	2
1904-5	GSWR				3		3	3
1903-8	GWR		97	97		2	2	99
1906	Isle of Wight Central				1		1	1
1905	LB & SCR					2†	2†	2†
1905-10	LNWR		7	7				7
1904-6	LSWR		15	15				15
1902	LSWR/LB & SCR Joint	2		2				2
1905-11	Lancashire & Yorkshire				17		17	17
1904	Midland		2	2				2
1905-6	North Staffordshire					3†	3†	3†
1907	Port Talbot					1§	1§	1§
1907	Rhymney				2		2	2
1904-5	SE & CR				8		8	8
1903-6	Taff Vale				16		16	16
	Totals	2	132	134	55	8	63	197

* The last British company to introduce the type.
† In effect an 'enclosed' locomotive portion but with 'external' chimney in front of the concealed portion.
§ The only British steam railcar with a *six*-coupled locomotive portion.

which, for convenience, may be described as 'open' or 'enclosed' in relation to the locomotive portion. In the former type, the powered end genuinely resembled a steam locomotive, albeit of diminutive size, whereas in the latter case the power unit was sheathed in an outer casing designed to look like part of the carriage itself. As part of the general attempt to keep down size, weight and cost, wheels were normally quite diminutive and the boiler itself could be either conventional (ie fore-and-aft), transverse or even vertical.

The three principal pre-group practitioners of the steam railcar were the Great Western (by far the most dominant single company), the LYR and Taff Vale, the GWR adopting the 'concealed' styling, the LYR and TVR going for the alternative mode. In both cases the influence of these companies turned out to be stronger than the rest, but, as Table 10 reveals, they were by no means the only operators of these characteristic vehicles. From the table it can also be seen that the rigid type outnumbered the articulated variety by roughly two to one and that, although both body styles could be seen in both structural patterns, the two predominant varieties were the 'rigid enclosed' and 'articulated open' variations.

Paradoxically, however, the first genuine railmotor design (discounting a few eccentric nineteenth century experiments) was not to either of the two common configurations, and its introduction was the brainchild of that celebrated Scotsman Dugald Drummond when, in 1902, as LSWR chief engineer he had built two for the joint services of the LSWR/LB & SCR between Southsea and Fratton. The GWR borrowed the first one and reported quite favourably, but in service they turned out to be feeble machines with insufficient steam raising power to keep going when fully loaded. In this respect they not only pioneered the railmotor type but also accurately anticipated its principal subsequent weakness, regardless of who built it, to what design, or for what purpose.

As built, these two vehicles were quite neat and tidy but the need to rebuild the locomotive portion gave rise to an ensemble which for grotesque ugliness would have taken some beating. One writer has described them as 'loutish' — most apt! Appearance notwithstanding, they nonetheless gave nearly twenty years of service in re-boilered form which was better than many. Nevertheless, the typical British railcar was not to be quite like either variant of these pioneer Drummond conveyances, and from this point it will be convenient to divide the discussion into the two principal structural forms, starting with the rigid type.

Although Drummond's prototype railcars had been of the rigid frame configuration, in the event they turned out to be the only such railcars to display an 'exposed' locomotive portion. All the rest were of the enclosed type and by far and away the leading light in this story was the GWR. In fact, its 'enclosed' rigid railcars made up just about half of the total British fleet of both kinds. They varied somewhat in both superficial appearance and detail design and, to be truthful, were not the most elegantly styled products of this celebrated railway, but they were probably the only really serious attempt on the part of a major company to persevere with a cheaper solution to real operating problems.

In terms of designed utilization, two main varieties were built, the so-called 'suburban' and 'branch line' types, and the nomenclature perhaps revealed a sort of uncertainty about the whole concept which was to bedevil all British steam railmotor building and was to be their subsequent undoing. Not to put too fine a point on it, it is hard to see how the same sort of vehicle could simultaneously be thought to be the right answer both for a lightly trafficked branch *and* for the busy suburbs, even given different seating capacity. However, the GWR (and others) went along with a sort of theory that one way to compete with the suburban tramcar was to provide a vehicle of somewhat similar capacity which, because of the very nature of the railway, could traverse the suburbs at frequent intervals much more quickly than a vehicle on the public highway. It could and it did, and it became so popular that it often turned out to be too small to carry the resultant loads. The generally feeble power of the dedicated locomotive portion was usually incapable of pulling an extra trailer to carry the greater load, thus resulting in a sort of conceptual stalemate. We shall come back to it later.

In the context of the GWR, however, the steam railcar obviously fulfilled a more than useful purpose — or else why build nearly 100 of them? This was especially true in the country areas, and the 'branch' type, always numerically stronger, well outlived the suburban variety by on average some ten years into the mid-1930s when it was often replaced, significantly one feels, either by the auto-train (see below) or the diesel railcar (See Volume 2). It is worth noting that the GWR steam railcar fleet remained at full strength for only the seven years between 1908 and 1914, and one cannot help but think that in the post-Great War era, the motor bus and motor car helped kill it off. However, many of them (most, in fact) had a second lease of life as auto-trailers.

After the LSWR/LB & SCR experiment, the GWR became (in 1903) the first company to embrace this new idea and, that company being so influential, it is likely that some at least of the other railways followed suit on the 'imitative' principle. In terms

Right *NBR horse-drawn Port Carlisle 'Dandy' No 2, built in 1908, must surely have been the most surprising new carriage ever built in the twentieth century for a British main-line company. It was broken up* circa *1914.*

Below *Drummond's pioneering LSW and LB & SCR joint steam railmotors: No 1 with its original too feeble boiler of 1903, and No 2 as rebuilt in a most grotesque fashion a year later.*

Bottom *GWR flat-sided 'enclosed' steam railcar No 17, characteristic of the earlier examples from this company.*

This page top to bottom *Later GWR railcars embodied more traditional vehicle styling with 'proper' panelling. This is No 61 hauling trailer No 34.*

The running gear of LSWR steam railcar No 5 reveals its derivation from Drummond's original efforts, but the enclosed body is far more typical of 'enclosed' steam railmotor practice at the time.

One of the neat Furness railmotors with its equally neat four-wheel trailer at Coniston. The clerestory styling was a distinctively different and attractive stylistic feature (Author's collection).

The LNWR steam railmotors were distinctly handsome as can be seen here at Bicester. No 3 was one of six broadly identical 57-foot cars; the engine portion is at the far end.

Right *The final LNWR railcar was a solitary 60-foot example with rather more power and designed to run with a trailer. In this view at Lees, near Oldham, in 1910, and now renumbered 507, it had also acquired a horsebox. Unfortunately, this degree of versatility was rare in most rigid steam railmotor designs.*

of those which adopted the enclosed rigid railcar, most seem to have done so on an experimental one-service-only basis if the quantities listed in Table 10 are any guide. Conceptually, all had much in common and some were distinctly stylish, but aside from the GWR the only two railways which tackled the rigid railcar in more than penny numbers were the LSWR and LNWR, and even these two seemed to have their doubts.

The LSWR built a total of fifteen whose running gear was much influenced by the prototype Drummond pair but whose bodywork was somewhat cleaned up in style, with a neatly enclosed portion. The first two of this new style had somewhat brutal, all-encasing platework at the powered end, but the final thirteen were treated in 'coachbuilding' style to vastly better effect. The LSWR seems to have seen them as fulfilling something like the GWR 'branch' role, but in 1906 Drummond moved to his version of the auto-train and the railcars quickly withered on the branch. Three only were left by 1916 and all had gone by 1919.

The LNWR, although much the same size as the GWR, seemed not to espouse the railcar cause with any great enthusiasm, but the few which it did build (six in 1905-7 and an extra one in 1910) were perhaps the most stylish enclosed steam railcars ever seen in Britain. Their nearest rivals in this respect were those of the Furness and GCR, and all three railways seemed to produce a more visually harmonious unit than did the otherwise far more significant GWR. The LNWR examples were particularly well built in body construction terms and were technically interesting in embodying an *inside*-cylindered locomotive unit which made them not only marginally less grotesque when in motion but probably smoother riding than most of their kind, if only because the cylinders were closer to the longitudinal centre-line. For all their small numbers, they lasted better than most and even the unsentimental LMS found use for most of them until the late 1920s or early 1930s. One lasted until BR days in 1948 and was the final survivor of any of its kind in revenue service in Britain, having outlived its far more numerous GWR contemporaries by some fourteen years.

As for the other rigid railcars, they can be realistically disregarded (except by their devotees) save perhaps for the Midland's experiment, and even then only by accident of history. The MR steam railcars were not the best of the bunch; there were only two of them and internally they displayed a particularly nasty form of pierced plywood seating which they shared with their equally unmemorable electric contemporaries (page 255 above). Their power units were unreliable (one, indeed, if not both had to be changed), but one of them was converted to an officer's saloon which, by one of those strange quirks of history, has survived and is now in the National Collection. It is, ironically, the only such vehicle in Britain which has any remote chance of being restored to its original and once quite characteristic form. It will need a vast sum of money and, at the time of writing, I am unable to state whether it will ever be possible; but it is better than nothing. If only there was a genuine GWR or LNWR example.

Turning now to the articulated form, this approach fared little better than the rigid railcar. It was very much a child of the Lancashire and Yorkshire via the Taff Vale in the person of Mr Hurry Riches who designed the first example for the TVR in 1903. As far as can be seen, Mr Riches, an enthusiastic supporter of the steam railmotor who, *inter alia,* delivered a paper on the subject to the Institution of Mechanical Engineers in 1906, felt that a more powerful unit, articulated to the passenger-carrying portion, might prove to be a better solution to the problem, and he designed a most unusual locomotive portion for TVR examples with a *transverse* boiler with

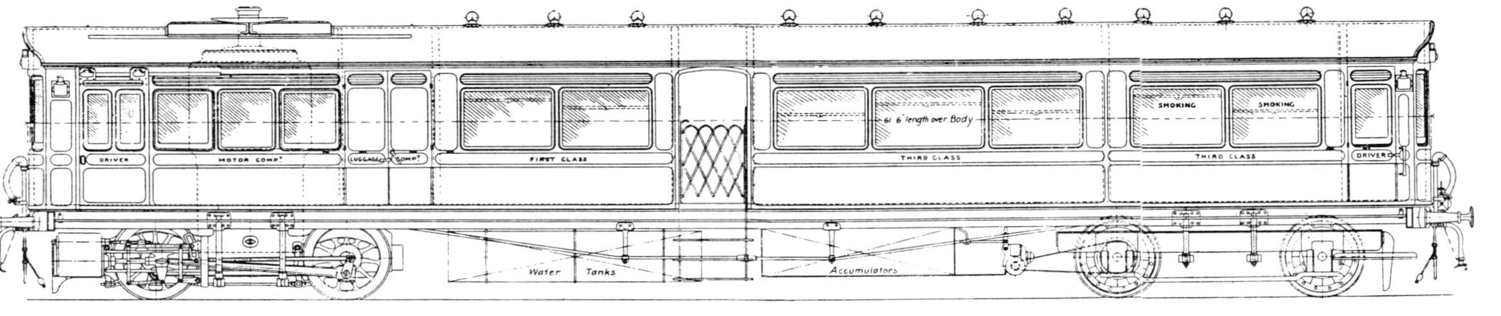

Figure 64 Scale 3mm = 1ft

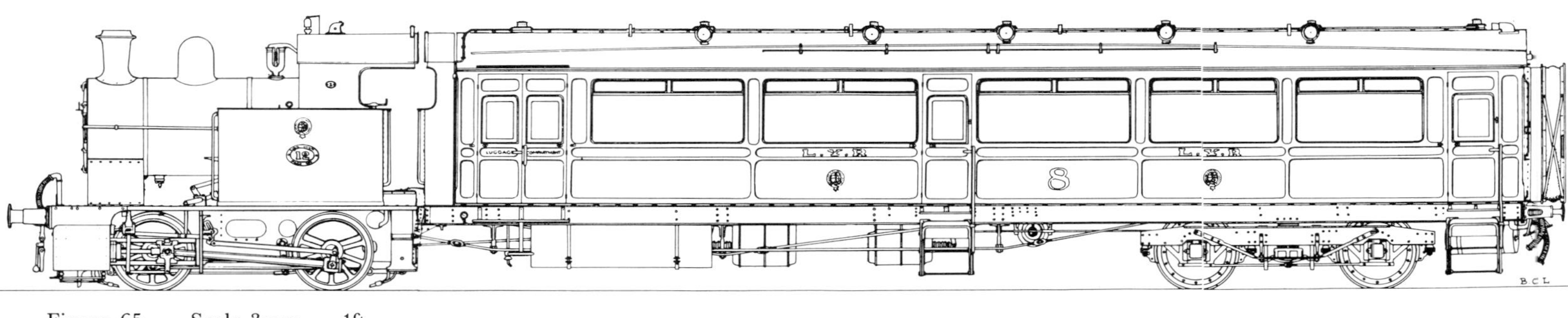

Figure 65 Scale 3mm = 1ft

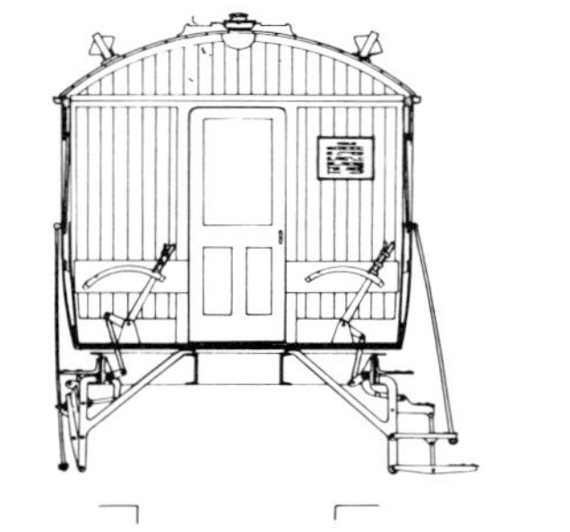

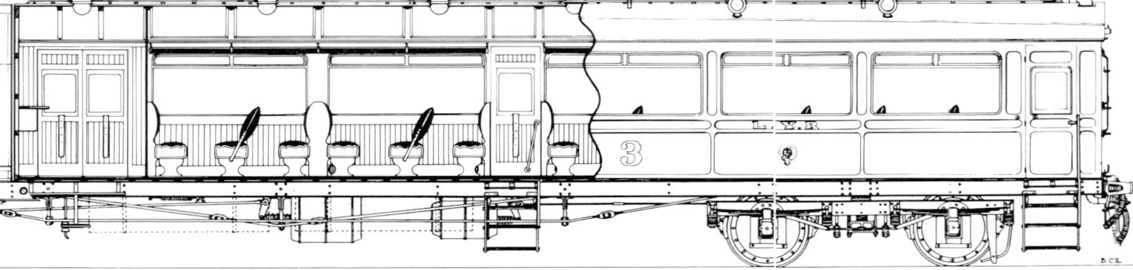

Figure 64 *This drawing of the GCR composite steam railmotor design reveals that it rivalled that of the LNWR for handsomeness of outline.*

Figure 65 *The upper drawing shows the final form of the LYR railmotors in 1921 livery. The wider chimney on the locomotive and corridor connection to the carriage were pre Great War alterations, but the wide bearing bogie was a later substitution. The lower, sectioned, drawing shows the first of Hughes's carriage sections with the 'truss rod' narrow bearing bogie and fully glazed driving end as built. Numerous other smaller modifications took place through the years to the lighting, gas supply tanks, steps and even the frames* (Drawing by B.C. Lane based on LYR originals).

Above right *Midland steam railmotor No 2234 is seen here receiving attention at Hellifield* circa *1904. The slightly tedious method of taking on water is readily apparent.*

Right *Mr Hurry Riches's pioneering articulated steam railmotor No 1 of the Taff Vale Railway. Its unorthodox boiler worked well on the TVR but did not fully withstand translation to the LYR* (Author's collection).

two short 'drums' fed by a single central firebox. By all accounts they had quite formidable steam raising power for their size, and the LYR was persuaded to go for a couple of similar machines in 1905. Avonside and Kerr Stuart were the favoured TVR manufacturers, and the LYR procured two Kerr Stuart examples to the basic TVR design; but, it has to be said, the LYR Chief Engineer, George Hughes, did not seem too enchanted with his new purchase! Accordingly, he decided he could do rather better himself and forthwith designed the LYR variant — a typically neat and efficient Horwich engine unit married to an altogether better-looking passenger-carrying component. This became (marginally) the most numerous, and undeniably the best, articulated steam railmotor ever built in Britain, and by far the most long-lived. Not for the first time, as this narrative has averred, the oft unsung 'Lanky' turned out to know best.

If the Taff Vale and the LYR vied with each other for *primus inter pares* in this form of alternative steam railcar technology, they were not exactly alone, for the articulated option seemed to attract the attention of more than a few eminent designers. In consequence, although numerically less significant than the rigid option, the articulated railcars seemed to sprout just as many varieties, most of which somehow seemed to be rather better regarded in their day. Perhaps it was because they looked more like 'proper' trains, since most of them had a very visible and obviously 'engine-like' powered end, that they were taken more seriously! Moreover, to be truthful,

Left *Detail view of LYR steam railmotor No 9 in 1920. Another view of this type will be found on page 78.*

Below *SE & CR steam railmotor No 1, built in 1904 and seen here labelled for service on the Isle of Sheppey Light Railway.*

many of the designs were of more than normally pleasant visual aspect, however useful or not they may have been in their primary role.

Of the many which might be mentioned, we can perhaps single out a few of particular interest, partly on numerical terms but also in the context of design originality. The surprising leader of the pack, after the LYR and TVR, was the SE & CR, which built no fewer than eight beautifully stylish examples under the supervision of Harry Wainwright. The carriage portion of the final six differed slightly from that of the first two. As with many other companies, these neat units found work for less than a decade, all being withdrawn by the end of 1914, although the carriage portions were converted for auto-train work.

The only other railway to build more than a token number of articulated railmotors was the GNR with six, built in three pairs and apparently intended by Ivatt for evaluation — there were two contemporary petrol railcars too. All three steam pairs differed slightly in detail, although the basic carriage layout was pretty well the same. Perhaps the most interesting structural feature was the full elliptical roof sported by the first pair (the other four had what amounted to a Howlden roof profile). This was the first use of the soon to be familiar GNR roof shape, and, although Ivatt is credited with the design, the influence of his carriage and wagon chief, Nigel Gresley, was clear. None of the designs was repeated but the GNR railmotors enjoyed twenty years of life before withdrawal — better than most — and, as was quite common, the carriage portions were recovered for further use. Unsurprisingly, Gresley turned pairs of them into articulated 'twins'.

Of the rest of this group, those of the LB & SCR and the NSR had much in common, with a curious

Above *GNR steam railmotors Nos 2 and 8, both built in 1905, show the two carriage styles adopted, the body of No 2 being the first Gresley bow-ended elliptical roof vehicle for the GNR. The power unit of No 8 was built by Avonside, and in both cases the carriage portions were later converted to articulated 'twins'.*

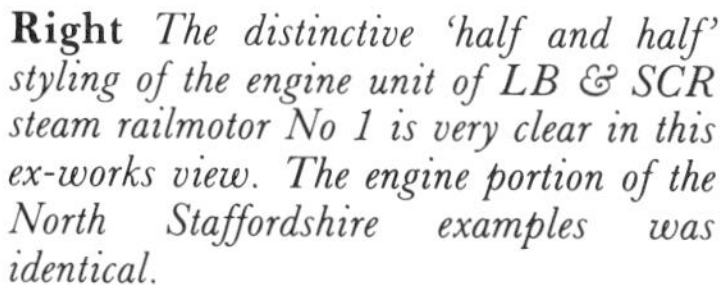

Right *The distinctive 'half and half' styling of the engine unit of LB & SCR steam railmotor No 1 is very clear in this ex-works view. The engine portion of the North Staffordshire examples was identical.*

'cross-bred' engine section, neither fully open nor fully enclosed. The engine portions were identical, but the carriage elements were different with the Brighton probably having the stylistic edge. However, their life was exceedingly short (four years or so) whereas the NSR trio survived until 1922. They were curious, ungainly looking ensembles compared with most of their type but at least they did manage to earn some revenue before going the way of the rest. Mention too should be made of the solitary GWR excursion into this type — a pair of Kerr Stuart units with hideous enclosed cabs and somewhat non-GWR-style bodies. One of them was sold to the Nidd Valley Light Railway in 1920 and outlived all the other GWR steam railcars (of any kind), not being withdrawn until 1937, by then named *Hill*. It was still in existence in a Leeds scrapyard some 25 years later!

Below *This picture reveals the unique hemispherical boiler design adopted by the GNSR for its steam railmotor No 29.*

Bottom *LB & SCR 'Balloon'-type carriage coupled to a 2-4-0T* Boxhill *represents the engine-plus-single-coach form of push-pull train.* Boxhill *was converted to this wheel arrangement from its original 0-6-0 styling for this type of use. It later reverted to an 0-6-0 type and, as such, is preserved at the NRM* (Author's collection).

Amongst the rest, perhaps the most interesting, if least successful, design was that of a GNSR pair which used patent boilers with a hemispherical firebox. It gave them a distinctive appearance but they were really rather ineffective and survived only a few years. In this they were in marked contrast to the solitary and quite successful 'enclosed' Port Talbot example, Britain's largest steam railcar of any design. It lasted until 1926, latterly with the Port of London Authority.

All told, however, the articulated railcar fared no better than the rigid type. The GSWR trio lasted until *circa* 1917 and the solitary Isle of Wight example only until 1912 so, apart from the LYR fleet, this interesting experiment was born, matured and died pretty well within the period encompassed by this volume. However, the LYR examples were different. For one thing, they had a powerful enough engine portion to allow a trailer to be attached to the main unit, and this gave them added flexibility in coping with busier traffic. The two Taff Vale units were

quickly consigned to oblivion (the carriage parts were retained) but the rest survived to the LMS and withdrawal was quite leisurely, not starting until 1927 and only slowly thereafter. The last example, like that of the LNWR (see above), just managed to reach BR.

The steam railmotor, rigid or articulated, was a fascinating if generally abortive attempt by the railways to make a quantum change. It failed because of its inflexibility. Whether in the suburbs or in the country, it was only viable as long as it did not generate too much patronage. The moment that overloading became a problem, the generally feeble engine portions proved unable to cope, and only those with a little extra power could survive. However, the moment one began to think of using a more powerful unit to cope with the extra loads, then most railways concluded that one might as well use a conventionally styled locomotive and separate carriages again. This, in fact, is precisely what happened in the form of the Auto-train, or such other name as the owning railways chose to call them.

This type of operation looked, superficially, rather like the sort of train which the steam railmotor had been designed to replace, but there was a strong technical linkage and this turned out to be the vital factor. More than once, this narrative has remarked on the time-wasting caused by marshalling carriages and by engines having to run round their trains for the return journey. The steam railmotor could be driven either from the locomotive *or* the opposite end of the carriage portion, and the technical modifications to allow this could without too much difficulty be applied to conventional engines and carriages. Thus was born the so-called 'Auto-train', 'push-pull train,' 'motor-train' or whatever.

It consisted of a suitably adapted engine and carriage(s) which remained semi-permanently

These views show the exterior and interior of a rather rare solution to the auto-train problem adopted by the LSWR — using a purpose-built engine rather than adapting an existing type. The neat and stylish exterior was somewhat marred by the frugal interior with its pierced plywood seats.

Most auto-trains were of a substantial nature with carriage and locomotives to full main-line standards. This handsome NER example only really reveals its push-pull status by virtue of the engine being located between the carriages (B.C. Lane collection).

coupled. The driver worked either from the engine itself or a specially modified 'cab' at the opposite end (usually located at the outer end of a brake-ended vehicle), and there was no need to run round. However, at the end of the day, the engine *could* be uncoupled if necessary for other work and the railways rapidly discovered that it was possible to convert *existing* stock for motor-train working if they chose not to build new vehicles for the task. Many companies actually did both, and this push-pull style of operation became a very widespread feature of the British scene almost to the end of steam.

However, its origins were in the hey-day of the steam railmotor and its success undoubtedly hastened the demise of the single-unit railcar. Indeed, as has been more than once remarked, the carriage part of many erstwhile steam railcars was often converted to the new mode. In this role they were often called 'trailers', 'auto-trailers', 'control trailers', 'motor trailers' or some such, and it was perfectly possible to have a push-pull train with several such vehicles, two or three being very common and four not unheard of. During the early days, many distinctly attractive formations were to be seen, some depicted here; in the 1930s the GWR in particular was regularly characterized by a branch line train consisting of a pair of auto-trailers (often ex-railcars) flanking a small engine, or with the engine at one end, either option being possible. The LYR's twelve railmotor trailers were 'ready-made' motor train vehicles and found several decades of use in North Lancashire in 'twin' or even 'quad' sets; as such they lasted until BR days.

Thus the steam railcar lived and died almost within a generation, save for a mild revival in a slightly different form during the 1920s and 1930s (see Volume 2), but it did leave its legacy in the form of the motor-fitted train, a much more useful solution to a real problem. Furthermore, the railcar left its mark on vehicle design too and this seems an appropriate theme with which to round up our pre-group survey.

The steam railcar was almost always of open interior configuration, a style it shared with contemporary electric stock. Seats were usually a mixture of transverse and longitudinal and often quite spartan. There was some attempt to produce composite 1st/3rd accommodation but predominantly and not surprisingly, this was a third class sort of business and thus it remained. In terms of what I have called carriage 'architecture', the railcar — and indeed many of the purpose-built push-pull 'trailers' — often broke new visual ground, sometimes with very pleasing results. There is little doubt in my mind that there is at least some design linkage between this type of operation and the move to electrification in terms of vehicle interior layout; the LNWR, for example, adopted a near identical vehicle body style both for its electrical services and in its push-pull operations.

Thus it is not perhaps too fanciful to state that in the various alternative approaches considered in this chapter, the railways began to sow the seeds of the now customary layout for the shorter-distance train, be it diesel of electric multiple unit or whatever. The traditional compartment, of course, died hard, and many hundreds were still built (or converted) for both EMUs and push-pull trains. However, a new idea was there, just as in the case of the longer-distance carriage (see Chapter 10), where some railways had begun to pioneer the now normal centre passageway open carriage.

And there, for the moment, we must leave the passenger-carrying vehicle in all its manifold variety. Much has, perforce, remained unsaid and much more was to happen in the next few decades; but that was after the great amalgamations of the early 1920s and will have to wait its turn for the moment.

Bibliography and sources

Although nothing like as comprehensive as that devoted to the locomotives, there is a surprisingly large amount of published material on the subject of railway carriages for those prepared to seek it out. Much has appeared over the years in article form in the various railway journals, and noteworthy in respect of this first volume are the early-twentieth-century issues of the much lamented *Railway Engineer*. This was a particularly fine source of drawings and most of those reproduced in this book have been culled from it, courtesy of the NRM. Most railway journals occasionally mention carriages in their pages, albeit often in the form of notes and news paragraphs. A little time spent searching through these sources by the dedicated researcher will be well repaid.

There are very few really comprehensive general works on the subject, other than the famous Hamilton Ellis title already recommended, and most carriage literature is of the semi-dedicated kind, ie confined to one or at most a few specific companies. The range in this field is quite catholic, and although there are a few noteworthy gaps, the breadth of coverage already in existence is considerable. A representative selection is offered below:

British Steam Railcars, R.W. Rush, Oakwood Press, 1971

Carriage Stock of Minor Standard Gauge Railways, R.W. Kidner, Oakwood Press, 1978

Carriage Stock of the LB & SCR, P.J. Newbury, Oakwood Press, 1976

Carriage Stock of the SE & CR, D. Gould, Oakwood Press, 1976

Gresley's Carriages, M. Harris, David & Charles, 1973

Great Western Coaches 1890-1954, M. Harris, David Charles, 1966

GWR Absorbed Coaching Stock, E.R. Mountford, Oakwood Press, 1978

LNWR Coaches (An Illustrated History of), D. Jenkinson, Oxford Pub Co, 1978

Maunsell's SR Steam Passenger Stock 1923-39, D. Gould, Oakwood Press, 1978

Midland Carriages, an Illustrated Review, D. Jenkinson/R.J. Essery, Oxford Pub Co, 1984

Midland Railway Carriages, Vols 1 & 2, R.E. Lacy and George Dow, Wild Swan, 1984 and 1986

Palaces on Wheels (Royal Carriages at the NRM), D. Jenkinson/G. Townend, HMSO, 1981

Pullman, J. Morel, David & Charles, 1983

Pullman, Travelling in Style, B. Haresnape, Malaga Books (Ian Allan), 1987.

Pullman in Europe, G. Behrend, Ian Allan, 1962

Railway Carriage Album, G.M. Kichenside, Ian Allan, 1966

Railway Carriages in the British Isles 1830-1914, C.H. Ellis, Allen & Unwin, 1965

Railway Carriages, 150 years of, G.M. Kichenside, David & Charles, 1981

Southern Electric 1909-79, G.T. Moody, Ian Allan, 1979

Southern Suburban Steam, R.W. Kidner, Oakwood Press, 1984

Steam to Silver (London Transport Surface Stock), J.G. Bruce, Capital Transport, 1983

Tube Trains Under London, J.G. Bruce, London Transport, 1977

Index

Note: For the most part, references in this index relate to the areas of the book where the subject concerned appears in more than passing reference. No attempt has been made to index every single occurrence of a specific subject. Most of the larger railways have a sub-index with, as their last entry, a list of illustrations for that company. Where these coincide, within a page or so, of a subject sub-reference for each company, they may be taken to relate to that subject, otherwise they should be assumed as illustrating a more general point not specific to that company. In the case of smaller companies and other references, entries in *italics* indicate illustrations.